THE INVENTION OF JOURNALISM ETHICS

McGill-Queen's Studies in the History of Ideas
Series Editor: Philip J. Cercone

1 Problems of Cartesianism
Edited by Thomas M. Lennon, John M. Nicholas, and John W. Davis

2 The Development of the Idea of History in Antiquity
Gerald A. Press

3 Claude Buffier and Thomas Reid: Two Common-Sense Philosophers
Louise Marcil-Lacoste

4 Schiller, Hegel, and Marx: State, Society, and the Aesthetic Ideal of Ancient Greece
Philip J. Kain

5 John Case and Aristotelianism in Renaissance England
Charles B. Schmitt

6 Beyond Liberty and Property: The Process of Self-Recognition in Eighteenth-Century Political Thought
J.A.W. Gunn

7 John Toland: His Methods, Manners, and Mind
Stephen H. Daniel

8 Coleridge and the Inspired Word
Anthony John Harding

9 The Jena System, 1804–5: Logic and Metaphysics
G.W.F. Hegel
Translation edited by John W. Burbidge and George di Giovanni
Introduction and notes by H.S. Harris

10 Consent, Coercion, and Limit: The Medieval Origins of Parliamentary Democracy
Arthur P. Monahan

11 Scottish Common Sense in Germany, 1768–1800: A Contribution to the History of Critical Philosophy
Manfred Kuehn

12 Paine and Cobbett: The Transatlantic Connection
David A. Wilson

13 Descartes and the Enlightenment
Peter A. Schouls

14 Greek Scepticism: Anti-Realist Trends in Ancient Thought
Leo Groarke

15 The Irony of Theology and the Nature of Religious Thought
Donald Wiebe

16 Form and Transformation: A Study in the Philosophy of Plotinus
Frederic M. Schroeder

17 From Personal Duties towards Personal Rights: Late Medieval and Early Modern Political Thought, c. 1300–c. 1650
Arthur P. Monahan

18 The Main Philosophical Writings and the Novel *Allwill*
Friedrich Heinrich Jacobi
Translated and edited by George di Giovanni

19 Kierkegaard as Humanist: Discovering My Self
Arnold B. Come

20 Durkheim, Morals, and Modernity
W. Watts Miller

21 The Career of Toleration: John Locke, Jonas Proast, and After
Richard Vernon

22 Dialectic of Love: Platonism in Schiller's Aesthetics
David Pugh

23 History and Memory in Ancient Greece
Gordon Shrimpton

24 Kierkegaard as Theologian: Recovering My Self
Arnold B. Come

25 An Enlightenment Tory in Victorian Scotland: The Career of Sir Archibald Alison
Michael Michie

26 The Road to Egdon Heath: The Aesthetics of the Great in Nature
Richard Bevis

27 Jena Romanticism and Its Appropriation of Jakob Böhme: Theosophy – Hagiography – Literature
Paolo Mayer

28 Enlightenment and Community: Lessing, Abbt, Herder, and the Quest for a German Public
Benjamin W. Redekop

29 Jacob Burckhardt and the Crisis of Modernity
John R. Hinde

30 The Distant Relation: Time and Identity in Spanish-American Fiction
Eoin S. Thomson

31 Mr Simson's Knotty Case: Divinity, Politics, and Due Process in Early Eighteenth-Century Scotland
Anne Skoczylas

32 Orthodoxy and Enlightenment: George Campbell in the Eighteenth Century
Jeffrey M. Suderman

33 Contemplation and Incarnation: The Theology of Marie-Dominique Chenu
Christophe F. Potworowski

34 Democratic Legitimacy: Plural Values and Political Power
Frederick M. Barnard

35 Herder on Nationality, Humanity, and History
Frederick M. Barnard

36 Labeling People: French Scholars on Society, Race, and Empire, 1815-1849
Martin S. Staum

37 The Subaltern Appeal to Experience: Self-Identity, Late Modernity, and the Politics of Immediacy
Craig Ireland

38 The Invention of Journalism Ethics: The Path to Objectivity and Beyond
Stephen J.A. Ward

THE INVENTION OF JOURNALISM ETHICS

The Path to Objectivity and Beyond

Stephen J.A. Ward

McGill-Queen's University Press
Montreal & Kingston · London · Ithaca

ISBN-13: 978-0-7735-2810-9 ISBN-10: 0-7735-2810-5 (cloth)
ISBN-13: 978-0-7735-2811-6 ISBN-10: 0-7735-2811-3 (paper)

Legal deposit fourth quarter 2004
Bibliothèque nationale du Québec

Printed in Canada on acid-free paper.
First paperback edition 2006

This book was first published with the help of a grant from the Canadian Federation for the Humanities and Social Sciences, through the Aid to Scholarly Publications Programme, using funds provided by the Social Sciences and Humanities Research Council of Canada.

McGill-Queen's University Press acknowledges the support of the Canada Council for the Arts for its publishing program. It also acknowledges the financial support of the Government of Canada through the Book Publishing Industry Development Program (BPIDP) for its publishing activities.

Library and Archives Canada Cataloguing in Publication

Ward, Stephen John Anthony, 1951–
The invention of journalism ethics: the path to objectivity and beyond/Stephen J.A. Ward.

(McGill-Queen's studies in the history of ideas; 38)
Includes bibliographical references and index.
ISBN-13: 978-0-7735-2810-9 ISBN-10: 0-7735-2810-5 (bnd)
ISBN-13: 978-0-7735-2811-6 ISBN-10: 0-7735-2811-3 (pkb)

1. Journalistic ethics. 2. Objectivity. I. Title. II. Series.

PN4756.W37 2004 174'.90704 C2004-903241-0

This book was typeset by Interscript in 10/12 Baskerville.

To Glenda

Contents

Acknowledgments

I have many people to thank for their help in this project. First and foremost, I owe an enormous debt to my wife, Glenda Thomson, for her confidence in my ability to complete this book over its ten years of gestation. We have been co-travellers on a remarkable journey. What is more, her skill in editing and her judgment on matters of language have been an invaluable source of firm, clear-headed advice. I thank my parents, Harold and Macrena, posthumously, for their unconditional love and their irrepressible optimism about my future when I was still young and finding my way. Similarly, I thank the rest of my family for constant encouragement.

I received sage advice and support from three mentors who taught me philosophy at the University of Waterloo – Professors James Van Evra, Rolf George, and William Abbott. I sustained my motivation to write this book by reflecting on two inspiring teachers during my undergraduate days at St Thomas University in Fredericton, NB – Professors Leo Ferrari and Frank Cronin. These teachers and scholars showed me how to think and act philosophically. Also I wish to recognize Mr. Charles Post, whose enthusiasm for my academic development came at a crucial juncture in my career and ultimately made this book possible.

At the University of British Columbia, I have received generous support from members of faculty and staff at the School of Journalism. In particular, I thank Professor Donna Logan, director, and Professor Mary Lynn Young. I wish to acknowledge the intellectual stimulus and encouragement provided by the University's Peter Wall Institute for Advanced Studies, especially its founding director, Professor Kenneth MacCrimmon.

Finally, I extend my gratitude to those students whom I have had the privilege to teach. I have learned much from them. The energy, integrity, and intelligence of this new generation of journalists fill me with hope for the future of the democratic profession of journalism.

THE INVENTION OF JOURNALISM ETHICS

INTRODUCTION

Reinventing Journalism Ethics

This book brings a philosophical and historical perspective to the study of journalism ethics. As a work in the philosophy of journalism, the book is a systematic attempt to understand the editorial standards espoused by journalists since the invention of the printing press. The result is a theoretical framework for conceptualizing the evolution of journalism ethics and a new concept of journalism objectivity.

I call the framework a *rhetorical theory of value change* in journalism. It views the ethical assertions of journalists as a form of persuasive, rhetorical speech. Journalists appeal to ethical norms as part of a rhetorical strategy to defend their practices. The aim of editors' ethical rhetoric is to establish, maintain, or enhance their own credibility and that of their publications. Ethical rhetoric is a crucial factor in the maintenance of a healthy communicative relationship between journalist and reader or between journalism and society. Without a solid, credible, communicative relationship, journalists run afoul of social critics and regulators and lose the support of readers. My rhetorical theory asserts that this communicative relationship largely determines in any era the kind of ethics that defines journalism – the norms to which editors appeal rhetorically. In turn, a number of factors shape this communicative relationship: the available technology, accepted practices, and economic, social, and political conditions.

A history of journalism ethics therefore must examine how journalism's communicative relationship with the public has evolved and how these changes have prompted the espousal of particular norms. We need to adopt this broad perspective on journalism in order to comprehend how ethical norms such as editorial independence arise and evolve. Such insights require an interdisciplinary approach employing philosophy, ethics, science, economics, and social history. To understand journalism ethics fully, we must plunge into the complex history of western culture.

This book pays special attention to the evolution of one of these ethical norms – the ideal of objectivity. It exposes journalism objectivity's long roots in Western culture, as far back as ancient Greek philosophy and early modern science. Having set out this history in chapters 1–6, I develop my theory of journalism objectivity, or "pragmatic objectivity," in chapter 7. I defend without apology this concept, but not the traditional idea of objective reporting as a neutral description of "just the facts." Instead, this book proposes a theory of objectivity that stresses the testing of journalistic interpretations in various contexts. The upshot is a conceptual reworking of the familiar notion that journalists should be objective by providing accurate, balanced, and unbiased news, without fear or favour. Within the following chapters, readers will find both an apologia and a critique of objectivity, a history of objectivity and a look into the future.

A reformulation of objectivity is important because the traditional notion of journalistic objectivity, articulated about a century ago, is indefensible philosophically, weakened by criticism inside and outside of journalism. In practice, fewer and fewer journalists embrace the ideal of traditional objectivity, while more and more newsrooms adopt a reporting style that includes perspective and interpretation. Traditional objectivity is no longer a viable ethical guide.

Pragmatic objectivity will not satisfy the extreme viewpoints that fuel the debate surrounding objectivity. No doubt, academic sceptics of objectivity will regard my proposal to invigorate objectivity as too little, too late. For them, several decades of trenchant criticism of the "myth" of objectivity in science, law, ethics, and journalism has discredited the concept or sent it into irreversible retreat. For adherents of traditional objectivity, my theory of pragmatic objectivity, with its leniency towards interpretation and value judgments, will appear to be an abandonment of objectivity. Nevertheless, I believe that my reformist position is the path to follow. We cannot return, conservatively, to traditional notions of objectivity constructed for other news media in another time. Nor is abandoning objectivity a viable option. Journalists continue to need a clear, vigorous norm of objectivity to guide their practice.

The best option is to reform objectivity to meet valid criticisms and preserve important practices of objective reporting. Without a thoughtful reform of objectivity, we risk losing a much-needed ethical restraint on today's news media. What we require is a progressive and philosophically sophisticated notion of objectivity that corrects stubborn misconceptions that have deep historical roots. We need a notion of objectivity that reflects our current understandings of knowledge and inquiry. The ideal of objectivity, properly understood, is vital not only for responsible journalism but for responsible scientific inquiry, informed public deliberations, and fair ethical and legal judgments. The peculiar Western attempt to be objective is a long, honourable tradition that is part of our continuing struggle to discern significant, well-grounded truths and to make fair decisions.

I became entangled in the web of ideas that surrounds objectivity as a foreign reporter for the Canadian Press news agency based in London during the first half of the 1990s. During this period, I began to question my adherence to traditional objectivity as I read the criticisms of objectivity. My reporting on war, ethnic hatred, social injustice, and radically different cultures raised for me questions about the universality and appropriateness of objectivity in journalism. At the same time, an apparent increase in non-objective, irresponsible journalism disturbed me. It seemed to me that abandoning all pretence of objectivity would only exacerbate journalism's problems and open the door to biased reporting. In this manner, the difficult theoretical and practical questions surrounding objectivity began to occupy me. I realized that they called for philosophical analysis. That analysis became a journey down the corridors of history to ancient Greece and back to where we stand today. My research has only scratched the surface of this issue. I hope that this book encourages others to deepen these reflections.

The book consists of seven chapters (arranged in three parts) and an epilogue. In part I, chapter 1 explains the idea of journalism objectivity as traditionally understood, the main senses of objectivity in our cultural history, and the rhetorical theory of value change. Chapter 2 examines three milestones in the development of objectivity: the origin of rational knowledge about an objective world in ancient Greek philosophy and science; the rise of "discourses of fact" and objective science in the early modern era; and the idea of a "pure," fact-driven objectivity developed by nineteenth century positivists.

Part II (chapters 3–6) traces the history of journalism ethics, century by century. Chapter 3 locates the invention of journalism ethics in the periodic press of seventeenth-century England and shows how the norms of these primitive news publications reflected prevailing ideas about objectivity. Chapter 4 examines the impact of the daily press of the eighteenth century on journalism ethics. The chapter explores interpretations of a new "public ethic" by four types of journalists – partisan essayists, spectators on society, reporters, and revolutionary writers. Chapter 5 describes how the doctrine of journalism objectivity grew out of the revolution in journalism during the nineteenth century. A commercial press bent on providing news to the masses encouraged the development of norms such as non-partisanship in reporting and independence in opinion. Chapter 6 explains the emergence of traditional objectivity as a dominant principle of North American reporting in the 1920s.

Chapter 7 (part III) provides the philosophical basis for a new concept of objectivity that both employs and improves on the ideas of objectivity examined in the book's historical survey. Like other ethical norms, pragmatic objectivity is a rhetorical response to new forms of journalism, to new social trends, and to recent changes to the journalist–audience relationship. The epilogue considers the future of objectivity in the context of emerging global and interactive news media. It outlines a new ethical framework, called "global journalism ethics."

PART ONE

The Roots of Objectivity

1

Objectivity: Senses and Origins

From such crooked wood as man is made of, nothing perfectly straight can be built.

Immanuel Kant[1]

Mankind is an inventive species; and where an invention is obvious and absolutely necessary, it may as properly be said to be natural.

David Hume[2]

This chapter explores first the senses of objectivity – the problem of objectivity, its three senses, and traditional and pragmatic objectivity. It then considers ethics as fair agreement, journalism ethics, and invention and rhetoric in journalism.

SENSES OF OBJECTIVITY

The Problem of Objectivity

Journalism, at its best, is one of the arts of democracy. Journalists provide the news and analysis by which a society communicates with itself, allowing it some measure of self-government. The public absorbs a daily barrage of news images that over time help to define its sense of place in society and within a global community. Fleeting news stories parade injustices, vanities, power struggles, disasters, accomplishments, and peculiar interests. Citizens, following the major issues in the press, become aware of their shared and competing values. Through journalism, a society debates how to reform its institutions

1 Kant, "Idea for a Universal History," 17–8.

2 Hume, *A Treatise of Human Nature*, 484.

and face the future. Journalism should be the lifeblood of a deliberative democracy.

Journalism, at its worst, is an art of the demagogue and the despot. It is the propaganda tool of powerful interests that subvert popular self-governance by manipulating the channels of information. Journalism becomes debased if it falls into the hands of unethical media owners and journalists or when editorial resources are squandered on merely entertaining stories. It falters when it fails to question the powers that be and when budget cuts strangle investigative journalism. It degenerates when its business overwhelms its democratic functions, seeking profit through every cheap trick in the history of popular printing – jingoism, sensationalism and fear-mongering. Journalism is an anti-democratic art when news organizations wield power without responsibility and journalists forsake their public responsibilities for fame and money. Five centuries after the first periodic papers, journalism still struggles to avoid debasement, let alone live up to its democratic duty.

It is an irony of history that Western society, which first regarded journalists as questionable writers-for-hire, has come to depend so heavily on the uneven standards of its newsmongers. Post-industrial society runs on information and communications. The vigour of its public sphere is directly proportional to the diversity and quality of its media and the professionalism of its journalists. Internationally, the performance of global news media directly influences public support for wars, human rights, famine relief, environmental treaties, and the cessation of ethnic conflict. Such awesome journalistic responsibilities are in the hands of global news corporations that face intense market competition and pressure from stockholders.

The problem of ensuring democratic self-governance is, in large part, the problem of ensuring that the news media properly inform people. The problem is not new. About 80 years ago, newspapers invented the doctrine of objectivity to assure the public that its news was factual and fair. American columnist Walter Lippmann, unhappy with the press of his day, put the problem in stark terms. He argued that if liberty and democracy depended on reliable, factual information from the press, then liberty and democracy were truly in trouble. The press, he argued, was one of the few powerful institutions that lacked a strict method for verifying facts, highly trained personnel, and enforceable standards. Journalism, Lippmann claimed, could serve democracy only if it provided objective information about the world, not fictions or "stereotypes."

From the beginning, this ideal of objectivity was contentious. Henry Luce, who founded *Time* magazine in the 1920s, dismissed it as a myth and claimed that events in a complex world needed explaining and interpreting. In the 1960s, an "adversarial culture" that criticized institutions and fought for civil rights was sceptical of objective experts and detached journalism.

Investigative journalism challenged objective reporting, while other journalists practised a subjective, "personal" journalism that looked to literature for its inspiration.

In academia, doubts about objectivity per se arose mid-century. Philosophers, social scientists, activists, and others challenged the objectivity and authority of scientific rationality. An ahistorical philosophy of science led by Rudolph Carnap and Karl Popper, which studied the logic of scientific explanation, came up against a new philosophy of science that stressed the social, historical, and cultural factors in change and acceptance of theories. The older tradition believed that the physical sciences, especially physics, were the best examples of precise, objective knowledge and scientific rationality. The tradition postulated a sharp distinction between observation and theory and between the psychological process of discovery and the logical justification of theory. Scientific truth was cumulative, and scientific explanation had a tight, deductive structure. Science was a "unity" in method and concept. All sciences employed (or should employ) the same general methods and forms of reasoning. Conceptually, the concepts of the social sciences would reduce eventually to the concepts of the physical sciences.

The new school, inaugurated by historians and sociologists of science, such as Thomas Kuhn, saw no sharp distinction between observation and theory, and no tight, deductive structure to science. Nor was science necessarily cumulative. Kuhn's influential writings were interpreted as showing that scientific change was a non-rational "conversion" to a new set of beliefs.[3] The new school rejected the ideal of unified science and believed that the processes of justification could not be completely separated from the processes of discovery. Science, rationality, and standards of objectivity are *in* time and evolve from era to era.[4] By the 1980s, the debate had degenerated into the so-called science wars – a squabble within the social and natural sciences about which disciplines were objective.

3 Kuhn, *The Structure of Scientific Revolutions.* Kuhn rejected this interpretation of his book.

4 The contrast between these two perspectives on science is explained by Hacking, *Representing and Intervening,* 1–17.

Did certain sciences, such as anthropology, need to follow the objective methods of the detached investigator?[5]

These challenges to the idea that scientific rationality transcended culture and history appealed to social scientists, who resented the suggestion that their theories reduced to more fundamental natural sciences. In the late 1970s, leading sociologists put forward a relativistic sociology of knowledge that explained claims to knowledge by reference to social causes.[6] They dismissed as Western arrogance the idea that science discovered *the* truth about the world because it had an objective method. All knowledge, even science, was theory-laden and redolent with values; all knowledge, "socially constructed."[7] Forms of thinking, including the standards of objectivity, were valid only in specific contexts, disciplines, or eras. Philosophers questioned an objectivity that assumed an absolute, or "God's eye" point of view outside history. Hilary Putnam talked about well-supported belief within a conceptual scheme, while Richard Rorty attacked a "Platonism" that believed in absolute, transcendent truth and saw objective knowledge as a "mirror" of nature.[8]

Meanwhile, objectivity became a lightning rod for attacks from the 1960s on by intellectual movements dissatisfied with the scientific establishment and the "Enlightenment" ideas that presumably supported the status quo – the superiority of objective, scientific truth and the scientist's detachment. The Frankfurt school of sociology decried the influence of both Enlightenment ideas and mass culture.[9] Postmodernists such as Lyotard and Baudrillard questioned the ideas of detached truth and philosophical "metanarratives" – large historical narratives that make sense of human experience.[10] Some feminists portrayed objectivity as the value of a patriarchal society that "objectifies" women and devalues imagination, caring, and intuition.[11] Debunking objectivity became a favourite intellectual pastime, with claims to objective knowledge "deconstructed" as claims to power. Questions about logic and evidence gave way to political questions

5 See Weinberg, *Facing Up*, and Brown, *Who Rules in Science?*

6 Barnes and Bloor, "Relativism, Rationalism and the Sociology of Knowledge," 21–47.

7 For a philosophical critique of the idea of social construction, see Hacking, *The Social Construction of What?*

8 See Putnam, *Realism with a Human Face*, and Rorty, *Philosophy and the Mirror of Nature* and *Objectivity, Relativism and Truth.*

9 Adorno and Horkheimer, *Dialectic of Enlightenment*, 3–42.

10 Connor, *Postmodernist Culture*, 27–64.

11 Hawkesworth, "From Objectivity to Objectification," 151–77.

about who controls science and who defines truth, rationality, and objectivity. Objectivity became a target for radical intellectuals, a scapegoat for what was wrong with academia and society.

By the 1960s, academic scepticism about objectivity was seeping into the study of journalism. Media scholars treated objectivity as the tainted dogma of dominant corporate media.[12] The restraining rules of objective reports, they said, reinforced the values of corporate capitalism and prevented the discussion of alternative ideas. Both journalists and media experts claimed that news objectivity was impossible because reporters were political actors, not neutral observers.[13] Objectivity was too much to expect, because journalists are under intense commercial pressure to sell the news, please their bosses, and write their stories according to the political slant of their news organization.

Critics pointed out endlessly that journalists do not just report facts; they also select their facts, their sources, and their "angle" on a story. Even if objectivity were possible, critics said that it was undesirable because it encourages reporting routines that carry their own biases, such as quoting only official sources. Some scholars argued that objective routines were popular because they protected journalists from criticism.[14] They blamed objectivity for sterile reporting that fails to get behind the facts and rejected it as equivalent to tepid neutrality that had no room for attachment or commitment.[15]

Logically, many of these criticisms missed their mark. Many assumed a simplistic or erroneous idea of objectivity. Many were partial truths or sweeping generalizations, biased exaggerations or ideologically tainted perspectives. Some received an unwarranted plausibility because they were intellectually fashionable. Nevertheless, the attacks cast a pall over the idea of objectivity. Journalism objectivity, once dominant and confident, was now a problem.

The weakening of objectivity did not solve any ethical issues. The criticisms rarely provided guidance on what standards should guide responsible, democratic media. Academics excelled in "deconstructing" objectivity as a theory but failed miserably in constructing new norms to guide practice. The practical impact of the debate on journalism was not their main concern. Tough questions remain today. If objectivity is

12 Hackett and Zhao, *Sustaining Democracy?*

13 Cook, *Governing with the News.*

14 Tuchman, *Making the News.*

15 Bell, "The Truth Is Our Currency," 102–9. See my "Answer to Bell," 121–5.

bankrupt, what should replace it? What, if any, of the practices of impartial journalism are worth maintaining? Should some form of objectivity remain a part of journalism? These questions need answers because the decline of objectivity has left a vacuum in ethics, just as journalism undergoes rapid, disorienting change. The market-driven demand for attention-grabbing news encourages entertainment disguised as news. It encourages a specious form of opinionated journalism, from "hot talk" radio shows to tabloid television newsmagazine shows. The popular idea that journalists should write with an "edge" or "attitude" is an invitation to bias, without restraining standards.

The norms of impartiality, balance, and attention to evidence have only a precarious foothold in online journalism – a medium that encourages subjective forms of writing, from first-person diatribes to multimedia forms of persuasion. Jon Katz, an American online columnist, has said that journalists should "abandon the false god of objectivity" for new forms of communication.[16] The public journalism movement in the United States argues that the ideal of the journalist as a detached, objective critic should give way to that of the journalist as a fair but engaged "catalyst" of civic conversation.[17]

Yet, despite the movement of journalism away from objectivity, opinion surveys show that a substantial portion of the public continues to expect reporters to provide fair, objective information. Paradoxically, some critics attack the news media for not being objective and, at the same time, dismiss objectivity as a myth.

The question of objectivity remains vexed, despite the criticism. It is a problem that we cannot leave dormant. Ethical theory must address it. The problem of objectivity is not just an intellectual debate between academics, media experts, and journalists. It is a problem with serious consequences. It raises practical questions about what norms should guide journalists as they construct stories that affect the public sphere.

The Three Senses of Objectivity

Any solution to the problem of objectivity must begin with clarifying the many senses of objectivity inherited from the evolution of language and culture. The term "objectivity" does not have one, unchanging meaning. As historian Lorraine Daston has said, to study the history of objec-

16 Katz, "No News Is Good News."

17 Rosen, *Getting the Connections Right.*

tivity is to study layers of meanings, much as the archaeologist studies the layers of ruins.[18]

The etymological history of "objectivity" and "subjectivity" reveals these shifting senses. In the medieval era, objectivity and subjectivity meant the opposite of what we mean by these terms today. The English noun "objectivity" goes back to the classical Latin verb "obicere" – "to oppose" or "to place a hindrance before." By medieval times, the Latin noun "objectum" referred to a visible object placed before someone.[19] The English verb "to object," and its noun form, "objection," took over these senses. "To object" meant to place something in opposition before a person. In medieval philosophy, "objective" referred to the objects of consciousness – an idea present before the mind. "Subjective" referred to real, external objects outside the mind – the subject of thought.

The medieval philosophical sense of objectivity continued into the early modern era, but by the seventeenth century the modern subjective–objective distinction was emerging. Logic texts began to distinguish between a belief that had subjective (psychological) certainty and one that had objective certainty, based on external evidence. Galileo, Locke, and Descartes distinguished between primary, objective properties of external objects and secondary, subjective properties that exist in the mind. Immanuel Kant made "objectivity" a popular philosophical term in the late eighteenth century because of his inquiries into how the mind experiences an objective world. By the mid-nineteenth, "objective" was a common term in science and philosophy. In 1856, De Quincey noted how ubiquitous "objective" had become. "The word, so nearly unintelligible in 1821, so intensely scholastic ... yet, on the other hand, so indispensable to accurate thinking, and to *wide* thinking, has since 1821 become too common to need any apology."[20]

For clarity, we need to establish the senses of objectivity used in this book. In ordinary usage, the noun, "objectivity," and the adjective, "objective," may refer to either psychological phenomena, such as objective beliefs, attitudes, and decisions, or non-psychological phenomena, such as objective (external) objects and facts. We also refer to people as "objective," but this usage is secondary – it amounts to saying that these people have objective beliefs or are able to adopt an objective attitude.

18 Daston, "Objectivity and the Escape from Perspective," 598. See also Daston, "Baconian Facts," 37–63.

19 See the *The Cambridge Dictionary of Philosophy* and *The New Shorter Oxford English Dictionary*.

20 De Quincey, "Confessions of an English Opium-Eater," 3: 44 on.

Therefore, we can divide the senses of objectivity into three kinds: *ontological* (external objects, facts), *epistemic or epistemological* (beliefs and attitudes), and *procedural* (decisions).[21] "Objectivity" in all three senses contrasts with its opposite, "subjectivity." To say that a belief, decision, or object is objective is to say that it is *not* subjective, and vice versa. Let's consider each sense of objectivity.

Something is ontologically objective if it exists independently of experience. Something is ontologically objective if it is a fact, not a fiction; a reality, not a subjective appearance. A belief is ontologically objective if it denotes an independently existing object, property, fact, lawful regularity, or state of affairs. Something is ontologically subjective if it is nonexistent, is illusory, or exists only the mind. Ontologically subjective phenomena include perceptual illusions, hallucinations, dreams, and erroneous beliefs, such as a belief in witches. Typical questions about the ontological status of objects – Is this real? Does this belief correspond to a fact? – presuppose that we can be mistaken about the objects of thought.

What one regards as ontologically objective depends on the era in which one lives and one's overall conceptual scheme. For modern people with a scientific worldview, chromosomes have ontologically objective existence, but not woodland fairies. Common sense regards trees, houses, and other people as the most obvious examples of objective entities. They are part of the furniture of the world. But doubt is always possible. Philosophers have found ways to cast doubt on the objective status of ordinary mid-sized objects by reducing them to collections of mental sensations or of sub-atomic particles. Individuals' view of the world usually designates some properties as more objective than others. For scientists of the early modern period, scientifically quantifiable and measurable properties, such as mass, weight, and shape, were more objective than the perceived properties of colour and warmth, which were relative to the condition of the senses and the perceiving conditions. At any given time, what is ontologically objective varies across disciplines. In addition, some disciplines are thought to be more objective, ontologically, because they have methods that test the objectivity of their knowledge claims. For example, physics supposedly refers to hard facts of the natural world, while ethical statements are expressions of subjective feelings or value judgments. On this view, ethical beliefs do not refer to an ontologically objective fact. Moreover, what a discipline considers onto-

21 For a discussion of the senses of objectivity, see Megill, *Rethinking Objectivity*, 1–20, and Newell, *Objectivity, Empiricism and Truth.*

logically objective changes as inquiry continues. The primary objects of study for ancient natural science were the elements of water, earth, air, and fire – a far cry from the arcane objects of contemporary physics, with its quanta of energy, sub-atomic particles, and fields of forces.

Epistemic objectivity is a property of people's beliefs and methods of inquiry. It refers to well-supported beliefs and stringent methods for testing hypotheses. Epistemic objectivity is a normative concept. It is what good beliefs (and inquiry) achieve. Beliefs are epistemically objective if they satisfy best practices and standards. The methods of objectivity can be the practices of common sense or the technical methods of scientific research. My belief that there is a green house on my street is epistemically objective because I (and others) have observed it many times under varying conditions. The hypothesis that a gene contributes to aggressive behaviour in mice is epistemically objective if it is the outcome of careful experiment and satisfies methodological standards.

Ontological objectivity explains the subjective–objective distinction as a difference between reality and appearance. Epistemic objectivity explains the distinction as a difference between well-supported and not well-supported beliefs. Epistemic objectivity comes in two forms, absolute and fallible. A method of inquiry is fallible if its standards do not guarantee truth (or certainty) but lead to more accurate, reasonable, better-evidenced beliefs. On this view, beliefs may be epistemically objective but false. Error or change in what we consider to be objective belief is always possible. A method is absolute if its proponents claim that it leads to truths that are known with certainty.[22] Both fallible and absolute forms of epistemic objectivity stress correct methods, but they differ on what these methods can achieve.

Procedural objectivity deals with fair and reasonable decisions in the practical, public areas of life, such as law, government, and institutional administration. The goal is not so much theoretical understanding as correct decisions. One uses practical reasoning to arrive at correct action-guiding conclusions. A decision procedure is objective if it satisfies

22 William James described absolutism as the view that reality "stands ready-made and complete," leaving our intellects with "the one simple duty of describing it as it is already." Absolutism believes that truths can be absolute in two senses – unchanging principles that are not relative to time and place, or truths about a hard-to-understand reality. Absolute truths take us beyond appearances, misconceptions, and prejudices to the real nature of the world. Lynch, *Truth in Context*, 9.

a number of relevant criteria that reduce the influence of irrelevant considerations or bias. Objective decision-makers must not only have a firm grasp on the facts of the case. They must act impartially towards the parties affected by the decision. They must weigh competing rights, principles, and the probable consequences of courses of action.

The primary step is to establish objective criteria for evaluating these factors. For example, the criteria for admitting students to a university program may range from past academic record, external references, and publications to community service and social skills. The criteria are objective not because they somehow "correspond to reality," but because the criteria are relevant to the program's purposes and are consistent with notions of fairness. The focus of procedural objectivity is fairness and the best means to established objectives, not scientific discovery or metaphysical truth. Which criteria are objective depends on the normative issue of what sort of institution (or society) the participants wish to construct. If one lives in an egalitarian, pluralistic society, then criteria that evaluate a job applicant on the basis of race or religious belief will be judged to be subjective and unfair. "Objectivity" in decision-making means following agreed-on criteria that are grounded in fact and reflect ethical and political values.

Although we can conceptually distinguish the three senses – ontological, epistemic, and procedural objectivity – they are closely related. Truth and method are hard to separate. To claim that one's belief is ontologically objective – a truth about reality – one usually has to explain the methods that establish one's claim. Confusion about what beliefs are true or false, caused by rival theories and sceptical arguments, have prompted philosophers to develop methods of inquiry. The enterprise of epistemology originated in the hope that epistemic objectivity leads to ontological objectivity. In science, researchers follow detailed methods because they believe them conducive to truth or to approximating the truth. Epistemic objectivity is also important to those who aspire towards procedural objectivity. As we saw above, correct procedural criteria require a foundation of facts established by objective methods.

Which of the three senses of objectivity will dominate in any context will depend on whether the goal is theoretical or practical. It will depend on whether one is seeking action-guiding conclusions or theoretical understandings of natural phenomena. Ontological objectivity tends to dominate when the argument concerns the reality of various types of sub-atomic particle. Procedural objectivity dominates in practical decisions. Epistemic objectivity occupies the terrain between ontological and procedural objectivity, able to assist inquirers in both theoretical and practical spheres.

Traditional and Pragmatic Objectivity

The doctrine of journalism objectivity, with its stress on facts, procedures, and impartiality, is a hybrid of the three senses of objectivity. According to traditional journalism objectivity, reports are ontologically objective if they are accurate and faithful descriptions of facts or events. Ontological objectivity in journalism involves telling it "the way it is." Reports are epistemically objective if they adhere to good reporting methods and standards. Reports are procedurally objective if they present information in a manner that is fair to sources and to rival viewpoints. The ideal objective report displays all three forms of objectivity.

By "traditional objectivity" I mean the original notion of journalistic objectivity that began to gain currency in the American journalism of the early twentieth century. At the heart of traditional objectivity lies the idea that reporters should provide straight, unbiased information. Its justification is that it enhances journalism's informing function. Commentary and argumentation are the business of editorialists and columnists, not of reporters.

The concept of traditional objectivity still plays several roles in journalism. It acts as an ideal, a set of standards, a set of practices that implement the standards, and a basis for distinguishing between types of story and types of journalist.

Six related standards define the ideal and help journalists decide whether a report is objective or subjective:

(a) *Factuality*: Reports are based on accurate, comprehensive, and verified facts.
(b) *Fairness*: Reports on controversial issues balance the main rival viewpoints, representing each viewpoint fairly.
(c) *Non-bias*: Prejudices, emotions, personal interests, or other subjective factors do not distort the content of reports.
(d) *Independence*: Reports are the work of journalists who are free to report without fear or favour.
(e) *Non-interpretation*: Reporters do not put their interpretations or opinion into their reports.
(f) *Neutrality and detachment*: Reports are neutral. They do not take sides in a dispute. Reporters do not act as advocates for groups and causes.

These standards support the three senses of objectivity – ontological, epistemic, and procedural. As we move from standards (a)–(f), objectivity imposes increasingly restrictive conditions on reporters and the content of their stories. The most controversial aspects of traditional objectivity are the standards (e) and (f). Most people would agree that reports should be factually accurate, as complete as possible, unbiased, and independently written. Serious disagreement begins over non-interpretation, neutrality, and detachment. Traditional objectivity insists that reports should contain *only* facts and exclude the reporter's opinion and interpretation. The severity of these standards, especially (e) and (f), is the distinguishing feature of traditional objectivity. The traditional language of journalistic objectivity is a normative language of self-denial, restraint, and exclusion. The reporter must, in an almost-Calvinist manner, keep a steady watch on his or her impulses to comment and interpret. Reporters provide an undistorted mirror on the world; they are passive recorders of facts.

Traditional objectivity is more than an ideal set of standards. It is a practical and comprehensive set of practices and rules that implement the above-mentioned standards in newsrooms. The rules determine what information to gather and how to construct stories. For example, rules of attribution and quotation govern how to insert opinion into a report. Many reports deal with disputes between several parties. So, although a reporter does not include his or her opinion in the story, he or she cannot avoid informing readers about the opinions of the contending parties.

The rules require clear attribution of all opinion to the source, accompanied by direct quotation and careful paraphrasing of the source's remarks. Someone's opinion is simply another fact. Readers know that it is not the reporter speaking and do not confuse fact with opinion. But attribution, direct quotation, and careful paraphrasing are not enough. To avoid bias, a report must balance one point of view with another. This gives rise to the rules of balance. Objective stories should present all major viewpoints, represent them fairly, and contain comment from people whom a report may damage. The rules of balance allow for exceptions. In some cases, recognized experts do not require balance by other experts.

But how do we know that a source is telling the truth or is reliable? Here, rules of attribution and balance lead to rules of sourcing and verification. Traditional objectivity calls for authoritative sources and persons who can speak for a group or institution. Also, objective practice asks reporters to verify alleged facts by reference to documents, scientific studies, government reports, and numerical analyses. The rules of attribution, balance, and verification provide an epistemically objective method of gathering news.

Another set of rules deals with the style of the report. Traditional objective reporting hides from view the extensive selection and editing process of news writing. The reader or audience sees only the end product. The report seems to be a straightforward description of the facts – what anyone would observe if present at the event. To enhance the appearance of objectivity, reporters use the detached tone of the third person, not the first person. Their language contains no personal observations, wit, or sarcasm, thereby minimizing their voice in the story. They eliminate any adjectives, adverbs, verbs, or phrases that might indicate a bias or an unjustified inference, or they translate them into neutral language.

No-nonsense, objective editors reject colourful, literary devices. The aim is not riveting narrative but factual news. For example, the neutral "said" replaces verbs such as "admitted" or "tried to claim" to describe someone's assertions. Reporters must avoid inferences when describing behaviour: instead of "The police chief lost control when asked," the reporter writes, "The police chief appeared to grow angry when asked." "The prime minister was stung by the accusation and struggled to recover" gives way to "The prime minister appeared surprised by the question." In the traditional objective style, news-writing genres provide a format for story construction. One long-standing format is the so-called inverted pyramid, which conveys the most important facts tersely and quickly. From the opening paragraph to the last, the story presents facts in a descending order of significance. The inverted pyramid suits objectivity because it encourages an impersonal writing style focused on fact.

The doctrine of traditional objectivity has long helped journalists and readers to distinguish between types of journalists and types of stories. By the early twentieth century, most mainstream newsrooms had news sections, operating according to the rules of traditional objectivity, and editorial sections, which generated subjective opinion and where the rules of objectivity did not apply. Journalists were either reporters of objective news or non-reporters (editorialists, columnists) who debated, argued, and opined. Their newsroom division of labour shaped the news product. Newspapers contained both objective news columns and subjective editorial pages. Anything that was not news was opinion. In theory, the perspective of the newspaper publisher and his or her columnists should not influence the news columns. Newspapers could campaign, but the news columns were to be an autonomous realm of impartial fact. News served journalism's informing function; commentary, its advocacy and watchdog functions.

Traditional objectivity, however, never received a precise definition and never developed into a detailed, explicit theory. The idea of objectivity was developed not for the philosophy classroom but for the practical purposes of the newsroom. Journalists borrowed the term from science to distinguish news from commentary. They did not feel the need to articulate their own elaborate theory of objectivity. They defined objectivity in a common-sense manner. Reporters were to stick to the facts and avoid partisan comment. The meaning of objectivity seemed obvious, as determined by concrete practice. Journalism objectivity was what reporters did in the newsroom. Milton's *Areopagitica* and Mill's *On Liberty* are intellectual landmarks that helped to define the notions of free speech and a free press. There are no similar landmarks for the doctrine of traditional objectivity. Lippmann's writings on objective information are as close as we get to a philosophy of journalistic objectivity. Journalistic objectivity did not need philosophical justification as long as the prevailing culture supported the idea.

My own theory – pragmatic objectivity, which I explain in chapter 7 – is similar to traditional objectivity in stressing factuality and fairness. But there the similarities end. Pragmatic objectivity rejects standards (e) and (f) of traditional objectivity. Pragmatic objectivity rejects traditional objectivity's demand that reports be factual descriptions of events without any interpretation, evaluation, or drawing of conclusions. It sees all forms of journalism, from straight reports to editorials, as interpretations. Objectivity is not the absence of interpretation. It is the *testing* of interpretations by the best available methods and restraining standards. Journalists are objective when they submit their writings to critical evaluation. Moreover, pragmatic objectivity allows varying degrees of journalistic detachment in different circumstances. That reporters be strictly neutral, across the board, is neither possible nor desirable.

ORIGIN OF JOURNALISM ETHICS

Ethics as Fair Agreement

By "journalism ethics," I refer to a set of ethical principles, norms, and standards that guide journalists in their practice. These ethical principles can be the principles of an individual journalist, a news organization, a form of journalism, or an entire era of journalism. I use the terms "ethics," "ethic," and "morality" interchangeably, as synonyms. My stress on practice means that journalism ethics refers, to some extent, to the mores of a group. But by "ethics" I mean something more than the accepted, perhaps unreflective, mores of a social group – not simply the static values that journalists pick up through entrance into the craft of journalism. Rather, I mean norms and principles that journalists espouse to explain and defend their actions and their profession. These principles are open to critical, self-conscious evaluation. They are supported by, and evolve in response to, rational argument, among other factors.

There is another sense of ethics, however – as a philosophical theory or sustained ethical reflection on principles. Ethical philosophy is the systematic study of moral experience and the justification of moral notions, beginning with those that historically and by current estimation are the most important.[23] I attempt to avoid confusion by referring to this sense of ethics as philosophical ethics. A good deal of journalism ethics does not amount to an explicit, philosophical system of ethical principles. The ethical principles of journalism may be explicit in varying degrees. Journalists may not completely articulate these principles, yet we can see them operating in their decisions and practices. At other times, journalists may appeal explicitly to specific principles to explain their actions or to advance their profession.

Journalists reflect on their principles, but they seldom develop a rigorous conceptual system or an ethical philosophy such as utilitarianism. Instead, journalism ethics sometimes amounts only to the espousal of a principle such as the liberty of the press. At other times, it refers to a group of related principles that cohere under one phrase. For example, the late-eighteenth-century idea of the press as a "fourth estate" brought together a number of principles about the role of the press in society, the validity of press criticism of government, and so on.

This is not to say that journalism ethics never seeks to become more systematic. In the early-twentieth-century United States, several pioneering codes of journalism ethics attempted to gather the norms of professional journalism into a single document. However, even there, the codes did not achieve the logical unity of a philosophical system – some were merely lists of loosely related principles.

My philosophical ethics is a species of contractualism, as found in the writings of John Rawls and T.M. Scanlon. Contractualism informs my approach to journalism ethics. Historically, contractualism stems from notions of social contract in Thomas Hobbes, John Locke, Jean-Jaques

23 Rawls, "Kantian Constructivism in Moral Theory," 200.

Rousseau, and Immanuel Kant.[24] For contractualism, ethical reasoning provides principles of fair and equitable co-operation. What is "right," "obligatory," or "wrong" in any domain of society is determined by principles that attempt to define a reasonable co-operative framework. Social morality, where valid, is reasonable agreement.

A contractualist therefore does not identify morality with existing principles. Moral agreements are something for people to achieve. Existing principles in domains such as journalism may be vague or inconsistent. They may be dubious rules that evolved historically and perpetuate biases. Morality is not the status quo. It is the set of legitimate principles that *ought* to govern the practice in question. A moral principle is legitimate if all parties could regard it as impartial and fair for all.

Facts are important elements of ethical reasoning and key determinants of ethical choice. Yet ethical principles find their justification or truthfulness not because they correspond to external moral facts or to a moral order in the universe. Moral statements are evaluative judgments about how to act. They provide reasons for appraisal, approval, and sanction. Objectivity in ethics is not a description of reality from "the point of view of the universe."[25] Objectivity in ethics is the activity of providing others with the best available reasons for types of actions. We reason among ourselves about means and ends, duties and consequences. We seek what is reasonable but not certain; what is workable in practice and agreeable to many; what is consistent with our deepest aspirations.

In most cases, we begin ethical reflection by clarifying concepts latent in practice. Where existing practice is uncertain, we propose principles

24 Contract theory has two main traditions: contractarianism and contractualism. The traditions differ on the conditions necessary for moral agreement. Contractarians, from Thomas Hobbes to David Gauthier, take a minimalist position, aimed at a non-moral justification for morality. They justify rules and rule-following by showing how they advance the interests of individuals. Parties to a contract do not have to approach agreements with a genuine moral concern for others or adopt an impartial viewpoint. Contractualists are not minimalists. They require moral agreements to have additional features. Individuals are to deliberate from an impartial moral stance motivated by a regard for others and a desire for fair agreements. See Darwall, ed., *Contractarianism/Contractualism.*

25 The phrase comes from Sidgwick's *The Methods of Ethics,* quoted in ibid., 215. Putnam has stated that many evaluative statements are "correct" or "warranted" but are not descriptions of fact. Such statements are "under rational control, governed by standards appropriate to their particular functions and contexts." Putnam, *The Collapse of the Fact/Value Dichotomy and Other Essays,* 33.

that capture our central convictions. Practically, we aim at right action. Intellectually, we aim at equilibrium between our ethical principles and our considered judgments about cases. Objective ethical principles are based on nothing more – and nothing less – than informed intersubjective agreement obtained from prolonged public deliberation, in the light of common purposes, facts, and standards of reasoning.

Thus ethical philosophy and ethical reasoning are not primarily theoretical enterprises, although they must face theoretical difficulties. Nor is ethical philosophy a factual science, although it must consider facts. The aim of ethical reflection is not the epistemological quest to ascertain a special moral truth about the world. It is not the metaphysical yearning for a moral order behind the appearances. Ethical reasoning is part of the practical social task of constructing fair principles of co-operation for a species fragmented by cultural differences, conflicting interests, and moral pluralism.

Journalism Duties

Journalism duties, like all ethical duties, arise out of agreements. Given a fair moral agreement, rational agents claim moral rights and impose moral duties on themselves and others. Given an agreement, implicit or explicit, people have legitimate ethical expectations of others, and vice-versa. An ethical duty is what one owes another, whether or not the law supports it.

Ethical expectations arise from formal or informal agreements, such as marriage vows, promises, oaths, written contracts, and verbal agreements.[26] Expectations do not have to be on paper. I may not endanger the passengers in my car by driving recklessly, even though we did not sign a contract before setting out. Duties can be general or specific. Ethical systems recognize duties for all normal adults, such as the duty to speak truthfully and to avoid unjustified violence against others. Specific duties arise when people enter into special relations with others, such as agreeing to keep a promise or to provide a service; or when they enter a profession or occupy a social role such as that of a parent.

The ethical duties of the profession of journalism are the duties that arise from the distinct social role of journalists. We can consider that

26 Contract-based duties are the bedrock of social morality. Yet they do not exhaust morality. Ethics also includes our relationship to animals and nature. Ethical behaviour includes superogatory acts of courage and sacrifice and the pursuit of personal ideals. Superogatory acts are praiseworthy, not obligatory.

role as defined by a contract between journalists and their society. To seek the duties of journalism is to look for the legitimate principles that *ought* to govern the social practice of journalism – principles that free and equal participants in the journalism–public process could recognize. We ask what journalists promise the public through their social contract and what the public can legitimately expect from them. A social contract in journalism is an agreement that journalists make with the public to balance the freedoms and the responsibilities of their profession. The interpretation of the social contract may vary according to society, but in all contracts journalists promise to act responsibly in return for some measure of freedom and independence. "Responsibly" usually involves both a negative and a positive dimension: a negative responsibility not to do harm by reporting inaccurately, sensationally, and recklessly; a positive responsibility (or general promise) to provide a public benefit. In becoming a journalist, a person enters into that contract. He or she takes on duties to the public in the same way that a person acquires duties by becoming a physician or accountant. A journalist must dedicate himself or herself to the public's 'informational' well-being in the same way that a public health officer dedicates himself or herself to the public's physical health.

Journalists have special duties because of the distinct social role of their profession. The social contract calls on journalists to be impartial, independent communicators. Journalists come under the general duties of truthful communication that apply to all public communicators. However, they also inherit duties specific to their profession. They must speak to the public in a manner that is different from partial public communicators such as social advocates, government officials, lobbyists, and public-relations people promoting a product or lawyers representing a client. Professional journalism is the organized, socially recognized activity of communicating *to the public for the public,* from the impartial perspective of the public good. Journalism has the task of acting as an independent communication link between all parts of society – civil and consumer society, military, government, and business.

The journalist's role is to attempt to discern, amid the clash of partisan voices, what is reasonable and factual and how such facts may affect the public good. In Western journalism, the social contract of journalists takes on additional duties defined by reference to democratic ideals. Journalism is not the politically neutral activity of disseminating bits of data. It is the dissemination and analysis of the most important information for a self-governing polity or for a polity that aspires to be self-governing. The ethics of Western journalism reflects the fact that journalism should be a "particular kind of democratic practice."[27]

Invention and Rhetoric

My contractualism places special emphasis on the remarkable human ability to construct and invent conceptual schemes, norms, and rules. The ethical perspective that stands behind my contractualism is a Kantian view of value. We confer value on the objects of our rational choices.[28] Our notion of persons as "ends-in-themselves" is a conferring of value on ourselves as autonomous, rational beings. We are, in a Sartrean way, condemned to choose, as rational beings in a causal, natural world.

When we think about our choices, we reason from the standpoint of practical reason, which starts from the view of ourselves as rational agents. We do not scientifically discover ourselves as "ends-in-themselves"; rather we confer on ourselves that value. We decide, through reflection, to see ourselves in this manner and to respect what we see. What brings objectivity to the realm of values is not some metaphysical fact about humans but objective constraints on our deliberation. Ethical arguments are not so much about us as *for* us or addressed *to* us. Practical reason is not so much something that we find in the world as something that we bring to it.[29]

I see ethical reflection as *reason in social practice.* It is the construction of ethical frameworks to guide difficult decisions in practical domains. Ethics is not the passive act of obeying an unchanging set of rules handed down to us. It is the dynamic activity of imagining new norms and adapting old principles to changing social conditions and human purposes.[30] Ethics is the never-completed project of inventing, applying, and critiquing the basic principles that guide human interaction, define social roles, and justify institutional structures.

In this book, I use the concept of invention in two contexts – that of normative ethical theory and that of journalism history. In normative theory, invention means the pursuit of fair and equitable principles for

27 Carey, "Some Personal Notes on US Journalism Education," 22.

28 Korsgaard, *Creating the Kingdom of Ends,* ix.

29 Ibid., x, xv.

30 Moral philosophers and psychologists, from Plato and John Dewey to Jean Piaget and Lawrence Kohlberg, have described the moral growth of individuals. Here, I am concerned with the evolution of moral frameworks as a social phenomenon.

practices and professions, as these practices exist today. In journalism history, it refers to how journalists constructed ethical principles to define and defend their work and their social status. I discuss invention in the normative context in chapter 7 and the epilogue. Discussions of historical invention occupy chapters 3–6, on journalism history. The two contexts have obvious differences. Historical discussions tend to be more factual. They deal more with actual journalism practice and how the espousal of principles related to economic and social factors. Historical invention is a story of contingent evolution, mixed motivations, and unintended consequences. In contrast, discussions of contractualist invention tend to be ideal, with proposals on what ought to be. They appeal more to ethical theory and justification, rather than to historical causes and personal motivations. Yet the two contexts are related. The main historical factors that gave rise to journalism ethics continue to work on journalism today and to influence attempts to construct new principles.

My approach to historical invention starts from two premises. The first appears in the book's title. Journalism ethics is an invention. The principles articulated in any era are a normative response to problematic situations. The second premise is that a rhetorical model of value change is a fruitful way to understand these inventions.[31]

The first premise asserts that problems, challenges, and changes force journalists to develop new norms, abandon old norms, and reinterpret principles to fit new situations. The invention of a journalism ethic or a new ideal is not just a reworking of existing ideas. Nor is it a creation out of nothing. It is a creative human response, developing new ideas out of the materials at hand. To call an ethic an invention does not imply that it is arbitrary or irrational. There can be good reasons for a new ethic.

Journalism ethical invention derives from factors specific to the profession, yet it is not unique. It is a form of conceptual creativity that occurs in other areas, such as theory change in science.[32] We live in a time of rapid invention and dissolution of values, but value change is nothing new. The ancient stoics developed the moral ideal of a universal brotherhood of man, which became a principle of Christian humanism. Jean-Henri Dunant of Switzerland popularized the moral ideal of humanitarian treatment for all combatants, after watching French and Austrian soldiers slaughter each other in northern Italy in 1859. His moral ideal founded the Red Cross and its doctrine of neutrality. Some philoso-

31 See Tindale, *Acts of Arguing.*

32 Thagard, *Conceptual Revolutions*, 34–61.

phers, such as Friedrich Nietzsche, have believed that some individuals were capable of a revaluation of all values.[33]

Modern journalism not only undergoes value change, it is an agent of moral change. Journalism changes our perception of the world and alters our moral experience. The emergence of the telegraph and the photograph in the mid-nineteenth century did not just speed up and enhance the process of reporting. It helped to close the gap between the reader and the battlefield. It showed readers the fearful killing power of new technology, such as the Gatling gun. Graphic, continuous news coverage helped to create a moral ambivalence towards the "glory" of war. The rise of television in the second half of the twentieth century brought foreign wars, disease, and famine into our living-rooms. Such coverage raised the issue of whether Western societies had a moral obligation to help or intervene. It supported an ethic of universal human rights.[34]

In our historical survey, we examine several moral inventions within journalism: the invention of the first norms in the seventeenth century (chapter 3), the emergence of a public ethic in the eighteenth century (chapter 4), the creation of a liberal theory of the press in the nineteenth century (chapter 5), and the arrival of objectivity in the twentieth century (chapter 6). In the process, we look at other inventions such as the assertion of editorial independence. History shows these familiar notions to be what they really are – inventions contingent on major developments in journalism.

My second premise places rhetoric at the centre of ethical deliberation among individuals, in professions, and in society at large.[35] By "rhetoric," I do not mean empty claims, tricks of language, or the unethical manipulation of opinion. "Rhetoric" refers to a type of interactive, social argumentation that is vital to a thriving, open society. Rhetorical theory is the study of this type of argumentation.

The classical source of rhetoric is Aristotle's *Organon,* which distinguished three forms of arguing – logic, dialectic, and rhetoric. For Aristotle, logic is the study of formal demonstration, especially the syllogism,

33 See Nietzsche, *Beyond Good and Evil.*

34 Ignatieff, "Is Nothing Sacred?" 9–33. As Ignatieff points out, television news also can lead to a shallow, short-lived, and partial moral outrage. It can make war seem "virtual" as we become fascinated by smart bombs and other technology. Television can induce a "compassion fatigue" that makes us feel that we cannot help warring groups far away because they are beyond reason.

35 See Tindale, *Acts of Arguing.*

where conclusions follow with necessity from the premises. Logic's aim is valid argument, where the argument is a product – a finished text that one can examine and analyse. Dialectic is the study of procedures for participating in rational debate on a wide range of subjects. Dialectic is the game of argument and counter-argument, where victory is forcing your opponent to admit to a contradiction. Through dialectic, we move from probable premises to opinions that most people consider reasonable.[36] Dialectic is useful in teaching rational thinking, promoting critical discussions, and resolving disputes.

Rhetoric is the art of persuasive speech. It is persuasion about issues in the public sphere. It can incorporate elements of logic and dialectic but has its own aims and features. The aim of rhetoric is neither formal demonstration nor logical victory over an opponent. Rhetoric's aim is less ambitious, and its methods involve the use of informal communication processes – of daily conversation and discussion among citizens. Rhetoric is the persuasion of reasonable people on the reasonableness of one's position on matters that elude proof. Rhetoric seeks to obtain and maintain the adherence of a designated audience(s) to one's position or to the legitimacy of one's actions.[37] The natural location of rhetorical argumentation is not the logic course or the academic lecture hall but the wider arena of "persuasive and investigative discourse that arises in the marketplace, in the media, on the Internet, and in the everyday conversations of citizens."[38] We engage in rhetoric when we argue about public policy, new laws, political choices, institutional procedures, or the performance of the news media.[39] Rhetoric focuses on the "communication processes inherent in argumentation, or the means by which arguers make their cases for the adherence of audiences to the claims advanced."[40] Rhetoric is one of the important "arts of discourse" in society.[41]

At the centre of rhetoric lies the complex relationship of speaker and audience as they interact over an extended period. To engage successfully in rhetoric, one must take the full, "real-world" context of argumentation into account. For the audience, the character (ethos) and

36 Aristotle, *Topics*, 104b10–11.

37 Perelman, *The New Rhetoric.*

38 Tindale, *Acts of Arguing*, 1.

39 For a rhetorical analysis of journalism on the internet, see Ward and Tindale, "Rhetorical Argumentation and the New Journalism."

40 Tindale, *Acts of Arguing*, 4.

41 Richard Andrews, *Teaching and Learning Argument*, 30.

personality of the speaker is important. For the speaker, the makeup of the audience – its beliefs, assumptions, values, and emotions (pathos) – is crucial. The rhetoric must identify and meet the audience's expectations. What reasons is it likely to accept as relevant? What behaviour does it expect of the speaker? The rhetorical context includes background information, such as previous arguments, past events, and what data are available to the audience.

The rhetorical relationship of speaker and audience is not the relationship of a lecturer to note-taking students. It is not the dialectic relationship of duelling lawyers. It is a less formal, conversational relationship. It is a process of interaction between speaker and audience. The speaker attempts to lead the audience towards certain conclusions, but the audience influences how the speaker acts and how the discussion turns out.

A rhetorical model of persuasion is a useful framework for understanding why journalists invent and strongly assert ethical norms. It is also useful, as we see below, in defining a notion of truth that is appropriate for journalism. Journalists make ethical assertions in an attempt to establish and maintain a relationship with an audience. Trust, credibility, and reliability are the basis of this relationship. Editors therefore use ethical rhetoric to persuade audiences that their journals are credible, that their journalism is reliable, and that their behaviour is justifiable. They always aim their rhetoric at an intended audience with known beliefs and attitudes. Moreover, broader political, scientific, and moral values in society usually influence the ethical rhetoric of editors. For example, the rhetoric that established the liberal theory of the press in the nineteenth century found its inspiration in the values of an emerging liberalism in Western society. The editor of the eighteenth-century English newspaper knew that his audience would respond well to his ringing appeals to liberty and public opinion.

The context of persuasive speech, such as readers' expectations and beliefs, determines what conceptual materials are available for invention and rhetoric. In many cases, the stimulus to ethical rhetoric has been some perceived threat to the journalist–reader relationship. The threat could be increased public scepticism about the press, the possibility of government censure, or something as specific as public criticism of an inaccurate article on a sensitive topic. The rhetorical model sees ethics as arising out of the stresses and strains on the journalist–reader relationship. Journalists invented new norms as their role changed from seventeenth-century partisan and eighteenth-century public representative to nineteenth-century liberal reformer and modern mass informer.

The usual vehicles for persuasive speech in journalism have been the prospectus of new publications, editorial comments inside journals, public speeches of leading journalists, and attacks on the ethics of editors. The rhetoric often consists of assertions about the high social purpose of the press and journalism's commitment to impartiality and truth. Contemporary critics often dismiss these assertions as hype or hypocrisy, not to be taken seriously. From a rhetorical perspective, however, these statements reveal the role of ethical language in the practice of journalism. These assertions are evidence of various rhetorical strategies designed to maintain readers' patronage, week in and week out, and to cast doubt on the ethical respectability of competitors. The editor, through rhetoric, establishes his or her credibility within a rhetorical space occupied by other editors and other forms of journalism.

If the journalist–audience relationship determines the articulation of norms, what determines the journalism–audience relationship? How does it change? The simple answer is that changes in journalism audience reflect changes in journalism practice (and forms of media) and in society. Shifts in journalism practice include new ways to gather news caused by the invention of new communications technology. These alterations in practice in turn are responses to more fundamental changes in society, such as a sharp increase in literacy levels, economic growth, better transportation, larger urban centres, and greater political freedom. For example, there was no talk of objective news reporting until highly efficient news-gathering practices came into being. But these new practices could never have come about without social, technological, and economic changes in society.

My rhetorical model therefore has three levels of analysis: rhetoric, actual practice, and social conditions. The ethical-rhetorical level deals with the relationship between journalist and audience, in terms of journalists' values and attitudes and the audience's values, interests, and expectations. The level of practice is that of actual journalism – the type of news media available, daily reporting routines, editing procedures, and newsroom organization. This is the level of production. The level of society refers to the economic, cultural, and political structure of society. This third level includes the dominant social values of the era and the prevailing view of the proper role of news media in that society.

A complete explanation of a change in journalism ethics must take all three levels into account. All three interact. The lines of causal influence run in all directions. Rhetoric influences practice, and practice and society shape rhetoric. Rhetorical norms are not reducible to or "explained away" by underlying economic pressures. An ethical commitment to objectivity may well have an economic cause, such as the belief that impartial reporting sells more newspapers. But the commitment to objectivity does not thereby become just a rationalization for profit-making. The adherence to objectivity may have other causes and legitimate reasons. Journalists may have a sincere belief that objectivity is important to the proper informing of the public, even if part of the original motivation was economic or political.

Many media commentators are so impatient to unmask the economic and selfish motives behind the espousal of a journalism norm that they fail to stress that the rhetorical level can also influence practice and, ultimately, social conditions. For example, once a norm such as objectivity becomes dominant, for whatever reasons, it comes to shape news practices. The emergence in North America in the 1920s of many journalism codes of ethics, with their adherence to objectivity, influenced professional practice. The ideal of objectivity received support from both the professional ethics of journalists and the economic value of impartial news.

My three-level rhetorical framework entails a multi-factor explanation of journalism objectivity. Objectivity is not the result of just one factor, such as the desire of newspaper owners for neutral copy or the impact of a new technology such as the telegraph. I explain objectivity as a rhetorical invention that emerged from a new journalism–audience relationship – the journalist as impartial mass informer. This new role grew out of a revolution in journalism practice and the nature of society in the nineteenth century. New technology, the commercialization of news, professionalism in journalism, fears about the manipulation of public opinion, and the advent of 'objective' society were among the many motivations for the construction of objectivity.

We can see how these factors work together in the rise of a periodic news press in the seventeenth century. The demands of periodic news, which was the product of technological and social change, changed the communicative relationship between journalist and reader. As a result, editors increased their rhetorical emphasis on norms of factuality and reliability. Periodic news eventually altered society's view of the press's role. At the same time, the periodic news press had to justify its existence and defend its practices against other segments of the population. Editors had to reply to public criticism (often from rival editors), escape government censure, and fulfil readers' expectations. In such a climate, rhetorical skills were crucial. Editors appealed to ethical norms of truth, impartiality, and fidelity to enhance their relationship with readers and the rest of society. In this manner, ethical rhetoric in the seventeenth and subsequent centuries played a very substantial role in developing the norms of journalism into what became an explicit set of principles and doctrines.

In addition to the ideas of invention and rhetoric, I weave a number of other themes into the fabric of the following chapters. One theme is my "imperfectionist" approach to ethics. Imperfectionism and perfectionism are general attitudes that one can apply to almost anything in life. One can be a perfectionist or an imperfectionist with regard to what to expect from knowledge, institutions, human nature, ethics, or journalism. A perfectionist tends to expect that knowledge is absolute, that professionals follow the strictest of standards, that humans do not betray their ideals, and that institutions fully achieve their objectives. The perfectionist has little tolerance for a gap between ideals and actual behaviour.

Perfectionism in life and religion has led thinkers to seek a more perfect reality beyond the imperfect world of everyday experience. Perfectionism in ethics leads to the demand that people observe to the letter the strictest of principles, without compromise. Perfectionism in knowledge leads to an expectation that any reasoning worth engaging in must lead to scientific proof. The trouble with perfectionism is that it devalues ordinary, practical activities, where theoretical precision or human perfection is not possible. Perfectionists tend to view non-demonstrable reasoning, as in ethics or rhetoric, as a second-class rationality rather than a valuable feature of a central area of life. Perfectionism can slide into cynicism or apathy. For example, if a strict scientific objectivity is not possible in practical activities, then the perfectionist tends to conclude that all is lost and objectivity is a myth. The perfectionist is likely to see the gap between ideals and practice in journalism as a reason for despair, rather than for reform.

Imperfectionism reduces expectations but does not settle for the status quo. It recognizes that institutions, imperfect forms of reasoning, and imperfect spheres of human activity may still contribute something useful to society. It refuses to run away from life to a perfect, transcendent reality. It sees value in seeking the most reasonable beliefs and the best, but imperfect, practices in many areas of life; it values practical reasoning and non-absolute forms of inquiry, even if the conclusions are fallible. My ethical imperfectionism is inspired by Aristotle's insistence that we must not be discouraged by the fact that ethical judgment lacks the rigour of formal logic or scientific proof. The ethical person exercises what Aristotle called practical wisdom, or *phronesis*. This form of context-bound practical reason is still of value even if its conclusions come from generally accepted maxims that apply "for the most part."

An attitude of imperfectionism helps us to evaluate realistically the potential of the press. If we bring perfectionist expectations to our evaluation of the press, we end up with an overly negative evaluation. For example, some media critics see any commercial influence on journalism as necessarily a bad thing, a contamination of its ideals to serve only the public impartially. This perfectionism blinds the critic to the long-term, positive contribution of the imperfect commercial press to the public sphere. The fact that journalists must work in a corruptible environment does not discourage the imperfectionist.

Corruptible environments are areas of society that put standards and ideals under strain. They can encourage unethical or selfish behaviour or press individuals to accept an unsatisfactory compromise of principle. Journalists, like many other professionals working in the real world, face a host of pressures. Because it is both a business and a public service, journalism will always struggle against non-ethical pressures. Given that journalists work within a manipulative public sphere, an imperfectionist attitude will help them retain their ideals yet acknowledge that the real world often does not allow full satisfaction of those ideals. The attitude of imperfectionism helps the journalist avoid cynicism or apathy. The journalist who adopts imperfectionism can more readily work for reform and continue to care about principles over the long term.

This book derives several lessons from the history of journalism. One is that journalism ethics includes but is not identical with a set of austere, philosophical principles. It is about how standards and values influence (or fail to influence) the messy practice of journalism in the real world. Ethical principles are among the many norms and values that define the practice of communities of journalists. Like all communities of practice, journalists follow, implicitly or explicitly, a "paradigm" or general approach to their work. This approach includes much more than ethical principles – practical goals, standard newsroom procedures, and methods of investigation. To understand the ethics of journalists, you have to pay attention to how the practitioners carry out their daily tasks and the presumptions embedded in their decisions. You have to see how ethical principles relate to non-ethical norms, ideas, methods, forms of media, and commercial pressures.

A second lesson is that the type of objectivity required in journalism is not the theoretical, philosophical conception of objectivity as absolute standards or absolute knowledge – what I call the "ways of truth." Journalism objectivity is closer to the imperfect form of objectivity that characterizes "ways of practice" such as law and other professions. The historical survey below also teaches us that the origin of journalism ethics is much earlier than previously recognized. Journalism ethics did not begin with journalism associations and codes of ethics in the nineteenth century. It goes back to an unlikely source – the partisan English newsbooks of the seventeenth century. Finally, our historical investigations point out the need for a more nuanced understanding of the liberal theory of the press. The liberal theory is not a monolithic doctrine spanning most of the eighteenth and nineteenth centuries. The "liberal ethic" is a distinctly nineteenth-century phenomenon, distinguishable from the "public ethic" of the eighteenth-century press. The liberal newspaper of the nineteenth century is actually several kinds of newspaper. This recognition changes our understanding of the origins of journalism objectivity.

2

Objectivity: Ancient, Early Modern, Positivist

It is a mark of the trained mind never to expect more precision in the treatment of any subject matter than the nature of that subject permits.

Aristotle

Objectivity did not originate with journalism. When modern journalism began to appear in the seventeenth century, Western culture's pursuit of objective knowledge in the form of philosophy, mathematics, and science had been under way for about 2,000 years. Philosophers, logicians, theologians, sophists, and sceptics had debated the relative worth of reason and faith, sensibility and intellect, theory and practice. They had debated the difference between cultural convention and nature, universal and parochial standards, reality and appearance, objective knowledge and subjective opinion. Ontological objectivity was the primary sense of objectivity in antiquity and medieval Europe. With the rise of modern science, epistemic objectivity became the dominant meaning of objectivity from the seventeenth century on. By the nineteenth century, epistemic objectivity was virtually synonymous with the methods of positivistic science and its alleged "pure objectivity." Meanwhile, procedural objectivity would become an ideal of mass, bureaucratic society, beginning late in the century.

These varieties of objectivity influenced journalism. In the eighteenth century, factual, disinterested science prompted journalists to claim that they too were factual and disinterested. In the nineteenth, a positivistic objectivity was part of a realism pervading Western culture, literature, and art. This realism found expression in the mass, commercial press as an empirical attitude that valued news and the reporting of facts. This attitude was the forerunner of journalism objectivity. To explain the roots of journalism ethics and objectivity, this chapter examines three milestones: the ancient idea of rational knowledge, discourses of fact in the early modern period, and pure objectivity in the nineteenth century.

RATIONAL KNOWLEDGE IN ANTIQUITY

Early Sources of Objectivity

The history of objectivity begins with the Greek invention of rational inquiry into society and nature. Rational inquiry first appears in the seventh century BC in the writings of physicians, historians, and natural philosophers who constructed speculative theories about a lawful nature. The natural philosophers gave way to the philosophical systems of Plato and Aristotle, and to theories in mathematics, logic, and geometry. The Pythagoreans, for instance, believed in an order of numbers and ratios that explained geometric figures, the order of the heavens, and musical harmony. Nature had a mathematical basis.[1]

These philosophical constructions departed from religion and myth, which based their stories on revelations, oracles, and the weight of tradition. The shift, however, was gradual. Ancient Greek philosophy is a mixture of proto-science, literature, rhetoric, logic, abstract metaphysics, and elements of mysticism. Many philosophers shared with religious leaders the perfectionist's quest for higher knowledge of a higher reality. Both were prone to posit an unchanging reality behind changing sensible appearances. Much of ancient philosophy and religion emerged from the feeling that ordinary beliefs were false or illusory and that ordinary life was evil or imperfect. Just as philosophers sought a heaven of intellectual truths, religious leaders looked for spiritual enlightenment. Some philosophers joined holy men in seeking to purify the soul from bodily contamination. Yet Greek philosophy was a new quest for truth, through reason. Philosophers offered logical explanations, not myths; they appealed to natural causes to explain events, not to gods. They put forward ideas for logic and experience to test. They told stories that gave events meaning but were not closed to rational critique.[2]

The Greek idea of disinterested, rational inquiry drew from divergent sources. Hannah Arendt has claimed that objectivity dates back to Homer's *Iliad*, where he praised the defeated Hector as well as Achilles, the hero of Homer's kinfolk. Objective thought took a step forward with natural philos-

1 Kitto, *The Greeks*, 192.

2 Aristotle divided the early Greek writers into two groups: "theologi," explained the world by appeal to the gods, "physici," by natural principles. The poet Pindar explained the annual flooding of the Nile as the result of a god moving his feet, while Herodotus considered natural causes, including the melting of snow on distant mountains. See Frankfort et al., *Before Philosophy*, and Graves, *The Greek Myths*.

ophers such as Thales, Anaximander, Empedocles, and Democritus, from the seventh to the fifth century BC.[3] They thought that the unifying principles of nature were material elements such as water, air, and fire, or atoms, or a universal matter that took on many forms. Thales of Miletus made the famously obscure statement that water is the principle of all things. The statement is not as foolish as it may sound. Water takes on different forms and is indispensable to life. Thales treated it as a sort of naturalistic hypothesis. He did not personify water and make it part of a creation myth, as did the Babylonians and Egyptians. He tried to give reasons for his hypothesis, holding that the earth rests on water because, like wood, it floats on water. Anaximander's *On Nature* gave explanations of the origin of the universe, the causes of natural phenomena, and the development of life. Anaximander posited an invisible basic stuff of the world, which he called the "indeterminate" – a raw material that took the shapes of objects. More naturalistic speculations followed. The basic stuff for Anaximenes was air; for Heraclitus, fire; for Empedocles, the four elements of water, fire, air, and earth. Democritus proposed an unseen world of atoms moving in a void. The belief in atoms, though speculative, was a rational conjecture.[4]

The stress on reason coexisted with an empirical curiosity. The Greek medical tradition associated with Hippocrates of Cos is an early source of empiricism. It approached the human body as a lawful, physical system. It treated diseases by physical means, not by rituals of purification. It saw epilepsy not as a divine madness, but as a puzzling natural phenomenon. One doctor hypothesized that epilepsy resulted from a blockage of air that was transmitted through the veins to the brain. These pioneers criticized philosophers for relying too much on reason: "One must pay attention not to plausible theorizing but to experience and reason together ... theorizing is to be approved, provided that it is based on facts."[5]

3 Arendt, *Between Past and Future*, 263. The objective turn of these natural philosophers can be difficult to appreciate because we have only fragments of their writings. Many natural philosophers lived on islands in the Aegean Sea and along the coast of Asia Minor. Some created schools, and some wrote books, and some wore splendid clothes and drew large audiences to their talks. Stimulated by contact with Egypt, Persia, and Babylon, these philosophers were freethinkers who had no emperor to placate or sacred book to defend. See Boardman, Griffin, and Murray, eds., *The Oxford History of Greece and the Hellenistic World*, 126–41.

4 McMullin, ed., *The Concept of Matter in Greek and Medieval Philosophy*, 1–54.

5 *The Precepts of Hippocrates*, cited in Kitto, *The Greeks*, 189. On the role of fact and theory, see Lloyd, *Magic, Reason and Experience.*

Historians followed the objective turn in thinking. If natural principles governed nature, facts about humans and their circumstances could explain historical events. To explain the Greek victory over the Persians, Herodotus travelled to Egypt, Persia, and Greek cities and made careful notes and recorded interviews. Sounding like an objective journalist, he wrote: "My job, throughout this account, is simply to record whatever I am told by each of my sources." But he did not just record – he imagined the thoughts of his historical actors. He intervened as narrator to warn the reader that an account may not be completely true. He saw himself as a researcher who composed the most plausible story about an event. His interventions display a "careful, critical distance ... toward his data."[6]

Thucydides' account of Athens's disastrous war with Sparta was methodologically self-conscious. He compared the Peloponnesian War with previous wars. He presented the factual causes for events. He criticized Herodotus for not being careful about his sources. Thucydides, like a journalist, assured the reader that he offered a reliable account. "With regard to my factual reporting of events ... I have made it a principle not to write down the first story that came my way, and not even to be guided by my own general impressions; either I was present myself at the events which I have described or else heard of them from eyewitnesses whose reports I have checked with as much thoroughness as possible."[7]

Objectivity therefore drew ideas from three aspects of early Greek thought: rational explanations, collections of fact, and an attitude of impartiality. Impartiality meant the ability to seek truth with disinterest, apart from practical application. Egyptian geometry became a method to mark fields after the annual inundation of the Nile. Babylonian astronomy predicted the future. Greek geometry and astronomy became intellectual pursuits for their own sake. Pythagoras compared intellectual impartiality with the detachment of a spectator at the Olympic Games. The knower as spectator would become a central metaphor in Western epistemology. In Rome, centuries later, Cicero argued that philosophers best trained the cultured mind because they were spectators without self-interest.

The Way of Truth

Out of ancient Greece came not one but two forms of objectivity: an objectivity of theory and an objectivity of practice. The former derived

6 Herodotus, *The Histories,* 144, xxvii, xxx.

7 Thucydides, *History of the Peloponnesian War,* 35.

from philosophical reflection – the pursuit of absolute or universal knowledge that transcended the relative beliefs of ordinary experience. It followed a rigorous "way of truth" to scientific truth or philosophical understanding. Objectivity of practice involved the pursuit of reasonable but fallible judgments in public assemblies, courts, and professions.

Parmenides, in the fifth century BC, described the way of truth in its purest form. He writes that, while he was on a search for knowledge, a goddess taught him the difference between absolute truth and the beliefs of ordinary people. Truth lies far "from the beaten track of men." The opinions of mortals are false, yet they have the "semblance of being."[8] The way of seeming is what happens to be the case, while the way of truth is knowledge held fast by "necessity" such that "no judgement of mortals may outstrip you." Parmenides uses reason to deduce truths that are paradoxical to common sense. He starts with a single premise – "it is" – and deduces that reality is one: complete, unchanging, and eternal. Our belief that the world has many things that move and change is an illusion. Parmenides meant his puzzling "proofs," and his student Zeno intended his paradoxes, to undermine faith in the senses, in favour of reason.

With Plato, a Parmenidean emphasis on rational truths about transcendent reality became the philosophical paradigm for knowledge. In Plato's youth, at the end of the fifth century BC, natural philosophy was on the defensive, having produced conflicting theories. Scepticism and relativism were in fashion as sophists debated the relative meanings of virtue and justice. Xenophanes wrote: "No one has ever known or ever will know for sure, for even if what he says is exactly right, he does not know it – it is all a matter of opinion." Plato constructed a comprehensive philosophy in response to the philosophical and political confusion that he witnessed in Athenian society after the Peloponnesian War. At 28, Plato withdrew from politics after watching a court condemn Socrates to death. In ethics, Plato attacked the relativism of the sophists. In physics, he rejected mechanical atomism for a rational, purposeful order. Drawing inspiration from the Pythagoreans, he defined knowledge as the enlightenment of the intellect as it moves, by dialectic reasoning, from uncertain opinion to certain, philosophical knowledge.

The *locus classicus* of Plato's view of knowledge is his discussion of the philosopher-king in Book V of his *Republic*. The philosopher's intellect grasps perfect universals, while the ordinary person perceives imperfect,

8 Kirk, Raven, and Schofield, *The Presocratic Philosophers*, 267.

particular things.[9] Things belong to a particular class of objects because they share a universal form. Things that are beautiful instantiate the form of beauty; actions that are just "participate" in the form of justice; all perceptible triangles have the form of triangularity. These perceptible things are poor copies of the universals that they embody. Whereas the form of justice is one and unchanging, the many acts of justice realize justice in varying degrees. The triangle that a person draws is not as perfect as the pure form of triangularity. Reflection on perceptible things, however, can lead the mind to knowledge of the forms. In the *Symposium,* Socrates says that the soul, by reflecting on beautiful things, comes to a vision of "wondrous beauty" that is "beauty only, absolute, separate, simple, and everlasting."[10]

Why is Plato attracted to unchanging universals? One reason is that they explain objective knowledge. Plato is a perfectionist with a "longing for objective values."[11] Knowledge must be clear, unchanging, and able to justify itself. There is no relative or probable knowledge. What is relative is belief or opinion. Stable knowledge requires a stable object: a class of unchanging universals such as beauty itself, triangularity itself. The universals are absolute standards for objective judgments of justice, goodness, equality, and so on. The pluralism of cultural norms and laws does not entail relativism because there is an absolute truth about what is good and what is real. Philosophical knowledge is objective because it is a secure apprehension of objective reality. "Knowledge," Socrates states, "has for its natural object the real – to know the truth about reality."[12] Knowledge is a rationally secure state of mind about real things, while belief is a rationally insecure state of mind about objects that exist in "twilight" – appearances that are neither wholly real nor wholly non-existent.

Plato uses two devices to explain the way to truth – the diagram of the line and the allegory of the cave. He represents the four levels of cogni-

9 The use of ocular metaphors to explain knowledge, such as the "eye" of the mind, encouraged the image of the knower as uninvolved observer. Dewey called it the spectator theory of knowledge. For Plato, knowing was an intellectual "seeing" of universals, which is analogous to the physical eye that sees particular objects. "Seeing" universals seemed necessary to explain general knowledge – for example, the difference between knowing that Socrates is good and knowing what goodness is.

10 Plato, "The Symposium," 354.

11 Flew, *An Introduction to Western Philosophy,* 78.

12 Plato, *The Republic,* 185. Here I am referring to Plato's "middle" dialogues. In his later dialogues, Plato questions the theory of forms. Yet "Platonism" – the

tion by dividing a line into two sections, representing belief and knowledge. Each of these sections he divides into two segments. The belief section's two segments represent the perception of images and the perception of objects. Knowledge's two segments represent mathematics and the highest cognition of all – the philosopher's knowledge of the forms. Each of the four segments, from the visual images to the forms, represents a more stable form of cognition about a more real object.

In the allegory of the cave, the line receives a dynamic interpretation. Plato portrays the path to knowledge as a confusing journey from the darkness of appearances inside a cave to knowledge of reality outside the cave. The allegory begins with prisoners chained in a cave who mistake the images of objects for reality. Only if they make the difficult journey out of the cave do they see the external world, illuminated by the blazing sun. The benighted denizens of the cave represent ordinary people living in a world of appearances. The people who escape the cave are philosophers who see real objects – the forms. The sun, which allows us to see the forms, is the highest universal – the Good.

The conception of objectivity in Plato's *Republic* is a form of absolute, ontological objectivity. Only the philosopher whose reason is not distracted by appetites and interests can judge what is truly valuable and real. Only reason has the independence and insight to evaluate our conflicting desires. The philosopher reaches a "standpoint of perfection" that is necessary for knowledge and a rationally ordered soul.

It is difficult to underestimate Plato's contribution to the tradition of objectivity in theory. His subtle dialogues examine the nature of reason and praise theory over practice.[13] His philosophy anchors knowledge in an ideal, objective order that provides absolute standards for

belief in absolute knowledge of a transcendent reality – has exercised a profound influence on Western philosophy, from the Neo-Platonism of Plotinus to the Christian philosophy of Augustine. The influence continues today. Physicist Roger wrote: "I imagine that whenever the mind perceives a mathematical idea, it makes contact with Plato's world of mathematical concepts." Penrose, *The Emperor's New Mind*, 428.

13 In Plato's *Republic*, Socrates says: "Nothing imperfect is a measure of anything, though sometimes people think that it is enough." Plato's praise of "pure" theory over practice appears in such dialogues as *Philebus, Republic,* and *Statesman.* In *Philebus,* Socrates praises the "purity" of education over the impure technical arts. Socrates notes the superiority of people who use mathematics in the arts over those who employ guesswork and rules of thumb. Nussbaum explores Plato's "standpoint of perfection" in *The Fragility of Goodness.*

judgment and society. Plato's exercise of objective reason, however, is not cold and aloof. It carries a sense of urgency and expresses an "eros" for wisdom. Plato's dualisms of universal and particular, reality and appearance, knowledge and belief shaped the thinking of philosophers, theologians and scientists for centuries. Some 2,000 years after Plato, René Descartes cast philosophy as a system of necessary truths. Western culture never lost what John Dewey called the "quest for certainty."

The Way of Practice

As philosophers of antiquity took the austere path to absolute truth, other people followed the way of practice. The latter included an assortment of sophists, magistrates, political leaders, and, later, the pragmatic Hellenistic philosophers of life. While development of objectivity in theory gained impetus from bold attempts to explain the world rationally, objectivity in practice developed via practical, social problems.

The way of practice was not the search for universal laws or theoretical principles to understand reality. It was the quest for imperfect tests and practical procedures to determine the most probable opinion or best decision in a specific context. The problem was not the logical validity of abstract theory but the evaluation of conflicting arguments and evidence so as to reach a reasonable, action-guiding judgment.

The problem, and importance, of wise judgment and reliable evidence was clear. State security depended on reliable reports from the battlefront and spies. Biased testimony in the courts could kill an innocent man. No one had to remind the ordinary Greek (or Roman) about the biasing influence of political allegiances and ambitions. The debates in the agora, and the disputes between rhetoricians and philosophers, demonstrated how the same facts could be interpreted in different ways.

The political structure of the city-states made the practical evaluation of claims central to the Greek public sphere. In the late archaic and classical periods, roughly from the seventh to the fourth centuries BC, the Greek world consisted of autonomous, if unstable, city-states. There was an unprecedented discussion of legal codes. The democratic Athenian constitution included the election of magistrates by lot, the referring of policy decisions to general assembly, and the choosing of military leaders by a show of hands. The same people who valued rhetoric in the assembly enjoyed witty dialogue at the theatre and symposia and public lectures at the pan-Hellenic festivals. The Greeks extended the range of issues for public debate to include politics, morality, law, and medicine.

As Lloyd said, "testing arguments, weighing evidence and adjudicating between opposing points of view were ... a common part of the experience of a considerable number of Athenian citizens."[14]

This critical spirit created a need to discuss and evaluate ideas publicly that would not exist under an authoritarian regime. For example, testing the objectivity of informants was a preoccupation of Greek institutions. In the courts, judges evaluated the testimony of litigants and witnesses on the basis of their reputation, economic status, and lack of personal interest in the matter. A public evaluation of facts and testimony tested a candidate's eligibility for a public office, such as magistrate. The Greek word for evidence is of legal origin and, in English, means "to bear witness," "make trial," and "testimony."[15] Greek expressions for testing an idea derive from the cross-examination of witnesses. But testing did not guarantee truth. The aim of a Greek trial was not to establish the truth, but to decide between rival descriptions of events.

The spread of literacy and written news promoted a more objective approach to practices and to the understanding of events. In the fifth century BC, people communicated primarily by spoken word, although texts were available for consultation and books were being collected. Socrates criticized learning from books, but he did not mention that written materials assisted the rational evaluation of beliefs. Speeches on paper could be analysed logically, and original statements retrieved. In 451 BC, the Roman Republic curbed the patrician class by writing laws on 12 tablets.

News, of course, proliferated. Non-literate tribes and literate societies from the earliest times have exchanged news by mouth, papyrus sheets, drum, sea signals, tribal meetings, and messengers.[16] News in ancient Greece, like today, was about battles, murders, athletic contests, and gossip about the powerful. News travelled with soldiers and merchants, to be exchanged at marketplaces, agora, symposia, the Olympic Games, and festivals.

The Greek city-state distributed official news by messengers, heralds, and scouts.[17] The original marathon was run in 490 BC by a naked messenger who carried news from Marathon to Athens of victory over the Persians. Anyone could be asked to report the latest news. In Plato's *Charmides*, Socrates, returning as a foot soldier from the Peloponnesian

14 Lloyd, *Reason and Experience*, 252. Buxton, *Persuasion in Greek Tragedy*, 5.

15 Lloyd, *Magic, Reason and Experience*, 129. Placing conflicting testimony before a judge was a feature also of Roman civil and criminal courts. See Jolowicz, *Historical Introduction to the Study of Roman Law*.

16 Stephens, *A History of News*.

17 Lewis, *News and Society in the Greek Polis*.

War, stops at a gymnasium, where someone asks him for news of the war. News gradually distinguished itself from rumour and supernatural tales. Aristotle's works traditionally include a slim volume called *De mirabilibus auscultationibus,* not written by Aristotle – a miscellaneous collection of brief reports about marvellous things in other lands, from mice that eat iron to a fountain that can heal wounds "in a moment."[18] Theophrastos's play *Characters* satirized the many Athenian newsmongers, or *logopoios,* as people who circulated false accounts of events to impress friends. Military leaders, politicians, and historians complained about unreliable reports circulated in the streets, while official publications, such as the Roman newsletters, were known to be propaganda vehicles. The Greeks and Romans had no more faith in the objectivity of the newsmonger or newsletter writer than modern audiences have in their own journalists.

The two great empires of antiquity – of Alexander the Great and the Roman Empire – established systems of oral and written news exchange to bind their territories together and to co-ordinate military campaigns. The Romans set up the first efficient, large-scale Western system of communication, sending written newsletters on its wide roads deep into the provinces. The Forum in Rome was the centre of empire news, as were the baths. In 59 BC, Romans read the first edition of *acta diurnal,* or the "daily gazette." Written on papyrus, this facsimile of a modern newspaper went up in public places and eventually went by post across the empire. In 1 BC, Cicero, then governor of Cilicia, asked his friend Caelius Rufus to send him news from Rome. Caelius tells Cicero that he will hire a correspondent to write a newsletter on the decrees of the Senate and other events. Cicero soon complained about the newsletter's gossip. "Do you think this is what I commissioned you to do, to send me reports of the gladiatorial matches, the adjournment of trials ... and such tittle-tattle?"[19]

Despite the propaganda and gossip, written news was more reliable than word of mouth. Writing about events as news helped to distinguish factual events from the tales of myth. Newsletters gave events a date and a place. They named sources. The newsletters developed a terse style to chronicle facts. Written news portrayed events as natural occurrences, related in chronological or causal order. To be sure, writing news on papyrus was slow and difficult, yet something called "news," a factual description of timely events, was coming into existence.

18 Aristotle, "De mirabilibus auscultationibus," 830b–847b. The work is part of *Opuscula* – a compilation of nine short works on topics ranging from the nature of colour to the transmission of sound.

19 Giffard, "Ancient Rome's Daily Gazette," 106–9.

The "street philosophers" of the way of practice were itinerant teachers known as sophists. A series of sophists, from Protagoras to Thrasymachus, converged on Athens during the second half of the fifth century BC, attracting large crowds to their orations. For a fee, the sophists provided a higher education in grammar, music, law, and human affairs. They taught rhetorical excellence in moral and legal discourse to young Athenians, showing students how to argue any side of an issue. Protagoras tells Socrates that he teaches the management of personal affairs so that the student can become "a real power in the city, both as speaker and as man of action." A philosophy of relativism justified sophistic practice. The sophists doubted universal truths. They pointed to the plurality of opinion on any subject. This relativism fit the fifth-century Greek "enlightenment," where regular contact with other cultures had made obvious the plurality of belief-systems.[20] Xenophanes had said that the Thracian gods resembled the Thracians and that if cows and horses could draw they would depict their gods as cattle and horses. Protagoras's famous statement that "man is the measure of all things" meant that truth was how the world appeared to each individual. Necessary laws ruled nature, but customs and conventions ordered human societies. "The laws of men are fixed by agreement, not by nature," wrote the sophist Antiphon.

Sophists came into conflict with philosophers, who insisted on objective truths. Plato, in his dialogues *Georgias, Protagoras, Euthydemus,* and *Sophist,* criticized sophists for charging fees, for seeking victory in argument, not truth, and for teaching relative opinion rather than true knowledge. The sophists also met resistance from traditionalists, who feared that rhetoric undermined confidence in religious and social practices. Many ordinary Athenians saw little difference between Socrates, the sophists, and the natural philosophers, who all espoused puzzling theories and practised a corrosive scepticism.

The Plato–sophist confrontation is a defining moment in Western intellectual history. It is a clash between the tradition of objectivity in theory, inspired by a perfectionist attitude, and the tradition of objectivity in practice, motivated by an imperfectionist view. Plato pushes forward the perfectionist view that knowledge must be absolute truth reached through dialectical reasoning. He distinguished philosophers from sophists in terms of their disinterested attitude towards truth-seeking. Anything *less* than knowledge that was rationally secure, objective, and universal could not satisfy Plato. The sophists, on the contrary, were

20 Guthrie, *The Fifth Century Enlightenment.*

practical, worldly imperfectionists who enjoyed the pluralism of opinion, the cut and thrust of public debate. They sought well-spoken, reasonable opinion that persuades others.

Plato's characterization of the sophist as a clever but self-interested showman has dominated over the centuries. Unfortunately, Plato's interpretation blinds us to the fact that the sophists were putting forward a new philosophical attitude that would grow into the idea of objectivity in practice – of reasonable belief achieved through public discourse, rhetoric, and imperfect procedures. In retrospect, we can see sophistic practice as pointing towards notions that are very modern – the social nature of thinking, the importance of concrete experience and cultural diversity, and the idea of "situated" rationality. The sophists, for all their faults, embody a different sort of reasonableness that is appropriate to purposive, social action. We forget that sophistic practice requires a quasi-objective attitude towards one's own beliefs. The sophist must be able to adopt the perspectives of others or to switch sides in an argument. The sophist stands back from his or her own place and time, viewing his or her own norms as one set among many.

The sophists were not systematic philosophers. A philosophical interpretation of objectivity in practice would wait until Aristotle, Plato's greatest student. Aristotle is able to find philosophical value in practice because of his view of reason, his naturalism and empiricism, and his pluralistic view of the sciences. For Aristotle, humans are distinct in their ability to use reason in two ways – to attain theoretical knowledge and to reach goals through deliberate action.

Reason has two parts: a theoretical reason that discovers the necessary causes, or "first principles," of natural phenomena and a calculating, deliberative, practical reason that generates action-guiding judgments. Theoretical reason aims at disinterested truth as a system of propositions, apart from practical interest, while practical reason seeks to discern the right action in a particular circumstance. Practical reason is interested in ideas insofar as they can be useful. For Aristotle, the distinction between theoretical and practical reason divides knowledge into the theoretical sciences – philosophy, mathematics, and natural science – and the practical and productive sciences – ethics, politics, and the arts. Scientific inquiry moves from observations to general principles and back to observations. The world becomes intelligible through this synthesis of observation and intellect. Aristotelian science presupposes an ontological objectivity – the objective structure of the world is intelligible to human thought.

Aristotle's interest in inquiry goes beyond theoretical, scientific knowledge. Science, or *episteme*, is the ideal, but not all inquiries reach the ideal. Aristotle argues that there are domains of inquiry where scientific objectivity and necessary knowledge is neither possible nor desirable. His writings describe a form of rationality and wisdom that is appropriate for these domains. His interest in non-necessary knowledge is evident in his empiricism – his love of nature, especially the study of biological species, and his delight in observation. His copious observations on marine life coexist with abstract thinking on metaphysics, logic, and scientific method. His interest in non-necessary knowledge is evident in his works on ethics, rhetoric, and politics.

We can understand Aristotle's contribution to objectivity in practice by looking at his imperfectionist approach to ethics. Ethics, for him, involves the study of how to act as good people, or how to achieve the good life. Politics studies how to structure society to make possible the good life. The issue of objectivity in ethics comes down to two questions: Is there an objective "end" (*telos)* for human action, towards which we should direct all our actions? Are there objective restraints and guides to particular ethical judgments?

Aristotle saw an objective end for action based on what is distinctive about human nature. That end he calls happiness. Adopting a biological perspective, he argues that humans, like horses, lions, and snakes, must have a discernible nature. Human happiness is whatever fulfils human nature. What is distinctive about humans lies not in perception, pleasure, self-movement, or nutrition, because humans share these faculties with plants and animals. Nor can we determine the end of human life by studying what is idiosyncratic and personal for each individual human. The end must be universal for everyone, yet distinctive to the human species. By isolating that common, distinctive nature, we will be articulating an objective good for humans. In his *Ethics,* Aristotle states that this objective good is the most complete and virtuous exercise of the most distinctive part of man – rationality. Happiness is not conformity to a moral code, but the fullest exercise of rationality, through the intellectual and moral virtues. Happiness is the activity of the rational soul in accordance with virtue, over a lifetime.[21] This is the objective *telos* by which to judge all activities. It is a goal not relative to individuals or social convention, but based on facts about the human species.

What about the second question of objectivity? How do we know that specific ethical judgments are objective, or in accordance with

21 Aristotle, *Ethics,* 75–6.

this general telos? Aristotle does not provide a detailed set of ethical rules that hold universally and objectively. Instead, he discusses what virtues a person must possess to live in excellence and to make wise judgments in various situations. The ethical actor will need practical wisdom, or *phronesis*, to arrive at correct action-guiding conclusions. Good deliberation and virtuous character are the only rational bulwarks against erroneous decisions.

The deliberation of practical reason is a combination of four kinds of skill and knowledge:

- the skill of applying general maxims that hold in most circumstances
- the skill of identifying all the relevant facts of the circumstance and all the available options
- knowledge of one's own desires and character
- knowledge of the excellences that make up the telos of life.

These factors are rational restraints on ethical judgment. They enhance the objectivity of the judgment.

There are serious limits to the precision and objectivity of ethical judgment. Ethical reasoning is an imperfect form of objectivity – objectivity in practice, a form of objectivity appropriate to the domain of human action. But, in the final analysis, ethics never achieves the certainty or universality of objective knowledge in the theoretical sciences. Aristotle repeatedly warns readers not to expect theoretical precision from the practical sciences. Ethics will never be a science with ethical theorems deduced from self-evident principles, by syllogistic reasoning. Expecting scientific precision in ethics is a serious mistake, because it misunderstands the nature of ethics. Such expectations inevitably produce disappointment, leading the inquirer to reject ethical study as subjective and simply a matter of opinion. "It is a mark of the trained mind never to expect more precision in the treatment of any subject matter than the nature of that subject permits," Aristotle writes.[22] One reason for the imprecision is that general principles never completely characterize situations in advance. Ethical statements, such as "every courageous act is praiseworthy," must sooner or later meet an exception.

Aristotle does make the famous statement that the right choice may be a mean between extremes. But some virtues have no mean, and the mean is relative to the circumstances of the act and relative to the individual's

22 Ibid., 65.

physical and mental nature. Aristotle states that at every turn in ethics we deliberate about the effects of our actions in much the same way as we do about our actions in medicine and navigation. In medicine and navigation, practitioners "are compelled at every step to think out for themselves what the circumstances demand." Deliberation is about "that which happens for the most part, where the result is obscure and the right course not clearly defined." In addition to the uncertainty of ethical reasoning, there are also social factors that may help or hinder ethical judgment and the pursuit of the good life. Aristotle notes that a great deal of ethics, especially the moral virtues, must be inculcated into people by habit and social training. Moreover, a good life will need luck, friendship, good children, money, and leisure.

Aristotle contributed substantially to both objectivity in theory and objectivity in practice. He gave a scientific interpretation of ontologically objective knowledge by replacing Platonic forms with "first principles" that govern phenomena. At the same time, he philosophized about the ways of practice. He showed that some degree of objective thinking was possible in domains that Plato considered irredeemably subjective. His tolerant imperfectionism allowed him to admire the exactness of science but also to see that exactness is not a primary value in many areas of study. In ethics, he grounds reasoning in an objective human nature and in the fallible application of general maxims to contexts. This is a modest objectivity in practice, with a human face. Aristotle does not force on us the false dilemma of philosophical absolutism *or* illusory opinion. A deep Platonic scepticism about the world of becoming is absent in Aristotle.

Philosophies of Life: Detachment and Plausibility

The three main Hellenistic philosophies that followed Aristotle – the epicurean, stoic, and sceptical – inherited this rich collage of ideas from the ways of practice and the ways of truth. Their practical philosophies of life redefined the role of rationality and detachment. They opened "schools" and wrote manuals that promised a happy life, or tranquillity. The epicureans taught a balanced life of pleasure and pain, without troubling beliefs. The stoics valued a virtuous life of reason that accepted the dictates of fate. The sceptics sought tranquillity through the suspension of judgment about the truth of philosophical dogmas.

The epicureans and stoics believed that a correct understanding of the world, as it truly is, was necessary for peace of mind or self-control. In 307 BC, Epicurus established his school in an Athenian garden. He taught a moderate hedonism that defined happiness as the intelligent pursuit of pleasure and the avoidance of pain. Epicurus did not teach unbridled pleasure. Happiness is *ataraxia,* or tranquillity, achieved by the right pleasures in the right amount, through "sober calculation."[23] *Ataraxia* needed correct knowledge of human nature so as to avoid false, worrying beliefs. Epicurus adopted atomism to banish worries about revengeful gods or life after death. If humans are material beings in a universe of atoms, they should not fear death, because the soul does not survive the body's demise.

The stoics, even more than the epicureans, put objective knowledge at the heart of the good life.[24] The stoics believed in a rational order or *logos* in the cosmos behind the appearances. God is the soul of the world, an eternal, subtle fire (*pneuma*) that acts on, orders, and permeates matter, including our bodies. Human reason consists of the same fiery substance and animates our material bodies. Humans make up a universal brotherhood because they share the spark of divine Reason. God determines what will happen according to "natural" law or fate. Stoic virtue, then, is a matter of "living according to nature" or God. "Freedom is to obey god," wrote Seneca. The wise person is free because of self-control and knowledge. The stoic knows the nature of fate (or God) and has the character to obey it. To not fight fate is the stoic notion of negative freedom.

Stoic self-control implies a mental detachment from desirable objects and unfortunate events. The stoic aimed at a virtuous management of the soul, through reason. The Roman stoic Epictetus wrote that one should care only for things that one can control. Within our power are our opinion, desire, and aversion. External things, such as our body, property, and reputation, are not properly our own affairs. Marcus Aurelius advised humans to "withdraw into oneself" and adopt a detachment that allowed one to sleep with equal happiness in a palace or a hovel.

23 The Hellenistic period is the 300 years or so between the reign of Alexander the Great (336–323 BC) and that of Augustus, the first Roman emperor (31 BC–AD 14). The Romans referred to Epicurus as "the pig." His opponents spread rumours of scandalous behaviour inside epicurean communities. See Inwood and Gerson, eds., *The Epicurus Reader,* Inwood, *Ethics and Human Action in Early Stoicism,* and Striker, "Following Nature."

24 Stoic ideas were elaborated over 500 years from the third century BC to the second century AD. The stoic writers of antiquity ranged from Zeno and Chrysippus in Athens to Seneca, Cicero, Epictetus, and Marcus Aurelius in Rome. See Colish, *The Stoic Tradition from Antiquity to the Early Middle Ages.*

Epictetus advised: "Never say about anything, 'I have lost it,' but only 'I have given it back.'"

The sceptic also emphasized detachment, but from dogmas about how the world really is – the sort of knowledge sought by the stoics. Some observers wrongly regard scepticism as an inconsistent, debunking philosophy that undermines all claims to truth and objectivity.[25] The sceptics did not attack all forms of belief. Instead, they trained their guns on the "conceit of the Dogmatists" – the spinners of theory, such as the Platonists, the natural philosophers, and the atomists. The sceptics attacked anyone who claimed to know the nature of reality, underlying the appearances. The Pyrrhoneans called the dogmatists "rash ... self-loving ... fools."[26]

The ancient sceptic was an imperfectionist who thought that the most important segment of Plato's line – absolute philosophical knowledge – is beyond human reach. Sceptics opposed the clash of dogmas because it disturbed the soul's tranquillity. Since no one could decide objectively between these rival theories, the clash of dogmas was an unproductive and irresolvable disturbance. The sceptic therefore practised a form of detachment called *epoche*, a suspension of judgment about the truth of philosophical theories. Scepticism was not another theory; it was a therapeutic practice. Sextus Empiricus, who was a physician, compared sceptical arguments with "purgative drugs" that removed unnecessary intellectual trouble. In his *Outlines of Pyrrhonism,* Sextus defined scepticism as a "mental attitude" that "opposes appearances to (absolute) judgments" and is justified by its utility.

The sceptic's *epoche* of dogma did not leave him or her without any beliefs on which to act. A sceptic guided his or her conduct by what appears to be the case, acting according to "the tradition of customs and laws." Nature, habit, the avoidance of pain, and the need to live in society require the sceptic to be a "believer" in what is apparent and plausible.[27] Pyrrho, the first sceptic, guided himself by the "apparent facts" of

25 Scepticism begins with Pyrrho of Elis in the third century BC and becomes the official philosophy of Plato's Academy under Arcesilaus (315–240 BC). Bertrand Russell called scepticism a "lazy man's" philosophy, while C.I. Lewis referred to it as an "intellectual disaster," because it is "nonsense to hold or imply that just any empirical judgment is as good as any other – because none is warranted." Russell, *A History of Western Philosophy,* 6, and C.I. Lewis, "The Given Element in Empirical Knowledge," 175.

26 Sextus Empiricus, *Outlines of Pyrrhonism,* 61. Groarke, *Greek Skepticism,* 85–6.

27 Hookway, *Scepticism,* 1–20, and Popkin, *The History of Scepticism from Erasmus to Spinoza,* xix.

experience. "That honey is (in itself) sweet I do not affirm," Pyrrho said, "but I agree that it appears so." When Arcesilaus took over the leadership of Plato's Academy, he talked about the acceptance of reasonable "subjectively defined" belief. Carneades and Sextus were "mitigated sceptics" who held that we cannot prove some fundamental beliefs, such as the belief in an external world and the principles of reason, and so must accept them. Some sceptics made plausibility a criterion for acceptance of belief. According to the sceptics, when we judge an experience (or belief) as plausible, we assess only its apparent truth, as it appears to us. Plausible beliefs may guide us in unimportant actions. But plausible beliefs *tested* by experience should guide us in significant matters, such as the pursuit of happiness. Cicero, for example, thought that one could extend the sceptics' criterion of plausibility to deliberations about whether to marry or have children.[28]

This appeal to what is plausible and tested may sound flimsy and unsubstantial. Yet this pragmatic criterion of belief pointed towards the future. Centuries later, it would re-emerge as the idea of plausible, yet fallible knowledge. The idea of a fallible, epistemic objectivity would support the idea of probable knowledge.

EARLY MODERN DISCOURSES AND SCIENCES OF FACT

Naturalism Revived

The second landmark in the history of objectivity, following antiquity, was the establishment of scientific objectivity in the discourses and sciences of fact of the early modern period. Science gave birth to a methodological, empirical objectivity that was based not on philosophical speculation or casual observation but on a powerful mix of experimen-

28 Carneades distinguished three types of impression: implausible; plausible, seeming true to "an intense degree"; and seemingly irreversible, resulting from a "concurrence" of impressions, such as the doctor's judgment about disease because of the presence of many symptoms. Impressions are more plausible if one considers the conditions of the perception and the state of the observer. Sextus Empiricus explained the testing of plausible beliefs with the following example: On seeing a coil of rope in a dark room, a man jumps over it, thinking it is a snake. Turning back, he finds it motionless. He remembers that snakes are motionless at times, so he prods the coiled mass with a stick. The coil does not move, so he concludes that it is not a snake. Groarke, *Greek Skepticism*, 114.

tal fact and mathematics. A wide gulf separates Hellenistic philosophers from seventeenth century scientific thinkers – the "dark ages," the medieval era, and the Renaissance. I avoid analysis of those periods because journalism objectivity has its roots in ancient rationalism and in modern fact, not in medieval Christianity. However, it is important to review how intervening eras – medieval and Renaissance – served as a bridge to modern objectivity.

The medieval period gave a religious definition to ontologically objective knowledge. On the whole, it advanced a pessimistic view of human nature that allowed faith to eclipse rational inquiry. Truth became the Word of God, and the way of truth became the way to God and salvation. Christ had said, "I am the truth."[29] All of nature was a divine creation, where visible things were signs of an invisible world. Behind the objective world of nature lay a world of spirit, divine design, and divine will. Gradually, the lived "truth" of early Christian communities after the death of Christ became intellectualized and shaped by church leaders into dogmatic truth and intolerant theology. What was truth, and who could determine the truth, became a question decided by an institution. Knowledge was not plural or merely plausible. Knowledge was a uniquely correct truth determined by the Christian church. The faith of loosely organized, early Christian communities crystallized into the dogma of a church, an institution of the Roman Empire.

Dogmatic truth extended church power and prevented fragmentation of the faith. Europe under Charlemagne began to conceive of itself as a universal society, a Christendom united doctrinally. Dogma was truth for all society, enforced by a universal church.[30] We can hear church absolutism of the thirteenth century in Innocent III's excommunication of Markward of Anweiler: "We excommunicate, anathematize, curse and damn him, an oath breaker, blasphemer, incendiary, as faithless and as a criminal and usurper, in the name of God the almighty Father."[31]

29 In answer to Thomas, Christ says: "I am the way, and the truth, and the life." Truth is not a scientific proposition but a spirit that dwells within oneself: "This is the Spirit of truth, whom the world cannot receive, because it neither sees him nor knows him. You know him because he abides with you, and he will be in you." *The New Oxford Annotated Bible,* John 14:6 and 14:17.

30 Fox, in *Pagans and Christians,* examined the problem of dissent for the early church. The apex of dogma-making is the Nicene Creed of the fourth century. The bitter Arian heresy on the nature of the Trinity forced Constantine to call a church-wide council at Nicaea in 325, and it laid down a creed of universal Christian beliefs.

31 Paul Johnson, *A History of Christianity,* 199.

The Christian world order received its definitive articulation in Augustine's philosophy, the basis for medieval theology. Augustine's life and works in the fifth century point to a subjective and an objective path to Christian truth. The subjective path appears in his *Confessions*, an intimate memoir addressed to God about his error-strewn path to conversion. Augustine rues the fact that pride and desire caused him to deny his dependence on God. Knowledge is possible only when the mind is ready to receive the illumination of God's grace. The objective route is the path of rational theology, as outlined in Augustine's *City of God*. Augustine places the sack of Rome in AD 410 within a divine cosmology. History is leading towards an eternal City of God. His subjective journey secures his faith inwardly. The theology secures it outwardly, by providing a historical explanation of humanity.

The main features of the Christian way of truth were:

- a pessimism about humanity's ability to discover truth or act morally, unaided by God;
- a non-naturalism that found truth and value in a spiritual world;
- a hierarchy of knowing that placed faith, contemplation, and theology on the highest rungs;
- an absolutism that believed that there was one set of truths.[32]

Contrary features did exist. Christian thought is not without the optimism of St Paul, the rationalism of Thomas Aquinas, or the scientific naturalism of Roger Bacon. Augustine himself is a source for both rational optimism and severe pessimism. However, in total, the four features outlined above were dominant values that humanists and scientists overcame as the medieval worldview crumbled.

32 "Naturalism" has many senses. The term may refer to the ontological doctrine that only natural causes operate in the world or to the view that science determines what exists in nature. It may also refer to a psychological attitude that has confidence in humankind's powers and finds value in the world, as opposed to spiritual realms. Giovanni Pico della Mirandola, *Oration on the Dignity of Man* (1486) – trans. A. Robert Caponigri (Washington, DC: Regnery Gateway, c. 1956) – is an example of Renaissance naturalism. It asserted that God gave human beings a free choice to fix "the limits of your own nature" and be "your own sculpture and maker." Recently, Dennett defined naturalism as "the idea that philosophical investigations are not superior to, or prior to, investigations in the natural sciences, but in partnership with these truth-seeking enterprises." Dennett, *Freedom Evolves*.

The first cracks in religious absolutism came from within the church during the revival of learning, trade, and architecture in the late medieval period. Theologians planted the seeds of an intellectual revolution in the eleventh and twelfth centuries with their renewed interest in logic and rational standards, independent of revelation. The revival of reason is evident in Anselm's rational theology and in Peter Abelard's logical method of resolving inconsistencies in scripture. The scholastic method, developed for teaching theology, bolstered rational inquiry, despite its abstruse reasoning and endless commentary.

In the twelfth century, interest in learning flourished in response to a flood of translations of Jewish, Arab, and Greek books in philosophy, mathematics, and natural science following the Christian conquest of Arab-held Spain and the establishment of universities in Europe. The revival of reason was impossible to control completely. Books banned in one decade were university texts the next. Aquinas's ideas earned criticism and then support. Newly recovered books by Aristotle forced the tension between faith and reason into the open. How should Christian faith respond to Aristotle's philosophy, which did not believe in divine creation or the soul's immortality?

Aquinas's *Summa theologica* responded by synthesizing reason and faith into a grand theological system. Aquinas used Aristotelian concepts, argued that reason was one way to theological truth, and put rationality at the centre of the good life. His synthesis was never accepted unanimously. Theologians John Duns Scotus and William of Ockham tried to protect theology by separating the superior truths of faith and the inferior truths of reason. This doctrine of "two truths" unintentionally aided the "new learning" of humanism and early science. It gave rationalists the freedom to create knowledge in their own "inferior" domain, while medieval theology declined.

The Renaissance, that fifteenth-century flowering of learning, culture, and society, revived ancient naturalism. The world was not a Christian "vale of tears," but a platform for inquiry and action. New towns, industry, and a bourgeoisie in the emerging nations of western Europe undermined the feudal system. Voyages of discovery broadened the horizons of Europe. The Renaissance cosmos remained full of "signs" and magical forces, and society was still Christian and ordered according to "natural" hierarchies. But writing, art, and civic reforms exuded a powerful sense of human potential, as old restrictions fell away. Life need not be a painful passage to heaven or hell. Original sin did not condemn humanity to everlasting ignorance. The humanists returned to the original texts of a Graeco-Roman culture – not to relive the past, but to construct new learning, as Gutenberg's printing press began to shatter church control on ideas.

The overall direction of Renaissance thought was not upward to heaven but outward towards nature. Painting, sculpture, and literature (written in the vernacular) depicted religious ideas and secular themes with more realism and feeling.[33] The first rule was to observe the world, not to write scholastic commentaries. Alberti's rules of linear perspective were a method for painting the world from a human perspective. Michelangelo's sculpture exhibited a detailed knowledge of the body. Leonardo told artists to study the weather so that they could paint realistic landscapes. "It is safer to go direct to the works of nature," he wrote. "For he who has access to the fountain does not go to the water-pot."[34] Spanish humanist Luis Vives urged natural philosophers to learn from the techniques of engineers, architects, and navigators. When craftsmen and military engineers wrote down their knowledge, they helped to establish the ideas of applied theory, method, and progress. Renaissance naturalism also created an intellectual space for scientific naturalism. Nature was a realm open to discovery. A revival of mathematics, made possible by the discovery of ancient texts by Plato and others, set the stage for Galileo and Kepler. Even Renaissance magic, alchemy, and astrology encouraged scientific inquiry by holding out the possibility of knowledge that could control nature.[35]

By the mid-sixteenth century, the upheavals of the Protestant Reformation emphasized the primacy of personal conscience and independent judgment in religion. But this positive appeal to individualism was balanced by a renewed negative emphasis on humans' limitations. Reformers such as Luther and Calvin gave new life to medieval non-naturalism. Luther and Calvin were interested not primarily in furthering natural knowledge but in serving God. They recognized that reason and observa-

33 The Renaissance begins in the fourteenth century, reaches it height in the fifteenth, and extends into the sixteenth. The term "Renaissance" emerged in the eighteenth century. The paintings of Titian and Leonardo, the sculpture of Donatello and Michelangelo, the architecture of Brunelleschi and Palladio, and the writings of Montaigne and Shakespeare put the human condition at the focus of things. See Burke, *The Italian Renaissance.*

34 Quoted in Gottlieb, *The Dream of Reason*, 410.

35 Westfall, *The Construction of Modern Science.* For Renaissance notions of knowledge, see Seigel, *Rhetoric and Philosophy in Renaissance Humanism*; Kristeller, *Renaissance Thought*; Garin, *Science and Civic Life in the Italian Renaissance*, and Gilbert, *Renaissance Concepts of Method.*

tion were necessary to daily living but insufficient for salvation or correct theology. For Luther, reason was "a whore" because it could serve unholy purposes. Where reason and faith come into conflict, faith should prevail. "Since God is true and one, he is utterly incomprehensible and inaccessible to human reason," said Luther. The German reformer started from a dark, Augustinian pessimism about humankind. Since humans are corrupt, fear and discipline must rule, every inner thought requires scrutiny, and every sin needs absolution. Calvin had an almost pathological fear of disorder. "All human desires are evil," he declared. "We affirm that they are inordinate because nothing pure or sincere can proceed from a corrupted and polluted nature."[36]

By the end of the sixteenth century, the Reformation had liberated the protestant religious conscience and challenged the power of the pope. But it had also sown confusion about objective truth and how to discern it. The Reformation created a crisis of knowledge that eventually found resolution in science's favour. The humanist tradition opened the door to new thinking, but it did not seek to create a new system of natural knowledge. The humanist too closely associated "science" with the dreaded scholasticism and Aristotelianism of the universities. Meanwhile, the Reformation splintered into factions, each claiming the truth.

Amid this confusion, there was no escaping the sceptical question: If the pope could be wrong, why not Luther? What was the criterion of truth? Was it reason and experience? scripture? clerical authority? The crisis produced such extreme doctrines that Richard Hooker, Henry More, and others used reason to defend the new Church of England from the "enthusiasms" of sects.[37] Yet the confusion spread. If religion lacked rational foundations, so did secular beliefs. In the 1560s, the translation of Sextus Empiricus into Latin made scepticism an attractive doctrine. Montaigne's diary-like essays introduced the sceptical, humanistic attitude to the public. Scepticism debunked authority, but where could one find hope for new knowledge?

36 When Luther was asked whether only he had knowledge, he replied: "I am a Christian theologian ... I want to believe freely and be a slave to the authority of no one, whether council, university, or Pope." Quoted in Bainton, *Here I Stand*, 119. On Calvin's fears, see Bouwsma, *John Calvin*, 36.

37 Beiser, *The Sovereignty of Reason*. On the Renaissance crises of knowing, see MacIntyre, "Epistemological Crises," 453–72.

A Culture of Fact

The answer lay in pursuit of sciences and discourses of fact. Barbara Shapiro notes that in England there was a broad interest in all manner of fact during the sixteenth and seventeenth centuries.[38] Discourses and sciences of fact developed a wide range of methods – criteria to detect bias, ingenious instruments, careful experiment, mathematical modelling, quantification, and peer review. The pursuit of fact prompted the invention of norms: disinterestedness and impartiality, repeatable experiment, intersubjective evidence, intellectual modesty, plain language, and self-restraint.

The sciences of fact provided a direct challenge to the medieval view that the human ability to observe and understand nature was an inferior, limited capacity. Two things were necessary to make the case for a renewed empirical science, independent of Aristotelianism and animism. Scientists had to show that a new method was possible, and they needed a new model of knowledge that explained the method.

The discoveries of Copernicus and Galileo on the Continent provided impressive examples of the new method. In England, Harvey, Hooke, and Boyle showed how experiments and calculations led to discoveries and laws. The discourses of fact – travel writing, chorography, and a primitive journalism – showed that impartial, factual methods were feasible in practical professions. Behind these inquiries lay a new philosophy of knowledge that was eroding the long-standing dichotomy between a necessary knowledge of universals (or essences) and "mere" probable opinion.

A third option was emerging: well-grounded empirical, or "morally certain" belief. The erosion of this dichotomy was crucial to making a systematic investigation into nature a worthy enterprise. As long as knowledge involved the apprehension of universals, empirical inquiry was a second-class occupation. It produced only specific observations or unreliable generalizations.

Scientific naturalists in the sixteenth and seventeenth centuries eroded the knowledge–opinion dichotomy. They arrived at useful empirical truths through scientific discoveries that ignored the medieval concern for essences. Copernicus's simpler, heliocentric astronomy did not ask about the essential "nature" of the planets; it described their orbits.[39] Galileo did not seek the essence of matter but mapped

38 Barbara Shapiro, *A Culture of Fact.*

39 Butterfield, *The Origins of Modern Science,* 17–36.

the mathematical relations between quantifiable features of phenomena. Meanwhile, throughout the seventeenth century, philosophers and mathematicians developed a logic of empirical knowledge based on notions of probability, statistical inference, and induction. The notion of evidence, hitherto equated with verbal testimony or a "sign" of things to come, received a scientific sense – logical support for an empirical belief, a support that came in degrees.[40]

The discourses and practices of fact took two forms. On the one hand, there were new literary genres as products of the printing press – travel writing, chorography, and journalism. All three genres claimed to be factual narratives. Their emphasis on facts made them different from other genres, such as fictional poetry and biased commentary. On the other hand, social practices such as law and academic disciplines such as history adopted an orientation towards fact and methods for determining fact.

Shapiro argues that the idea of impartial fact-determination in England first took root not in science but in the common law of the fifteenth and sixteenth centuries. Eventually, the legal "fact" became the editor's "newes" of the Thirty Years War, the explorer's "chronicle," the experimenter's "matter of fact," and the merchant's facts of finance.[41] In English law, a "matter of fact" was any act of legal significance, such as murder or theft. Factuality was important for three reasons: the law made a crucial distinction between matters of fact and matters of law; lay jurors had to evaluate alleged fact; and courts were supposed to be impartial proceedings. The distinction between fact and legal interpretation underlay the twelfth-century proverb: "You give me the facts, I give you the law." A fact was not an established truth. It was what had to be proved against the accused.

Early legal manuals laid down criteria for assessing witnesses. Witnesses were more credible if they were male and well-educated, owned property, and were of good character and even temper. In criminal trials, the accused and friends were "suspect" witnesses. In civil cases, courts disqualified witnesses with a financial interest. They first applied "impartial" to judges and jurors. From the late fifteenth century on, they instructed jurors to give their verdicts "according to your evidence and your conscience." Hale urged the judge to display an "entire absence of passion, affection, and

40 Hacking, *The Emergence of Probability*.

41 Mary Poovey argues that the modern fact began in the double-entry bookkeeping of sixteenth–century merchants. Poovey, *A History of the Modern Fact*, 29–91.

perturbation so that he may come to the business with clearness of understanding and judgment." Law reformer William Walwyn praised juries for "judging the cause of rich and poor without fear or favour."[42]

On this account, the courtroom was the site of the first modern attempts to define objectivity in practice. Legal decisions employed deliberative reason under conditions of uncertainty and lurking subjectivity. The juror who put facts "on trial" was an analogue of the scientist who tested ideas before nature. Objectivity was a practical matter. The legal system supported the objectivity of the judge's or juror's judgment by constructing a procedure-bound process focused on the impartial determination of fact. The courtroom combined impartial jurors with partial, disputing parties. Legal procedures sought a morally certain judgment that was neither absolutely certain nor arbitrary.

Other disciplines adopted the same norms of factuality. Historians claimed their writings were factual chronicles – not poetry, speculative philosophy, or partisan commentary. For Francis Bacon, the historian must "freely and faithfully" report with "impartial veracity" and follow "the rule of writing nothing but Matter of Fact." Chorography, as in Camden's nationwide study, *The Britannia* (1586), and John Stow's survey of London in 1598, provided a systematic description of places and societies. Travel writing reported on exotic journeys and the customs of natives.[43] Fraudulent reports of monsters and marvels were so common that some writers were called "travel liars." Therefore news reports and travel pieces stressed the writer's commitment to truth, impartial accounts, and reliable sources. Defoe stressed that he based his *Tour Thro the Whole Island of Great Britain* on his "Eye-witness." But inaccurate stories continued, forcing the Royal Society of London (founded 1660) to impose its own rules on fact gathering.

Legal practice and discourses of fact made the notions of factuality and impartiality familiar to the general culture. But a deeper notion of empirical objectivity was the work of the new sciences. English experimentalists in the seventeenth century developed a notion of fact that surpassed the ancient idea of "what generally happens." Philosophers from Aristotle to Aquinas had recognized observation as a source of information, and medieval science was not lacking an empirical spirit.[44]

42 Barbara Shapiro, *A Culture of Fact*, 27, 24.

43 The first important travel collection was Richard Hakluyt's *Principal Navigations, Voyages, Traffiques and Discoveries of the English Nation* (1589; reprint Glasgow: J. Mac Lebase and Sons, 1903), a collection of documents, letters, and first-hand accounts.

44 Crombie, *Science in the Middle Ages*, vol. 1.

But most philosophers did not regard facts as the basis of science, and few conducted experiments to force nature to reveal new facts. The experimentalists did. Experimental fact replaced the bishop or Bible as an authority on nature. Boyle said that, if matters of fact were not the whole of knowledge, then they were the most trustworthy part, having the greatest degree of probability or "moral certainty." He distinguished facts from uncertain inferences about their causes. "I dare speak confidently and positively of very few things, except of matters of fact," he said. Daston called Bacon "the patron saint of objectivity" because of his stress on facts as a neutral evaluator of hypotheses.[45]

It is difficult to separate the history of scientific objectivity from that of scientific instruments. In early modern science, instruments were the generators of objective facts. The air pump, telescope, and microscope were showpieces of the new scientific method, appearing in numerous paintings.[46] Instruments allowed people to see certain things for the first time: the rings of Saturn, the structure of the fly's eye, the spots on the sun. Tycho Brahe, in the late sixteenth century, established a scientific laboratory on the Danish island of Hven where inquirers observed comets, made new tools for astronomy and map-making, and published findings on their own printing press. The new scientists saw themselves as surpassing the ancients by virtue of their printing press, guns, mariner's compass, and other inventions. Scientific work, Bacon said, should be "like mines, where the noise of new works and further advances is heard on every side." Sprat enjoined scientists to learn from the "Shops of Mechanics; from the Voyages of Merchants; from the Ploughs of Husbandmen."

The new experimentalists were not isolated intellectuals but part of an international "Republic of Letters," whose members believed that their work transcended factions and countries. Moreover, their intellectual detachment coexisted with an active intervention in nature.[47] Nature would reveal its secrets only if "under constraint and vexed" by experiment. In 1699, the *Histoire* of the Royal Academy of Sciences in Paris said that scientists wrenched "matters of fact" from nature by a

45 Davis and Hunter, *Robert Boyle*; Daston, "Baconian Facts," 37.

46 Shapin and Schaffer, *Leviathan and the Air-Pump.*

47 On the Republic of Letters, see Burke, *A Social History of Knowledge.* On experimentalism, see Butterfield, *The Origins of Modern Science,* 77–95. Butterfield notes that interest in experiment was strong among sixteenth-century medical students, especially those at the University of Padua, where Copernicus, Galileo, and Harvey had studied.

"kind of violence."[48] But how to test the claims of experimenters across Europe in an age of slow communications and fledgling scientific routines? One answer was to test the latest experiments before gatherings of scientific societies; another was to publish them in a scientific journal. At meetings and in publications, scientists described their experiments so that others could identify errors or do the experiment themselves. Sprat said that meetings of the Royal Society made "the whole process (the experiment) pass under its own eyes," correcting idiosyncrasies of observation and judgment.

From the beginning, the test of scientific objectivity was a combination of the test of nature and the test of public scrutiny. Objectivity required facts and intersubjective agreement. The social aspect of objectivity was crucial.[49] A fact was not recognized as such until it met the norms of the relevant scientific community. "It is not I who says this; it is all of us," Sprat said, referring to experiments sanctioned by the Royal Society. However, since not everyone could attend the meetings or replicate the findings, much depended on trust and the scientist's reputation. The experimentalist inspired trust by displaying impartiality, by showing "indifferency" with regard to where the facts might lead and civility towards other scientists. Impartiality took the form of a sober style that made modest claims. Impartiality and civility were not attributes of disputes in theology and philosophy in previous centuries. But in the seventeenth century, revolution devastated England, and partisan politics wracked it. Impartiality and public procedures held passions at bay, creating a safe place for scientific discussion.

Science retained the abstract idea of truth as correspondence to reality but now gave truth a pragmatic meaning. Experimentalists showed how empirical objectivity was possible. They described their methods and identified sources of bias, such as Bacon's "idols" of the mind. Sciences of fact worked out "standards for well-founded, reasonable, highly probable, but non-certain belief."[50]

48 Quoted in Daston, "Fear and Loathing of the Imagination in Science,"75.

49 In modern times, Karl Popper developed the idea of scientific objectivity as a method with an intrinsic social aspect in *The Open Society and Its Enemies*, 2:217–20. Popper states that scientific objectivity is "not a product of the individual scientist's impartiality, but a product of the social or public character of scientific method."

50 Barbara Shapiro, *Probability and Certainty in Seventeenth-Century England*, 4–5: "By the end of the seventeenth century, most English thinkers, no matter what their field of inquiry, had ceased to believe that their labours would produce the certitude or 'science' that had for centuries been the goal of the philosopher."

Philosophies of Objective Knowledge

By the end of the seventeenth century, science was the most successful model of inquiry, able to boast about Galileo's laws of motion, Harvey's discovery of the circulation of the blood, and Newton's dynamics. But these theories did not constitute a unified philosophy of science. Aristotelian academics, religious reformers, and sceptics questioned the new learning.[51] Scientists disagreed on questions of method, and their findings had troubling implications for religion. These implications stimulated Locke, Descartes, and others to take the "epistemological turn" and construct theories of human understanding to explain how science was possible.

The disagreements coalesced around the differences between rationalists and empiricists. Both groups agreed that reason and the senses played a part in natural knowledge, but not about their relative importance. Just as medieval philosophers had debated the roles of faith and reason, natural philosophers debated the roles of reason and the senses. Most rationalists were Continental thinkers, represented by Descartes, Gassendi, Pascal, Leibniz, and Spinoza. The application of mathematics and formal reasoning to science impressed them. "Was not Plato perfectly right," asked Galileo, "when he wished that his pupils should be first of all well grounded in mathematics?"[52] Leading empiricists were English experimentalists and philosophers such as Bacon, Hooke, Boyle, Locke, and later Berkeley and Hume.

By "reason" the rationalists meant more than the ability to draw inferences or to figure out the means to an end. Reason was a special faculty that provided knowledge of necessary truths of logic, mathematics, or philosophy. They justified necessary truths not by induction over observations but by reason's logical analysis of ideas, some of which were innate to the mind. The rationalist's model for knowledge was Euclidean

51 The phrase "natural philosophy" gave way to "sciences of nature" only in the eighteenth century. The first scholar to write of "scientific method" appears to have been the sceptic and philosopher Francisco Sanchez (1552–1623), in *Why Nothing Can Be Known* (1581). He argued that humans can make only limited claims about appearances – a cautious approach that he called "scientific method."

52 Galileo, *Dialogues Concerning Two New Sciences,* 137. For Aristotle, mathematical concepts were abstractions of physical properties – ideally straight lines and perfect circles. These unchanging formal concepts could not explain the causes or "essences" of physical things. Instead, Aristotle applied his concepts of substance, matter and form, and potential and actual being. Galileo showed how mathematics could be useful for scientific discovery.

geometry, where axioms led deductively to theorems. But rationalism went beyond formal deductive systems and applied formal thought to the objects of experience. Galileo, for example, used idealized mathematical models to interpret natural events such as sunspots, the swinging of pendulums, and Jupiter's satellites. Experience was useful to science once it had been mathematically described. Facts must be embedded within a rational system. In spirit, the rationalists followed the ancient way of truth. Reason and mathematics promised to fulfil a "yearning for certainty and consensus" in a time of scepticism and religious wars.[53] Galileo said that knowledge by mathematical proof "equals the Divine in objective certainty, for here it succeeds in understanding necessity."[54]

English empiricists, in contrast, tended to be imperfectionists who followed the way of experience. Empiricists stressed the origin of ideas in sensation, the importance of habit, and the psychological association of ideas. Science progressed not by constructing systems of reason but by accumulating facts, experiments, hypotheses, and inductive generalizations. Most empiricists did not share Descartes's dream of a great deductive system of knowledge. Boyle claimed that he avoided knowledge of theoretical systems, such as atomism or Cartesian philosophy, so "that I might not be predisposed with any theory or principles."

We must not push the rationalism–empiricism distinction too far. Empiricists and rationalists agreed on several basic matters. Both groups were naturalists who believed in the authority of rational thought in science. Echoing Galileo, Boyle said: "I could be very well content to be thought to have scarce looked upon any other book than that of nature."[55] Both groups agreed that the new science differed from previous inquiry by stressing what was new, useful, empirical, and clear. All believed that science was capable of benefiting humanity.

In actual inquiry, empiricists and rationalists combined reason and experience. They used facts, hypotheses, logic, and mathematics. Newton's dynamics was a remarkable synthesis of these elements. Descartes, the arch-rationalist, made many observations in optics, physiology, and psychology. For Descartes, once reason had established secure founda-

53 Toulmin, *Return to Reason*, 32. Toulmin notes how Descartes wrote as Europe suffered through the Thirty Years War (1618–48), which killed one-third of Germany's population and destroyed half of its cities.

54 Clavelin, *The Natural Philosophy of Galileo*, 383–461. Galileo dismissed rhetoric as "probable arguments, conjectures ... and other sophisms."

55 Shapin and Schaffer, *Leviathan and the Air-Pump*, 68.

tions for knowledge, the sciences could employ empirical forms of inquiry for the "good of mankind."

Empiricists attempted what Bacon called a "lawful marriage" between reason and observation. Neither the light of natural reason nor passive experiencing would create science. Both rational and empirical methods must shape experience. Hooke described the experimentalist's method as a circular process involving the senses, memory, understanding, and reason. Bacon pointed out two erroneous approaches to inquiry: the "empyrick," who like an ant gathers useless facts without principle or design, and the "reasoner," who like a spider spins dogmas that ignore nature. Inquirers should act like the bees that gather material from the flowers of the field but digest the material by a power of their own. Science was the achievement of an active rationality that brings several faculties to bear on the world.

Empiricists and rationalists sought to reconstruct the language of science. Prevailing discourses, such as scholastic logic and the eloquent letters of humanists, they thought, blocked a clear apprehension of the facts or made people vulnerable to poetic devices. Science needed a plain language that referred directly to fact and assisted clear reasoning. For some practitioners, scientific language was mathematical. Galileo said that the "grand book, the universe ... is written in the language of mathematics." Leibniz wanted an "exact" language for reasoning about all issues: a universal language would resolve the "Babel of doctrine" in seventeenth century Europe.[56]

Others sought a plain language, stripped of adornment, as developed by chorography, travel writing, and journalism. The printing press received frequent praise as an agent of plain fact. Empiricists wanted a factual language – a transparent medium between mind and object. Sprat distrusted the "cheat of words," and Bacon warned about the "juggleries and charms of words." The Royal Society's statutes proclaimed: "In all Reports to be brought into the Society, the Matter of Fact shall be barely stated, without Prefaces, Apologies, or Rhetorical Flourishes."[57] Locke said that a clear language would let the things themselves determine truth. Philosophers could learn from the clear speech of "merchants and lovers, cooks and sailors." Objective reality and numbers, it seemed, would overcome the fog of words.[58]

56 Toulmin, *Return to Reason*, 67–76.

57 Sprat, *History of the Royal Society*.

58 Ray Porter, *Enlightenment*, 54–5.

Disengagement and Transcendence

Two philosophers, Descartes and Locke, deepened the notion of scientific objectivity through their reflections on method. Despite Locke's scepticism towards acquiring knowledge by reason alone, both men approached knowledge as the analysis and combination of ideas.[59] Moreover, correct method depended on the adoption of an objective attitude – that of disengaged reason. Objective knowledge was the product of a subjectivity disciplined by method and disengagement.

Descartes said that only correct method could lead to science's goal of "true and evident cognition." "By method," he explained, "I mean certain and simple rules, such that, if a man observe them accurately, he shall never assume what is false as true ... but will gradually increase his knowledge and so arrive at a true understanding of all that does not surpass his powers." Descartes's method consisted of the analysis and synthesis of ideas. Through analysis, the mind breaks down complex ideas into clear and simple ideas. It intuits simple ideas – for example, that some thing exists, that three lines only bound a triangle, that nothing which is "A" can be "not A." Synthesis works in the opposite direction. The mind takes simple ideas and deduces more complex ideas. The method of analysis and synthesis "springs from the light of reason alone" and is the only way to "sure and indubitable knowledge."[60]

Locke conducted a psychological study of how the mind constructs complex beliefs from ideas originating in sensation. The mind is empty of ideas until external objects cause bodily sensations of colour, heat, shape, pain, and so on. The mind reflects on these sensations and produces the ideas of colour, heat, shape, and pain in the mind. It then combines these ideas into judgments, such as cause and effect. It can also reason, moving by inference, from ideas to other ideas. Locke concludes: "Knowledge then seems to me to be nothing but the perception of the connection and agreement, or disagreement and repugnancy of any of our ideas."[61] Locke's inquiry discovers two types of knowledge: direct awareness of ideas caused by particular objects acting on us; and discursive reasoning, which expands knowledge through demonstration or probable inference (by analogy or induction).

The pursuit of truth, however, involves more than analysing and combining ideas. For Locke and Descartes, the inquirer must disengage

59 Schouls, *The Imposition of Method,* 5.

60 Descartes, *The Philosophical Works of Descartes,* 1:9, 1:7, 1:3.

61 Locke, *An Essay Concerning Human Understanding,* 2:167.

from conventional thinking. The thinker starts as an embodied subject with false ideas inculcated by society. Correct thinking begins with a mental disengagement from one's current beliefs. Disengagement means opening up a critical distance between oneself and one's culture. Once disengaged, the inquirer follows a method to reach objective truths, based on logic and evidence. Such beliefs receive rational certification. They are not merely the effect of causal factors in society. The disengaged thinker transcends his or her situation. Descartes, echoing Plato's disappointment with opinion, complains that he travelled the world and found either conflicting beliefs or consent to "extravagant and ridiculous" opinions. Unlike the sophists, Descartes does not appreciate the pluralism of thought, and he resolves to "believe nothing too certainly of which I had only been convinced by example and custom," which "rendered us less capable of listening to Reason."[62]

Descartes adopts the liberating attitude of disengagement during his meditations before a fire. Analysis and radical doubt allow him to step back from his beliefs. They lead him to clear, indubitable ideas, such as the fact that he and a benevolent God exist. Then he uses these ideas to deduce fundamental truths about the world – the philosophical basis for science. For Descartes, correct method and disengagement aim ultimately at an "absolute conception" of the world: to know things as they really are, independent of historically and socially conditioned perspectives.[63]

Locke expresses a more modest variant of disengagement: "I have not made it my business, either to quit, or follow any Authority in the ensuring Discourse. Truth has been my only aim." He adds: "The floating of other men's opinions in our brains, makes us not one jot the more knowing, though they happen to be true."[64]

For Descartes and Locke, disengagement was the first step in the rational reconstruction of beliefs. The key was reason's autonomy. If reason was not autonomous, it could not adopt an objective attitude, it could not discover its own truths, it could not transcend its entanglement in tradition. In Augustine, God's grace illuminates confused minds. In Descartes, the "natural light of reason" provides its own illumination.

The growth of science in the seventeenth century led to a reconception of nature. Since scientific method favoured properties that were

62 Descartes, *The Philosophical Works of Descartes*, 1:87.

63 Williams, *Descartes*, 65.

64 Locke, *An Essay Concerning Human Understanding*, 2:115.

observable and measurable, nature came to be conceived of as mathematically lawful and materialistic. Descartes separated the world into extended matter and non-extended mind. A law-governed, mechanical, material nature stands over and against mind as mental substance.[65] Galileo distinguished between objective, primary properties – an object's shape, size, and motion – and subjective, secondary properties – an object's colour, taste, sound, and smell. "Tastes, odours, colours, and so on, are no more than mere names so far as the object in which we place them is concerned, and that they reside only in consciousness."[66]

For these modern pioneers, science is objective not only because it follows objective methods but also because its methods deal with objective properties. The epistemic objectivity of natural science complements the ontological objectivity of the mechanical world, known by natural science. In contrast, ethics, art, and other non-scientific activities are subjective, because they deal with the subjective qualities of objects. At this point, the scientific and human images of the world begin to diverge. The world according to science begins to look quite different from the world known by ordinary experience.

ENLIGHTENMENT AND OBJECTIVITY

The Common View

The Enlightenment's emphasis on reason shaped empirical objectivity in two ways. In ethics, an objective thinker was an impartial judge who adopted a "common view" when considering the rightness or wrongness of an action. In philosophy, objectivity in knowledge became correct representation.

Enlightenment "reason" was a broad term, including the use of judgment, interpretation, and imagination. Voltaire's history of human development, for example, was a sweeping narrative – part literature, part rational conjecture. "Reason" referred to the ability and right of humans to think for themselves, to search for reasons rather than accepting the dictates of authority. "Reason" was also a political slogan. The French *philosophes* sang the praises of reason in defiance of absolute monarchy and entrenched church hierarchy. They did not regard scientific reason as the enemy of creativity or of the imagination. In fact, eighteenth-century England discovered the "pleasures of the imagina-

65 Burtt, *The Metaphysical Foundations of Modern Science*, 105–24.

66 Quoted in Clavelin, *The Natural Philosophy of Galileo*, 435.

tion" through the commercialization of culture.[67] Scientific knowledge was thought to rely on more than facts – the scientist's creativity, skill, and experienced judgment. What mattered was the proper use of imagination. A disciplined imagination was a source of discovery and genius; an undisciplined imagination eroded judgment. A French scientific commission, which included Lavoisier and Franklin, attributed the public's belief in animal magnetism to overwrought imagination.

The Enlightenment of the first half of the eighteenth century saw a confident application of reason and science to society and natural phenomena. In England, both mainstream and radical elements of the early Enlightenment sought to clear away "the rubbish" of old traditions, from scholasticism and Catholicism to Protestant sectarianism.[68] Newton's *Mathematical Principles of Natural Philosophy* (1687) was the paradigm of exact science; English liberty, the paradigm of progressive society. Across Europe, scientific societies and sciences, such as chemistry, emerged. Diderot and d'Alembert proudly collected the new learning into the *Encyclopédie,* printing pictures of farm machinery alongside analysis of Newtonian physics. By late in the century, this confidence was succumbing to worries over the bounds of reason and the implications of a Newtonian world. Kant's limitation of science to sensible appearances demoralized Voltaire, who wrote that every substance is unknown because "we see appearances only; we are in a dream."[69]

67 Brewer, *The Pleasures of the Imagination.*

68 Israel, in his *Radical Enlightenment,* argues that the early Enlightenment had a moderate stream represented by Locke and Newton and a radical stream represented by Spinoza. The moderates placed their philosophy within a Christian framework. Descartes saw the mechanical philosophy as supporting God's rationality. Locke wrote *The Reasonableness of Christianity* in 1695. The radical branch could not be incorporated into Christian orthodoxy. In France, d'Holbach and La Mettrie espoused a brash materialism. Other thinkers stressed the wonders of a providential God. As Pope wrote in *Essay on Man,* "whatever is, is right."

69 Kant's motto for the Enlightenment was uplifting: "Sapere aude!" Have courage to use your own understanding, which is "man's emergence from his self-incurred immaturity." But Voltaire opened his *Philosophe ignorant* as follows: "Who are you? Where do you come from? ... This is a question one must put to every creature in the universe but none of them gives us any answer." His sardonic *Candide* barely masked the disillusionment of an ageing, exiled Voltaire with optimistic views about God's providence. Diderot ended his *Interpretation of Nature* with a strange prayer: "O God, I do know if you exist ... Here I stand, as I am, a necessarily organized part of eternal and necessary matter ... or perhaps your own creation." Quoted in Hampson, *The Enlightenment,* 95–6.

The spread of scientific philosophy did not crush belief in a rational ethics. Instead, some of the best minds of the age constructed ethics on presumed facts about human nature and on conjectures about the origin of society. Naturalistic morals found new principles in human sentiments, utilitarian facts, social contracts, and impartial judgment.[70] Moral naturalism began with a psychological interpretation of ethical notions. Locke identified good and bad with our desire to achieve pleasure and avoid pain. Hobbes defined "good" and "right" as objects that psychologically attract or repel us, respectively. Hume argued that emotion, not reason, sets the ends of action. Bentham's utilitarianism was empirical and reformist, reducing decisions to the calculation of pleasures and pains, "the greatest good of the greatest number."

But this approach begged large questions. If everyone acts according to their interests and sentiments, why should anyone act for the benefit of others? Conceptually, how do we get from the preferences of self-interested individuals to the duties of morality? Hobbes's answer had been an authoritarian version of the social contract: it is in everyone's interest to place power in the hands of a Leviathan to enforce contracts. Another response was to emphasize a counter-balancing sentiment of benevolence or sympathy. Condorcet believed that nature endowed all people with "benevolence ... and generous sensibility." Hume said that, to judge another person as vicious, one must persuade others by appealing to common feelings of sympathy and antipathy towards certain actions, arguing from a "common point of view." Vanity or ambition may at times overwhelm these feelings, "yet, being common to all men, [sympathy] can alone be the foundation of morals ... (for) the humanity of one man is the humanity of every one."

Adam Smith, in *The Theory of Moral Sentiments,* put forward an ethical naturalism that placed feelings of sympathy, imagination, and impartial judgment at the centre of his moral system. Smith's moral system sought to answer the question of human society – how is it possible that humans are "fit" for society? After answering this question, Smith moved on to consider economic activity in *The Wealth of Nations* (1776). He departed from the teaching of his instructor in moral philosophy, Francis Hutcheson, who had argued that virtue consisted in benevolence and that benevolent actions are alone worthy of moral approval. Smith saw other virtues, such as the more demanding virtue of "self-command." Also, mankind's imperfection meant that humans must act from many other motivations. Smith emphasized mankind's self-love or

70 Taylor, *Sources of the Self,* 248–65.

self-regarding propensities, which are not always anti-social. In fact, they often lead people to enter into social relations. The self-regarding economic activities of individuals, for example, can help produce a more productive, wealthy society. In a famous passage, Smith noted, "It is not from the benevolence of the butcher, the brewer, or the baker that we expect our dinner, but from their regard to their own interests. We address ourselves, not to their humanity but to their self-love." Many of our wants are supplied "by treaty, by barter, and by purchase."[71]

For society to exist, however, there must be controls on self-love. Smith's controls included the ability of individuals to put themselves imaginatively in the place of others and to feel sympathy for them. "(Sympathy) is the source of our fellow-feeling of the misery of others, that it is by changing places in fancy with the sufferer, that we come either to conceive or to be affected by what he feels."[72] But sympathy is not sufficient. In ethics, it is never enough to feel sorrow or joy. One must also judge whether someone's actions display propriety or impropriety, given their situation. To judge of someone's propriety, we must view the actions and their circumstances "at a certain distance from us." We look on the actions from the perspective of an external, impartial judge. We do the same when we judge of our own actions. The actions are proper or improper to the degree that impartial spectators can agree or sympathize with them. If they agree, the actions appear as just and proper.[73] Yet even the ability to feel sympathy and to judge impartially would not be sufficient control on individuals unless humans cared about the judgment of others and their conscience. Smith therefore argues that humans incline naturally to seek the approval of others and to be worthy of that approval.[74]

Hence Smith's moral philosophy holds that individuals are subject to two forms of restraint – the judgment of other people and the judgment of their own consciences, or the "man within." The "impartial spectator" is the impartial judgment of conscience within the human "breast."[75]

71 Adam Smith, *The Wealth of Nations* (1776), 119.

72 Adam Smith, *The Theory of Moral Sentiments* (1759), 3.

73 Ibid., 22.

74 Ibid., 248.

75 Smith argued for a similar impartial voice in the marketplace, in the form of government, which should act as an impartial agent to stop unfair competition.

Philosophers of that era gave impartial judgment a role beyond ethics. Hume, for example, advised the art critic to take the position of a "man in general, forget, if possible, my individual being, and my peculiar circumstances." He believed that historians must "have no particular interest or concern to pervert their judgment." In politics, Hume encouraged impartiality and public zeal, not the "ends of ... faction."[76]

Impartiality, established earlier by discourses of fact, now formed an essential part of moral, political, and aesthetic reasoning. Impartial judging replaced or supplemented appeals to God's will. The "ought" of morality was the combined compulsion of sympathy and an impartial attitude. Impartiality and sentiment became linked. Sympathy for others induces one to take the other person's viewpoint. Conversely, by adopting an impartial viewpoint, by "standing in someone's shoes," one is moved by feelings of sympathy.

Impartiality, civility, and sentiment had political and social value for a growing public sphere. However, the appeal to society and sentiment gradually became problematic. By the mid-eighteenth century, in France, Rousseau was challenging the restraints of sentiment and polite society. He claimed instead that society corrupted natural feelings. True sentiment had to be rediscovered beneath the false and contrived layers of feeling and manners of sophisticated society.

Representing the World

The idea of objectivity also entered the conversation of Enlightenment thinkers through epistemological quarrels over how the mind could know nature. Locke and Descartes interpreted knowledge as the correct mental representation of objects. But the idea of representation stirred a hornet's nest of sceptical questions. Most basically, how do we know that our ideas represent material objects, as they exist? Berkeley concluded that if we know objects through ideas, we can know only that minds and ideas exist. Moreover, empirical epistemology seemed to make knowledge of nature a conjecture. If empirical reasoning is induction over past experience, why do we believe that the past will resemble the future? How can the observation of empirical regularities justify the belief in a necessary causal structure of the world? Hume settled for a mitigated scepticism that went back to antiquity: we have to presume, not prove, some principles of reason, such as induction.

76 Hume, *Essays: Moral, Political and Literary*, 562, 278–9.

Kant responded to the epistemological quarrels by writing three critiques between 1781 and 1790 that placed objective judgment in science, ethics, and art at the heart of Western philosophy. Kant's "Copernican revolution" in philosophy started with the mind, not the world. Psychologically, how do humans come to believe in an objective world? Epistemically, how much of that experience is warranted knowledge? His answer was that we construct a representation of an objective world by using the faculties of understanding and reason to organize sensory intuitions. Epistemically, we have warranted knowledge of objects only as "appearances" or how they appear to us, through the mediation of the categories of understanding and reason.

Kant combined elements of empiricism and rationalism to explain the psychological construction. All experience is rationally interpreted experience. The mind does not receive raw sensory input from objects, which it then interprets by concepts. Sensation and conceptualization operate together, from the start.

Kant claimed that the mind comes equipped with basic categories without which no experience would be possible. These categories, such as space, time, and causality, determine the structure of all experience. Kant calls these categories "a priori" or "transcendental," because they do not derive from empirical experience – they belong to the structure of all minds. We construct an experience of an objective world though these categories. Reason therefore cannot know "things-in-themselves" – how things are – apart from how they appear. Nor can reason know "supersensible" objects, such as God, that go beyond the appearances. Science knows nature as a lawful system of appearances, filtered through a priori categories. By drawing limits around reason, Kant believed that he had left room for faith, freedom, and morality in a deterministic, scientific world.

Kant defined truth in the traditional way as the "agreement of knowledge with its object." But he then asked what the "criterion of truth" could be.[77] Judgments can be false, distorted, or the product of bad reasoning. Experience becomes objective knowledge when we do two things – when we keep reasoning within the bounds of experience, properly applying categories to sensible intuitions, and, more particularly, when we order and test our judgments by observation, logic, and mathematical analysis.

77 Kant, *Critique of Pure Reason* (1781), 97.

For Kant, scientific knowledge is universal, necessary, and systematic. The laws of science, such as the laws of planetary motion, are not relative to person, place, or time. The ideal form of knowledge is a deductive system. Kant's second critique, on morals, took the form of definitions, principles, and theorems.

In Kant's ethics, objectivity is the agreement not of judgment and object but of a specific judgment with the principles of practical reason. Kant agrees that our will is influenced "empirically" by desires and consequences, but he denies that such considerations can be the foundation for morality. At best, they provide hypothetical rules that hold here and there, and for the most part. Fundamental ethical principles must be imperatives that are universal and categorical, not hypothetical. They must be based solely on considerations of duty, not "subjective" factors such as pleasure, sentiment, or utilitarian consequences. Kant believed that if we use our practical reason properly, we will arrive at such categorical imperatives, or "fact(s) of reason." How do we recognize a fact of practical reason? The rule must have a universal form. Kant writes: "Act only on the maxim through which you can at the same time will that it should become universal law."[78]

A principle becomes an objective duty, then, if reason regards it as a duty for all rational beings. Universalizability, impartiality, rational consistency – these are the signs of agreement with practical reason. Not all moral maxims are (or must be) objective in this rigorous way. But fundamental moral laws must be facts of reason. These imperatives will have "objective reality" if they determine our will. Reason must give the moral law to itself. Kant, Hume, and Smith agreed on the virtues of reciprocity and impartiality. They agreed that morality derived from some aspect of human nature. But Kant makes the "voice" of morality not sentiment but the stern voice of self-legislating reason. By impartially determining the morals that guide us, we become conscious of ourselves as free, rational creatures, not determined by the laws of nature. To violate duty is to betray one's nature as a self-determining being. Acting objectively in ethics is an expression of autonomous human nature and of human dignity.

Kant also uses the term "objective" to refer to claims tested by "publicity" – the scrutiny of rational inquirers. Intersubjective validity assures us that our judgment goes beyond our idiosyncratic experience. In his first critique, on knowledge, Kant says that one holds a judg-

78 Kant, *Critique of Practical Reason*, (1788), 17, 30.

ment with "conviction" after seeing that others think one's reasons valid. His second critique challenges those people who have metaphysical knowledge to "present it for public testing." His third, on aesthetic judgment, comes close to Hume's "common view" by saying that people check their judgments by "think(ing) in the place of everybody else." However, Kant warns, "universality of assent does not *prove* the objective validity of a judgment." Rather, objective knowledge supports agreement.[79]

Despite Kant's philosophical labours, the problem of objectivity – of how ideas represent objects – would live on. A long line of philosophers attempted to explain the presumed gap between mental idea and external object. The Scottish "common sense" philosopher Thomas Reid said that the mind had an irresistible tendency to believe that ideas "suggest" the presence of external bodies. John Stuart Mill said that the mind constructed the perceived object as an association of actual and expected sensations. Matter was the "permanent possibility of sensation," and the world was "the world of possible sensations succeeding one another according to laws."[80] But none of these philosophical answers silenced sceptical doubts. Mental representation, as a theory of objective knowledge, remained a philosophical problem.

QUEST FOR PURE OBJECTIVITY

The Positive Spirit

By the mid-nineteenth century, the term "objectivity" was popular in the academy and in the public sphere. It became popular at about the same time as the term "scientist" entered common usage. "Objectivity" in this era emerges with a modern, scientific meaning.[81] Part of its popularity was the result of Kant and the epistemological debates of the late eighteenth century. Part of it was the nineteenth century's admiration for scientific fact and what appeared to follow from objective fact – advances in technology. Another reason was the growth of the sciences and their interest in distinguishing themselves as disciplines that "let nature speak for itself." To be objective was to accept the coercion of facts.

79 Kant, *Critique of Pure Reason*, 645, *Critique of Practical Reason*, 5, 13.

80 Quoted in Passmore, *A Hundred Years of Philosophy*, 32.

81 "Subjective" and "objective" enter German, French, and English dictionaries as a pair of terms in the 1820s and 1830s.

The concept of objectivity evolved throughout the nineteenth century towards what I call "pure objectivity." The attempt to inoculate science from bias launched the quest for pure objectivity. Objectivity became narrower in concept and stricter in method. Pure objectivity conceived of the scientist as a dispassionate observer of nature. It favoured procedures and new instruments that grasped the facts. It reconceived the role of facts. Ontologically, a fact was a hard nugget of data that no one could invent or manipulate. The truth of a factual statement followed from a direct correspondence of the sentence and the state of affairs that it describes. Facts could be the objective, evidentiary basis of science only if science could draw a hard line between facts and value, facts and interpretation. Science, of course, interested itself not in common, everyday facts but in new facts revealed by precise method that took safeguards against bias. Objectivity thereby acquired a negative meaning. "Objectivity" was *not* being subjective, *not* interpreting. "Sit down before a fact as a little child," wrote Thomas Huxley. "Be prepared to give up every pre-conceived notion, follow humbly wherever and to whatever abyss nature leads, or you shall learn nothing."[82]

The first expression of pure objectivity in the nineteenth century was positivism – a philosophy of science and a general climate of thought. Mill said that positivism was "the general property of the age." Positivism was, first and foremost, anti-metaphysical. It wanted to move beyond theoretical speculations and the philosophical systems of German idealism. Positivists took to heart Kant's dictum that science knew only appearances, not things in themselves.[83] Scientific thinkers should deal only with the facts of experience. Mill wrote: "We have no knowledge of anything but phenomena, and our knowledge of phenomena is relative, not absolute. We know not the essence, nor the real mode of production, of any fact, but only its relations to other facts in the way of succession or of similitude." Fourier's mathematical laws of the diffusion of heat, for example, formulated regularities among phenomena without assumptions about the nature of heat.

Epistemically, positivism took over Hume's view that meaningful statements were of two kinds: matters of fact, as in observation and science; and relations of ideas, as in logic and mathematics. In

82 Quoted in Stevens, *A History of News*, 221.

83 By 1834, Schilling had given his last philosophical lectures, and Hegel was dead. The term "positivism" first appears in 1831 in a document published by followers of the French utopian socialist Saint-Simon.

France, Auguste Comte said: "Any (empirical) proposition which does not admit of being ultimately reduced to a single enunciation of fact, special or general, can have no real or intelligible sense." For Comte, science was the culmination of the march of human thought from theology to metaphysics to positivistic science. The accumulation of facts would lead to predictive laws of society that would guide political reform. Comte's talk of fact was not new. But his worship of facts and his strident rejection of other forms of thought pointed towards pure objectivity.

Positivism's uncompromising empiricism suited an increasingly confident science that was supposed to be factual and directed towards results. Positivistic philosophy was compatible with new scientific movements, such as nineteenth-century materialism. Karl Vogt's *Physiological Epistles* of 1847 had shocked many readers with its declaration that "the brain secretes thought, just as the liver secretes bile."[84] In the second half of the century, physical materialism and Comte's positivism gave way to broader, historical theories of nature and society by Darwin, Spencer, and Marx. Yet the movement towards stricter empirical approaches did not lag. By the end of the century, Spencer's principles were too broad for many scientists. Experimental procedures were making further inroads. In psychology, psycho-physics and Wundt's experiments on introspection suggested a quantification of the mind – the abode of consciousness.

Mechanical and Neutral Objectivity

Comte's positive philosophy gave the attitude of pure objectivity a name and an ideology. But the strongest force behind the invention of pure objectivity was the development of science as a powerful institution, linked to the economy, the education system, the military, and the race to develop new technology. By 1900, scientific inquiry was a professional, salaried occupation established at universities and industrial laboratories. Scientists also worked at schools that taught the applied sciences. Social acceptance of science depended on impressive discoveries in physics, physiology, medicine, and chemistry, along with new technologies, from the locomotive to electricity.

As the institution of science expanded, it fragmented into specialized disciplines. Science became "the sciences," natural, historical, and social. The modern sciences of biology, psychology, economics,

84 Quoted in Passmore, *A Hundred Years of Philosophy*, 36.

sociology, and statistics emerged, and new disciplines abounded: phrenology, haematology, toxicology, climatology, ethnology, epidemiology, topology, and criminology. Specialization made scientists impatient with system-builders. Progress in a scientific career required the learning of specific methods and a more narrow focus of inquiry. It became scientific to be cautious about speculating on the wider, philosophical implications of one's experimental results. The sciences distinguished themselves from the "subjective" non-sciences and arts by objective methods, suspicion of theorizing without empirical control, and devotion to facts.

The movement towards pure objectivity received additional support from science's nineteenth-century internationalization, which encouraged the search for objective standards and terminology so that scientists could communicate across national borders. Scientific congresses established standards of measurement, from the ohm to standard time.

Scientists gave birth to at least three species of epistemic objectivity: mechanical, aperspectival, and procedural. First, mechanical objectivity was objectivity through machines. Machines recorded facts automatically, uncontaminated by interpretation. Among the instruments used were the camera obscura, lithographs, photoengraving, photographs, and X-rays. Scientists employed machines to create images of the body, biological and botanical species, and eventually elementary particles, stars, and embryos. The camera obscura, for example, projected images of a bone or plant on to a surface where a researcher drew its form on a piece of paper. In an industrial age, scientific machines seemed tireless, ideal observers, ignorant of theory and devoid of personal ambition. Atlases, which proliferated from 1830 to 1920, were symbols of objectivity. In 1874, Gaston Tissandier, the French popularizer of science, said: "That which man cannot do, the machine can accomplish." Edgar Allan Poe wrote how the daguerreotype, compared with a work of art, discloses "a more absolute truth, more perfect identity of aspect with the thing represented." In 1885, William Anderson said that medicine no longer needed artists to construct atlases of the body because cheaper photographic methods "reproduce the drawings of the original object without error of interpretation." In 1875, the ophthalmoscope helped two authors, Hermann Pagenstecher and Carl Centus, to create an atlas of the eye. About their atlas they said: "[We] have kept it purely objective ... to preserve to the reader the advantages of unprejudiced view and unbiased judgment." In 1878, French physiologist E.J. Marey said that machine-made pictures are "patient and exact observers, blessed with senses more ... perfect than our own ... they accumulate documents of an unimpeachable fidelity." Charles Babbage praised machinery because it avoided "the inattention, the idleness, or the dishonesty of human agents."[85]

Second, objectivity for many scientists meant the transcendence of partial viewpoints – aperspectival objectivity was not the copying of facts but the reduction of distortion caused by local perspective. The scientist needed to "escape from perspective" to apprehend nature as it really is.[86] One way to do so was through peer review by scientific societies and journals. Another way was to study phenomena in teams of scientists. Yet another was to insist that experiments be replicable by other scientists. Aperspectival objectivity increased when many "subjectivities" reasoned together – when many scientists worked on the same problem. Early experimentalists had recognized the need for scientific societies. Kant had talked about "publicity."

In the nineteenth century, these norms developed into practices that defined scientific objectivity. In the United States, pragmatist Charles Peirce said that truth was what emerges in the long run from communal inquiry. Claude Bernard declared: "L'art c'est moi, la science, c'est nous." Ernest Renan observed that scientists were "transported to the viewpoint of humanity," while philosophers provided "the subjective fact of the solitary thinker." By the late nineteenth century, pure objectivity took on a moral tone, of Victorian self-discipline. British physicist Michael Faraday wrote: "The world little knows how many of the thoughts and theories which have passed through the mind of a scientific investigator have been crushed in silence ... by his own severe criticism."[87]

Third, inquiry and decision-making in the social sphere called forth procedural objectivity, which had two parts: the numerical analysis of social problems and of public policy, and the deployment of fair rules for political decisions and the administration of institutions. In the late nineteenth century, numerical analysis took many forms: surveys,

85 Daston and Galison, "The Image of Objectivity," 81–127.

86 Daston, "Objectivity and the Escape from Perspective," 597–618.

87 Peirce, "A Critical Review of Berkeley's Idealism," 81–3. See also Daston, "Objectivity and the Escape from Perspective," 609, and Daston and Galison, "The Image of Objectivity," 118. Scientists such as Faraday were among Samuel Smiles's heroes.

equations, graphs, measurements, statistical inferences, cost–benefit analyses and the application of probability theory to decisions. Numbers were considered objective because they were abstract, impersonal entities, governed by formal rules of calculation that hold for all rational beings. Numerical facts were as objective as the images of scientific instruments.

This "trust in numbers"[88] created new social facts and revealed patterns in welters of data. People could use numbers to characterize social groups and economic trends, to predict the consequences of actions, and to calculate mortality rates for insurance premiums. Procedural objectivity was a professional ideal for the expanding ranks of experts, officials, and sociologists. An "objective society" based on facts, not on patronage, seemed possible. Governments, politicians, and interest groups appealed to the numerical facts to justify decisions or to deflect complaints. For example, the U.S. Army Corps of Engineers early in the twentieth century explained its plans for major public works projects by developing detailed cost–benefit analyses. The results helped to create a consensus among engineers and to persuade politicians that the corps could do the job.

Meanwhile, procedural objectivity as objective rules became an ideal for large, urbanized democracies, which could not leave decisions to trust or to the discretion of dominant elites. Rival groups insisted on non-arbitrary policies.[89] Decision-makers had at least to put on the façade of objectivity. Governments set up public procedures for hiring staff and for awarding contracts. Sociologists have argued that objectivity is a matter of formalizing disciplinary routines.[90] But aperspectival and procedural objectivity went beyond routines, to provide norms for discourse across borders, disciplines, and societies. They acted as a bridge of communication between potentially rival groups. The search for objectivity is not just a quest for routines. In many cases, it was a search for a common ground where subjectivity, mistrust, and confusion otherwise confound us.

88 For the rise of probability theory and statistics, see Theodore M. Porter, *The Rise of Statistical Thinking* and *Trust in Numbers.* See also Stigler, *The History of Statistics,* Gigerenzer, et al., *The Empire of Chance;* and Hacking, *The Taming of Chance.*

89 Theodore M. Porter, "Objectivity as Standardization," 197–237.

90 Bloor, "A Sociological Theory of Objectivity," 229–45.

Towards the end of the nineteenth century, the social sciences contributed an additional norm to pure objectivity – the idea of a completely neutral, or "value-free," science. Robert Proctor has shown how a campaign for neutral social science grew in Germany (and elsewhere) in the late nineteenth and early twentieth centuries. Max Weber, among others, tried to rescue German social science from the control of socialists, politicians, and industrial leaders. Neutrality and objectivity were to act as shields against those who would politicize social theory.

Weber argued that social science had practical application, yet it should study social phenomena from a neutral perspective. Scientists might determine the consequences of different programs, but they should not judge the value of the rival programs. Citizens, not scientists, would resolve major questions of value. Weber said that a sociologist studying the conditions of factory workers should not see this as an opportunity for political pronouncements but should observe them "simply as a phenomenon ... whose progress it is his business objectively to explain." The ideal of neutrality assumed the objectivity of facts and the subjectivity of conceptions of the good. "Whenever the man of science comes forth with his own values, full understanding of the facts ceases," Weber wrote.[91]

During the nineteenth century, many scientists moved to pure objectivity as a response to the proliferation of scientific theories. The growth of sciences generated a plethora of conflicting theories in physics and other sciences until it seemed that no theory was safe. In this climate, "pure facts, severed from theory and sheltered from the imagination, were the last best hope for permanence in scientific achievement."[92] Furthermore, pure objectivity was a scientific antidote to the romantic movement and to existential philosophy, which valued the will, imagination, and inner feeling.

In philosophy, Kierkegaard insisted that human life was about the "individual" and his or her unique subjectivity, which people could not understand by a Hegelian system of history or by universal scientific knowledge. Schopenhauer wrote how the "world" was a reflection of the will. Nietzsche attacked "the dangerous old conceptual fiction that posited a pure, will-less, painless, timeless knowing subject." The more that philosophers and artists defined thinking as the product of unruly

91 Quoted in Proctor, *Value-Free Science?* 139, 150, 151.

92 Daston, "Fear and Loathing of the Imagination in Science," 91.

genius, or of emotional contact with creative nature, the more that scientists defined science as the domain of reason, logic, and fact. Objectivity became associated with science; subjectivity, with philosophy, art, and poetry.

Pure objectivity would receive its definitive expression in the philosophical movement of logical positivism. Like the earlier positivism, it was anti-metaphysical, but it used new logical techniques for analysing language and knowledge. After the First World War, a group of scientists and philosophers gathered around Moritz Schlick in Vienna – the "Vienna Circle." Between 1920 and 1960, the movement spread from Austria and Germany to England and the United States, to become the leading form of analytical philosophy.

Like its nineteenth-century predecessor, logical positivism caught the spirit of its times. In the 1920s, the political left and right in Austria and Germany were calling for a radical reconstruction of society after a disastrous war. A modern society would be built on uncompromising new modes of thought that were practical, scientific, and technological. Rudolph Carnap issued a call for "clarity, for a science that is free from metaphysics," for an attitude that "will win the future."[93] Logical positivism, with its austere methods, resembled the austerity of Bauhaus architecture. Philosophy would give up its pretension to providing special, metaphysical knowledge about the world. Instead, it would explain the logic of science by clarifying the language, methods, and empirical foundations of science. Philosophers would work "within the one unified science." Knowledge consisted either of synthetic truths about the world, known through experience, or of analytic truths of logic, language, and mathematics, grasped through conceptual analysis. Science discovered synthetic truths, while philosophy discovered analytical truths about concepts and rules of language. The statements of ethics, which were *not* translatable into or verifiable by experience, were literally meaningless – they were neither true nor false. At best, they expressed subjective emotions or attitudes.

In 1967, John Passmore wrote in the *Encyopaedia of Philosophy* that logical positivism "is dead, or as dead as any philosophy ever be-

93 Carnap, *The Logical Structure of the World and Pseudoproblems in Philosophy*, xviii. Carnap described how individuals, starting with their subjective streams of experience, arrived at a common knowledge of the world. See Richardson, *Carnap's Construction of the World*, and Galison, "Constructing Modernism," 17–44.

comes." What had happened to the bold program? Logical positivism fell prey to external criticism and internal differences. Appreciation was growing for the complexity of the process by which theories are changed and evaluated. Kuhn's *The Structure of Scientific Revolutions* emphasized the history and practice of science. Social, historical, and psychological factors were as important as the logic of science. Epistemologically, the positivist's hope for a hard distinction between fact and theory evaporated. Philosophers struggled to draw clear lines between observation and theory, between synthetic fact and analytical meaning. As well, the attempt to reduce theoretical statements to experiences stumbled.

In sum, logical positivism could not explain the complex relationship between theory and its empirical base. At the same time, more sophisticated theories of science pushed logical positivism to the philosophical sidelines. Quine offered an influential, alternative view of science as a fabric of self-supporting, theoretical beliefs that touches on observational evidence only along the "edges." With the death of logical positivism, a century-long movement towards pure objectivity ended.

The Legacy of Pure Objectivity

We have traced the history of objectivity through a maze of intellectual and social movements, philosophers and scientists. To guide our path across this shifting landscape, we found two landmarks: the invention of critical rationality in ancient times, in theory and in practice, and the development of a culture of fact and a scientific objectivity in the early modern period. We then saw how scientific objectivity evolved into a pure objectivity by 1900.

Given this historical perspective, we can regret the narrowing of objectivity into pure objectivity. Some narrowing of objective method for scientific purposes was natural and progressive. It strengthened the focus and method of particular sciences. But when it went beyond such laudable scientific purposes it became a negative influence. Objectivity became a dogmatic, divisive, and at times arrogant pure objectivity. It became a rhetorical device to humble "softer" disciplines and to foster unnecessary science wars. This militant pure objectivity, in the long run, helped to undermine not only pure objectivity but also the very idea of objectivity. Objectivity became identified, wrongly, with an extreme interpretation of the ideal – the idea of pure objectivity. The false and vulnerable conception of pure objectivity could not avoid entanglement in thorny epistemological problems, beginning in the 1960s. When its inadequate concepts underwent sustained attack, it crumbled, leaving the impression that objectivity per se was refuted or passé.

Today, many people that still incorrectly assume objectivity entails the unrealistic norms of neutrality, severe detachment, and "just the facts." They too often ignore the possibility that objectivity may be compatible with impure facts and non-absolute standards. Any new notion of objectivity must build itself on the ashes of pure objectivity. In chapter 7 I attempt to rescue objectivity from the strait-jacket of pure objectivity by providing an alternative theory. But first, we must examine how journalism ethics and journalism objectivity arose against the background of this history of objectivity.

PART TWO

The Evolution of Journalism Ethics

3

The Invention of Journalism Ethics: The Seventeenth Century

I am no Romance-Monger to present the world with Tragi-Comedies of my own invention.

Moderate Intelligencer

JOURNALISM AS A DISCOURSE OF FACT

Identifying an exact point at which journalism ethics begins is as hopeless a task as attempting to say when modern journalism begins. In the early modern period, there is no "first work" of print journalism. Nor is there an official date when a group of practitioners began to call themselves "journalists" and carried out activities clearly distinct from the work of printers, publishers, pamphlet writers, or ballad composers.[1]

1 The term "journalist" first appeared in the seventeenth century, vis-à-vis men of letters who wrote in learned journals. See Burke, *A Social History of Knowledge.* The term became associated with members of the popular press in the early eighteenth century. In 1712, Addison, in his *Spectator,* called a correspondent "a journalist." The term "reporter" referred initially to an official who recorded court proceedings by short-hand. Only later in the century did "reporter" begin to apply to a group of newspaper journalists covering the courts, Parliament, fires, and other notable events. For most of the eighteenth century, a reporter was called a "news-gatherer," or "news-writer."

Similarly, "editor" first appeared outside news journalism. In the eighteenth century, the term referred to someone who prepared a new, authoritative edition of an author's works, as Pope would do for Shakespeare in 1725. The editor's role developed slowly in newspapers. For much of the century, newspapers were operated, administratively and editorially, by a publisher, who hired the services of a few people to produce his paper.

The rise of journalism ethics begins with the emergence of a set of skills used in the production of printed news for a public.

Histories of modern journalism usually begin with the creation of a periodic news press in the seventeenth century – the "newspaper" in the form of a weekly (or bi-weekly) newsbook or newssheet.[2] I will argue that the weekly newspaper is where an embryonic journalism ethics starts to be asserted, including the first articulation of a "proto-objectivity" – a commitment to factuality and impartiality. Talk of impartiality begins to gather momentum in journalism at a time when Western culture's tradition of rational inquiry was being enriched by a scientific form of empirical objectivity examined in Chapter Two. In the first half of the 1600s, English weekly papers claimed that their reports were impartial "relations" of the truth and based on "matters of fact." The story of journalistic objectivity, therefore, begins in the most unlikely of places. It begins with a primitive, periodic, seventeenth century press shaped by England's violent path to a parliament-restrained monarchy.

As we have seen, the norms of impartiality and factuality did not originate in journalism but in the discourses and sciences of fact, and the rise of a "detached" Republic of Letters. A culture of fact had an impact on the seventeenth-century newsmonger. Ethical language gave the periodical editors a way of conceptualizing and justifying their activity in the face of the English government's nervousness over publicity on matters of state. Also, a culture interested in the exchange of information and matters of fact was likely to be receptive to publishers' claims that their fact-oriented activities were legitimate.

Early editors' assertions that they produced reasonable reports based on observation and testimony were comprehensible to a culture shifting towards a fallible, epistemic sense of objectivity. Periodic news journalism was, in effect, claiming to be another discourse of fact, with a particular interest in informing the general populace. Did the newsbooks not report on particular matters of fact, or "newes," like the chorographer or travel writer? It required no great effort to link prevailing ideas about matters of fact, faithful witnessing, and impartial judgment to the journalistic chronicling of events. The virtues of the ideal editor were not far from those of the "faithful" historian, the factual court witness, or even

2 "Newspaper" surfaced in England in the 1670s but was not a popular term until the eighteenth century. A letter dated 10 September 1670 contains the first known use of "newes paper." In Germany, *Zeitung* (newspaper) did not enter common usage until 1850. The German "presse," which emerged after 1500, referred to the machinery of printing.

the disinterested experimentalist. The spirit of early journalism was, like other discourses of fact, empirical, naturalistic, and, by necessity, pragmatic.

The lines of cultural influence ran in both directions. The culture of fact supported news journalism, which supported the culture of fact. News reports created excitement about explorations, while helping to disseminate scientific findings. The periodic press was both a product and a contributor to the ascending print culture of western Europe in the sixteenth and seventeenth centuries. Elizabeth Eisenstein has shown how the printing press did not just increase the quantity of books. It gave birth to a culture of print that changed the attitudes and practices of scholars, editors, and writers and created a new "objective" approach to knowledge and the world.[3] It was now possible to analyse printed texts objectively and to reproduce them endlessly with accuracy, creating in effect a database on which other inquirers could build. With its serially numbered newspapers, full of "occurrences," journalism contributed to the print culture and the scientific mindset by portraying the world as a sequence of datable events – an independent, objective realm of social and natural facts open to description, analysis, and further study.

Nevertheless, the periodical news of the seventeenth century was only a marginally respectable discourse of fact. Many people saw it as not much better than the partisan, often-hysterical broadsides of the previous century. Editors' claims to be reporting impartial facts and true opinion never carried as much weight as the same claim made by celebrated authors, philosophers, and scientists or the reports of the Royal Society. Journalism was a precarious commercial enterprise without a rigorous method for verifying its stories, compromised by an ever-present temptation to sensationalize or moralize. The facts of news journals were always suspect. Editors' strident claims of printing the real "truth" and "undeceiv[ing] the people" were assertions by men of dubious social status and of known political bias. It was easy to dismiss them as self-interested entrepreneurs who appealed insincerely to high-minded principle only to promote their "staple of news." Yet this fledgling, imperfect, periodic journalism was a new "way of practice" in society. Because it communicated directly with the public, it did more than most other discourses to spread among the populace the notions of fact, reasonable belief, and impartiality.

The birth of modern print journalism, and of journalistic ethics, occurs in England in the seventeenth century at the convergence of three

3 Eisenstein, *The Printing Press as an Agent of Change.*

cultural streams. One stream, as we saw, was the development of an enlightened culture of fact and its associated print culture. A second was the constellation of a number of social, economic, and technological conditions that made the periodic press possible. The third was the rise of the news press as an essential component of a public sphere, especially in the eighteenth century.

This chapter charts the invention and evolution of journalism ethics in England across the seventeenth century in relation to these three streams. Using my rhetorical framework, I show how journalism ethics emerged in England within the context of an evolving, three-stage relationship between journalist and reader. A pre-periodic press, up to the 1620s, gave way to periodic news publishing, from the 1620s to the 1650s, and finally to the Restoration-era press, which effectively terminated with the end of licensing in 1695. Chapter 4 follows this transition into the eighteenth century, where a new journalism ethic – a public ethic – resulted from further changes in the relationship between journalist and reader, the product of daily publishing in a growing public sphere.

THE PRE-PERIODIC PRESS, TO THE 1620S

Building a Periodic News Press

The periodic news press followed a diverse pre-periodic press established in Europe between the mid-fifteenth and early seventeenth centuries. The spread of printing after Gutenberg introduced his press was so swift and far-reaching that almost from the start a wide variety of printed matter claimed to provide "newes" and information. The main forms of publication were the pamphlet, the broadside, the polemical tract, and the ballad. But printed media did not operate in a vacuum. These printed publications circulated alongside oral media and other forms of communication. People sang printed ballads and read broadsides aloud to their illiterate fellows; printed petitions were part of public protests at the English Parliament.

The newspaper took its format from these prior publications, especially from the pamphlet and the broadside. Pamphlets were small books, or "newsbooks," usually 14 by 22 centimetres in size and containing 4 to 28 pages. Large initial letters and woodcuts made them look like written manuscripts. Unlike the newspapers, pamphlets dealt usually with one topic: a trial, a natural disaster, a sea battle, a prodigy, or a government announcement.[4] The pamphlet went back at least to the late fifteenth century, when 2,000 newsbooks were printed on Europe's wars with the Ottoman Empire. In 1486, 10 years after Claxton established his press in England, Henry VII printed a pamphlet containing the pope's bull confirming his claim to the throne after he killed Richard III in battle. Broadsides were large, single sheets. They could be a government decree mounted in a public place, a polemical sheet circulated illegally, or a "relation" that gave news of an event. In 1587, an illustrated broadside extolled the "worthy and valiant exploytes" of Francis Drake as he attacked Spanish ships. In 1607, another broadside interpreted a flood in Wales as God's anger at sinners.

In tracing the origin of news and public communication, one can go back as far as the "oral" and "visual" public sphere of Italian city-states, such as Florence, during the fourteenth and fifteenth centuries. Florence's squares were sites of political discussion, where orators appealed to *il popolo* ("the people," defined as members of trade and craft guilds). In the fifteenth and sixteenth centuries, the pamphlet was a vehicle of information and propaganda. Protestants in German city-states during the Reformation, such as Nuremberg and Strasbourg, gave printed matter its first major ideological role. In 1517, pamphlets ignored official censors and spread news of Martin Luther's 95 theses across Europe.[5]

4 These pamphlets became more frequent in the late sixteenth and early seventeenth centuries. The earliest known English news pamphlet recounted a victory over the Scots on Flodden Field in 1513. Censorship in England meant that there were few printed news pamphlets in England during the late sixteenth century, although the number in London increased after 1590. Between 1590 and 1610, about 270 pamphlets were produced in England, most of them containing news about events on the continent.

5 In France, "occasionnels" – mainly formal government statements and official announcements – appeared between 1488 and 1529. Charles VIII used the press to persuade a sceptical public of the merits of his 1494 invasion of Italy. He wrote at least 41 newsbooks on the fighting, but the propaganda could not hide the fact that the 11-month campaign was a disaster. In Germany, the Edict of Worms found Luther to be an outlaw and attempted to restrict printing. Yet the Reformation went forward. At the end of the sixteenth century, German printers were producing pamphlets of political and other news, plus almanacs that summarized recent events. In Mexico City, beginning in 1535, the printing press helped Europeans conquer the new world by producing maps of the new territory and religious material for the conquered. Newsbooks called *hojas volantes* (flying pages) appeared there for 100 years before England set up the first press in America at Harvard University.

Reformers took part in a vicious pamphlet campaign against the pope – an effort that joined forces with other media. For example, printed texts carried images of Luther, with a halo around his head. Anti-pope woodcuts embellished religious tracts. Protestants held public "rituals" that mocked Catholic practices, such as the collecting of relics. A pamphlet war also erupted in France during the sixteenth-century conflict between Catholics and Protestants and again in the Netherlands during its revolt against Spain. In the late sixteenth century, Christopher Marlowe based his play *Massacre at Paris*, about the killing of Protestants, on accounts found in pamphlets. Between 1614 and 1617, when French nobles rebelled against their king, 1,200 anti-monarchy pamphlets appeared.

Religious and political conflict ensured the popularity of printed matter and the wide use of small printing presses. But news publishing, and the craft of the news writer, gained firmer ground with commercial printing in publishing centres such as Venice in the sixteenth century, Amsterdam in the seventeenth, and London in the eighteenth. Venice in the sixteenth century had 500 printing establishments, plus hundreds of bookshops. Amsterdam became a publishing magnet as part of the new Dutch Republic. The Dutch East India Company made it an information centre about East Asia. With its religious toleration, the city became a news entrepot, exporting printed material in many languages. By the second half of the seventeenth century, it had over 270 booksellers and printers producing maps, travel books, atlases, English Bibles, and marine charts for English sailors. By 1620, it was the centre of European journalism. Brusque "corantos" were published mainly for merchants and traders and then translated and exported to France, England, and other countries.[6] Because of controls on printing, London did not become the leading publishing centre until the 1770s, when it had over 70 booksellers.

It was inevitable that these printers and publishers would try their hand at newspapers as a relatively low-cost branch of their main business of selling books. The concentration of publishers in cities created a demand for literary and editing skills that could be applied to news pub-

6 Amsterdam was a cosmopolitan city of merchants, traders, and bankers. The East India Company was chartered in 1602, an exchange bank in 1609, and the (Dutch) West India Company in 1621. By 1645, at least eight weekly or biweeklies were on sale. Amsterdam's freedom of the press also attracted intellectuals such as Descartes, who published books in the city.

lishing. In Venice during the sixteenth century, printers needed the services of book editors and proof readers. Agencies that provided newsletters for clients hired writers, who could make a living independent of patrons. In France, after Louis XIV revoked the Edict of Nantes in 1685, Protestants emigrated or converted to Catholicism. Many French Calvinists set up printing shops in Amsterdam and published papers attacking the French king. A number of them, such as the philosopher Peter Bayle, set up learned journals, while others experimented with printed sheets of news for sale across Europe. Newspapers evolved from this print culture of irregularly published pamphlets and broadsides, and regularly published newsletters.

Shaaber's survey of printed news in England from 1476 to 1622 shows the remarkable range of news and gossip in the pre-periodic press.[7] The excitement that surrounded the arrival of fresh news was already evident. A newsbook reporting on a 1548 military expedition into Scotland attempted to satisfy "the thursty desyer that all our kynde hath to know." News about ordinary life and ordinary people was scant. The earliest forms of printed news celebrated the achievements of great people and reported the acts of government and important trials. Often, reports on military operations came from an unnamed officer of the royal court. Court officials also wrote propaganda justifying the monarch's actions, such as the king's claim to Scotland or his condemnation of an opponent. Also popular were "illegal" partisan tracts by religious and political groups, secretly printed inside or outside England.

Commentary was dangerous. When ballad writer Thomas Deloney protested against a famine in England, authorities forced him into hiding. Many pamphlets played it safe by offering a yellow journalism about the royal court's social events, ghoulish murders, witchcraft, and conspiracies. Reports interpreted unusual events as omens or miracles and appeared under titles such as "Strange and Miraculous News from Exeter." Comets seen in London in 1580 and 1583 inspired a torrent of books and ballads that interpreted them as signs that the end of the world was near or that strange events would follow. Illustrated pamphlets reported on Sussex dragons, humans with the head of a bird, or the birth of deformed children, which they blamed on "incestuous copulation."[8] The plague prompted many printed prayers to ward off the dreaded disease.

7 Shaaber, *Some Forerunners of the Newspapers in England.*

8 Jackson, *The Pictorial Press.*

Yet these experiments in publication did not lead immediately to a periodic news press. More than 150 years would pass between Gutenberg's movable-type press and the first periodic English newssheets of the 1620s. A stable, periodic press requires conditions that go beyond the prerequisites of a book trade or the sporadic issuing of broadsides. It needs a strong demand for a constant supply of news, a sufficiently large and literate public, cheap and plentiful paper, adequate transportation, a public sphere with some measure of tolerance for freedom of expression, the prospect of publishing profits, and a network of publishers and correspondents. Variations in these conditions go a long way to explaining why the press grew faster in some European countries than in others.

Consider some of the main conditions for a periodic press. Weekly newspapers would not have been possible without a growth in population and an improvement in the general level of literacy and education. Between 1600 and 1650, the population of Britain increased from about six million to 7.7 million. Large urban centres were rising along the main routes of Europe, as England, Holland, France, and Spain benefited from trade and exploration. In the early seventeenth century, London, Amsterdam, and Paris had populations of about 225,000. By 1700, London had 500,000 residents. Economic growth supported the new institutions of a cosmopolitan capitalism, from stock markets to international banking houses. The new classes of people mixing in Antwerp, Augsberg, London, Paris, and Venice – craftsmen, exporters, financiers, lawyers, merchants, and soldiers – had a stake in obtaining the latest "intelligence" on wars, voyages, and government decisions. Retailers needed publicity to reach buyers. Civil, religious, and colonial wars deepened this thirst for news.

By the late sixteenth century, transportation and communication links between European urban centres, including new postal services, improved the distribution of news.[9] The postal services were operated by governments, universities, financial houses such as the Fuggers of Germany, or families such as the Thurn and Taxis of Italy. The postal companies served monarchs, institutions, and the wealthy before becoming national public services. In the early sixteenth cen-

9 In the seventeenth century, several European governments set up general postal systems. Denmark did so in 1624; England had its first postmaster general in 1533, but the post office did not exist until 1637, when Thomas Witherings set up a public "Letter Office."

tury, Franz von Taxis, postmaster to Maximilian I of Germany, the Holy Roman Emperor, began to expand of his family's postal service into a supranational company that spanned most of Europe, employing 20,000 people.[10] In the decades leading up to the first weekly newspapers, scheduled horse-drawn couriers and coaches moved government dispatches, diplomatic reports, and other official material. They also moved broadsides and pamphlets, newsletters compiled by agencies, and letters from correspondents to editors. In addition, postmasters wrote their own newsletters for clients, based on the news that passed through their offices. Post offices and publishing premises in large cities became clearing houses for news from their region. It would not be long before commercial publishers, seeing this regular supply of news, would start printing the first newspapers using the postal service to transport their papers across Europe. Their papers mention casually the arrival of reports from many "pens" and contributors across Europe, assuming a news system familiar to the reader.

A large reading public, connected by post, was still not enough for a periodic news press. A seventeenth-century periodic newspaper needed government approval – or de facto tolerance – to publish for a wide circulation. A periodical is a public enterprise. It must hawk its papers on the streets and provide an address for subscribers. Its editor must be known to correspondents, and it must openly seek out information from officials. It is much more vulnerable to official censors than a secret press cranking out sporadic broadsheets.

Conversely, a periodic newspaper that reported and commented on all manner of events for a public created a special threat to monarchs who regarded printing as their prerogative. As the seventeenth century opened, European governments controlled printing and suppressed offending publications by a combination of licensing, censorship, prison, torture, the forced bankruptcy of wayward editors, and charges of seditious libel. The news publisher in England, for example, laboured under a system of licensing and censorship initiated

10 The Italian family of Thurn and Taxis began a courier postal service in the Italian city-states about 1290. The service lasted until the nineteenth century. In the early sixteenth century, Franz von Taxis gained permission to establish a postal network linking cities in Spain, France, Germany, Italy, and Austria. The firm's postal coaches could cover 166 kilometres a day, travelling from Augsburg to Venice in six days.

by the Tudor monarchs of the sixteenth century in concert with the church, judges, Parliament, and printing associations.[11]

Early news publishers had to shape the content and style of their newspapers to prevailing political sensitivities. Luckily, pockets of relative freedom in cities such as Amsterdam allowed a periodic news press to exist. In Paris, the periodic news press was an official gazette newspaper, which alone could print political news. In London, the first newspapers were careful weekly digests of foreign news that skirted controversial domestic news. Throughout the seventeenth century, the freedom of the English news press expanded and contracted according to political developments. When freedom contracted, as in the Restoration, the press was small and careful in reporting; when central control of the press declined, as in the civil war, the press multiplied and reported more boldly.

Despite press controls, demand for news was so great, and the prospect of fast profits so alluring, that news publishers took the risk of printing weekly papers. Most of the papers were a list of brief news items. In Amsterdam, they tended to be printed on a single sheet of paper, like a broadsheet; in Germany, printers used the pamphlet form. The new medium spread quickly in the late sixteenth and early seventeenth century, appearing first in Holland and Germany. By the end of the 1620s, there were weekly and bi-weekly papers in Amsterdam, Antwerp, Basil, Berlin, Cologne, Frankfort, Hamburg, Leipzig, London, Paris and Vienna, and post and ship transported them to other commercial centres. The pre-periodic press, and the right socioeconomic conditions, had so well prepared the arrival of the weekly newspaper that it occasioned no announcement that a radically new form of publication had arrived.

11 England subjected printing to strict licensing and censorship after 1586 and allowed presses only in London, Oxford, and Cambridge. There were only 15 printers in London in 1615 and only 20 in 1637, when Charles I banned all periodicals of news. The Star Chamber enforced censorship through the Company of Stationers in London – a group of printers, publishers, and booksellers around St Paul's Cathedral. The archbishop of Canterbury and his colleague the bishop of London had the exclusive right to nominate new master-printers. The Company of Stationers registered every work and exercised the right to search all premises suspected of infringing its privileges. Only approved printers received lucrative contracts to publish certain types of material, such as Bibles and law texts. See Siebert, *Freedom of the Press in England, 1476–1776*.

The Ethics of the Pre-Periodic Press

No form of journalism is without an ethic. Any publication expresses (or exhibits) the values, intentions, and interests of its publisher and journalists. Such values may be implicit or explicit. They may be codified into a statement of principles or exist as practical rules of thumb. During certain eras, journalists come under pressure to embrace explicit codes of conduct. During others, they feel no compulsion to construct an explicit ethic. The scattered broadsides and pamphlets of the pre-periodic press never developed anything resembling an explicit ethic. There are many reasons. First, the pre-periodic news press was, as I have said, scattered. The publishing of news was too primitive and underdeveloped to have an explicit ethic. The press was in the hands of entrepreneurs, officials, universities, and warring factions who did not see themselves as part of an institution or system called the "press," with professional obligations. Second, the press was sporadic. As we see below, a periodic relationship with a recognizable public is a crucial factor in developing a journalistic sense of obligation and a commitment to norms and reliable practices. The pre-periodic press largely lacked this relationship. Pamphlets came and went, printed by officials or by secret presses operated by unknown editors. Sensational pamphlets were ephemeral entertainment, even if the publisher's intention was to moralize or educate. Readers could not easily hold *anyone* responsible for errors, and it was not possible to send a "message" by refusing to buy the next regular issue. With shadowy publishers producing ephemeral publications, there was no firm ground on which to build a journalistic ethic or even consider one necessary. If the publication had no licence, its aim was to express a political or religious viewpoint or to tell a sensational tale, not to meet the informational needs of a regular readership. If the publication had a licence, its main obligation was meeting the demands of the censor.

This is not to say that the pre-periodic press of the fifteenth and sixteenth centuries did not have an implicit ethic or that publishers never asserted a normative claim about how they ought to act. Pre-periodic news exhibits a variety of values and motivations. Political authorities and religious reformers used broadsides and pamphlets to spread propaganda, demonize opponents, and control society. Moralists seized on prodigies and strange events to draw theological lessons; some printers entertained the masses with ballads.

Much of the sensational news derived not from "a public spirit, or enlightened self-interest, or intelligent curiosity," but from the desire to sell a pamphlet by feeding a naïve wonder or a religious nervousness about the world. The impulse to interpret was overwhelming, stimulated by partisanship and the lack of reports. The news-ballad was "not so much a record of events as a commentary upon them ... expressing the opinion of the mass of people about it."[12] Much of the interest in events concerned how to understand them or how they exemplified religious truths. For many English readers, a reformer's diatribe against a bishop was more interesting than a careful, factual report by a court official.

We should not read modern values into the past. In the sixteenth century, publishers were starting to use the language of matter of fact. But there was little news that was strictly impartial in the modern sense of being written by disinterested journalists solely for the information of the public. The early news publishers were not self-appointed watchdogs for a liberal society, and their publications were not forums for the expression of many views. Polemical pamphlets published "The Truth" and sent those who disagreed to the devil.

A PERIODIC PRESS, 1620s–1650

Inventing Ethics

The story of Western journalism is by no means confined to the English newspaper. However, the English press of the seventeenth and eighteenth centuries, especially its battle for freedom and independence, had a powerful influence on the European press, the American newspaper, and, as the British Empire expanded, the press of far-flung colonies such as Canada. English press traditions have been the largest single influence on North American journalism. For this reason, I locate the origins of Western journalism ethics in the English newspaper. Historians usually treat journalism ethics as a development of the early twentieth century, with the establishment of schools of journalism and professional associations. In fact, journalists were talking about their social roles, norms of practice, and public duties long before the written codes of ethics in the 1920s. The codes built on journalistic traditions originating in the seventeenth and eighteenth centuries.

As Chapter 1 explained, by "ethics" or "ethic" I do not mean a systematic set of ethical principles, based on philosophical theory and argumentation. I mean a set of principles and norms that, at least to some degree, guided journalistic practice and that editors espoused. In this

12 Shaaber, *Some Forerunners of the Newspapers in England,* 138, 194.

sense, the early newsbook publishers, and then the editors of daily papers, invented an ethics by their actions and their words. They espoused publicly a set of norms that they claimed to follow in gathering, selecting, editing, and publishing their news. They made a variety of promises, pronouncements, and assertions about the aims and standards of the publications in question. Some editors clearly and unequivocally asserted what we may call "norms of publication." I label this invention "strange but marvelous," to echo the period's fascination with marvels. It is indeed remarkable that editors should insist on impartiality in a factional age, when objective reporters did not exist.

These early news publishers and editors did not advocate principles simply because they wanted to appear virtuous or to gloss over dubious practices. They did not adopt these principles simply because they personally believed in certain ideals. The origin of journalism ethics is social and lies in the complex relationship *between* journalist and society. Journalism ethics in the seventeenth century was neither an invention of the journalist as an individual nor simply the inevitable effect of some social factor. It was the result of both terms of the journalist–society relation interacting and mutually influencing each other.

Editors adopted ethical discourse in response to changes in journalism and to the economic, political, and social conditions around them. The impulse to speak ethically, or to use normative language, came from general cultural factors plus specific constraints on periodic publishing. As we have seen above, the general cultural climate of the seventeenth century encouraged a stress on impartial matters of fact. But there were other, more specific factors, including the use of ethical language to placate the censor and assure sceptical readers.

The penchant of early editors to proclaim loudly that they were spreading the impartial "truth" was partly an attempt to persuade nervous government officials that their publications were "safe" for society. Often a claim to report the "truth" about some event was "code" for the claim that the newspaper reported the event according to the view of authorities. The normative language of truth and impartiality helped the journalist rationalize the role of the news periodical.

But other pressures stimulated the use of normative, ethical language. Such language served as a way to build up and maintain the journalist's relationship with readers. The editor used ethical rhetoric to address the concerns and expectations of readers. Readers' concerns about the reliability of reports prompted editors to adopt – or at least to *say* that they adopted – a range of careful practices and high standards in putting together the news.

The early newspapers therefore contained editorial comments to the reader. Editors frequently asked readers to try to understand their difficult task of balancing conflicting accounts of events, verifying alleged facts, securing reliable correspondents, and draining religious and political bias from reports. For example, the editor of a London newspaper knew very well that a report of a Catholic victory in the Thirty Years War would upset his Protestant readers. They would discount the report if it came from a writer in a Catholic region of Europe. The editor therefore was at pains to reassure the reader that his correspondents were reliable and that his paper did what it could to eliminate bias.

In this way, editors began to articulate an ethics of journalistic practice that stressed impartiality, unbiased eyewitness accounts, and matters of fact. To keep readers loyal, editors attempted to reassure them about the credibility of reports. In so doing, they made use of ethical rhetoric. The tenuous, difficult relationship between periodic news publisher and society was the ground from which this embryonic ethics grew.

The seventeenth-century English press presents us with an imperfect, proto-ethics that is a fascinating mix of puffery, opportunism, toadying to authority, and concern for truth. The editors could be both insincere and committed; their publications both biased and surprisingly factual. For ill or good, here is where journalism ethics starts.

The journalism ethics of the seventeenth century helps us understand other ethical inventions in journalism in other periods. The invention is never a creation *ex nihlo.* Fresh ideas arise through the creative adaptation of new and existing "materials." The ethics of journalism changes when existing norms interact with new social trends and new public expectations for their news media. We cannot "explain away" the use of ethical terms by journalists in any period as just insincere adoption of ethical language. Inventing journalism ethics in the seventeenth century, or today, is part of the crucial activity of redefining commitments in the light of changing social contexts. Inventing ethics is a necessary, reinvigorating process for institutions of any significance.

The Pre-Revolutionary and Revolutionary Presses

In the rest of this section on the period 1620s–1650s, I pay attention to two types of English newspapers: the cautious "corantos" and newsbooks of the 1620s and early 1630s; and the more vigorous, partisan newsbooks of the Civil War–era 1640s and early 1650s. In both periods, English readers were thirsty for news about war, a thirst that the non-periodic press could not slake. In the 1620s, the English followed the Protestant cause in the Thirty Years War through newsbook reports about battles, sieges and princes. In the 1640s, newsbooks covered the tensions between Charles I and Parliament, the Civil War, and the aftermath of a divided Commonwealth and Oliver Cromwell's protectorate.

However, the presses of the 1620s and of the 1640s differed in their aims, their freedom, and their content. The first weekly newspapers in England would be foreign imports – newssheets called "corantos" from the Netherlands.[13] The first Dutch import arrived in London in 1620, published by Pieter van den Keere, an Amsterdam publisher and map engraver. He sent his paper, which lacked a consistent title, to London by post, after he had translated its foreign news into English. It was a single sheet, with two columns on each side. Between 2 December 1620 and 18 September 1621, he issued 15 corantos in London. Other Dutch imports followed. Between December 1620 and September 1621, London received 27 different corantos. These imports quickly gave way to papers printed by a handful of London publishers, starting in August 1621, with Thomas Archer's coranto.[14]

Within a year, the newsbook (pamphlet) format emerged, and it remained the style of the English paper until the *Gazette* newssheet in 1665. At any given time in the 1620s, men such as Archer, Nicholas Bourne, and Nathaniel Butter were publishing one or two series of newsbooks. The papers sold for one, two, or three pence in the booksellers' shops and eventually on the streets and went by post to other parts of England. In the first half of the century, the average circulation of a newsbook, which cost half a penny to print, ranged from 250 copies to 3,000. The publisher needed a translator, an editor, and a postal service that brought him other publications and letters from correspondents. After checking the paper for offensive material, he registered the issue with the Company of Stationers and began to print it.

13 "Coranto" is related to the English "current" and may be of Italian origin. Originally, it may have referred to a type of running, perhaps a messenger. For the history of the early news press, see Shaaber, *Some Forerunners of the Newspapers in England,* and Frank, *The Beginnings of the English Newspaper.*

14 Sometime about August 1621, bookseller Thomas Archer began issuing corantos resembling the weekly Dutch publications, and in September Nathaniel Butter received a licence to print corantos, publishing seven issues in September and October. See Frank, *The Beginnings of the English Newspaper*, 1–3. Dahl has estimated that, between 1620 and 1642, at least 1,000 separate issues, or "numbers," of papers were printed in England. The average run for an issue was 400 copies. Dahl, *A Bibliography of English Corantos and Periodical Newsbooks,* 22.

In style, the first corantos were by modern standards poor in appearance and dull in content. They resembled the news briefs produced by today's news agencies. Since the publishing of domestic news was illegal, the papers were a "grocery list" of foreign news about governments, monarchs, and armies, produced quickly on cheap paper by men of limited literary talent. The news items, enhanced by a woodcut, were in narrow columns. Much of the news appeared in a dreary official style that was fond of the third person – "we are informed" – and the passive tense.

An item from Van den Keere's first English coranto read as follows: "Out of Weenen, (Vienna) the 6 November: The French ambassador hath caused the Earle of Dampier to be buried stately at Presburg. In the meane while hath Bethlem Gabor (prince of Transylvania) cited all the Hungerish States, to come together at Presburg the 5. of the present, to discourse aboute the Crowning (Bethlem was elected king of Hungary) and other causes concerning the Kingdom."

There was little comment on the news, and the papers bore sleepy titles, such as "A Continuation of our Weekly News." Logical organizing of items for the reader's ease was minimal. General headings, such as "Out of Rome" or "Out of Vienna," indicated only where the report had been written. So under "Out of Rome," a reader might find stories about a battle near Prague or a decision by a Germany diet. Printers set news as it came in; they crammed late items, no matter how important, at the end of the newsbook in small type. Editors promised to publish on a given day each week but waited until the postal service brought enough news to fill their pages.

If we think of the objective style of reporting as a dry recording of facts, this was "precisely the style of the first English newspaper."[15] The switch to the newsbook format gradually improved the paper's appearance. Publishers began to hire editors to construct more coherent stories from several reports and to insert "notices" to the reader. Editors also anticipated the modern headline by summarizing the main stories on the title page in headline fashion.

There were, of course, good reasons why the newsbooks were dull, timid publications. The publishers, operating with limited resources, were just learning about the periodic press. Newsbooks were not their main source of income. Printing a Bible took time and money; printing news was cheaper and more slapdash, with faster typesetting times and a

15 Shaaber, *Some Forerunners of the Newspapers in England*, 220.

quick return in cash.[16] Editorially, the publications aimed only to be digests for people anxious for any news. There was every reason for publishers to avoid inflaming the authorities with comment.

The newspapers of the 1620s came from a handful of London publishers and booksellers of the Stationer's Company. These men were not anxious to jeopardize their government-approved monopoly on publishing news. As they worked, publishers could feel the hot breath of the Stuart monarchs over their shoulder. James I, who considered matters of state unfit for public discussion, tried to stop the importation of foreign corantos. The state regularly revoked publication licences because of controversial items. Charles I, in 1632, banned the publication of all newsbooks for six years. The papers therefore skirted English news, including even major events such as the assassination of the Duke of Buckingham. Editors promised to "meddle with nothing but justifiable actions" and tell "nothing but shall be befitting" the readers.[17]

In the Civil War period of the 1640s, a more freewheeling journalism arose as central controls on the press weakened or broke down entirely. Hundreds of newsbooks flooded the country between the collapse of royal censorship in 1641 and the reimposition of controls by Cromwell. For the first time, the press carried a large portion of domestic news, much of it on parliament and military campaigns. The periodic paper still appeared as an 8- or 12-page newsbook, but it had a more personal and partisan style. Newsbooks combined blistering editorials with relatively accurate reports on battles and parliamentary decisions, plus the usual stories about marvels. The factionalism of the era found echoes in the factionalism of the press. Parliamentary and royalist newsbooks fought it out rhetorically, hammer and tong. Anti-royalist editors did their best to stay on the good side of parliamentary factions and their

16 The press that printed the news was a barely improved version of the devices used by Gutenberg in Germany and by Caxton in England. It used an oaken screw to impress a page of type on a single page, with letters inked between each impression. (There were no great changes in this technology until Koenig's cylinder press in 1812.) In Paris in the seventeenth century, a printer's shop began work at 5 a.m. and finished at 9 p.m., and its two presses could produce between 2,500 and 3,000 copies of a two-sheet publication. The printing of news began as a minor offshoot of the printer's business. So much capital went to the printing of books – the King James Bible would cost a printer £3,500 to produce – that printers looked to newsbooks for extra revenue, despite the political risks.

17 Frank, *The Beginnings of the English Newspaper*, 7.

military leaders. Royalist editors stayed one step ahead of factions attempting to arrest them and smash their presses.[18]

The newsbooks came in several styles: the sober "diurnal," which followed the day-to-day proceedings of Parliament; the racy "mercury," where the editor wrote strongly in his own voice; and the more official and intellectual "intelligencer." Newsbooks were ubiquitous, at least in London. By 1645, Londoners could choose from 14 weeklies of eight or more pages. In the heat of the Civil War, a newsbook might reach a circulation of 2,000, or 3,000, or more. In 1640, an anti-royalist tract sold 4,500 copies.

What sort of ethics did these early papers espouse? We can group the range of ethical claims into four kinds: statements of aims; claims to publish truth over fiction or misinformation; claims to adhere to methods that were factual, balanced, and reliable; and claims to adhere to disinterestedness and impartiality. The papers of the 1620s and 1640s wore their commitment to responsible journalism on their sleeve – their grandiose titles. Papers were called *A True and Perfect Informer*, or the *Impartial Intelligencer* or the *Faithful Scout, Impartially Communicating*. In the 1640s, *Mercurius Civicus* called itself London's "intelligencer or truth impartially related from thence to the whole kingdom."

These papers usually spelled out their aims in a prospectus or, retrospectively, in the final edition. The declared aims ranged from serving the monarch, a parliamentary group, or political idea to informing and entertaining the people. The front page of *The Parliamentary Intelligencer* asserted that it was "For Information of the People." But providing information was not just the innocuous delivery of neutral facts. In many cases it meant providing the real "truth" of political events, as defined by the editor and his political supporters. Many editors were more likely to regard the "people" as an unpredictable mob, rather than as a rational public. Nevertheless, the appeal to the "people" gained in popularity.

A commitment to truth and plain speaking over fanciful fictions was almost universal. Editors resolved to avoid "tart language" and give readers "simply a narration of affairs." Daniel Border opened the *Faithful Scout* in 1651 with a flourish: "Having put on the Armour of Resolution, I intend ... to encounter falsehood with the sword of truth. I will not endeavour to flatter the world into a belief of things that are not; but truly inform them of things that are." The *Weekly Account* promised to present news "without any gilded glossings, invented fictions, or flat-

18 For a review of these revolutionary newsbooks, see Raymond, *Making the News*.

tering Commentaries." The editor of the *Moderate Intelligencer* insisted, "I am no Romance-Monger to present the world with Tragi-Comedies of my own invention."

Despite these homilies to truth, editors acknowledged that journalism's truth was a partial, cumulative affair. News came late by post, from uncertain or conflicting sources, and in dribs and drabs. Editors sought probable opinion, not the demonstrations of philosophers. In 1643, Henry Walley, editor of the *True Informer,* said: "Truth (in the newsbooks) is the daughter of time. Relations of Battels, fights, skirmiches and other passages ... are not alwaies to be taken or credited at the first hand, for that many times they are uncertaine, and the truth doth not so conspicuoulsy appeare till a second or third relation."[19]

From the start, editors insisted that their news was more reliable and responsible than that of their rivals. Some coranto editors said that they were more reliable *because* they were licensed. On 14 September 1622, Butter assured readers that his editorial procedures, combined with the threat of punishment from the censor, ensured careful, reliable reports. He noted that he had not published a false report that had appeared in an unlicensed newsbook which had claimed that Count Mansfeld, a famous figure in the Thirty Years War, had 5,000 "whores in his Campe." Butter wrote: "Whatsoever is licensed is thoroughly examined and printed according to the high or low Dutch printed copies or out of Letters of the best credit from beyond the seas, and that whosoever hath or shall offend ... is liable to be severely punished: therefore expect no such bold attempt from any of us hereafter."

Editors attempted to compensate for their publications' limitations by announcing their commitment to norms such as factuality – a preference for plain facts, unbiased news, eyewitnesses' accounts, reliable sources, and judicious editing. In making these claims, journalists sounded like the travel writer, the chorographer, or even the experimental scientist. Factual techniques included giving the exact time, date, and place of the event reported. Even when the story was a preposterous tale – for example, about a monstrous fish caught near Suffolk – the editor would name the date and place of the event and the people who claimed to have seen it. The editor might even name a tavern where readers could go to talk to witnesses. The early press was not unfamiliar with the five "Ws" of journalism - who, what, where, when, and why. Moreover, in an age of poor communications and false rumours, newsbooks stressed that their reports came from an

19 Frank, *The Beginnings of the English Newspaper*, 54.

eyewitness, or "a very good hand," or with confirmation by "persons of unquestionable Credit."[20]

The desire of newsbooks to maintain credibility among a regular group of readers explains to a large extent the constant editorial harping on the impartiality of reports and the "faithfulness" of its editor and correspondents.[21] The words "faithful" and "impartial" appeared in newsbook titles almost as much as "true." Titles ranged from "Faithful Intelligencer" to the "Kingdomes Faithfull and Impartiall Scout." Civil War newsbook editors, such as Samuel Pecke, took pride in their ability to present factual reports in troubled times. In mid-century, newsbooks such as the *Mercurius Aulicus* began to separate news from editor's comments. *A Modest Narrative of Intelligence Fitted for the Republique of England and Ireland* alternated between editions full of commentary and editions with only news.

The Editor's Predicament

These kinds of ethical assertions are an abstraction unless we connect them to the lives of newsbook publishers and editors. The newsbook editor faced many pressures, including the economic pressure of keeping his enterprise alive in a competitive market. He had to face readers' demands for fresh news on major battles and campaigns. Sensational stories boosted sales but could undermine a periodical's reputation for reliability. The editor had to avoid shutting down by censors, military leaders, or factions. Publisher Thomas Audley of the *London Post* described the editor's life in 1647 as a precarious voyage: "Whosoever undertakes to write weekly in this nature, undertakes to sayle down a narrow Channell, where all along the shore on each side are Rocks and Cliffs that threaten him ... He onely is the happy steersman that can keep his course into the middle of the channell."[22]

20 *True Protestant Mercury,* no. 3 (London, 1674), quoted in Barbara Shapiro, *A Culture of Fact,* 100. When newsbooks reported a dubious story about a "strange and terrible" storm of two-pound hailstones at Exeter, the *True Protestant Mercury* claimed that "persons of unquestionable Credit" confirmed the hailstones.

21 The editor of the *Flying Post* declared: "I shall write with the greatest indifference, truth and modestie as shall satisfy the impartiallest that reades me, attributing to the Enemy no otherwise that truth will warrant it." Quoted in Jackson, *The Pictorial Press,* 127.

22 Quoted in Frank, *The Beginnings of the English Newspaper,* 131–2.

Let us look briefly at three leading editors – Thomas Gainsford, Samuel Pecke and Marchamont Nedham. I start with one of the earliest, Thomas Gainsford, who edited the corantos and newsbooks of Butter and associates for a brief but formative period in the early 1620s until his death from plague in 1623. Gainsford, a well-travelled army captain, improved the papers by adding titles, arranging news by topic, and blending reports into a single narrative. Gainsford gave impersonal newsbooks a more personal tone through his editorial asides. He reminded readers of how a story followed a previous report and what news might follow. He told the sceptical reader that he followed the best standards and procedures possible, under the circumstances. He informed readers that he scanned foreign reports on the Thirty Years War for blatant bias, and he attempted to reach a balance by using accounts from Catholic and Protestant sources. In one issue, Gainsford thanked a reader for correcting a previous erroneous story that located the Antichrist's birth in Babylon.

Gainsford insisted that he strove to be responsible. "I acquaint you with nothing but that is extracted out of true and credible Originals," he protested, to complaints from readers. "Either Letters of justifiable information, or Corantos published in other Countries." His comments suggest that he thought that he had a "contract" of trust with readers. It was a contract that brought complaints from all sides. "Gentle readers, how comes it then to pass that nothing can please you?" Gainsford lamented in one of his asides. "If we afford you plaine stuffe, you complaine of the phrase ... if the newes be forcible against the Emperour, you breake forth, it is impossible, and all is invention ... if we talke of novelty indeed, you make a doubt of the verity; if wee onely tell you what we know, you throw away the booke and breake out, there is nothing in it."[23]

Despite claims to impartiality, the bias of newsbook reports was hard to hide. Bias appeared not so much in intentionally fabricated reports or diatribes, but in the editor's selection of stories and how he reported on them. During the Thirty Years War, Protestant editors tended to magnify Protestant successes and minimize misfortunes. When a Protestant general slaughtered his defeated enemy, the sympathetic newsbook editor said that the general rightly punished the enemy. But when a Catholic general did the same, he was a "bloody Tyrant." Balance was limited by what censors and readers could stomach by way of bad news. One editor advised

23 Ibid., 300, 10–11.

readers that in coverage of the Thirty Years War "you and I must be contented with such ... newes, as we finde, and dare justifie in London."

Perhaps no editor of this period knew more about satisfying the readers' "news itch" while staying out of trouble than Samuel Pecke – the godfather of objective journalism. Pecke was a London bookseller with a little stall in Westminster Hall who turned to newsbooks for added revenue. He gradually built his paper, *A Perfect Diurnall of the Passages in Parliament,* into a sort of *New York Times* of the revolutionary-era press. His was an authoritative paper of record, with the most extensive reporting on Parliament and military affairs. It pioneered the straight news report, and even his rivals said that he tried to be impartial. At its height in the late 1640s, the *Perfect Diurnall* had large print runs of 3,000, requiring the use of two presses.

Pecke's impartiality amounted to careful neutrality on certain topics. He said enough to be interesting, but not enough to offend anyone seriously. His editorials stayed within accepted themes, and his discussion of religious issues skirted incendiary topics. He shrewdly adjusted to shifts in power and official opinion. When faced with a delicate political matter, he sometimes resorted to bafflegab, assuming that his contemporaries could read between the lines. For example, when the Earl of Essex was replaced as leader of the parliamentary army, Pecke wrote opaquely: "The Commons also had consultation touching some alterations and amendments for the better explanation and enlargement of Sir William Wallers Commission, and upon the result of all they appointed a Committee to treat with the Earl of Essex for his approbation and concurrence therein."[24] When Cromwell's New Model Army marched on London in November 1648, Pecke prudently printed only the official declaration justifying the intimidation of the city; then he gave four lines of copy on the troops' arrival. During heated parliamentary debates on religion, Pecke exercised self-censorship, saying for example that the members discussed "divers particulars ... not convenient to be published at this time."

Pecke's impartiality existed within a larger zone of partiality. His editorials reflected prevailing prejudice. Pecke was as anti-Irish and anti-royalist as other editors, to the point of supporting an ordinance to kill all captured Irish rebels. His devotion to facts did not preclude the common "apparition" story. He safely attacked the "popish superstition" of Archbishop Land's high church, but he was careful to avoid the power struggle between religious factions inside Parliament. Nevertheless, he

24 Ibid., 52.

often transcended his partiality. He provided relatively fair reporting of royalist military victories. He gave a balanced treatment to the rise of the Levellers and their democratic ambitions. He reported on atrocities by parliamentary soldiers. Pecke praised himself for his plainness, carefulness, brevity, and ability to get the news.

In the trial and execution of Charles I in 1649, we get a glimpse of how Pecke and other newsbook editors negotiated the tension between reporting and commenting, impartiality and partisanship. The newsbooks reported the facts yet wanted their readers to interpret the execution in various ways – as either the illegal killing of a head of state or the legitimate execution of a traitor. Moderate papers covered calmly the king's trial, describing his entrance into the court and his dialogue with the judge. Yet newsbooks' editorials, and their editorial remarks to readers, made it clear that they saw the trial and execution as necessary.

Editors covering the king's trial also showed an early awareness that the *manner* of presenting information was a powerful tool of persuasion. Newsbook editors were becoming conscious of their role in the "theatre" of the public sphere. With the trial of Charles I, the newsbooks functioned as a metaphorical "stage," where public figures appeared and were judged. The newsbooks were as much a public stage as the wooden stage on which Charles was beheaded with great ritual.[25]

Pecke's coverage of the execution was as matter of fact as one can imagine. He wrote an introductory paragraph on how the high court had met and decided on the place of execution. Then he began his account of the execution with a straight lead paragraph: "This day the King was beheaded, over against the Banquetting house by White-hall. The manner of Execution, and what passed before his death take thus." Pecke gives a plain account of the king's dignified approach to the scaffold, his instructions to the executioner, and his speech to the crowd. He ends with the sobering information: "On Thursday, the king's head was sowed on and his corpse removed to St. James ... a committee to consider the time of his Funeral, by his Ancestors, not yet agreed upon."[26]

Pecke's editorial caution paid off. His coverage of politics harvested readers interested more in news than in red-hot rhetoric. He succeeded perhaps as well because many Londoners were not zealots and shared his moderate political views as they muddled through difficult times. His paper became a respectable institution. His paper could have embraced

25 Raymond, *Making the News,* 207.

26 Ibid., 245, 249.

the motto of the *New York Times*, "all the news that's fit to print." But, for Pecke, what "fitted" was a *shifting boundary*, sensitive to prevailing political and religious opinions.

If Pecke was the objective journalist of the 1640s, Marchamont Nedham (1620–1678) was its greatest partisan who helped to define English political journalism. Critics either admire Nedham for his bold writing or dismiss him as a political opportunist. Born in Derbyshire in 1620 to genteel parents, he graduated from Oxford in 1637 and practised briefly as a school teacher and law clerk. At the age of 23, he landed his first newspaper job as editor of the *Mercurius Britanicus.* He is famous for several decades of strident political writings – he changed sides three times during the Civil War. He went to jail repeatedly and narrowly escaped hanging. His rivals condemned him as "Hell's barking cur," a "jack of all sides," a "political shuttle-cock," and a man with a "publique Brothel in his Mouth."[27]

Nedham took up the parliamentary side as editor of the *Mercurius Britanicus* – founded, he said, "for the better information of the people." It was much more than a journal of information. It was a rollicking, biting journal. Each week, Nedham levelled broadsides against the royalists. The royalists answered in kind through the writings of another Oxford graduate, John Birkenhead, in his equally popular *Mercurius Aulicus.*[28] The struggle was a no-holds-barred battle royal between two wits using the dark arts of slander, innuendo, selective facts, and propaganda. Listen to Nedham on Birkenhead. "But harke ye, thou mathematicall liar, that framest lies of all dimensions, long, broad and profound lies, and then playest the botcher, the quibbling pricklouse every weeke in tacking and stitching them together; I tell thee (Birkenhead) thou art a knowne notorious odious forger ... all the world knows thou art an underling pimpe to the whore of Babylon, and thy conscience an arrant prostitute for base ends. This is truth, not railing."[29]

Such railings had limits. Nedham, in one issue, directly attacked the person of Charles I for his stammer, his "bloody hands," and his cowardly flight from London. He called for the king's arrest. Even this was too much for some parliamentarians, who threw him in jail. Remarkably, in 1647, after a personal reconciliation with Charles, which included kissing the king's hands, Nedham switched to the royalist camp and began publishing *Mercu-*

27 Ibid., 338.

28 Thomas, *Sir John Berkenhead.*

29 Quoted in Frank, *The Beginnings of the English Newspaper,* 76.

rius Pragmaticus. Nedham attacked Cromwell as "Crum-hell." He poked fun at Cromwell's long nose, and he portrayed the parliamentary factions as dangerous tyrants. In June 1649, parliamentary agents caught him in Oxfordshire and arrested him.

Remarkably, again, he was persuaded to adopt the cause of the Commonwealth. In June 1650, Cromwell appointed him editor of his official newsbook. Nedham's *Mercurius Politicus* began its tenure as the longest-lived newsbook of this period.[30] Nedham declared that he had changed his mind after reviewing the affairs of the new government "with an impartial eye." *Politicus* published 500 numbers over 10 years. So effective was Nedham that he has been called Cromwell's press agent.[31] With the Restoration, Nedham fled to Holland, causing great joy among his opponents. He was 40 years old, and his newsbook days were over.

Nedham is a paradoxical figure, and it is too easy to dismiss him as a journalistic gun-for-hire. He was more than a press agent. His editorials in the 1650s were short, serious philosophical treatises that employed ideas from Hobbes and Machiavelli to justify the Commonwealth. The pieces were so serious and well written that some thought them the work of Nedham's friend John Milton. No doubt Nedham was adept at changing political horses in midstream to enhance his career or save his life. But he was also a sceptic and a political pragmatist, and this may help explain his willingness to attack almost any group over the years and to change his mind as conditions changed.

We should remember that newsbook publishers and editors were not independent professionals, but writers who took up many causes, prepared many types of material for various patrons, and dabbled in a string of occupations, from government spy to soldier. Editors might distinguish between news reports and their editorials, but they did not make a hard distinction between being objective and being partisan.

Indeed, Nedham could talk about being impartial and about being partisan in the same paragraph, with no seeming sense of contradiction. Complicating matters, he wrote in what he called his "joco-serious style," full of drollery, irony, and exaggeration, a blending of verse and prose. He thought this irony necessary to reach the ordinary person – to "undeceive the People, it must bee written in a Jocular way, or else it will never bee cryed up."[32]

30 The newsbooks of Nedham, under Cromwell's rule in the 1650s, were profitable ventures. Each earned about £570 per year.

31 See Frank, *Cromwell's Press Agent*, and Stephen and Lee, *Dictionary of National Biography* (London: Smith, Elder & Co., 1908–9), vol. 1, 159–64.

32 Raymond, *Making the News*, 335.

Journalism and journalism ethics trace their histories back to cautious entrepreneurs such as Archer, Butter, and Bourne and to more audacious political partisans such as Nedham. Some publishers, such as Pecke, were both business-like and partisan. The first journalists were a grab bag of unlikely ethical pioneers – tailors, army captains, doctors, Oxford graduates, clerics, and unrestrained propagandists. Some editors were talented, knowledgeable writers; others, dullards with a pen. Some were reasonable men; others, fanatics. Not a few were opportunistic, changing their tune with the winds of politics. Ideological passion drove others. Some made a tidy profit; others ended their lives in poverty.

To understand the origins of journalism ethics, we need to appreciate these editors' uncertain status in the literary and publishing establishment. The newsbook publisher was a new specialty in the printing business and another step forward in the commercialization of information for a wider public. By the early seventeenth century, printing, bookselling, and publishing were becoming distinct activities. Publishers were people who sought out things to publish, rounded up the capital to finance publications, and engaged printers. Newsbooks represented one of their ventures, among many. News publishers were part of the industry of "print capitalism."[33] The printing press had created an interest in making money from disseminating knowledge – including news. Socially, news publishers and editors were part of a rising bourgeoisie in urban centres. They were businessmen, members of the Company of Stationers.

Yet, despite their rising fortunes, the early news publishers and editors of England occupied a low rung in the social and literary hierarchy. True, the news publisher was entering a more flexible society, where land was no longer a guaranteed source of wealth and many yeoman and merchants no longer sought the trappings of gentility. But flexibility does not mean solid respectability, at least in the eyes of conservative clergymen, government officials, or literary figures. The news publisher was hard to define by the social categories of his time. He was part craftsman, part entrepreneur, part bookseller, part printer, and part writer. His ephemeral newsbooks also fell between existing literary categories.

Newsbooks were not full-length books on history and political theory. Nor were they identical with the sensational broadsides or pamphlets of previous decades. The newsbooks contained both popular superstition

33 Anderson, *Imagined Communities.*

and scientific fact. The first news publishers and editors attempted to locate their publications among the discourses of fact. They sought a place among chorographers, travel authors, and newsletter writers. But the more "serious" playwrights, poets, and philosophers regularly questioned their social status.

The Ethical Legacy of the Periodic Press

The newsbooks' legacy for journalism ethics is three-fold. First, it created a number of journalistic practices that would become the "standards" of journalism ethics in the centuries ahead. Second, it established an ethical lexicon for news journalism, including notions that anticipated journalistic objectivity. Third, it was a major player in the first public sphere, and therefore its ethical rhetoric anticipated a public ethic for journalism.

The newsbooks pioneered journalistic practices such as "headlines" on the title page, the sensational human-interest story, the leading article (editorial), the publishing of advertisements, and the use of correspondents in the field, especially during war. The weekly newsbooks began to separate news and commentary and initiated practices that sought to make reports more factual, balanced, and reliable. Editors questioned their sources for bias, tried to balance reports, preferred reputable correspondents and eyewitnesses, and gave the date, time, and place of story. Today, such practices are still the building blocks of an objective news report.

An examination of the English newsbooks of the seventeenth century may suggest that the early modern era saw a bland journalism of fact and a ridiculing, polemic journalism.[34] However, much of the press straddled these two categories and constituted a third type, which mixed fact and commentary in varying proportions. The newsbooks of the 1620s and 1640s give us examples of journalists who provided mainly facts and of others busy advocating, reforming, moralizing, and educating. Most editors both made news and made opinion. The difference between editors was the degree to which they emphasized one activity over the other. Both objective and partisan journalism started in this period, often side by side in the same newsbook. In the centuries to come, these practices would develop into separate traditions. Partisan journalism would develop into the essay journalism and revolutionary press of the eighteenth century; objective journalism, into the reporting of the *Times* (of London).

34 See Nigel Smith, *Literature and Revolution in England.*

From these practices, journalism inherited an ethical lexicon of which the primary terms were "truth," "faithfulness," "impartiality," "matter of fact," and "informing the people." These terms in the seventeenth century had meanings that do not necessarily correspond with modern senses. "Truth" for the newsbook editor could mean an absolute religious truth or the truth as his faction saw it. "Impartiality" had a narrow political sense – of not being partial to a faction. For Audley, impartiality involved steering a safe, middle course between factions; for Pecke, a limited neutrality on specific issues, which coexisted with more basic commitments. The editor's talk of his "obligation" to be impartial often meant nothing more than a prudent need to avoid dangerous commentary. "Having the facts" did not necessarily mean that the editor possessed a modern "fact" – a verified, scientific finding. It could mean no more than receiving a letter from a correspondent or testimony from an alleged witness. Moreover, what people accepted as fact depended on political and religious beliefs. Gainsford, the apparently careful, factual editor, printed a report on the birth of the Antichrist.

The final ethical legacy of the seventeenth-century news press was its contribution to the origins of an English public sphere. The newsbooks, and other products of the printing press, spread the idea that information and discussion about matters of state should be public. The people have a right to debate and discuss information. Such discussion was not the prerogative of the sovereign and his or her privy council. The idea grew that society was not necessarily a closed, hierarchical structure where everyone knows his or her "station." It was not divinely ordained that the powerful should be the only ones who know, debate, and decide.

Society should contain a sphere of public affairs, where people could take positions and follow events. David Zaret has noted that, in seventeenth-century England, the use of the printing press encouraged "new communicative practices," such as circulation of printed petitions to sovereign and Parliament, use of broadsides and pamphlets by religious and political groups, the spread of political messages through periodic newsbooks, and publication of sermons and speeches. These communication practices increased participation in politics and created a rudimentary public sphere.[35] Public participation in politics now went beyond watching symbolic displays of authority.

As with the ancient origins of objectivity-in-practice, modern democratic ideas began with a number of "ways of practice" – various social

35 Zaret, *Origins of Democratic Culture.*

practices. In the seventeenth century, many of these new practices either originated in, or gained support from, the news press and the field of printed communication. The circulation of newsbooks and petitions broke down the elites' control on the discussion of state business and undermined the secrecy and privilege of government. Such activities flew directly in the face of the prevailing view that saw printing as a privilege granted by the sovereign, reporting parliamentary debates as a crime, and state business as not for the ignorant masses.

Radical printers, news publishers, and others challenged those assumptions, intentionally or unintentionally, by using the press to spread ideas made popular by a plain or "joco-serious" writing style. Furthermore, the polemical and factual content of newsbooks stimulated public discussion and deliberation. Critical thought grew through the newsbook practice of referring to facts, events, history, and previous reports. Conflicting views went down on paper, ready for comparison and debate. Readers could think for themselves and refer to original sources, rather than relying on the mediating interpretation of church officials or the people's "betters."

The proliferation of these new ways of political practice resulted from an alliance between "commerce and controversy" – the engine of print capitalism.[36] Publishers competed to produce texts to meet public demand, and the resultant flood of relatively cheap texts made a return to authoritarian controls on information – and authoritarian attitudes towards governance – increasingly difficult. By the end of the century, such views were receiving philosophical treatment and justification. Locke, for example, was writing about the political authority of the public and the need for popular consent.

How do we explain this emergence of ethical lexicon in journalism? It is easy to speculate. Cynically, we can surmise that ethical language was a way for editors to puff themselves up. Or we can see the ethical language as, at least in some cases, the sincere expression of individual commitment to a set of values. Any complex human activity will contain some degree of hypocrisy and some degree of sincerity.

But there are deeper and more specific systemic reasons for the resort to journalism ethics, and they have to do with the nature of the press and its place in society. In particular, one needs to focus on the close connections between three "social" factors that historians of the press have not emphasized: periodicy, readers' scepticism, and the use of rhetorical argumentation in pragmatic contexts.

36 Ibid., 13.

These three features define the all-important relationship between newsbook editors and their readers. They define the communicative situation of newsbook publishers. "Periodicy" refers to the relationship between publisher and reader constructed through regular publication. "Scepticism" involves publishers' attempts to maintain that relationship in the face of readers' scepticism and expectations. "Rhetorical argumentation" refers to the editors' use of rhetoric in specific contexts to forge a niche for his newsbook (and its political perspective) within a space of competing newsbooks. Periodicy, scepticism, and rhetoric were, in varying degrees, constants for editors of the seventeenth-century news press, from the coranto publisher, through the revolutionary-era editor, to the gazette editor of the Restoration period. Once we reflect on these three features, we see why editors resorted to ethical language.

Everything stems from periodicy. The publication of a weekly or daily paper has to overcome economic, technical, and editorial problems. But, once established, the periodical then has to maintain a precarious "contract" of trust and presumed reliability with readers. Each week, newsbooks had to attract readers and assure them of their reliable news service and cogent opinion. They had to provide the sorts of information that readers demanded, in the style and tone expected. Commercial competition added to the pressure, prompting editors to characterize competitors as untrustworthy and devoid of editorial standards. Periodic news publishing "set up a continuing relationship ... between reader, printer, and the originator of the information."[37] The publisher of the occasional broadside or pamphlet lacked a constant and close relationship with a recognizable readership.

To get a grip on publishing, the language of journalism ethics required a journalism with a more robust relationship between publisher and public. The weekly newspaper was not a "one-off" broadside nailed to a tree. It was a continuous series of news reports by a single, identifiable publication with a business and a reputation at stake. Usually, such economic and social pressures seem to corrupt journalistic principle. However, periodicy and competition generated pressure on editors to espouse editorial norms and aims.

Once periodicy was in place, scepticism and rhetorical context became problems for the newsbook editor. Credibility was difficult to establish in the first half of the century, because of the political and general intellectual conditions. Scepticism about the validity of (and motivation behind) claims ran rampant in a society that questioned

37 Anthony Smith, *The Newspaper*, 9.

traditional authority and had little political consensus. Readers lived in a time of scepticism about sources of knowledge, as we saw in chapter 2. Subjectivity and uncertainty flowed from pyrrhonic scepticism about the criterion of truth and from the impact of the "radical enlightenment" on established belief.

Periodic journalism extended that philosophical scepticism to both politics and daily public life. Ordinary people, through the newspapers, saw the reality of conflicting political and religious opinion. Readers of the seventeenth century, like the denizens of classical Athens, were acutely aware of the influence of partisanship on judgment and the presentation of facts. In 1644, Richard Collings, editor of the *Kingdomes Weekly Intelligencer,* wrote: "There were never more pretenders to the Truth than in this Age, nor ever fewer that obtained it."[38]

What was most important was how people understood these differences of opinion. As traditional sources of certainty crumbled, the journals explained this conflict not so much as a matter of honest error or a lack of facts and knowledge[39] but by differences in personal bias, in "interests" and social status. Newsbook editors commonly rebuked rival publications by pointing out that the prejudices of the author motivated their editorials. The attempt by biased editors to claim impartiality only reinforced the tendency to look to the cause and motivations of claims. In this manner, journalism spread the idea of bias and the influence of society on knowledge claims long before modern sociologists of knowledge. Journalism attacked the views of opponents as partial, deceptive, and self-interested. Their own views, of course, were impartial, disinterested, and devoted to "undeceiving" the people. The craft of journalism – an agent and product of popular scepticism – engaged in ethical language to protect itself from sceptical voices.

Readers' scepticism grew as they read in the press about conflicting opinions among officials, clergymen, and scientists and as they grasped the subjectivity, unreliability, and partiality of the newsbooks themselves. The crude and limited nature of the periodic journalism, immersed in factional conflict, inspired little confidence in editors' objectivity. English newsbook readers were sensitive to and wary of political messages, implied or overt. They knew that many newsbooks started for political purposes. They could easily distinguish between a royalist and a parliamentary notebook. They were able to detect biases in allegedly

38 Quote in Frank, *The Beginnings of the English Newspaper,* 122.

39 On the cultural relativity of reliable knowledge, see Zinman, *Reliable Knowledge.*

impartial reports. Readers were also aware of the many false or "planted" stories, the dodgy character of the editor's "reliable" correspondents, the commercial and political pressures on publications, and the use of rumour and sensationalism to increase sales. As Gainsford found out, some of his "gentle readers" were quick to read into reports the editor's alleged religious sympathies.

Scepticism about periodic journalism was strengthened by a chorus of criticism of the new weekly press from courtiers, offended factions, literary icons, and outraged parsons. Our culture's long debate over journalism was well under way by 1700. Ben Jonson's satirical play of 1626, *A Staple of News,* portrayed the "newsmonger" as a person who sells lies to the credulous hoi polloi for credit. The writer Donald Lupton opined: "Ordinarily they (editors) have as many Leyes [lies] as Lines ... They are old and new in five days. They are busie fellows, for they meddle with other men's Affaires. No Pope, Emperour, or King but must bee touched by their pen."[40] Editors responded by making ethical claims on behalf of their craft and their newsbooks, and the more they protested their disinterestedness the more they contributed to readers' scepticism. The appeal to ethical norms was routinely unsuccessful in securing the faith of a regular readership.

Scepticism in turbulent times turned the English public arena into a tough rhetorical public sphere. Periodic journalists found themselves engaging in a rhetorical contest with readers, political enemies, and government officials. The opinions of newsbook editors were part of the cacophony of voices during the revolutionary period. England was on fire with radical ideas put forward not only by commercial newsbook editors but also by prophets, levellers, ranters, and other agitators. The world appeared to have "turned upside down."[41] Newsbook editors published their views within this context of fiercely contested beliefs.

In retrospect, we can see that the editors used rhetoric in print media to debate issues in much the same way as the ancient Greeks did to debate in public about contentious political decisions.[42] At times of

40 Quoted in Frank, *The Beginnings of the English Newspaper,* 277.

41 Hill, *The World Turned Upside Down.*

42 An example of how ancient Athenians used rhetoric occurs in the debate at the Athenian Assembly over the fate of leaders of an unsuccessful rebellion in Mytilene against Athens in 427 BC. Mytilene had been an ally of Athens in the Athenian League. Thucydides discussed the debate in his *History of the Peloponnesian War,* 103–19.

high tension, the rhetorical relationship spiralled downward into a vicious confrontation, such as the battle of words between Nedham and Birkenhead. At other times, messages were more subtle, and an editor would position himself as the only reasonable writer in a country of fanatics.

The content, language, and style of newsbooks bear the stamp of this rhetorical relationship. The editor's leading articles and arguments had to anticipate objections and responses from his imagined readers. Especially in the 1640s and 1650s, he rarely reported just the facts or constructed a logical argument, with premises leading to a conclusion. Instead, he showed how his facts led to certain interpretations, and he attacked other points of views as he made his argument. A good deal of newsbook content is not stand-alone arguments or stand-alone reports. One needs to understand the article as only the latest salvo in an ongoing rhetorical debate. One must bear in mind the events prior to the editorial, what else people wrote about the event, readers' reactions to past stories, and how the editor may have anticipated counter-arguments to his position in the next issue of a rival newsbook.

The rhetorical editor used a variety of devices to persuade readers and undermine other views. He questioned the presumed facts of other perspectives. He marshalled all the literary conventions of his age to the cause – wit, satire, caricature, poetry, humour, and the serious essay. He appealed to allegedly factual methods used to construct the story. He applied rhetorical tropes to express ideas powerfully, and he employed suggestion or innuendo to lead readers to an implied conclusion. He defined the task of telling the truth rhetorically as the "unmasking" of pretenders to knowledge.

Newsbook writers talked endlessly about their duty to "undeceive" the people about previous reports, and they attributed falsehood not so much to honest mistakes or lack of facts but to the partiality of "interests." They claimed for themselves the ability to transcend their interests and partialities, while denying it to their opponents.

To borrow terms from Aristotle, the editor appealed to the "ethos" and "pathos" of his rhetorical situation – to the writer's ethical character (ethos) and to the presumed values of his audience (pathos). Newsbooks tried to bolster their conclusions by invoking the editor's impartiality, his adherence to reasonable argument, and the "good character" of correspondents. Editors attempted to persuade readers by appealing to their values in two ways – in some contexts, to their blatant, specific prejudices (for example, hatred of the Irish or Catholics), and, in others, to their logic, universal principles, trust in facts, and ability to be impartial judges.[43]

The rhetorical context therefore encouraged the use of ethical terms as part of the language of persuasion. Appeal to ethical and logical norms added to the rhetorical power of particular writings. Overall, these rhetorical exercises helped to legitimate the editor's newsbook, and its arguments, as reasonable in the new rhetorical space created by periodic print media. The ethical legacy of the seventeenth-century press is largely an inventive response to the rhetorical relationship built into news publication. Some readers surely felt that the editors, in their claims to impartiality, protested too much. Yet, as we saw in the rise of scientific objectivity, such claims loom large where trust and consensus are lacking.

THE RESTORATION PRESS, 1660–1695

Historians sometimes depict the period from the Restoration in 1660 to the end of newspaper licensing in 1695 as an era of stagnation for the English press, after the chaotic expansion of the revolutionary newsbook. In 1662, Charles II introduced a new, repressive printing act. The clampdown was neither novel nor unexpected. Cromwell had imposed stiff press restrictions in 1655. Parliament had long opposed publicity of its proceedings. The House of Commons in June 1660 made reporting on Parliament a crime, thereby depriving newsbooks of a major source of news. Both Charles II and James II did their best to suppress all news publications except for an official weekly gazette and several other publications. They continued to restrict the operation of printing presses to London, Cambridge, and Oxford, while delayed the creation of a provincial press until late in the century.[44]

The Restoration brought a measure of political stability after the Civil War, the sects, and the rule of Cromwell and his army. But factionalism did not cease. It became a bitter contest between political parties, Whigs and Tories. Royalist rhetoric and poet laureate John Dryden too hastily

43 The editor could direct his rhetoric to either the high-minded or the low-minded dimension of his audience. As Perelman says, the rhetoric can appeal to a particular or to a universal audience – to parochial, biased interests or to reasonable, impartial principles respectively. In any rhetorical context, the speaker (or journalist) can address either type of audience. See Perelman, *The New Rhetoric.*

44 Cranfield, *The Development of the Provincial Newspaper*, 3.

proclaimed the Restoration as the end of factionalism: "At home the hateful names of Parties cease, and factious Souls are weary'ed into peace."[45] Amid this continuing factionalism, many subjects approved of, or at least did not oppose, the king's measures against the press.

By the autumn of 1666, the only weekly newspaper available was the government-sanctioned newssheet, the *London Gazette.* Published from "Whitehall," it eschewed (dangerous) comment in favour of foreign and government news. It reported on the king's activities, ministerial changes, visits by foreign princes, and the deaths of statesmen. It would remain that way for 13 years. The history of the Restoration weekly newspaper is not that of a free and independent press.[46] Its most positive aspect was the development of factual reporting in the gazettes. It saw also the return of repression and power struggles between a handful of privileged publishers and licensers of the press, such as Henry Muddiman and Roger L'Estrange. Their journalistic efforts were shaped by their obligation to the king, through whom they retained their positions. Their journalistic assertions, like those of the pre-Restoration press, formed part of their political rhetoric – a reflection of larger political battles between king and Parliament, Whig and Tory.

Press controls, however, did not eliminate the exchange of news and information. People shared political intelligence in the new coffeehouses and clubs. Unofficial broadsides and polemical pamphlets continued to appear. Newsbook ads and large placards posted in the streets advertised plays and other events. The tempo of publication of learned journals accelerated in England and much of western Europe. A diminished printed press meant a greater circulation for written newsletters full of unofficial gossip and news for the upper classes, compiled by well-placed professional writers, from Muddiman to Ichabod Dawks.[47]

45 Dryden, "Astrea Redux," 10.

46 The suppression of the press was so successful that in 1688, when William of Orange landed at Torbay and marched to Exeter, he could not find a printer in Exeter, the main city of southwest England, to publish a manifesto. No London printer would produce such a sensitive document with King James still in power. William finally located a printer in York. Cranfield, *The Development of the Provincial Newspaper,* 5.

47 Muddiman's long career as professional newsletter writer, confidant of secretaries of state, and publisher of the *Gazette* is described in Muddiman, *The King's Journalist.* For Dawks, see Morison, *Ichabod Dawks and His Newsletter.* The newsletters, which escaped the restrictions on print, replaced the revolutionary newsbooks as publications with "insider" news, commentary, and gossip.

Between 1660 and 1695, the press enjoyed two interludes of freedom. The first was from 1679 to 1682, when the printing act temporarily expired because of parliamentary gridlock between Whigs and Tories. The second was the uncertain period leading to the "Glorious Revolution" of 1688, when William III and Mary II replaced her father, James II, on the throne. Once again, the weakening of controls allowed a robust, scandalous press. During the first interlude, about 40 papers were appearing, some short-lived, others lasting for as much as two years. Most of the notable publishers, such as Benjamin Harris and Nathaniel Thompson, ended up in trouble with authorities.

The newspapers' excesses in both periods provoked support for William III's own crackdown on the papers. The Bill of Rights of 1689 made no reference to press rights. Elsewhere in Europe, press repression was the norm. Both the Catholic and Protestant churches in Europe had long been enforcing censorship.[48] Outside England, a licensed periodic news press produced cautious, official papers. In Germany, the many principalities imposed strict regulations on printers. In France, Cardinal Richelieu, wary of a rise in inflammatory pamphlets and newsbooks, granted an exclusive privilege for news publication to Théophraste Renaudot and his *Gazette de France*. Renaudot's paper, which lasted well over a century until the French Revolution, was a model for the English gazette.

Appeal to ethical and idealistic norms continued throughout this period. "In one thing," wrote Renaudot, "I yield not to anyone – in the search for truth." John Wallis's *London Courant* in 1688 promised to write "with the integrity of an unbyass'd Historian to do Justice to all parties, in representing things as they shall really happen." The gazettes represented a maturing of "objective" journalism. Given state controls, gazetteers learned to write the bare news without blatant moralizing or commentary. The gazettes had better information than the revolutionary press because their publishers had access to government reports and foreign intelligence. Renaudot's gazette was a model of authoritative, factual journalism. The gazettes' careful distinction between fact and opinion appealed to readers tired of partisan railings. Samuel Pepys described the *London Gazette* as "very pretty, full of newes, and no folly in

48 The Catholic church was one of the first bureaucracies of information-gathering and censorship. It gathered information for inquisitions. The Jesuits regularly sent to Rome their letters of information. The church's Index of Prohibited Books – an attempt to control printing and the spread of Protestantism – began in 1564. See Burke, *A Social History of Knowledge*, 117–48.

it." The *Currant Intelligence*, of the 1680s, told readers that it would present news "without any reflection upon either persons or things, giving only that are matter of fact."[49] The gazettes were also vehicles of government misinformation and propaganda, including "leaks" against rival countries and governments. Several of the supervisors of the *London Gazette* were government spies.[50] The gazettes tamed the news. They provided a vehicle for the transmission of inoffensive information. When criticized for his conservatism, Renaudot replied: "Was it for me to examine the acts of the government?"

The craft of reporting began during the Restoration period. London newsletters and newspapers deployed "newswriters" to track down stories, attend trials, and rush to fires, while "correspondents" outside the city supplied shipping news and other material. Papers started using the phrase "it is reported," which usually meant that someone had been heard to say it.[51] Macaulay described a newswriter as a man who "rambled from coffee house to coffee house, collecting reports, squeezing himself into the Sessions House at the Old Bailey if there was an interesting trial, nay, perhaps, obtained permission to the gallery of Whitehall, and noticed how the King and Duke looked."[52] Two or three men put together a paper, struggling to fill it and laboriously producing it by a hand press with manual typesetting.

The gazettes, written in a succinct, plain style, were primarily for middle-class readers – merchants, shopkeepers, financiers, bankers, and goldsmiths. Obituaries, shipping news, funerals, and government announcements had to fit into a two-page paper. The broadsides and newsbooks, when allowed to flourish, sought an even wider audience by focusing on crime, trials, executions, and occasional glimpses of public unrest, such as the marches of London apprentices, or fights between drunken patrons in theatres.

49 *Currant Intelligence*, 26 April 1681, quoted in Barbara Shapiro, *A Culture of Fact*, 95. By 1688, another publication, the *Present State of Europe: or the Historical and Political Mercury*, separated its "Advice" – news reports from abroad – from its "Reflections upon the Advice."

50 Burke, *A Social History of Knowledge*, 145–6.

51 Sutherland, *The Restoration Newspaper and Its Development*, 47. Reporting on fires and other events was helped by the development of postal service in London. However, finding the locations of fires was difficult, since houses were not numbered and travel across London was slow. London developed an extensive letter post by 1680, supported by sorting offices and collection sites. Reports could now reach newspapers within a few hours.

52 Macaulay, quoted in Cranfield, *The Development of the Provincial Newspaper*, 3.

The Restoration era inaugurated a debate between authoritarian and more liberal attitudes towards the press, several decades after Milton's plea for an unregulated press. The conservative view informed the licensing act of 1662, which set itself against the "general (press) licentiousness of the late times," which endangered the "peace of these kingdoms." L'Estrange, who argued that a free press would frighten the ordinary person out of his "wits," eagerly spied on and raided "seditious" printers, who then faced judges who made examples of them by applying harsh penalties.[53] L'Estrange rejected the idea that he should publish a popular mercury because it would make the public too familiar with its superiors and would encourage the dangerous belief that it had a "Right to be Meddling with the Government."[54] The main debate over the press took place in Parliament. In 1680, Sir Leoline Jenkins, secretary of state, said that any reporting on Parliament was dangerous – "a sort of appeal to the people." Sir Francis Winnington replied that people should know about the actions of parliamentarians.

Despite the dominance of the gazettes and officially sanctioned publications, the period was not without its press wars. Pamphlets and newssheets continued to appear unlicensed and then flourished during the two interludes of relative freedom. Editors continued to exchange claims and counter-claims. For example, Nedham attempted to prevent the restoration of Charles II by writing reports intended to divide the pro-restoration camp. Pamphlets written by L'Estrange and others almost immediately answered his reports.

The division of parliamentary politics into Whig and Tory groups in the late 1670s during the Exclusion Crisis only intensified the rhetorical use of journalism. "Truth" for a supporter of James, Duke of York, later James II, was a loyalist truth. In the early 1680s, ministers of Charles II hired "counter-writers" to publish racy pamphlets to counterbalance the anti-Stuart pamphlets. L'Estrange began publishing the *Observator,* using a question-and-answer format "to prevent Mistakes and False News, and to give you a true Information of the state of things,

53 Armed with a general warrant from the government, the press censor could raid a printer's shop on suspicion of illegal activity, destroy his printing materials, and send him before a judge. The judges shared L'Estrange's anti-press fervour. In 1663, Lord Chief Justice Hyde sentenced printer John Twyn to be hanged, drawn, and quartered for a critical pamphlet on English justice, as an "example" to the "Boldness" of the press.

54 Herd, *The March of Journalism,* 11.

and advance your understanding above the common rate of Coffee-House Statesmen."[55]

Ethical language and grand statements could not hide the low standards of the press, especially during the two interludes. Papers failed to verify stories and printed "hoax" letters. Newswriters gathered bogus stories from coffee-houses. Benjamin Harris, among other editors, played a disgraceful role in whipping up anti-Catholic feeling among London mobs during the "Popish Plot." The fictional Jesuit scheme to kill Charles II led to the execution of 35 Catholics, including the primate of Ireland. Harris gave detailed coverage to the gruesome executions. A free press could be ugly. Yet the periodic press's claim to be a discourse of fact did not succumb completely to politics. The licensed press was still relied on to bring forth new facts in its plain style. Robert Hooke, for instance, complained that the *London Gazette*'s report about an earthquake in the Antilles was too short.[56]

The end of press licensing in 1695 may appear to us as inevitable, given that society was moving towards more open, liberal arrangements. But throughout the 1680s, many people considered licensing a necessary condition for peace in a divided nation. Nevertheless, the licensing system came under constant stress as the public sphere expanded. In 1695, the Whigs in Parliament refused to renew the printing act, so it expired. The Whigs did not want the Tories in government to control the press. The Whigs' official reasons, apparently drafted by Locke and others, were mainly practical. The number of publications swamped the censors, causing delays for printers; the system did not eliminate seditious material; and there were legal measures to punish seditious papers after publication. Unsuccessful attempts to restore licensing would take place well into the eighteenth century. Meanwhile, the government found other ways to control the press, from taxes through bribery, to charges of seditious libel. The function of the press, particularly its political function and its freedom, would be a major stimulant for the development of journalism ethics in the next century. The development culminated in an explicit "public ethic" that claimed that the press was a fourth estate. Another stimulant was an explosion in the number of newspapers after the expiry of licensing. The pent-up demand for news and commentary had found release. The central public role of the newspaper could no longer be denied.

55 Sutherland, *The Restoration Newspaper and Its Development,* 18.

56 Barbara Shapiro, *A Culture of Fact,* 101.

4

The Invention of a Public Ethic: The Eighteenth Century

The nation is governed by all that has tongue.

Edmund Burke

In this chapter I explain the eighteenth-century invention of a public ethic in terms of three intertwined developments. Daily newspapers helped create a concomitant public sphere; a new breed of essayists wrote for, and helped crystallize, an English public; and a group of journalists radicalized a segment of the population of England – as well as many people in the American colonies and France. The epilogue looks at a crucial change in journalism's status in England and elsewhere – its emergence by century's end as a fourth estate.

DAILY NEWSPAPERS AND THE PUBLIC SPHERE

A public philosophy of journalism arose in eighteenth-century England as the daily newspaper emerged. Partisan voices in the press jostled politicians and aristocratic oligarchies for influence in the public sphere. This chapter explains how this public philosophy generated what I call a "public ethic" and how the major forms of journalism – the partisan, spectator, and reform presses in England, and the revolutionary press in America and France – expressed it.

During the early eighteenth century, the rapid expansion of the unlicensed press coincided with fundamental changes in English society. A public sphere created an almost insatiable demand for news, information, critical reviews, and political comment. A host of newspapers and journals in London, followed by weekly newspapers across Britain, met the demand obliged by the voracious readership. As our model of ethical change predicts, this new social context altered the journalist–reader relationship and led journalists to assert a distinct set of norms and ideals. As in the seventeenth century, journalistic assertions of factuality and impartiality abound in the eighteenth century. But a new element emerged. The reader became an actor in a public sphere that increasingly took on a liberal spirit. Publishers introduced new terms to describe their newspapers' relationship with this public. Newspapers called themselves "public watchdog," "tribunal of the people," "instrument of public opinion," and "bulwark" of the public's liberty. The journalism ethics of the eighteenth century is that of a press conscious of its enlarged role in shaping public opinion.

Whether acting as objective informer or reform advocate, the eighteenth-century paper is distinct ethically in its claim to be the public's agent and main representative. We must not reduce the century's changes in the press to a mere difference in quantity – more types of papers publishing more often for more readers. The papers' role shifted, as did publishers' aims and journalists' public personae.

The idea of a public ethic in journalism could not arise in Britain until seventeenth-century authoritarianism was in retreat. The idea of the press as a public tribune could not gain wide approval until new norms of publicity, public opinion, and public representation challenged political norms of secrecy and privilege. The English journalist's claim to an essential public role would gain acceptance only when a substantial portion of that society embraced the principle of government by informed public consent. Only then could the press begin to achieve recognition as a vital part of society.

Addressing a Public

In the eighteenth century, journalists began to conceive of readers as members of a public. The terms "public" and "public opinion" represented novel concepts, despite their familiarity to us today. Readers, as a public, had a political identity that went beyond the seventeenth-century idea of the "people." The rights of the English public went back at least to the Bill of Rights of 1689 and the enhanced powers of Parliament. In theory, members of the public were not just subjects of the sovereign, or members of a family, religious group, or political faction. They were citizens engaged in self-governance through the discussion of public issues and participation in public affairs. In debating issues, people were ideally rational and morally autonomous agents able to consider the public interest, not just their own self-interest. Together, they arrived at a public opinion that expressed their "general will," which government had to follow, or at least consider.

In reality, social and economic class determined to a large extent one's membership and participation in the eighteenth century public. For much of the century, the governing elites thought of the public as the aristocracy, the propertied upper class, and the educated middle-class – groups that dominated Parliament and other institutions. These were the people supposedly capable of reaching enlightened opinion and separate from what Voltaire called the lower-class "mob" – an irrational, violent group that "clamours" and needs policing. The concept of the public widened during the eighteenth century. For reforming journalists such as John Wilkes, the public was the "middling and inferior" people whose liberties needed protection. French revolutionaries talked about the political rights of all *mankind*.

The expansion of the idea of the public coincided with the development of a public sphere, consisting of members of the public, in their multifarious communications and interactions on matters of common interest. The English public sphere began in the seventeenth century and was completed in the next century. Habermas has claimed that a public domain arose in England in the 1690s as a bourgeois sphere between the private activities of family and the privileged precincts of Parliament.[1] Ever since Habermas, scholars have sought to push back its origins – towards the 1640s, the Reformation, even the Renaissance.[2] The public sphere of the eighteenth century consisted of physical spaces or "sites": a salon, a coffee-house or tavern, a public meeting, a bookshop, or a club. By 1739, London had 559 coffee-houses. There were separate coffee-houses for merchants, ships' officers, actors, writers, Whigs, and Tories. The newspaper was fodder for coffee-house conversation.

Politics was not the only driving force behind the public sphere. Equally important was the interest in culture, the arts, science, and news of all kinds. A striking aspect was the commercialization of culture, especially for the rising middle class. The public consumed many types of literature and art, from books to theatrical performances by David Garret. Culture was no longer only for the private appreciation of the upper class,

1 Habermas, *The Structural Transformation of the Public Sphere.* See also Calhoun, *Habermas and the Public Sphere.*

2 Briggs and Burke, *A Social History of the Media,* 74–105. Joad Raymond argues that the most "rapid development of informed popular debate" occurred in the 1640s, with revolutionary newsbooks. Raymond, "The Newspaper," 128.

sponsored by the royal court and patrons. People bought paintings to display in homes; Wedgwood copied artistic designs onto his porcelain; periodicals serialized novels. The public consumed culture at the theatre, from circulating libraries, and in public gardens.[3]

The press stimulated the non-political public sphere through reviews of plays, advertisements, essays on science, and articles on fashion and "polite" society. The non-political sphere included the meetings and publications of learned societies and scientists. Europeans set up some 70 learned societies concerned wholly or partly with natural philosophy in the eighteenth century. No fewer than 1,267 periodical journals were established in France between 1600 and 1789, many dealing with scientific and artistic matters.[4] Scientists, scholars, art dealers, and booksellers used the printing press to construct a web of communications across the public sphere.

Publishing news daily (or frequently) for a public sphere altered and intensified the relationship between journalists and their readers. As in the previous century, the publisher had to attract enough readers to maintain his journal economically. He had to position his journal rhetorically vis-à-vis other publications. The press now operated in a non-licensed atmosphere, where more journals published more often. For daily news publishing, editorial claims of reliability and impartiality were more important than ever.

But they were more difficult to maintain in an era when papers collected news in greater quantities and at a faster rate. The chance of making a reporting error (and having one's error detected) increased as did the quantity of hurried, poor-quality newspaper writing. Benjamin Constant in 1797 complained that the pressures of periodic publishing were downgrading journalism: "The necessity of writing everyday is the tomb of talent". Samuel Johnson described the difficulties well: "He that condemns himself to compose on a stated day, will often bring to his task, an attention dissipated, a memory overwhelmed, an imagination embarrassed, a mind distracted with anxieties, and a body languishing with disease: He will sometimes labour on a barren topic, till it is too late to change it; and sometimes, in the ardor of invention, diffuse his thoughts into wild exuberance, which the pressing hour of publication will not suffer judgment to examine or reduce."[5]

3 Brewer, *The Pleasures of the Imagination.*

4 Burke, *A Social History of Knowledge,* 47–8.

5 Samuel Johnson, "The Rambler," 188.

The relationship between journalist and reader intensified as more and more people acquired the habit of a daily paper. Readers came to expect their daily ration of fresh news from the press. But the daily coming together of reader and paper meant more than the establishment of a social habit or a private, economic exchange – individuals buying specific news products. Buying a paper was also part of the educating and informing of a public in the issues of the day and part of the public's activity as citizens.

The interaction of press and public was political and had far-reaching implications. The journalist and the reader were acting out roles that went beyond their actions as private individuals. The public, in buying a newspaper, was not acquiring just another product, like shoes or food. It was engaging in one of the new daily rituals of the public sphere – informing itself about the performance of its government and the general state of its country. The press provided information and comment on matters of general public interest, not just the specific interests of individuals. Information, then as today, was valuable to individuals who wanted to carry out political and cultural activities in the public sphere. Through the papers, individuals saw themselves linked to other individuals. They were part of a public, a party or a community of shared ideas. The journalist's status also changed gradually, from hack writer to indispensable informer and critic. The journalist was a spectator who attended events on the public's behalf.

The daily paper instilled in people the habits of a public. The habit created new expectations that people came, in time, to take for granted. By reading about public affairs, readers came to expect freer public discussion and more participation in the public sphere. The more they participated in public events, the more they wanted to be informed. The press and its readers found themselves caught up in a virtuous circle that strengthened the public sphere. The circle encouraged the press to articulate a public ethic – a set of principles that expressed its role in the public sphere. Newspapers helped to develop the idea of a public, which it then claimed to represent.

The newspaper was ideal for the activities of the public sphere. The daily newspaper claimed, with some justification, that it was the only form of media able to bring all of the public together regularly. The press provided a new space capable of linking a dispersed group of readers. Other "media" existed, such as novels, pamphlets, plays, and public festivals, but daily newspapers and regularly published journals appeared in most public places and sought out a wide range of readers through street vendor and postman. The papers could follow a sequence of events more or less as they happened. They could apply continuous pressure on officials. Abstractions such as the "public sphere" and "public opinion" became "something definite, tangible, manifested on a daily basis in the newspapers."[6]

The press could establish many sub-spheres within the public sphere. For example, it created "temporary" (or local) public spheres based around a region or issue or more permanent, national public spheres. The press in regions such as Brittany in France and London sparked interest in local issues over a short period, such as food prices or improvements to a main roadway. But it also linked people together on broader, long-term issues such as parliamentary reform and land enclosures. The press also gave the public sphere historical depth by printing important texts and histories and by keeping a permanent record of events and decisions. In this way, members of the public could refer back to original texts and arguments and compare their situation with other people in other times. They could remember how problems arose and see themselves as actors in campaigns that had deep historical roots. The radicals of revolutionary France, for example, looked back to Milton's *Areopagitica,* while they adapted the strategies of the revolutionary journalists in America. The U.S. Declaration of Independence could be seen as part of a long historical process that went back to the "great remonstrance" by the English parliament against Charles I.

We should not exaggerate the influence of the eighteenth-century press, nor forget the many other social forces at play. Yet the proliferation of newspapers and journals as a whole, despite the limitations of individual publications, developed the public's ability to reason and enter into dialogue about events, to think collectively about public affairs. We should not under-estimate this contribution to liberal, democratic society. Never before had so many journals existed. Never before were individuals inundated with so much information, news, commentary, advertisements, and satire. Never before had people met and discussed public affairs and matters of society in the many sites of the public sphere, from the spa to the public garden lecture. In the press, political essayists answered political essayists, readers questioned articles, high-church clergymen corrected dissenters, Hanoverians rebutted Jacobites, and Whigs denounced Tories.

It was the imperfect but vigorous rationality of the public sphere, which did not confine itself to arcane philosophy texts or elite discussions in the king's court. A claim in the public sphere was reasonable, or at least had

6 Baker, "Politics and Public Opinion under the Old Regime," 213.

to be taken seriously, if it was sufficiently persuasive to support certain courses of action. What was reasonable was a generally accepted conclusion reached through the hurly-burly, rhetorical process of public discourse. One's position was reasonable if it could persuade other reasonable people, withstand public scrutiny, and hold its ground amid claim and counter-claim. In the press, and at other public-sphere sites, arguments were not formal demonstrations. Beliefs were not unquestionable objective knowledge reached by impeccable methods. This form of public reason in practice, much like the public rhetoric in ancient Athens, could be admirable or disappointing. At times of political tension, public reason could degenerate into xenophobic ranting or personal abuse.

The press encouraged a practical, contextual approach to discussions of public policy, despite the well-known problems of bias and self-interest. A pure objectivity, or a strict scientific impartiality, was too much to ask of the participants. People could enter the public sphere with their own interests, partialities, and ideas. Since special interests and base motivations had potential influence, the debate took a pragmatic approach to the threat of bias. One could not expect perfectly objective public discourse. But one could improve public discourse by "unmasking" the interests, questionable facts, and specious reasoning of specific opponents in particular situations. The rhetoric of Parliament, with formal protocols and restricted types of interlocutors, was different from the rhetoric of the public through the medium of newspaper articles, editorials, and essays. The daily press was a new "way of practice" – a medium by which society could seek a reasonable, public discussion and perhaps a consensus.

Given the limits of this press-facilitated public discourse, we miss the importance of the press if we approach it from a perfectionist standpoint. If we evaluate it according to ideal standards of impartiality, reason, and inclusivity, the eighteenth-century public sphere looks to have been a biased, exclusive arena using a low-grade rationality.[7]

7 Scholars have noted that public communication in the seventeenth and eighteenth centuries does not live up to Habermas's normative requirements for a public sphere – that discussion of public issues should be rational, inclusive, open to all participants, and not distorted by particular interests. This approach lends itself to a perfectionist attitude whereby we evaluate the public sphere and its press according to strict, ideal standards. Not surprisingly, this view finds the public sphere and the press almost irredeemably flawed. The early partisan newspapers seem not to be contributors to a rational public sphere, and the ethical claims of early journalists appear hypocritical or a sham.

Public reason did not meet the standards of philosophical logic or an Athenian symposium led by Socrates. We also miss the press's importance if we think of the eighteenth century as represented by philosophers and poets who sought a higher knowledge about humanity, religion, and society than appeared in the arguments in the marketplace or in the short articles of the press. From this perspective, the eighteenth-century public sphere looks like a mere "shadow" of a truly rational and open public sphere, as real-world objects are shadows of Platonic forms. The political and commercial "interests" that lay behind debate and action in the public sphere appear only as regrettable, corrupting influences.

This ideal perspective gets in the way of a more realistic appreciation of the eighteenth-century public sphere and of the long-term, positive impact of an imperfect press. We need to adopt a pragmatic, imperfectionist approach that is neither too idealistic nor too cynical. An imperfectionist approach that does not *expect* an ideal rationality from social processes allows us to grasp the fact that arguments in the public sphere were not always worthless or totally biased or "below" the consideration of public philosophers.

Many settings required members of the public to argue in a reasonably impartial manner – to appeal to facts, to try to see others' viewpoints, to rise above their worst prejudices. In taverns and coffee-houses, there was more than bawdy talk. There could be witty, satirical, and intellectual discussion of the day's newspapers. Interlocutors at Dr Johnson's table, for example, would have to offer sharp commentary and analyses. In the salons of "polite" society, one displayed refinement by engaging in eloquent, rational debate. The newspaper publisher or essayist never presumed to be a disinterested philosopher following universal logical principles. The publisher was more like a sophist, addressing the contentious crowds of the English agora.

From a purely logical perspective, such arguments were flawed. But from a historical perspective, this imperfect clash of views sharpened the public's critical powers and made it willing to question the assertions of its government. Moreover, "interests" do not always thoroughly corrupt public reason and social progress. The economic and political interests that stood behind the commercialization of culture and the establishment of newspapers had unintentional, positive effects for liberal society. Commercial aims and the clash of political interests both distorted the press and the public sphere and helped to *create* a vigorous press and public sphere.

A more complex relationship between journalist and public in the eighteenth century called for a revision of the ethical lexicon of journalism, inherited from the seventeenth century. In the seventeenth century, publishers valued impartial reports that contained matters of fact because they maintained a readership, while keeping the censor at bay. In the eighteenth, factuality and impartiality promoted the public sphere, informing public opinion and effective criticism of government. These values became part of a more ambitious public ethic of journalism.

Eighteenth-century journalists interpreted the public ethic in various ways. The partisan journalist saw it as service to a political cause or party; the spectator journalist, as restrained, impartial analysis and accurate informing. For reform and revolutionary journalists it meant advocacy for a free, egalitarian public sphere or for reducing the powers of despots and aristocracies. We catch glimpses of the public ethic in editorials, newspaper prospectuses, essays, and pamphlets. We hear it in the statements of journalists (and others) before the courts, Parliament, and public forums. People appeal to it in disputes among editors and between editors and government ministers. The idea of the public role of the press receives a philosophical interpretation from Hume, Erskine, Paine, Condorcet, and Jefferson, among others.

Before analysing those ethical assertions, we need to review the progress of the eighteenth-century press and describe two types of journalist: the partisan and the spectator.

ESSAYISTS FOR AN ENGLISH PUBLIC

Journalism's Primordial Soup

Britain in the first half of the eighteenth century enjoyed a period of relative political stability and increasing national wealth. The succession of the Hanoverian house was secured during the reign of the first two Georges, from 1714 to 1760. George I and George II focused on foreign policy and large constitutional issues. They tended to leave the daily business of government to their powerful Whig "first ministers," such as Walpole and Pelham. After the Seven Years' War, Britain was the most powerful European power, no longer the poor neighbour of Enlightenment France. Its constitution, guaranteeing individual rights and the supremacy of Parliament, was an envious exception in a Europe of absolute monarchs.

We should not over-estimate the stability of the era, however. Tory ministers during Queen Anne's reign (1702–14) had to defuse a Jacobite rebellion and crack down on religious dissenters whom they accused of putting the Church of England "in danger." From the 1720s onward, Walpole's ministry became a symbol of corruption, patronage, and a ruthless commercialism that had caused the investment scandal called the South Sea Bubble. Wars increased the national debt and taxes, and Parliament too often descended into court intrigue and party politics. John Gay's *The Beggar's Opera* compared the morals of the upper class to those of a brothel. In 1737, political criticism in plays by Gay, Fielding, and others led Walpole to license the London theatres. In 1745, Charles Edward Stuart's (the Young Pretender) Jacobite forces marched into the heartland of England before being turned back. A sense of political drift and popular dissent set in by the 1760s, because of the inept George III, his unpopular policies and advisers, and later his loss of the American colonies. When the French Revolution encouraged radicalism, the British government, soon to be at war with France, restricted liberties and jailed reformers.[8]

The course of English journalism followed the contours of this social history. The journalism of the first half of the century saw experimentation both in news and in partisan comment, based on Whig–Tory antagonisms. News sales benefited from wealth, war, trade, and larger urban populations. London publishers circulated dailies, weekly journals, and tri-weekly newspapers. For an established printer, a newspaper was a low-cost experiment. Some papers offered news and ads, while others stressed political comment.

In the second half of the century, the same bifurcated development continued. On the one hand, journals and weekly papers continued the political warfare, but with a more radical edge. Journalists went beyond the usual party rhetoric to demand reforms that challenged the political system per se. On the other hand, readers, stimulated by the American and French revolutions, looked to daily newspapers for news, not comment.

By 1709, London had 12 tri-weeklies, 1 bi-weekly, 20 weekly journals, and, from 11 March 1702, the first daily newspaper – Samuel Buckley's *Daily Courant.* Many other titles had come and gone. In the 1720s, new daily newspapers arrived, such as the *Daily Post* and the *Universal Spectator,* selling for one or two pence per copy. In the 1730s the daily

8 Dickinson, *British Radicalism and the French Revolution.*

"advertisers" arrived, consisting mainly of ads and news of commerce. From the 1770s on, London dailies began to dominate the market, assert their independence, and develop reporting. The *Times* (London) and the *Morning Chronicle* were leading models of the daily newspaper and formed a growing political force. England was now at the forefront of journalism, and London was the centre of publishing. France would not have a daily newspaper until 1777. Most European countries lacked a significant daily press until the nineteenth century.

From one perspective, the eighteenth-century newspaper was a slow-changing, modest enterprise that depended on political patronage. The newspaper of the 1770s, for example, was larger and contained more ads than that of the 1730s. But its content was not much different. Politics, finance, trials, disasters, war, and shipping news were still the staple. A few people using hand-operated presses continued to put out the daily newspapers. With a small staff, editors obtained most of their news from external sources, such as politicians, diplomatic reports, reports in other papers, and events at the standard venues – courts, public speeches, funerals of great men, and so on.

Many parts of English society, including Parliament, were closed to reporters. News-gatherers picked up scraps of news outside the House of Commons and from people arriving at ports, in coffee-houses, or at the Stock Exchange. Additional material came from correspondents' letters, while the editor or an external writer prepared the commentary.

Historian Arthur Aspinall describes the eighteenth-century newspaper as short on news, full of ads, low in circulation, and too small a business to achieve independence from political subsidies. Other factors slowing the spread of papers in Britain included limited roads, low literacy rates, hostility from the governing classes, opposition to selling papers on Sundays, and stamp taxes that drove up the cost of printing and the price of papers.[9]

From another perspective, the papers and journals were numerous and audacious, the essential diet of gossip and discussion. Most forms of newspapering originate in this era: the first tri-weekly newspapers, the first evening papers, the first dailies, and the first Sunday papers. In this primordial soup of journalism, the newspaper metamorphosed from dry, official gazette to indispensable informer.

Although circulation grew slowly at times during the century, the news press fanned out from London, and by the 1760s London dailies

9 Aspinall, *Politics and the Press,* 1–6

or provincial weeklies served almost all of England.[10] The total daily circulation of (stamped) London newspapers at mid-century was over 45,000. The average circulation of individual dailies was about 5,000, up from 1,500 in the 1720s; a few papers exceeded 10,000.[11] Annual sales of all stamped London papers grew from 2.5 million in 1712 to 12.6 million in 1775. London had 6 dailies in the 1730s, 9 in the 1780s, and 14 in 1792.

London's press extended beyond the daily papers. For example, in 1760, it had 86 papers – dailies, weeklies, newsmagazines, magazines, and political journals. Johnson wondered how it was possible to subsist without a newspaper when almost every large English town "has its weekly historian, who regularly circulates his periodical intelligence."[12] The papers were not just numerous or popular. The press showed that it was a rising social force by celebrating landmark legal victories against government. The opening of Parliament to reporters in the 1770s only increased the press's political influence, as the newspapers subjected political decisions and debate to daily scrutiny.

Partisan, Spectator, and Register

The journalist as partisan, political warrior came early to the new unlicensed press. Between 1700 and 1730, the polemical essay became a centrepiece of newspapers and of weekly journals of news and comment. The essay signalled the rise of a partisan journalism connected closely to the era's religious and political struggles between Whigs and Tories.[13] The

10 Cranfield, *The Development of the Provincial Newspaper.* The provincial paper filled its pages by reprinting articles from the London papers.

11 Harris, "The Structure," 87.

12 *Cambridge Journal,* 9 May 1752. Quoted in Cranfield, *The Development of the Provincial Newspaper,* 69.

13 The political parties emerged in the late 1670s during the Exclusion crises, when groups of MPs attempted to pass legislation that would prevent James, the Catholic brother of Charles II, from becoming king. Party factionalism continued after the Glorious Revolution of 1688 ousted James II. The new Bill of Rights, which recognized the sovereignty of Parliament, encouraged party struggles within the Commons. Political differences reflected religious differences. Members of the Church of England tended to support the Tory party. The Protestant sects – Presbyterians, Quakers, Baptists, and Independents – tended to favour the Whigs.

"Glorious Revolution" had not healed deep divisions over the role of a national church, the monarch's religion, the power of Parliament, and the limits of liberty. Much was at stake in this struggle – careers, power, land, and ideology. The main instruments of persuasion were patronage and press propaganda.[14]

Nedham had pioneered the polemical essay long before, and the essay had remained the basis of the many pamphlets that still circulated in the eighteenth century. But the periodic press of the early eighteenth century extended the essay to more people. The English reader enjoyed the weekly papers' mix of news and essays, ads and serialized novels.[15] The essays came from leading editors such as Nicholas Amhurst and Nathaniel Mist, Grub Street journalists, government propagandists, and some of the best writers of the period – Daniel Defoe, Henry Fielding, Tobias Smollett, and Jonathan Swift. Some essayists were fired by ideology; others sought political favours, fame, or a regular paycheque.

Early forms of the partisan essay appeared in political journals of the first decade of the century, such as the *Examiner*, under Swift's editorship and Defoe's *Review*.[16] In the 1720s and 1730s, the essay moved to the front page of weekly news journals, such as Mist's Whiggish *Weekly Journal* and Amhurst's Tory *Craftsman*.[17] The decision by government and opposition parties to help finance and operate newspapers only intensified partisan journalism. Both Whigs and Tories spent thousands of

14 Visitors from the Continent, such as Voltaire, found English freedoms striking. But some British writers, such as Joseph Addison, worried about how the nation had divided itself into two groups of "strangers."

15 In 1731, the *Craftsmen*, with ads covering half of its pages, boasted a circulation of 12,000. The *Craftsman*, the *Weekly Journal*, and the *London Journal* had daily circulations of over 10,000 in the 1730s.

16 Swift edited the *Examiner* for a brief period in 1711. This conservative periodical challenged the more liberal views of Steele's *Guardian* and Addison's *Whig Examiner*. Swift was perhaps the most accomplished and prolific essayist of his time, writing dozens of stinging pamphlets on social and political controversies.

17 Mist's journal was one of the most successful of the weekly papers. It began in December 1716 as the *Weekly Journal Or, Saturday's Post*, and became *Mist's Weekly Journal* in 1725, surviving to 1737. During the 1720s, Mist was arrested, tried, fined, jailed, and sent to the pillory. In 1727 he was fined £500 and had to put up a bond for future good behaviour, which caused him to take refuge in France in 1728.

pounds to start journals, buy hostile papers, provide the salaries of journalists, pay critics to stay silent, and support friendly publishers. In 1722, Walpole's government purchased the *London Journal.* In 1726, Tory politicians financed the *Craftsman.* Amhurst hired Gay, Pope, and Swift to question the policies of Walpole's government.

Defoe's long and winding career epitomizes the life of the essay journalist. Defoe took up journalism about 1700 after failing as a merchant. His 1701 pamphlet *The True-Born Englishman* satirized the criticism of William III's Dutch nationality. Another satire in 1702, *The Shortest-Way with the Dissenters,* made fun of the high-church rhetoric against dissenters by proposing eliminating them. Defoe, a dissenter, landed in the pillory for libel.[18] He obtained release from prison after agreeing to be a pamphlet writer and spy for the Tory first minister, Robert Harley, Earl of Oxford. During his journalism career, Defoe wrote almost 2,000 short essays for at least 26 publications, managing to offend almost all political sides. One reason for Defoe's editorial flexibility was his need to feed his seven children. For a while, he wrote for Nathaniel Mist under pseudonyms such as "Eye Witness," attacking the government of George I. From 1704 to 1715, he produced a tri-weekly political journal, the *Review,* which opposed the high church and the Jacobites and criticized France.

In the 1720s Defoe turned to novel writing, travel writing, and reporting on events. He knew how to use plain language, and he had an eye for realistic detail that fit with England's "culture of fact." In the late 1720s, he wrote his *Tour through the Whole Island of Great Britain* – a vivid first-hand account of the state of the country, which combined travel writing and chorography. The journalism of an essayist such as Defoe blurred the line between fact and interpretation, between eyewitness reporting and imaginative reconstruction. He wrote about the London plague of 1666 using documents and his imagination. *Robinson Crusoe* mixed travel reporting and fiction.[19]

18 Defoe grew up during the tense Restoration era. Because he was the son of a Presbyterian butcher, he could not enter Oxford or Cambridge, which were reserved for members of the Church of England. His grandiose schemes to make money failed miserably, including an attempt to manufacture perfume from cat urine. See Novak, *Daniel Defoe.*

19 A similar mixture of journalism, ambition, and political service appears in other partisan journalists of the era. Henry Fielding was a pamphleteer and a justice of the peace. He edited his weekly, four-page satirical *Jacobite's Journal* to support the House of Hanover after the 1745 rebellion.

Not all essayists were partisan and polemical. Some saw themselves as sophisticated spectators commenting on the passing show of life. Factional discord induced some writers to promote journalistic civility and to write in a more literary, detached manner. The paradigm of spectator journalism was Joseph Addison and Richard Steele's *Spectator* journal (1711–14). The *Spectator* had an immediate impact, selling 4,000 copies a day. It flourished in the coffee-houses; it was discussed in Britain and colonial America; for decades it was reprinted in English school textbooks and manuals of conduct. In the United States, Benjamin Franklin copied its style. The *Spectator* eschewed heated, factional writing in favour of sophisticated observations on society. It occupied a middle ground between dry news in the official gazettes and the heated, partisan commentary in weekly political journals. Addison laid his observations before the reader gently and with wit, seeking not to incite partisan feelings. In the same way, a few years later, Hume asked historians and moralists to transcend their partiality and to place a critical distance between themselves and their topic.

By mid-century, another man of letters, Samuel Johnson, was practising an essay journalism that was less factional and more literary. Instead of flaying political figures, Johnson sought higher ground in his anonymously published series, the *Rambler*, which appeared bi-weekly from March 1750 to March 1752 and followed in the tradition of Addison's *Spectator*.[20] The *Rambler* offered essays on society and literature. Its topics ranged from the usefulness of biography to the difficulties of maintaining a reputation. Later, from 1758 to 1760, Johnson wrote his weekly essay, the *Idler*, which appeared in the *Universal Chronicle* newspaper. The essays in the *Idler* were shorter and more casual than those in the *Rambler*.

Johnson wrote elevated journalism adorned by wit, handsome phrases, and wide learning. From his Olympian heights, he could dismiss the partisan writers who sold their abilities "to one or other of the parties that divide us ... without a Wish for Truth or Thought or Decency, without Care of any other Reputation than that of a stubborn Adherence to their Abbetors."[21] But Johnson's journalism, for all its learnedness and condescension towards the paid writers of the press, was itself part of the press. In fact, Johnson got his literary start in the popular journalism that he criticized. He began his literary career at London in 1738 by joining a group of hack writers who made a living producing verse and short biographies

20 McAdam and Milne, *A Johnson Reader*, 159.

21 From Johnson's prospectus for the *London Chronicle* of 1757. Quoted in Anthony Smith, *The Newspaper*, 76.

for the reading public. He also put together reports on Parliament for Edward Cave's *Gentleman's Magazine.*

Johnson's conservatism affected his views on the liberty of the press. He felt that "political liberty is good only so long as it produces private liberty," and he questioned whether restraints on the printing of "thoughts" had any impact on the "private happiness of the nation."[22] He mocked the argument for the right of unrestrained printing because post-publication penalties existed. He said the argument was no more reasonable than the view that we should "sleep with doors unbolted, because by our laws we can hang a thief."[23]

Even Johnson – the "great cham of literature," this critic of Shakespeare and dictionary compiler – could not avoid the patronage politics of his age. He was not active in party politics, but he was a Tory by philosophy. He favoured the Protestant monarchy, the government's right to limit a licentious press, and society's restraining imperfect human nature. When George III became king in 1760, Tories were back in favour, and Johnson was one of the conservatives rewarded, receiving a government pension from Lord Bute. He told Bute that he received the money gratefully, as a man without "alliance or interest." In other words, Bute should not expect him to do anything for the money. Yet Johnson did go on to pen political tracts, including a defence of the king's acceptance of the peace terms for the Seven Years' War.[24]

A third journalistic persona was that of the spectator as a 'register' of events: the newsgatherer, or the editor of news. Although reporters would not proliferate until the next century, the "news-writers" and parliamentary reporters of the eighteenth-century London newspapers initiated the craft of gathering and writing news. Daily news began in an inauspicious manner. Buckley filled his dull *Daily Courant* with official news provided by government, items on London's port, and foreign news scalped from other publications.[25]

22 Boswell, *Life of Johnson*, 60.

23 Quoted in Rea, *The English Press in Politics*, 6.

24 Ibid., 23.

25 Buckley's paper is dull by modern standards, but the English public wanted to read everything that it could on the conflict with France over the Spanish Succession (1701–14). The government gave Buckley information on the conflict to maintain public support for the war. The first issue contained news of the "Marlborough Wars," where the Duke of Marlborough was enjoying a series of victories over the French armies of Louis XIV.

As other newspapers joined the market, editors started sending newsgatherers to fires and court trials. The *Spectator* noted in 1712 that the owners of papers gave a "Salary for better Advices" to "Collectors of Home News." In 1725, Defoe called the reporting of "Home News" a "new Common Hunt." Addison wrote: "There is no Humour in my Countrymen, which I am more inclined to wonder at, than their general Thirst after News." Nathaniel Mist's *Weekly Journal* was said to have had "an agent scraping the Jails in Middlesex ... another has a warrant for scouring the Ale-houses and Gin-shops ... and another in the Park to watch the Motions of the Guards."[26]

Reporting also began with the collection of the sober facts of commerce for shippers, financiers, and farmers headed to market. The *Daily Advertiser* announced on 26 February 1730: "This paper will consist wholly of Advertisements, together with the Price of Stocks, Course of Exchange, and Names and Descriptions of Persons becoming Bankrupts ... (and) the Several Species of Goods Imported into the Port of London."

Reporting could be both shoddy and stale. News writers began their salacious stories from coffee-house strangers with the phrase "We are informed." Others paid for information from "death-hunters" – men who gathered information on deaths by talking to undertakers. Editors reprinted old stories as new to fill space. News could not travel faster than sailing ships and the horses of the postal service. Winter ice delayed the arrival of ships from the Continent for weeks. At the start of the century, the minimum time to cross the ocean from England to Massachusetts was about 48 days.[27]

The greatest stimuli to reporting in the eighteenth century were the openings of the House of Commons to reporters in 1771, and of the House of Lords in 1775, although reporters were not allowed to take notes during debates for another 12 years. Newspapers hired reporters for extensive coverage of Parliament, requiring them to summarize hours

26 Anthony Smith, *The Newspaper*, 63.

27 Word of mouth was sometimes faster than the newspapers. A newspaper announcing the death of William III on March 8, 1702, did not reach Boston until May 28; weeks after rumours of his death were circulating in the American colonies. In the seventeenth century, the *Gazette de France*, with one of the world's best newsgathering systems, contained six-day-old news from London, week-old news from Brussels, and news from Constantinople that was 10 weeks old. Battles around Quebec between French soldiers and natives in October 1666 appeared in the *Gazette de France* in March 1667.

of debate, mainly from memory. Parliamentary reporting arrived at an opportune time for the expanding dailies, reinforcing a trend towards news over commentary.

By the 1780s the English newspaper had taken shape – a broadsheet with many long columns. The *Times,* with a daily circulation of 10,000, began to assign writers to "beats" such as the courts and to send their own reporters to major events in and outside London. On 20 August 1791, for a trial of rioters in Birmingham, the *Times* reported that it had sent "the gentleman, who takes the Law Reports for this paper, to write down the trials in short hand." By 1808, it employed at least six full-time reporters. In 1791, James Perry, owner of the *Morning Chronicle,* went to Paris to report on the French Revolution, producing an "amazing circulation." In 1794, John Bell, owner of the *Oracle and Public Advertiser,* travelled to Flanders to report on fighting between British and French troops. He told his readers: "I shall be my own Journalist."

The growing power of the press, however, did not translate into social respectability. The alliance between journalists and politicians, especially in the first half of the century, damaged the image of journalism for years. As late as 1810 the Benchers of Lincoln's Inn tried to forbid membership to anyone who had ever written for hire in newspapers. Sir Walter Scott wrote in his *Journal,* "nothing but a thorough-going blackguard ought to attempt the daily Press unless it is some quiet country diurnal."[28]

Variations on a Public Ethic

The partisan, the spectator, and the reporter justified their activities as beneficial to the public sphere. Their comments on the press were the first "theories" about the public newspaper. Newspapers claimed to fulfil a host of public functions, such as informing, analysing, entertaining, and educating the people. They aimed to expose official folly and social pretence, represent public opinion, protect liberty, "answer" misguided opinion, and act as a historian of the times. George Colman, in

28 The eighteenth-century paper was known for bribery and scurrility. For example, editors commonly charged "insertion and contradiction fees." A politician could print or "insert" an attack on his opponent for the price of an advertisement. The attacked person could reply in another advertisement for a "contradiction" fee.

the *Connoisseur* of 1754, observed that writers for periodical papers were among the "modern improvers of literature." The ancients, he noted, had no periodic publications, unless one supposes that "the history of Thucydides retailed weekly in six-penny papers; that Seneca dealt out his morality every Saturday."[29]

Assertions of public benefit, often exaggerated, surfaced most frequently when editors announced their new paper, when they had to defend their stories, and when they resisted government interference. According to the *Whitehall Evening Post*, people "writing papers of public intelligence" should guide themselves by the principle "not only to give intelligence, but that all [their] intelligence be calculated for the public good."[30] The *Craftsman* in the late 1720s claimed to be carrying out a vital political role as defender of "the public welfare" and "Pensioner of the People." The public, through the press, should be able to debate "the great affairs of peace and war."[31]

In the 1720s, Mist explained that his *Weekly Journal* of news and comment aimed to be both a "Paper of Intelligence," with impartial, accurate news, and a "Paper of Entertainment", with political analysis and satire on the foibles of the age. Using the model of the *Spectator*, Mist portrayed his journal as a moral educator that, like the theatre, instructs while providing pleasure.[32] It is a "History of the present Times" guided by "a love of truth." Mist declared that his journal's essays provided an education for young politicians because they supplied "comments, explanations" on the news.

Despite Mist's idealistic vision, the ethics of partisan journalism was ambiguous. The partisan press did not linger too long on the tension between the claim that it served the public in general and the fact that it also served political ideologies or masters. Political passions tainted the news of partisan journals. Essays displayed blatant bias, unfairness, and the intention to persuade by any rhetorical means. The essayist often "met" the reader through a veil of anonymity that eased the levelling of unproven allegations. For many writers, the essays were piecework or temporary employment, only one form of writing and revenue. Hence partisan journalism could be a transitory profession, reckless in spirit and prone to political influence. Journalism simply had not become a distinct professional activity, with norms of detachment and independence.

29 George Colman, *Connoisseur*, 14 Feb. 1754. Quoted in Black, *The English Press in the Eighteenth Century*, 1.

30 *Whitehall Evening Post*, 30 Dec. 1718.

31 *Craftsman*, 23 Sept. 1727; 25 Nov. 1727; 9 Dec. 1726.

32 *Weekly Journal*, 24 Jan. 1721; 28 July 1722; 29 April 1723; 29 Feb. 1724.

Yet the partisan press, for all its faults, did have a public ethic, and it did contribute to the public sphere over the long term. Mist believed that he served the public by "clarifying and solving the problems of the age."[33] A journal such as the *Craftsman,* with its mix of news and commentary, could claim to both inform and educate. Partisan journalism believed that it served the public sphere not through careful impartiality but by advancing correct political views and causes and by exposing the errors of the other party.

The partisan journalist helped to establish a tradition of critical journalism and free political comment. Amhurst, Defoe, and Mist risked prison and fines to function as journalistic watchdogs on power. The partisan press could be narrow in perspective, but it touched on issues that engaged readers across the country. It asserted its right to criticize authority on behalf of the public, thereby testing the limits of liberty. The press established itself as an extra-parliamentary forum that dragged decision-making into the harsh light of the public arena. The biased portrayals of political leaders and their policies diminished the ideal rationality of the public sphere. But public debate was here to stay, on a daily basis. The political essay "established journalism as a direct form of political power."[34] In this new age of public opinion, the "censor" became the disapproving editor. "What I approve I defend," wrote Defoe. "What I dislike I censure."

Addison's spectator journalism reflected a different public ethic. The ultimate aim was a "polite" public sphere for peaceful and rational discussion of issues. Addison opposed any excess in writing style, theatrical performance, or political action. When he staged his play *Cato,* based on the Roman conflict between republican freedom and imperialism, he tried to be politically impartial. He submitted the play to a Tory minister, Bolingbroke, for approval. To avoid any charge of partisanship, he had a Tory poet, Alexander Pope, write the prologue, and a Whig poet, Samuel Garth, write the epilogue. At its first performance in 1713, Whigs and Tories in the audience competed in applauding scenes where characters praised alternatively liberty and virtue.[35] Dislike of factionalism motivated the *Spectator,* which sought "to enliven morality with wit and to temper wit

33 Quoted in Black, *The English Press in the Eighteenth Century,* 34.

34 Anthony Smith, *The Newspaper,* 62.

35 Hampden, *The Beggar's Opera and Other Eighteenth-Century Plays,* viii, ix. This conservative attitude is noticeable in the London theatre of the early eighteenth century, with its lack of impressive new works. Addison, Defoe and Steele attacked the extravagance, immoral comedy, and bad behaviour of the plays and their audiences. Addison criticized the ornate costumes of kings and excessive use of "drums, trumpets and huzzas" in battle scenes.

with morality." Its sophisticated essays would bring "philosophy out of the closets ... to dwell in Clubs and Assemblies, at Tea-Tables and in Coffee-Houses."[36]

By "politeness," Addison did not mean good table manners. The term is close in meaning to "civility." Politeness and refinement meant impartial judgments on scientific theories and morality and "good taste" in art. Politeness led to amicable conversation and reasonable debate in public spaces. A dispassionate "Fraternity of Spectators" would enhance public civility. The *Spectator* embodied this ethic of detachment in its wry, restrained, conversational style. Writing as a spectator, a journalist such as Addison showed how a rational public sphere was possible.

Another form of spectator journalism, Johnson's literary essays, also supported public civility. Moral earnestness motivated his writings. In his last *Rambler* essay, he wrote that literature should provide moral education by setting before the public models of good conduct and moral character. The *Rambler* had tried to inculcate a "wisdom and piety" that was "conformable to the precepts of Christianity, without any accommodation to the licentiousness and levity of the present age."[37]

Meanwhile, it was obvious from the start that news reporting required a different public ethic. Reporters' contribution to the public sphere was the provision of accurate, timely information. Their skills in gathering information were different from essayists' ability to wield a "sharp pen" to unmask a government folly. Reporters described ephemeral events, resisting the impulse to interpret or persuade. We can see this in the parliamentary coverage of the day. Reporters did not intervene in events; they took down the debates in a notepad. They were spectators for hire.

An ethic of factuality came naturally, since the rapid digestion of large quantities of information recommended a concise, plain style, which contrasted with the more ornate, bombastic style of opinion writing. Britain's first daily declared this ethic publicly. Buckley's *Courant* promised "to give news, give it daily and impartially." The *Daily Courant* would not comment on news "but will relate only Matter of Fact, supposing other people to have Sense enough to make *reflections for themselves.*"[38] This is one of the earliest statements of news objectivity.

36 *Spectator,* 12 March 1711. Quoted in Black, *The English Press in the Eighteenth Century*, 33.

37 Samuel Johnson, "The Rambler," 14 March 1752.

38 *Daily Courant,* 11 March 1702. Quoted in Herd, *The March of Journalism,* 40.

By mid-century, newspapers grew increasingly fond of claiming that their factual news and impartial judgment were more important to the public than the polemics of the partisan journals. This made a virtue out of an economic necessity. Publishers had invested in papers that sought to attract a news-hungry population. In 1709, William Foster wrote that his *Miscellany* would mention "the smallest as well as the greatest Occurrences of trade, manufacture and finances." On 24 January 1721, London's *Daily Journal* began by warning readers that if they wanted "Party-Reflections" rather than news they should not bother reading its impartial pages. The *London Mercury* said that reasonable readers could not fault its "transactions ingenuously and faithfully deliver'd, contrary to the malignant manner partially made use of by contending (essay) writers." On 15 August 1745, the *Daily Post* said that it sought information "from both sides of the question" to give the best coverage. In 1733, both the *British Observator* and the *Newcastle Courant* said that many people, including members of the middle class, disliked the papers that carried a "political letter" on their front pages because they "want not to study politics" but "news rather than conjectures." They were "desiring to meet with facts instead of speculations" and to read foreign reports that have been "digest[ed] with the proper method." Even papers known for their political bias, such as the *Craftsman*, claimed to be impartial in their news. The *St. James's Post* promised a political interpretation of the facts. It would attach "remarks" to the facts to undermine the "vermin of the press" – the Whig papers.

The newspaper as an objective historian and vehicle of fact was a common theme. On 3 October 1719, Francis Clifton, in his *Weekly Medley*, promised to provide the exact and impartial judgment of a historian. His paper would not print news "trifles" such as the "hawking diversions" of princes. It would judge the significance of events using the historian's method of searching for "confirme'd and known authentic passages of the present times." Clifton would stand above the "common herd of news writers." Any partiality would violate his "duty" as "an historian." William Cuthbert and Isaac Thompson of the *London Evening Post* proclaimed on 22 January 1739 that their newspaper would be an enlightening discourse of fact. A paper should be "an historical rhapsody, or register, of civil, political and natural occurrences, and the present state of things." Theirs would provide "a description and account of the whole earth and seas" and about the "latest discoveries and observations."

In the late eighteenth century, the ethical ideal of the objective newspaper culminated in the idea that a daily paper was to be a great "register" of events, and the reporter its recording instrument. Large, daily newspapers were necessary for information and for the economy. In 1785, John Walters I started the *Daily Universal Register* of London, soon to become the *Times,* as part of his new printing business. The *Times* would be a "faithful recorder of every species of intelligence" for all readers and an aid to commercial transactions through advertisements.[39] The preference for objective reporting was a response to the demand for news and the need to please readers of varying political views. The objective style provided information in a style that conformed to the readers' larger social, aesthetic, and political values – but not just any readers.

The values that counted were those of the middle or upper class, whose literacy, status, and interest in public affairs made them attractive to newspapers and advertisers. These readers of the *Times* wanted the news, but in a certain form. It should be accurate and timely, of course, but also written with restraint and lacking obvious political bias. These readers wanted a respectable family paper that was politically moderate, was "decent," and avoided scandal-mongering. It became important to papers such as the *Times,* both economically and rhetorically, to talk about itself as a responsible "register," which formulated its editorial views independently. When Lord Derby defended Perry's *Morning Chronicle* in 1798 for breaching parliamentary privilege, he said that it was "distinguished by its regard to the decencies of life, by its disdain of all scandal on individuals ... by which the peace of families was disturbed."[40] The espousal of objective reporting helped the *Times* secure its daily contract with its most important readers. Objectivity found a home in the respectable journalism of such papers, in the same way and for the same reasons that objectivity found its American home in the *New York Times* a century later.

An analysis of the ethical assertions of partisan and spectator journalists reveals how the editorial norms reflected the changing relationship of

39 Woods and Bishop, *The Story of the Times,* 17. Walters started publishing pamphlets and books after his insurance business went bankrupt. He started the newspaper partly to demonstrate a new system of printing, called logography, which soldered together commonly occurring words and groups of letters to speed up composition.

40 Quoted in Anthony Smith, *The Newspaper,* 100. In 1823, William Hazlitt, a former *Times* employee, wrote in the *Edinburgh Review* that the *Times* had ceased to be the "handmaiden of a parliamentary faction and taken on the more mature role of independent actor in the political world."

journalist and reader. Daily or near-daily publishing in a competitive market created even more pressure on editors to resort to ethical language. Some of the motivations for ethical assertions were similar in kind to those of the previous century: the need to promote the paper and the publisher, to sustain credibility with readers, to deflect public criticism, and to combat government intervention. However, shifting circumstances changed the nature and intention of these claims. Editors issued the assertions not to please a licenser or official censor, but rather to rally public opinion behind some cause, such as the press's agitation for more freedom to comment and report. Editors' talk of impartiality and the variety of their news constituted an attempt to appeal to a larger variety of readers and to their changing social and political values.

Both the partisan and the spectator journalist justified their practices by reference to a distinctly eighteenth-century concept. Newspapers constituted a "press." The press, as a collective, was a quasi-institution that benefited the public and claimed for itself a heavy responsibility to its readers as citizens. The partisan stressed the value of free criticism and debate. The spectator emphasized the value either of "civility" or of factuality and impartial news. The press allowed the public sphere to operate as a field of opinion that restrained government. Just as parliamentarians had restrained the monarch's powers in the late seventeenth century, public opinion, through the medium of newspapers, would restrain parliamentarians in the eighteenth.

Journalists were not alone in arguing for the social indispensability of their craft. Philosophers and Enlightenment figures throughout the eighteenth century would argue for the value of a free press. Hume believed that a free press was an educator and a defence against the return of tyranny.[41] English jurists such as Blackstone defined the legal rights and duties of the press. Diderot, Rousseau, and Voltaire took up the cause of freedom of expression. "It is as much a natural right to use one's pen," wrote Voltaire, "as it is to use one's tongue." Diderot's *Encyclopédie* declared that "any country in which a man may not think and write his thoughts must necessarily fall into stupidity, superstition and barbarism."[42]

These claims had to be argued for and established rhetorically against criticism and scepticism. At times, ethical terms became so common and widely applied in journalistic discourse that they lost some of their

41 Hume, "Of the Liberty of the Press," 8–12.

42 Quoted in Anthony Smith, *The Newspaper,* 76.

rhetorical force. Every journalist in a jam and every demagogue seeking support abused the idea of liberty of the press. Journalists' strident insistence on their impartiality, despite the partiality of the press, must have left many members of the public feeling that the editors protested too much.

None the less, despite their abuse, ethical terms were key weapons in the battle for public opinion, now a serious factor. Attitudes towards the press were neither homogeneous nor settled. Readers complained alternatively that the papers contained too much "trivial" news and not enough serious analysis or had too much biased comment and not enough straight news. But for all their complaining, readers had a deep interest in, and even a fascination about, the news press. In the seventeenth century, L'Estrange had used similar complaints against the press to enforce pre-publication controls. But times had changed. Everyone from the country squire to the king complained about the "licentious" press. But the complaints did not recommend a new system of press licensing. By mid-century, serious attempts to bring back pre-publication controls had ended. For better or worse, the press was part of the public sphere. The real argument was over how far the press could go.

RADICAL JOURNALISTS: CREATING A RADICAL PUBLIC

The public ethic reached its strongest and most explicit expression in the reform and revolutionary journalists, from the 1760s onward. The creation of a public, free from despotism, was the cry of a new generation of journalists. Changes in the press and society called forth this radical journalism. By mid-century, public opinion, through the press, was crucial for governments bent on re-election and for politicians attempting to hold on to, or win back, power. Britain, France, and other societies were experiencing serious political dissent.

The dissent encouraged journalists to step forward as unabashed representatives of the public against established authority. Given this political turmoil, it was inevitable that the principle of a free press would become a major legal and social point of contention. In Britain, the roots of the dispute over a free press went back to the end of press licensing in 1695.

In the heyday of essay journalism, two writers argued for the freedom of the press. From 1720 to 1723, John Trenchard and Thomas Gordon published anonymously the famous "Cato" letters in the *London Journal.*

The 144 letters provided a theoretical basis for ideas about freedom of conscience and speech. In the name of Cato, the famous Roman republican, Trenchard and Gordon assailed "wicked ministers" who "enslave their country." The letters warned government to pay attention to the "affectations and opinion" and reasonable demands of the people, who had a "natural honesty" and whose judgment was "sound" if not misled. "Cato" argued that truth should be a defence against libel, opposing the prevailing common law that "the greater the truth, the greater the libel."[43]

On 4 February 1720, the fifteenth "Cato" letter presented its famous argument that freedom of the press was "inseparable from publick liberty." "Freedom of Speech is the great Bulwark of Liberty; they prosper and die together: And it is the great Terror of Traitors and Oppressors." This claim would re-emerge throughout the century.

Cato's arguments, republished in the American colonies by Benjamin Franklin, played a role in the acquittal of John Peter Zenger in 1735 for criticizing the governor of New York. Zenger's lawyer, Alexander Hamilton, argued that the people had a right to expose and oppose arbitrary power by speaking and writing the truth. He told the court that the case was "not just the cause of the poor printer ... It is the best cause; it is the cause of Liberty."[44]

As the press grew in scale and influence, such challenges could not be ignored. The stage was set for journalism's involvement in the politics of popular protest.

Liberty "for Whigs and Englishmen"

The British reform press of the unhappy 1760s helped establish the legal and political basis for a free, critical journalism of the public sphere. George III, the "patriot" king, had taken the throne amid great hopes. The Jacobite threat was past, and Britain was a colonial power. The middle-class was rising and growing wealthy, led by bourgeois entrepreneurs such as Josiah Wedgwood. As the industrial revolution laid down roots in the English Midlands, towns were being redesigned along Georgian lines, and the country was building a national system of turnpike roads.

Nevertheless, the decade saw brutal political battles, ministerial instability, crop failures, and riots. Politically, the reinstallation of Tories at court and in government caused rancour. Economically, the growth of

43 Hohenberg, *Free Press, Free People*, 38.

44 Quoted in Anthony Smith, *The Newspaper*, 72.

wealth among the middle and upper classes only emphasized the poverty of the lower class and its lack of political representation. The spread of culture within the middle-class did not diminish the grinding, uncertain conditions of the poor.[45] In the 1740s and 1750s, food and electoral riots had been tolerated. Some officials considered the protests a safety-value for pent-up anger. By the 1760s, the spread of discontent from London into the countryside took on a more ominous aspect. The anger culminated in the fearful anti-Catholic Gordon riots in London in 1780, which killed over 300 people within a week.

Throughout this period, journalists and government were at loggerheads over the bedrock political issues of freedom of speech and the liberty of the subject. The government poisoned relations with the press by attempting to control it through taxes, libel action, raids on publishers' premises by "messengers of the press," restrictions on parliamentary reporting, and the silencing of opposition papers. The government's creation of its own papers and its efforts to shut down others spurred the great Whig families to create their own papers. Lord Bute's *Briton* found an answer in John Wilkes's *North Briton*.[46]

In this tense climate, the polemical essay regained its vitality. Newspapers printed angry attacks on the king, Scotsmen such as Bute, the peace terms of the Seven Years' War, and the incompetence of the prime minister, the Duke of Grafton. Both the press and members of the public rebelled against judgments against the press by conservative chief justices such as Lord Mansfield. Journalists gave voice to a populist anger against arrogant authority, cider taxes, food prices, corrupt politics, and limited political representation. Artists such as William Hogarth captured the turmoil with, for example, his famous portrait of a leering John Wilkes. Government attempted to stem the tide of criticism by arresting publishers for seditious libel, but the efforts were in vain or their victories temporary. Anonymous writers were hard to prosecute, and when cases reached the court, judges and juries threw out the charges. Editors successfully sued government agents for illegal seizure of goods under the dreaded general warrants. Even where prosecutions of journalists succeeded, such action by an unpopular government made journalists martyrs.

45 For a study of popular dissent during this period, see Rogers, *Crowds*.

46 Rea, *The English Press in Politics*, 28–41. By the 1760s, politicians could not ignore public opinion. When Lord Bute started his own press in the 1760s, this provoked a full-scale war between government journals, such as Smollett's *Briton* and Arthur Murphy's *Auditor*, and Whig-financed papers, such as Wilkes's *North Briton*.

Papers, in their constant praise of the "liberty of the press," laid claim to a public role that questioned the principle of parliamentary supremacy. The principle had been the basis of the political system for much of the century. Many members of the governing classes did *not* recognize the press or public opinion as legitimate restraints on parliamentary supremacy. They did not recognize the social value of a free press. They did not recognize the press as a legitimate representative of the public. The prevailing view was that Parliament, through its three estates – nobility, clergy, and commons – was the supreme authority and the sole, legitimate political representative of the people. The public was *not* represented by some rag-tag group of lower-class journalists pretending to be a fourth estate. The governing elite did not feel obligated to answer regularly to public opinion or to an extra-parliamentary press. Henry Seymour Conway, secretary of state from 1765 to 1768, stated that parliament "constitutes the good people of England; ... the voice which denies our authority without doors, hurls a treason against the majesty of the British people."[47]

The doctrine of parliamentary supremacy gained support from a hierarchical social structure with a paternalistic attitude towards the public. The upper class was to govern, and the lower class to follow. Chief Justice Holt had argued in 1704 that press criticism of government was criminal because "it is very necessary for all governments that the people should have a good opinion of it."[48] The elites believed that they had a right to protect themselves from the critical eye of the press. A country that had robbed the king of supreme authority had placed it in the hands of a dominant segment of society.

A significant portion of the periodic press had opposed these entrenched attitudes for most of the century. But in the 1760s, the tension intensified, as observers began to question the limitations of the political framework. The result was a vigorous reform press. It is, of course, possible to overestimate the political impact of the reform papers – or the eighteenth-century paper as a whole. Jeremy Black has noted that conservative-minded ministers such as North continued to rule Britain despite the press opposition. The conservative nature of society made reform slow and intermittent.[49] But this conservative backdrop only highlights the press as a new force in the public sphere.

47 Quoted in Rea, *The English Press in Politics*, 1.

48 Ibid., 5.

49 Black, *The English Press in the Eighteenth Century*, 151–61.

The ability of journalism in the 1760s to tap into deep reservoirs of popular resentment is evident in the letters of Junius and the fame of Wilkes, self-proclaimed defender of liberty. Their sharp, devastating polemics claimed to be in the service of the nation and its suffering public. The 70 Junius letters appeared between January 1769 and January 1772 in London's popular *Public Advertiser*.[50] Junius's immediate political aim was to press the king to bring in a new Whig administration, headed by Grenville and Chatham. Junius's first letter attacked the Grafton ministry on behalf of "a nation overwhelmed with debt; her revenues wasted; her trade declining; the affections of her colonies alienated ... the whole administration of justice become odious and suspected to the whole body of the people." On 19 December 1769, Junius had the temerity to address his letter to the king on behalf of the nation. He urged the king to speak "with the spirit of a man" and remove his people's grievances. Junius told the king it was "the misfortune of your life ... that you should never have been acquainted with the language of truth, until you heard it in the complaints of your people."

This journalistic audacity struck a nerve. The letter to the king sold 4,800 copies, and Junius's broadsides against the alleged immorality of Grafton and other leading politicians were reprinted across the country. When court action against publishers of the letter to the king collapsed, Junius became a symbol of the political force of newspapers and of an expansion in society's tolerance for critical comment.

The phenomenon of Junius was a product of the new relationship between journalists and readers in the growing public sphere. The reform essayist claimed to articulate the voices of his readers. The reformist argued that the voices of this large public must be heard because they were a legitimate extension of Locke's notion of government by consent. Junius himself was acutely conscious of his relationship with readers. He declared that he refused to be humbly subservient to readers or to browbeat them with superior cynicism or learning. Instead, he assumed the role of a public watchdog who lived among the people. In the "Dedication to the English Nation" that prefaced his collected letters, he wrote: "I dedicate to You a collection of Letters, written by one of Yourselves for the common benefit of us all." He portrayed himself as a prophet of freedom with a rousing call to action. He produced all his

50 McCracken, *Junius and Philip Francis*. Scholars have debated the identity of Junius for years. Some believe that he was Philip Francis, a War Office clerk who became an MP and a councillor in India. Others think that he was colonial administrator Warren Hastings.

writings in the name of lofty freedom: "Let it be impressed upon your minds, let it be instilled into your children, that the liberty of the press is the Palladium of all the civil, political, and religious rights of the Englishman."[51]

Junius's letters fall within the tradition of partisan journalism, but they have a sharper edge. He directly urges the public, and the opposition, to action, and he questions the moral legitimacy of the political system. For George III, Junius was a dangerous man with too many readers. To persuade the public, Junius would use any rhetorical tool – caricature, personal abuse, satire, wit, innuendo. Some critics have compared his satirical portraits of Grafton and others to Aristophanes' rendering of Socrates suspended in a basket in the clouds. Coleridge observed that his letters "impel (readers) to action, not thought," through imagination and invention, more than through sober reasoning and facts. Junius had many conservative critics. Johnson remarked: "It is not hard to be sarcastic in a mask." Burke recognized the extraordinary power of Junius's printed oratory but rebuked him for his "inexcusable irreverence." Against his critics, Junius appealed directly to the public. "Is there no merit in dedicating my life to the information of my fellow-subjects?" he wrote. "What public question have I declined, what villain have I spared?"[52]

The government's repeated clashes with one man, John Wilkes, MP, editor of London's weekly *North Briton*, summed up the tenor of the times.[53] Wilkes used the intoxicating ideal of the liberty of the people to ride a wave of dissent to notoriety, public office, and journalistic immortality. On 25 April 1763, the famous issue Number 45 of the *North Briton* criticized the king's speech to Parliament for repeating the alleged falsehoods of Bute and other allegedly corrupt ministers. The article was not atypical for the times, but it was the last straw for the king and his government, who had endured Wilkes's attacks in Parliament and in print for several years. They charged Wilkes with seditious

51 Ibid., 115.

52 Ibid., 13, 116.

53 The weekly *North Briton* was born 6 June 1762. Wilkes and Charles Churchill were the editors. The paper was an answer to the *Briton*, edited by Smollett and financed by Lord Bute. Its name referred to the belief among some reformers that the Bute government employed too many "northern" Scots. The *North Briton's* 45 numbers, from June 1762 to April 1763, contained strident criticism of government.

libel, raided his premises, seized documents, and threw him into the Tower of London.[54] Such treatment made Wilkes and the "liberty of the press" a *cause célèbre.*

"My Lords," Wilkes cried at his trial, "the liberty of all peers and gentlemen, and what touches me more sensibly, that of all the middling and inferior set of people, who stand most in need of protection, is in my case this day to be finally decided upon a question of such importance as to determine at once whether English liberty shall be a reality or shadow." When the court dismissed the charge because it judged Wilkes, as an MP, to be immune from libel, a crowd of supporters left the court shouting "Wilkes and Liberty."

Although another court subsequently convicted Wilkes of libel, the case of Number 45 began a series of legal actions where the courts refused to convict publishers of libel. Instead, they imposed fines on officials for using general warrants to round up publishers and seize materials. These decisions weakened the threat of seditious libel against journalists and led to the end of general warrants, helping to establish the legal basis for a free press. The cases led to explicit recognition of a central part of the public ethic – that the press has an important political role both in informing and in commenting on public affairs.

Wilkes represents the public journalist as wily demagogue. During his long and tumultuous career, he was an outlaw from justice, a crisis-provoking MP, and a swaggering mayor of London. In his prime, Wilkes directed attention away from his own motivations by dedicating himself to "the rights of his fellow-subjects, and ... the liberties of WHIGS AND ENGLISHMEN." At the same time, he said privately to friends that "in this time of public dissension" he was "resolved to make his fortune."[55] Ideals and slogans were propaganda to advance Wilkes's self-interest and his favourite public causes.

Wilkes was able to get disgruntled citizens – artisans, shopkeepers, wage-earners, and the poor – to see his controversial actions as the actions of everyman. Infringements on his liberty were infringements on the liberty of everyone. A victory for Wilkes, in court or in Parliament,

54 See Rude, *Wilkes and Liberty.* Royalists claimed that Wilkes had called the king a liar. One of the offending passages of Number 45 read: "Every friend of this country must lament that a prince of so many great and admirable qualities, whom England truly reveres, can be brought to give the sanction of his sacred name to the most odious measures and the most unjustifiable public declarations from a throne even renowned for truth, honour and an unsullied virtue."

55 Rea, *The English Press in Politics,* 40, 29.

was a victory for the people. Wilkes sought damages of £5,000 against the secretary of state, Robert Wood, for illegal seizure of his papers. This was an astronomical claim for the times. Wilkes's lawyer justified it by arguing that the threat of seizure against his client was an implied threat against the "liberty of every subject of this country" and an "outrage to the constitution itself."[56]

When Wilkes fled to Paris in 1764 to escape additional charges, his reputation as a journalist of the people increased. His conviction and imprisonment on a second charge of libel, when he returned to England in 1768, made him a martyr. In the late 1760s, he provoked a constitutional crisis by trying to take his seat as elected member for Middlesex, on the outskirts of London, despite his expulsion from the Commons. When he finally took his seat in 1774, he was a symbol of the people's power over that of the aristocracy and other elites. In his final, declining years, he became a conservative who helped police attack rioters and who decried the French Revolution.

Although a rake, Wilkes had the courage to defy authority and advance a number of good causes – from the rejection of general warrants to his efforts to open up Parliament to reporters. He never claimed to be a radical or to condone extreme measures. But there was always a menacing defiance and the possibility of violence surrounding his actions. He was as close to a revolutionary journalist as England would produce.

Happily for the publishers, this public ethic of journalism coincided with their economic interests. Libel suits and government interference were costly and blocked the publication of material that resonated with the changing attitudes of their readers. Allegiances to political parties continued to influence the papers, but the government's ability to control the press firmly through subsidies waned as papers became more reliant on the public through circulation and ad revenue. The profits of the press occasioned sardonic comment. Johnson had said that only a blockhead would write for nothing. Walpole added a cynical corollary: "they who print for profit print only for profit."[57] Neither the reforming journalists nor their publishers sought a revolution. Henry Woodfall, the conservative-minded editor of the *Public Advertiser,* nervously printed the letters of Junius not because he agreed with the author but because they sold his papers. John Almnon, one of the most radical publishers of

56 Ibid., 68.

57 Ibid., 8.

the era, became more conservative as he grew wealthy and finally accepted a subsidy from the government.

Whatever their motivations, reform newspapers bound journalism to the public, in principle. The liberty-preaching reform journalist claimed legal protection for his role as a "stand-in" for the rest of the public. What the government could do to the journalist it could do to anyone else. But more than that, the journalists, in expanding on the value of a free press, constructed arguments about how to use that freedom to advance the public interest.

It began to appear that the press, in addition to its rights and liberties, had certain ethical duties to the public as reliable informer, watchdog of liberty, and critic of Parliament. The pursuit of press freedom and the recognition of press responsibilities arose at the same time. Press historians have emphasized the dramatic struggle for a free press in the eighteenth century. But the justification for the "liberty of the press" was never simply a libertarian argument – the natural right of expression of any individual. From Cato to Junius, writers justified the liberty of the press as a valuable instrument for political accountability, reform, and the operation of public opinion. Press liberty was the public's liberty. Journalism had taken a new and profound step towards a public philosophy for journalism.

A Tribune for the People

The revolutionary journalist took the political and polemical energies of reform journalism to a higher level of intensity and political engagement. The point of revolutionary journalism was not simply to inform readers. It was also to join forces with other segments of the population to change the system, not gradually modify it. All forms of journalism in the eighteenth century agreed that the newspaper was a force for enlightenment, information, and liberty. But revolutionary journalism went further and concluded that the task of enlightenment required direct political action against oppressors, where necessary.

The primary ethical principle of the eighteenth-century revolutionary journalist was the right and obligation to help the public create a more equitable society based on a new political constitution. All other journalistic activities derived their significance from this principle, in conjunction with the specific aims of the revolution. The press was a means to a revolutionary end. The ethic of revolutionary journalists therefore was based on journalist's unquestionable commitment to revolutionary ideals and their participation on one side of the conflict. Journalists should articulate and organize resistance to those who governed. They should move people to action. The journalist was strongly partial but justified the partiality by a vision of society, a political *summum bonum.* The journalistic norms of factuality, accuracy, restraint, and impartiality take second place to the journalist's goal of spreading revolutionary ideas.

Journalists in revolutionary America and France were participants in a dizzying cascade of protests, rebellion, and war. At the end of the fighting, they won constitutional guarantees of freedom. But when idealism flagged after the revolutions, and political divisions resurfaced, the press once again became an agent of conflict. In the sobering aftermath, press freedoms would be challenged and rescinded.

In colonial America, the newspapers were a driving force behind anti-British feeling long before the first shots of the War of Independence in 1775. By the 1760s, there were over 45 newspapers. The press had come a long way from the small, regulated colonial press of the first decades of the century. In mid-century, more and more papers in the American colonies joined in protest against British taxes on newspapers, tea, glass, and paper. The papers resented the fact that the colonies, which lacked representation in the British Parliament, had to pay taxes to finance Britain's wars and expanding debt. Serious unrest arose in 1773, when Britain allowed the East India Company to market tea directly to the colonies, with a price advantage over local merchants. The Boston Tea Party was planned in the house of Benjamin Edes, editor of the *Boston Gazette.* Britain's retaliatory Coercive Acts of 1774, called the "Intolerable Acts" by colonialists, only increased resentment.

Along the revolutionary path, pamphlet writers and newspaper editors, such as Samuel Adams, Thomas Paine, and Isaiah Thomas, used powerful rhetoric and images to stir up disenchantment. They created a revolutionary public with its own myths and ideals.[58] Adams, publisher of the *Boston Gazette and Country Journal,* covered the meetings of independence groups and attacked the character of colonial authorities. The papers repeatedly used anti-British woodcuts designed by Paul Revere that depicted skulls or coffins to represent the Boston Massacre, itself exaggerated for propaganda purposes. A popular cartoon, first

58 Like most wars, the revolution was good for newspapers. By the 1780s, the weekly *Connecticut Journal* had a circulation of 8,000, larger than any London journal. The war also helped to establish the British North American press. Editors in the American colonies who remained loyal to the British monarchy moved northward to what is now Canada.

published by James Franklin in the *Pennsylvania Gazette,* represented the colonies as a snake divided into nine parts, with the slogan "Join or Die."[59] Impartiality was difficult to maintain. The press branded British officials as "serpents" and "diabolical tools of Tyrants." Americans who imported British goods were "Enemies to their Country." The *Massachusetts Spy* asked: "Shall the island BRITAIN enslave this great continent of AMERICA?"

In this climate, facts served as fodder for journalistic broadsides. The actions of opponents became diabolical. Editors invariably interpreted the latest events as support for their grievances or as raising hope for their revolutionary cause. One series of articles, the "Journal of Occurrences," detailed alleged "outrages" by British troops in Boston, including rudeness to women. Another popular series – "Letters from a Farmer in Pennsylvania to the Inhabitants of the British Colonies" – was the creation of a Philadelphia lawyer, John Dickinson. In his diary, John Adams described how he spent a Sunday evening in 1769 with his second cousin, Samuel Adams, and John Gill, the editor of the *Patriot,* "preparing for the next day's newspaper – a curious employment, cooking up paragraphs, articles, occurrences ... working the political engine!" Even criminal acts received a political spin. The *Boston Evening-Post* of 4 November 1765 reported: "Saturday last was executed, Henry Halbert ... for the murder of the son of Jacob Woolman. He will never pay any of the taxes unjustly laid on these once happy lands." When the war was over, the American papers took credit for helping to create a free nation. Their revolutionary tactics and enviable freedom inspired editors elsewhere, especially in France. Thomas Jefferson called the newspaper "the only tocsin of a nation." In the *Providence Gazette,* "A Son of Liberty" wrote, "The Press hath never done greater service since its first invention."

The writings of American revolutionary Thomas Paine are a model of agitation journalism, justified by a public ethic. Paine, who grew up in England as a Quaker, combined partisanship with Enlightenment ideals of universal rights and reason. His incredibly popular pamphlet of 1776, *Common Sense,* was a manifesto to persuade anyone wavering between compromise with Britain and independence. The anonymous pamphlet "struck a string which required but a touch to make it vibrate." Pain declared: "the cause of America is in a great measure the cause of all mankind" because Britain had declared "War" against the "natural rights of all Mankind." Paine argued that the identity of the au-

59 Anthony Smith, *The Newspaper,* 72.

thor of *Common Sense* was irrelevant because the pamphlet was written by a man "unconnected with any Party" and influenced only by "reason and principle."[60]

Like Junius and Wilkes, Paine adopted the persona of public journalist. While in the revolutionary army, he wrote his series of *American Crisis* pamphlets, beginning in December 1776. They addressed the whole nation and were read out to troops before battle to maintain morale. After the fighting, Paine went to France to witness its revolution. For a while, he was a darling of the radicals and helped them draw up a constitution. He returned to England, where he became a leading exponent of British radicalism with *The Rights of Man* (1787) – a rejoinder to Burke's criticism of the French revolution.[61] Once again, he was the toast of radical groups, and the book sold an incredible 200,000 copies. Burke's *Reflexions on the Revolution in France* sold 19,000. The worried British government convicted Paine, in abstentia, of seditious libel. In 1794 Paine published *The Age of Reason*. He argued that Christianity would give way to science and a rational, deistic religion that was free of superstition. The *Age of Reason* made him notorious. He was attacked for undermining religion. When he returned to the United States, newspapers called him a "loathsome reptile" and a "lying, drunken, brutal, infidel." [62]

Chartists and the early trade unionists of the nineteenth century cited Paine's writings. But Paine was not a proto-socialist. His political ideology was classic, bourgeois liberalism, derived from Locke and others. He was an egalitarian democrat who opposed the "fiction" of aristocratic superiority. He had a liberal's faith in human rationality and people's ability to govern themselves. He believed that his ideal of an egalitarian society would help the poor. However, he did not envisage the elimination of all social differences. Society would "enthrone liberty" and the rights of man, ensure no unfair privileges or monopolies, and then allow individuals to compete according to their talents. Government would umpire the clash of "distinct, unconnected individuals" in a nation. Paine believed that the bourgeoisie, with its stress on individualism, private property, and enterprise, had the best chance to destroy aristocratic power.[63]

60 Foot and Kramnick, *The Thomas Paine Reader*, 9, 65–6. *Common Sense* sold an estimated 100,000 copies in 1776. It was a great success in Paris. But not all reformers were impressed. John Adams feared its radical spirit.

61 Doyle, *The Oxford History of the French Revolution*, 166–73.

62 Foot and Kramnick, *The Thomas Paine Reader*, 16, 17.

63 *Ibid.*, 22, 23.

Due to censorship, the French press did not play as great a role in formenting revolution in France as in the American colonies. Prior to the revolution, France's public sphere had, like England's, many "sites," from salons and coffee-houses to *nouvellistes à la bouche*, who dispensed news verbally at street corners. The mainstream consisted of a licensed (and censored) domestic press and a bolder, periodical press written abroad by exiled Huguenots, and others, and imported into France.[64] After 1750, it had become easier to publish domestic journals so long as they avoided political and religious issues. By the 1780s, the legal domestic press included several national papers and about 40 provincial "affiches" – weekly newssheets with business and official news. At the hub of the system sat three periodicals – the bi-weekly *Gazette de France*, with its monopoly on political and foreign news, the monthly *Journal des Savants*, for scientific information, and the literary and social weekly, *Mercure de France*. All three received information, editorial supervision, and funding from government ministries. The *Gazette* had over 12,000 subscribers in 1780, and the *Mercure* reached 20,000 in the mid-1780s. The *Gazette's* monopoly on politics ended in 1777 with the first daily, the *Journal de Paris*.

France's licensed press was a sophisticated information-gathering system. French officials abroad had to send news to the *Gazette*. France was a leader of the Enlightenment, and so it had a market for journals of science and of the arts, plus the bulletins of the salons. However, there were serious restrictions on political comment. An editor of the *Mercure* said that his publication "must always be neutral and never enter into cabals ... impartiality is the first of our Duties."[65] The press reached mainly a select, educated audience of clergymen, nobles, and bourgeois. In 1789, about half of the male adult population of France could read. Yet journal subscriptions were beyond the means of most people. Few pre-revolutionary journals attempted to write for readers who were literate but formally uneducated.[66]

For the "inside" news about French politics, people turned to imported periodicals, such as the *Gazette de Leyde*. French officials covertly

64 Anthony Smith, *The Newspaper*, 48. The censor system in France was at its height in the seventeenth century under Louis XIII and Louis XIV. In 1760, censors existed in 120 towns in the provinces aided by informers, police, and local authorities. Descartes and Voltaire felt the influence of the censor. Diderot spent a hundred days in a dungeon at Vincennes. One printer at Mont-St-Michel was placed in an iron cage until he died.

65 Quoted in ibid., 51

66 Jeremy Popkin, *Revolutionary News*, 24. See also Censer, *The French Press in the Age of Enlightenment*.

tolerated the periodicals so long as they toned down their hostility to the regime. The government had the means to put pressure on editors, if its officials wished to use their power. The government could, for example, interrupt the paper's deliveries to Paris or harass its Paris correspondents. It thereby maintained some control while allowing the press to satisfy the demand of elites for news and information. Between the domestic and international journals were the unlicensed papers – the scandalous broadsheets, newsbooks, and handwritten newsletters. Darnton called these secret presses a "literary proletariat" that insulted the king and even *philosophes*, infuriating Voltaire.[67]

A revolutionary press began in the late 1780s, as activists across France prepared for a number of dramatic meetings intended to deal with the deteriorating financial and political situation. In July 1788, the government took the gamble of calling the first meeting of the Estates-General in 175 years, open to deputies from the clergy, nobility, and commoners. The regime hoped that this broad assembly would undercut the refusal by the *parlements*, the sovereign law courts, to approve taxes to relieve the nation's fiscal crisis. The government lifted censorship restrictions and encouraged writers to discuss how the Estates-General should do its work.[68]

A national debate ensued. The press printed the declarations issued by the estates as they chose their deputies, and then it covered the Estates-General. Leading deputies, such as Jacques-Pierre Brissot and Honoré-Gabriel Riqueti, comte de Mirabeau, published their own papers and called for a free press. Probably more than 10 million copies of pamphlets circulated in France in the year before the Estates-General met in May 1789.[69]

But it was the unexpected fall of the Bastille in July and establishment of a provisional government that created, almost overnight, a radical revolutionary press.[70] As the regime's authority melted across the country, publishers scrambled to cover events. The *Revolutions de Paris*,

67 Darnton, *The Literary Underground of the Old Regime.*

68 Jeremy Popkin, *Revolutionary News,* 25.

69 Ibid., 28, 26. At least 767 pamphlets appeared between May and September 1788 and another 2,639 during the election of Estates-General deputies in the first four months of 1789.

70 Other forms of communication spread the revolutionary message. There was oral communication through intense debates in assemblies and clubs. There were public festivals and the production of images. Jacques-Louis David painted the assassinated Marat as a heroic martyr. The slogan "Long Live the Third Estate" was printed on French dishes and playing cards. Briggs and Burke, *A Social History of the Media,* 99.

a major revolutionary journal, gave hurried summaries of the Bastille crisis. Jean-Paul Marat put out his *Ami du peuple* in September 1789. In the provinces, the *affiches* added political news and published more frequently. In the years of press freedom – 1789–92 – up to 1,000 papers existed, spanning the political spectrum.[71] Royalist papers, which sometimes ignored or downplayed events, competed with red-hot revolutionary journals, which exaggerated them. "In fighting against the enemies of the state, I attack the cheats without fear, I unmask the hypocrites, I denounce the traitors," railed Marat.[72] The *Gazette de France* and the *Journal de Paris* continued as official publications, reporting on the discussions of the assemblies. The *Mercure de France* opposed all excess. Panckoucke's conservative *Gazette nationale, ou Moniteur universal,* provided a journal of record.

The freedom of the French press lasted about three years.[73] Article XI of the Declaration of the Rights of Man and the Citizen (1789) stated: "Free communication of thought and opinion is one of the most precious rights of man. Every citizen can therefore speak, write or print freely except in such cases as are provided for under the law." The law would soon intervene. Until 1792, a balance of opposing forces within the revolutionary groups secured free expression. Revolutionary factions wanted a press that provided propaganda for *their* ideals. Also, revolutionary leaders, facing war with other European powers, worried that the press might support reactionary forces. With France at war within and without, press freedom evaporated. In August 1792, the Paris Commune agreed to a formula that defined sedition and libel, reintroduced a system of press control, and arrested the editors of royalist journals such as the *Ami du roi.* Many journalists and writers, including Condorcet, would be executed during the Terror. Press controls returned with increasing strength throughout the 1790s, reaching their zenith under Napoleon.

In retrospect, we can see that revolutionary journalism transformed public perceptions of the press. The revolutionary press changed the

71 Jeremy Popkin, *Revolutionary News,* 33. At least 250 French newspapers were established in the last six months of 1789, aimed at different audiences. Some 335 appeared in Paris in 1790 alone.

72 Anthony Smith, *The Newspaper,* 197.

73 With the fall of Robespierre, a brief half-liberty returned to French press. But on 6 September 1797, after a failed royalist coup d'état, the government placed the press under police control. It proscribed some 44 Paris papers and deported their publishers, editors, and writers, some to the Americas.

journalist's image, while redefining journalism's relationship with its readers. The American and French revolutions helped to establish journalism as a distinct, full-time activity, widely admired or feared. In France, between 300 and 400 journalists were active in revolutionary Paris at any given time. These people worked and wrote in a manner different from the pre-revolutionary "men of letters," who prepared learned essays. They differed from the previously circumspect editors of licensed papers and the hack writers who produced material on erratic schedules.

Revolutionary publishing demanded a professional-like commitment to the regular publication of incisive commentary and the latest news from the national and regional assemblies, on deadline. Writers learned how to summarize the long assembly debates. Editorialists learned how to produce a rhetorical argument every day, often in a hurry. In the past, France had produced many celebrated writers, such as Voltaire and Rousseau, but none became so notorious so quickly as the revolutionary journalists, such as Brissot, Camille Desmoulins, Marat, and Thomas-Marie Royou. Some attained cult status. In 1793, eulogists compared the assassinated Marat to Jesus.[74]

The French revolutionary press was not a frantic, unstructured journalism. Revolutionary journalism worked according to a division between news and commentary. There was a divide between papers of news and journals of revolutionary comment. The term *journalist* applied to two types of writers: the well-known, talented, and well-paid editorialists; and the largely anonymous "news workers," who gathered news patiently from political meetings, and the editors who compiled news summaries. The median age of revolutionary journalists was 35, and most were educated bourgeois. They used their talent to advance themselves in dangerous times, practising a quasi-professional craft. They did not belong to any professional associations, and the press was not yet an institution in the full sense. Like the English essayists, many French revolutionary writers went into journalism attracted by ideology, a regular paycheque, notoriety, or a chance to report on dramatic events. The most famous could command a handsome contract from their publishers and made up to 25,000 *livres* a year, with added compensation if forced to take flight. They could make more money than as famous a writer as Rousseau, who sold the rights of his wildly successful novel *Emile* for only 6,000 livres in the 1760s.

The inflamed political debate of revolutionary times made American and French journalists self-conscious about their public role. Journalists,

74 In 1793, Charlotte Corday assassinated Marat.

from Adams and Paine in America to Mirabeau and Marat in France, gave the seventeenth-century idea of "unmasking" falsehoods a new and radical purpose. The Enlightenment's belief in the right of reason to evaluate all beliefs and improve society received a super-charged revolutionary spin that contained as much emotion as logic. The revolutionary took the doctrine of the "liberty of the press" and made it part of a utopian, perfectionist, revolutionary politics. The liberty of the press became a right to agitate, resist, and rebel with force of arms.

Revolutionary journalism also changed how editors saw their readers. Caught up in the passions of revolution, the editors did not regard their audience as a passive consumer of information. They imagined it as politically motivated and idealistic. The goal of a radical press was to radicalize the public. Revolutionary journalists addressed readers as citizens who presumably shared their political vision. The idea of the people as an irrational mob gave way before the Enlightenment notion of rational agents whose opinions constituted the "general will," the only legitimate political authority.

Revolutionary journalists expressed, emphatically and emotionally, the idea of service to a public. Their rhetoric argued that the authority of church and king had shifted to a public or "re-public" of citizens. Journalists were the tribunes of the public and among the trustees of revolutionary ideals. C.F. Volney, in a pamphlet series published in Brittany in 1788, was one of the first to designate himself as the people's watchman, or *sentinelle du peuple*. Paine claimed to speak for the rights of all men. Marat said that he wanted nothing more than "the glory of sacrificing myself for the country."

Revolutionary journalists saw the newspaper as the means by which to create a democratic public sphere in which citizens could "meet" regularly. The general will could operate only through representative institutions and regular mechanisms of publicity. In 1789, the galleries of revolutionary assemblies were open to spectators. Mirabeau, who had translated Milton's *Areopagitica* into French, had said, before the revolution, that newspapers "establish communications that cannot fail to produce a harmony of sentiments, of opinions and of actions that constitutes the real political force, the safeguard of the constitution."

Only the daily newspaper was capable of following the actions of law-making assembles so that, as one revolutionary editor claimed, the 600,000 Parisians and the other 28 million people in France would "virtually be present ... as if they were attending in person." Brissot said: "through the press, they [people] can discuss it [ideas] without tumult, decide calmly and give their opinion." Pierre-Louis Roederer, revolutionary politician and journalist, observed in a 1796 essay that newspapers reached more readers than did books and taught the same truth "every day, at the same time ... in all public places."[75] Pierre Retat, a historian of the press, has argued that the periodicy and circulation of the newspaper during the revolution made it a "continual functioning tribune ... to talk to the crowds, and this capacity resurrects an antique agora."[76]

But the revolutionary's praise of the newspaper had limits. A free press was wonderful so long as it preached the revolutionary's version of truth. Brissot was willing to give the Estates-General the right to punish journalists who offended it.

The revolutionary journalist's intervention in the public sphere could be "hot" or "cold." Radicals such as Marat and Tournon made the paper a hot "organ of incitement," attempting to short-circuit established authority by appealing directly to the people. Moderates such as Brissot emphasized the newspaper's more restrained role as educator and mediator between the public and its representatives.[77]

The French revolutionary's faith in journalism carried forward to modern times. Historian James Billington has noted that, for many of the leading revolutionaries of the nineteenth and twentieth centuries, "journalism was the most important single professional activity" through which they expressed their faith.[78] The first thing that Lenin did when he set out in 1901 to promote revolution in Russia was to start a newspaper. The periodicy of a paper and its need for a "regular supply of copy" made it more than a "collective propagandist and a collective agitator," Lenin argued. It was also a "collective organizer."[79]

Revolutionary journalists did not attempt to keep an objective distance from events. They interacted directly with their audiences, in person and

75 Quoted in Jeremy Popkin, *Revolutionary News*, 3, 28.

76 Retat, "The Revolutionary Word in the Newspaper in 1789," 93.

77 Ibid., 93.

78 Billington, *Fire in the Minds of Men*, 306, 308.

79 Lenin, "Where to Begin?" 15. In a series of articles after the Russian Revolution, Lenin stressed that the workers' press should write concise, factual articles in "telegraphic" form on the progress of the revolution – a style found in the bourgeois newspapers. Facts and the verification of claims by journalists would replace long-winded "political twaddle." Lenin compared the newspaper to the scaffolding that workers erect around a building under construction. Analogously, a newspaper would help revolutionary workers communicate with each other and view the results of their efforts. Systematic agitation required the aid of the periodical press.

in print. Camille Desmoulins and other editors climbed on to their chairs to preach to the crowds in the Palais-Royale. Their newspapers were read aloud at the meetings of political clubs. The journalists' rhetorical interventions took the form of patriotic addresses to the public, addressing it as an actor in a grand drama. The journalist's instrument was language – the "uprising of the word" – freed from previous constraints. The revolutionary printed word was the "piercing cry that stuns the tyrants."[80]

In the revolutionary public sphere, journalists developed their "ethos" by identifying themselves with the people. Newspapers became almost "sacred objects" that safeguarded the people. The press sought to claim the widest possible legitimacy before the widest possible public. The French newspapers of 1789 claimed that "all of Europe has its eyes" on Paris. The revolutionary journalist had the unique role of being both a chronicler of events and a passionate voice for what the revolution is and what it could become.

EPILOGUE: THE FOURTH ESTATE

Towards the end of the eighteenth century, Edmund Burke, theorist of the British constitution, rose in Parliament to talk about a new player in democracy – a fourth estate. Thomas Carlyle reported Burke's comments:

> Burke said there were Three Estates in Parliament; but in the Reporter' Gallery yonder, there sat a Fourth Estate more important than they all. It is not a figure of speech, or a witty saying; it is a literal fact – very momentous to us in these times. Literature is our Parliament too. Printing, which comes necessarily out of Writing, I say often, is equivalent to Democracy; invent Writing, Democracy is inevitable ... Whoever can speak, speaking now to the whole nation, becomes a power, a branch of government, with inalienable weight in lawmaking, in all acts of authority. It matters not what rank he has, what revenues or garnitures: the requisite thing is that he have a tongue which others will listen to; this and nothing more is requisite. The nation is governed by all that has tongue in the nation. Democracy is virtually there.[81]

The idea of a fourth estate was the last conceptual step in the eighteenth century's development of an explicit public ethic. To the three

80 Retat, "The Revolutionary Word in the Newspaper in 1789," 92.

81 Carlyle, *On Heroes,* 141. The passage quoted does not give the date of Burke's comment. However, it had to be after 1771, when the Commons allowed reporters to report from within Parliament.

estates of Britain's Parliament a fourth was added de facto – the press, as the voice of public opinion. The press and public opinion had arrived as social and political forces, less than a hundred years after the end of press licensing. It was one thing to claim that the press served the public. It was quite another to claim that it was one of the estates that governed the realm.

The public ethic at the end of the eighteenth century was no longer a new, audacious idea. It was no longer the scattered assertions of editors under political pressure. It was an explicit theory about the press, which combined the powerful ideal of liberty and the legitimate power of the public. The public ethic was advanced in opposition to a stubborn but fading authoritarian (and paternalistic) attitude towards the press and the public. By late century, leading journalists had espoused the public ethic in part or in whole; senior jurists had ruled on it; the best Enlightenment minds had considered it. An explicit ethic for newspapers was a natural development for a press that had grown from an unimpressive collection of newsbooks and gazettes to "the press," with enormous power over public opinion. Journalists were becoming "unacknowledged legislators" through their effect on government. Newspapers could spark riots, stir up revolutionary ferment, or inform objectively. Such a powerful instrument needed an explicit ethic to explain its social role and justify its freedoms.

The nineteenth-century press inherited the public ethic from the previous century as a cluster of ideas about the ideal role of the press in a liberal society:

- *Political role:* The press has a fundamental political (or constitutional) role in the public sphere. It allows dispersed citizens to come together as a public, form public opinion, and make better-informed electoral decisions. It represents public opinion to government, and government to the public. The press is a fourth estate, part of the people's self-governing process.
- *Service to the public interest:* The press should serve the general interests of the public, not the interests of the state, the elected government, or particular groups.
- *Importance of publicity:* Events in the public sphere should be as public as possible and disseminated through the publicity of newspapers.
- *Stimulant of non-political communication:* Newspapers also serve the non-political activities of the public sphere. They stimulate the economy by linking buyers and sellers through advertisements. They inform readers

about financial news, entertainment, the arts, the sciences, and culture. The press educates the populace by spreading ideas, facts, and didactic texts.

- *Liberty of the press:* The press can serve the public only if it is free from government censorship, intimidation, and excessive controls.

As the public sphere developed through evolution or revolution, the relationship between journalists and readers also changed. Journalists became full-time, professional providers of information. Readers became consumers of news and members of a public. This change in the journalist-reader relationship was broad enough to allow different interpretations of the public ethic – the public ethic according to the partisan, spectator, or revolutionary.

The construction of the ethic was neither easy nor uncontroversial. Even in the late eighteenth century, the ethic was contested. Each component of the ethic was challenged by conservative elements of a hierarchical society – politicians, judges, clergymen, journalists, and members of the public. At times, the political corruption of the press made a mockery of newspapers' claims to be impartial public servants. Yet change was in the air, and many traditionalists failed to appreciate that the political ground under their feet was shifting. Some were simply confused by the turmoil and new brazen attitudes. "What time do we live in when a parcel of low shopkeepers pretend to direct the whole Legislature?" asked George III.[82]

A succession of conservative-minded British prime ministers in the second half of the eighteenth century despised the press and saw it as a "luxury" to tax more and more. Smollett said that the idea of the liberty of the press, like that of "Protestant religion," often served the "purposes of sedition."[83] He wrote in his *Briton* about "forlorn grubs and gazetteers, desperate gamblers ... These are the people who proclaim themselves free born *Englishmen,* and ... insist upon having a spoke in the wheel of government."[84] Other observers correctly grasped the implications of a polity responsive to a press and public opinion – the diminishment of Parliament as the sole agent of the public. "It [Parliament] may still do a little good or prevent a little harm itself, but it is the public opinion which decides, which the House of Commons must obey," wrote

82 Quoted in Rea, *The English Press in Politics,* 3.

83 Ibid., 6.

84 Tobias Smollett in *Briton,* no. 15, Sept. 1762. Quoted in Rea, *The English Press in Politics,* 3.

the Earl of Shelburne.[85] Even by the early nineteenth century, large segments of the British populace would have no truck with the positive image of the press found in the public ethic. The Tory *Anti-Jacobin Review* in 1801 declared: "We have long considered the establishment of newspapers in this country as a misfortune to be regretted."

The embryonic journalism ethics of the early seventeenth century had culminated in a public ethic. The public ethic had begun with the rather simple notion that a periodic press wrote for readers and therefore owed the public reliable and factual news. The public ethic, by about 1800, had become a more complex theory based on the idea of a free press, as enshrined in the American and French constitutions. The conceptual elaboration of this ethic would not end in the 1790s. The public ethic was the platform of ideas from which the liberal theory of press would spread in the nineteenth century and from which the idea of objectivity arose as one variant of this evolution.

85 Quoted in Rea, *The English Press in Politics*, 3.

5

Anticipating Objectivity: The Nineteenth Century

The world has grown tired of preachers and sermons, today it asks for facts.

Clarence Darrow

To be a fact is to be a failure.

Oscar Wilde

The nineteenth-century newspaper set the stage for the arrival of objectivity early in the twentieth. The doctrine of objectivity emerged from two notions of newspaper function: educator of public opinion and informer of the masses. These ideas in turn emerged from two forms of liberal paper in the nineteenth century – the elitist, middle-class, liberal newspaper of England and the egalitarian, popular press first developed in the United States in the 1830s. From the English paper, objectivity took the idea of the informed public educator and opinion creator. The English paper anticipated objectivity insofar as it aspired to be an independent educator of the public, resisting the distortions of partiality. From the U.S.-style popular press, objectivity in England took the idea of the newspaper as the impartial provider of news for the masses. News was the product of an independent paper for all the people, not just for one class or political party.

The two traditions do not fit together smoothly. In the long run, this dual heritage caused a quarrel within journalism about the newspaper's primary function. Liberals argued that its "glory" was its robust opinion. They decried the emphasis on news and entertainment as a betrayal of journalism in favour of profit. Leaders of the popular press, in contrast, saw the modern paper's glory as its ability to disseminate factual news quickly. Both forms of liberal newspaper saw servile party partisanship as a relic of the past.

The liberal newspaper (examined in the first section of this chapter) represented yet another revolution in journalism. The revolution was the result of far-reaching developments in journalism and in society. The upshot of these many changes was the creation of the commercial popular press in England, the United States, Canada, and other countries (subject of the second section). It embraced the "business of news" – the systematic pursuit of news by large newsrooms with many types of journalists, aided by the latest inventions and technology. The commercial popular press in England, the United States, Canada, and other countries embraced this business of news and quickly left the smaller liberal newspaper of opinion far behind.

As my rhetorical theory of journalism predicts, the revolution in news in turn transformed the ethics of journalism (third section). The popular press developed norms (fourth section) that are part of today's notion of "objectivity" – factuality, non-partisanship, and independence – and launched a movement towards professionalism with associations, codes of ethics, and training programs. Objectivity was just around the corner. This chapter explains the development of these two forces – the liberal paper and the popular press. It shows how they revolutionized ethics and anticipated the twentieth-century rise of the objective newspaper and the doctrine of objectivity.

THE OMNIPOTENT LIBERAL NEWSPAPER

The nineteenth-century press of Britain, the United States, France, Canada, and other British colonies had a strong liberal orientation, born of conflict. Between 1815 and 1880, newspapers fought and won a struggle for freedom from harsh laws and crippling taxes. Their struggles were part of the liberal movements that sparked revolutions across Europe in 1848. The uprisings showed that the European newspaper had survived a clampdown on free speech and political agitation after the French Revolution. In England, as the taxes on newspapers slowly eased, the press began to operate like any other business, until the newspaper became ubiquitous. London commuters in the 1880s fought over newspapers at railway stations and at the end of the working day left tube (subway) cars strewn with papers. "Newspapers have become almost as necessary to our daily life as bread itself," effused Mason Jackson.[1]

The majority of newspapers supported a liberalism of enlarged individual liberties, greater freedom of the press, greater accountability of Parliament to the people, free trade, and fewer social restrictions. In London, the *Times* and the *Morning Chronicle* were model liberal papers at

1 Jackson, *The Pictorial Press*, 3.

mid-century, followed soon by the *Daily Telegraph*. The liberal provincial press featured such papers as the *Birmingham Daily Post, Bristol Daily Post, Leeds Mercury, Manchester Guardian,* and *Sheffield Independent.* [2]

The newspaper was not just ubiquitous. It was apparently omnipotent. Observers praised it lavishly as an instrument of progress and educator of public opinion. Only the railway rivalled it for superlatives. Both represented the spirit of enterprise. Both were "vehicles" reshaping the economy, the city, and public communications. The power of newspapers over public opinion seemed obvious. "The true Church of England at this moment lies in the Editors of its newspapers," Thomas Carlyle wrote in 1829. Editor Charles Peabody, in *English Journalism and the Men Who Have Made It,* said that the press "raised the tone of our public life; made bribery and corruption ... impossible."[3] British press historian Alexander Andrews spoke of the "Giant [newspaper] which now awes potentates ... this mighty Mind-Engine ... this tremendous moral power."[4] Charles Dickens and Joseph Paxton, builder of the Crystal Palace, brought out their *Daily News,* saying that its purpose was to push for "principles of progress and improvement ... the bodily comfort, mental elevation and general contentment of the British people."[5]

The lower class also saw the paper as an agent of social change. The motto of Hetherington's *Poor Man's Guardian* was "Knowledge is Power." Samuel Smiles said that the "mighty educator, the Press," would "teach working men that they must be their own elevators, educators, emancipators." Some even argued that a cheap press, unrestricted by taxes, would reduce drunkenness and labour unrest, because "readers are not rioters."[6]

The English newspaper from the 1840s to the 1860s represented the economic and political aspirations of an ascendant middle class. Britain was in the midst of an industrial revolution. It had avoided political revolution through repression, war, a relatively stable social structure, and horror at the chaos of the French Revolution. Agitation for reform, led by an unstamped radical (or "pauper") press, had flared up after Napoleon's defeat at Waterloo and had culminated in the Chartist rallies of the late 1810s and the 1820s.

2 Alan J. Lee, *The Origins of the Popular Press in England,* 282.
3 Quoted in Anthony Smith, *The Newspaper,* 143.
4 Alexander Andrews, *The History of British Journalism,* 2:347.
5 Quoted in Anthony Smith, *The Newspaper,* 122.
6 Smiles, "What Are the People Doing to Educate Themselves?" 230.

However, by the 1840s, economic growth was reducing the threat of serious upheaval and establishing the basis for a peaceful liberal revolution. Britain was a newly urbanized and industrialized nation with an economy dependent on international trade. A surging middle class of traders, factory owners, bankers, and manufacturers was confident in the ability of rational, scientific human beings to subdue nature. In 1829, the *Edinburgh Review* wrote: "We remove mountains, and make seas our smooth highway; nothing can resist us. We war with rude nature; and by our resistless engines, come off always victorious, and loaded with our spoils."[7] The gleaming Crystal Palace of London's Great Exhibition of 1851 symbolized Britain's commitment to liberalism.

Liberalism required freedom: free trade, minimal government, fewer restrictions on land use, fewer restrictions on educational and career opportunities (especially for religious non-conformists), and a free press to win over the public and to pressure government. The liberal class demanded political reforms that reduced the power of the aristocracy over Parliament. The mantras of "free trade" and "laissez-faire" were shorthand for an entire liberal philosophy.[8] By 1874, under William Ewart Gladstone, Britain had translated much of this philosophy into law.[9]

Liberalism valued the rational, informed individual who was free to make his or her own way in the two marketplaces of life – that of ideas and that of the economy. Individualism had intrinsic and instrumental value. A life of liberty was valuable in itself, while the competition of free individuals was a means to the best society possible. Associated

7 Matthew, "The Liberal Age (1851–1914)," 420, 463–522.

8 J.S. Mill expressed the spirit of mid-Victorian liberalism in 1848: "Laissez-faire, in short, should be the general practice: every departure from it, unless required by some great good, is a certain evil." *Principles of Political Economy*, 2:950. Mill was not a libertarian, however. He states that he does not believe that the function of government should be limited to protecting individuals from violence or fraud. He discusses at length the need for government intervention in such areas as education, public charity, the care of the mentally disabled, and the regulation of water and gas utilities. Later in life, he softened further his enthusiasm for laissez-faire liberalism by adopting a "qualified socialism" that supported representative democracy over "pure" democracy. See his *Autobiography*, 102, 115, 136-8.

9 Matthew, "The Liberal Age (1851–1914)," 466. By 1874, religion tests for entry to Oxford and Cambridge were abolished, the franchise was extended, entrance to the civil service was based on competition, and education reform was underway.

with freedom and individuality were the values of self-help and self-discipline. Since liberals opposed government interference, progress was to arrive through education, good "character," the "elevation" of public opinion, and useful knowledge. Liberalism was attractive to both the radicals, such as Jeremy Bentham, and to the conservative army of clerks, factory managers, teachers, and bureaucrats who sought careers and social respectability. On the bright side, liberalism challenged the pre-industrial, aristocratic ethic of public life, based on partisanship, tradition, and privilege. The middle class argued that the civil service, universities, and the economy should operate on the basis of merit, knowledge, and professionalism. On the dark side, it used the idea that unrestricted competition was "natural" to justify Social Darwinism and imperialism.

The tenets of liberalism were attractive to publishers and editors. A free marketplace of ideas made a newspaper of opinion possible. Political liberalism removed government restrictions on the newspaper's operations. Better public education promised a new generation of newspaper readers. Free trade stimulated economic activity, increasing circulations and advertising. Many editors were middle-class liberals who served as mayors and members of Parliament. They were "the standard-bearers of their class in the struggle for domination, and they were conscious of the fact."[10]

Liberalism also implied a theory of the press that explained the function of newspapers in a liberal society – a privately owned, self-regulated free press protected individual rights, informed citizens, acted as a watchdog, expressed public opinion to government, and helped to oil the economy. The theory drew inspiration from John Milton, John Locke, and Thomas Paine. The liberal theory received its definitive nineteenth-century form from J.S. Mill and journalists such as Walter Bagehot, John Delane, and C.P. Scott. As the British Empire expanded, the idea of a free, liberal press accompanied political liberalism as it spread around the world. The idea of a liberal press has endured. On 21 November 1970, the London *Times* announced: "We believe in reason, in the power of rational processes to determine truth and to present real choices in human affairs. We do not have any illusion that reason always prevails. The *Times* is ... a Liberal newspaper."

Talk about a liberal theory of the press can be misleading. The phrase "*the* liberal theory of the press" implies incorrectly that there was only one form of liberal paper. Moreover, expositions of the theory

10 Alan J. Lee, *The Origins of the Popular Press in England*, 52.

fail to explain how nineteenth-century press liberalism went beyond the eighteenth-century "public ethic." How did liberalism differ from a general Enlightenment belief in reason? Political liberalism agreed with the Enlightenment in its preference for "natural rights" and reason over authority and hierarchy. But liberalism was more than that. It was a specific interpretation of what Enlightenment meant in the mid-nineteenth century. Liberalism was more than a philosophical doctrine about the value of reason and liberty. It was a practical, political movement that sought to bring into existence a rational, liberal society. It made demands for a range of reforms that an entrepreneurial middle-class championed in the newspapers and in Parliament. The liberal press advocated such changes.

The liberal theory of the press gave a liberal interpretation to the premises of the public ethic: an unlicensed press, service to a public, and a fourth estate. It magnified the importance of an uncensored press. The press must be not only uncensored but also *maximally* free of pre- or post-publication restrictions. Laissez-faire was the government's proper attitude in dealing with the economy and the press. Service to the public meant service to the construction of a liberal society. The liberal press pushed the idea of a fourth estate to the limit. The *Times* described itself as a "perpetual committee of the legislature," since, unlike Parliament, it "sat" every day. Henry Reeve wrote that the press was a better vehicle for public opinion than the pamphlet, the public meeting, or Parliament.[11] *Times* editor John Delane summed up press responsibilities in the strongest terms possible: "The duty of the Press is to speak; of the statesman to be silent."

The liberal paper was not a monolithic entity. It had at least two forms: the elitist, middle-class liberal newspaper of England in mid-century, and the liberal-democratic, popular paper in the United States from the 1830s onward. The liberal paper interpreted the liberal theory differently from the popular, liberal-democratic press that would supplant it. Both agreed that the press must inform the public. But they differed on the meaning of "informing".

For the English paper, it meant educating the public in the correct, liberal attitudes, mainly through political argument, opinion, and analysis. Informing involved not just the dissemination of neutral information but the "improving" and "elevating" of the beliefs and tastes of the general populace. The paper's primary purpose was not the provision of

11 Reeve, "The Newspaper Press," 470-98.

isolated bits of news, advertisements, news from the racetrack, or stories of crime. The heart of the English liberal paper was its political criticism and weighty opinion. A paper that was neutral or uninterested in politics did not advance the liberal cause.

For the egalitarian popular paper, informing was providing "news for all" in an accessible format. It meant offering the sorts of information that readers wanted, even if it was not necessarily "improving." The popular paper claimed to be enlightening the populace, but not by bringing the masses up to the level of their "betters." It sought instead to be the voice of the masses, reflecting their interests, opinions, and concerns. The dramatic format and accessible writing of the cheap popular press expressed the spirit of egalitarian liberalism. The format was neither "intellectual" nor elitist. The duller format of *The Times* in mid-century reflected the spirit of an elitist liberal press that saw itself as a serious educator and political commentator. The *Times* featured political analysis and editorials. It carried long articles on political speeches, introduced by small headings crammed between narrow columns.

Some papers found a niche between the two forms. At the penny *Manchester Guardian*, C.P. Scott was a transitional liberal editor. While he praised "facts," he thought of his paper as a "quality" sheet distinguished by its opinion. It was not until 1952 that the paper put news on its front page.[12] In addition, the elitist ideal of a morally uplifting press also existed in the United States. John Marmaduke told the Missouri Press Association in 1873 that the press was "too ready" to accommodate "a perverted public taste." The press's mission was "to elevate, not debase; to enlighten, not darken ... to promote the welfare of our race and bear us on to a higher destiny."[13]

The elitist liberal theory made two large and precarious assumptions. One was that the press, once freed from government taxes and censure, would propagate elevating opinion and serious political information. The other was the Miltonian idea that the formulation of public opinion through the press would lead to the triumph of the most rational, progressive ideas. Liberal editors assumed that the best ideas were liberal ideas and that Liberals would guide the formulation of public opinion. The well-educated elites would determine the best opinion and pass it on

12 Briggs and Burke, *A Social History of the Media,* 185. Many publishers put advertising on the front page to make their papers look more like a respectable magazine than a sensational newspaper.

13 Banning, "Truth Is Our Ultimate Goal," 23.

to the masses. Many liberals assumed optimistically that public opinion would naturally move towards liberalism. "The form of government becomes liberal," wrote William A. Mackinnon, "in the exact proportions as the power of public opinion increases."[14] Charles Knight, publisher of *Penny Magazine* and advocate of popular publishing, thought that the press should disseminate middle-class ideas down to the lower class. Such education "from above" would reduce any negative influence that the press might have on a poorly educated public.

Mid-Victorian Liberals, despite their apparent confidence in a marketplace of ideas, feared irrational popular opinion. The old Platonic distrust of the masses and the fear of a democratic "levelling" of opinion lay close to the surface of nineteenth-century English liberalism. In 1821, James Mill, a follower of Bentham's utilitarianism, supported the principle of a free press because it allowed "the sufficiently enlightened" and "the greatest number of qualified persons" to engage in open discussion. His son, John Stuart Mill, though a frequent contributor to journals and newspapers, worried that public opinion in large societies "depends not upon what a person is, but upon what he seems."[15]

THE BUSINESS OF NEWS AND THE EMERGENCE OF THE POPULAR PRESS

Exploding Circulations

The business of news created a different liberal paper – a cheap popular sheet. Making papers "pay" changed their aim from dissemination of opinion by an editor for political purposes to dissemination of news by a large news organization for profit. The public had always demanded news, but two things were necessary to meet that demand. Newspapers required the technological ability to gather, edit, print, and

14 Mackinnon, *On the Rise*, 6–7. Knight, *The Old Printer and the Modern Press*, 29.

15 James Mill, "Liberty of the Press," 21–8. J.S. Mill, "Civilization," 165, 168. As a young man, and throughout his life, J.S. Mill was an active "opinion journalist." He wrote for his own utilitarian journal, the *London and Westminster Review*, and for London newspapers such as the *Morning Chronicle*, edited by John Black, a Benthamite editor. Mill was sceptical about the ability of newspapers and the growing power of the masses – the "uncultivated herd" – to determine rational public policy. Mill, *Autobiography*, 119, 137.

distribute the news to thousands of readers morning, noon, or night. Newspapers also needed an elaborate system of newsroom production that put technology to work. By the 1880s, most of these technological, organizational, and business structures were in place. The mass-circulation paper employed a hierarchy of editors and reporters working to immovable deadlines, constructing news according to standard styles. The era of "personal journalism" – the newspaper as the organ of an editor – was receding.

Meanwhile, the nineteenth century provided the technology: steamship, railway, telegraph, kerosene lamp, steam-powered press, pulp paper, linotype, camera, telephone, and electricity. Papers had become *news*papers, the first mass medium. They were no longer revolutionary agitators worthy of repression, but essential cogs of the economy. The impressive buildings of newspapers stood tall in the centres of the largest cities.

The popular press differed in style, content, distribution, and readership from the more earnest, low-circulation papers. Editors slashed the price of a newspaper to one penny and sold copies on the street to a large diaspora of urban readers, rather than relying on annual subscriptions. News, dramatized by banner headlines and illustrations, took over the front page. The types of stories expanded to encompass crime, sports, business, gossip, humour, fashion, and family matters. Then the many types of articles were grouped into separate newspaper sections. Turgid prose gave way to engaging "stories" that employed short sentences and plain language. News began to appear in a crisp, factual style.

Between the 1830s and the 1880s, the popular press emerged in Britain, France, the United States, and Canada, although the rate of development varied.[16] All four countries provided favourable conditions for a mass press: decreasing legal restrictions, economic and population growth, scientific advances, and better public education. The trend was towards more newspapers for more readers, a larger newsroom staff, faster presses, higher costs, but greater profits. Eventually, the heavy costs shifted ownership from individuals and family firms to joint-stock companies, chains, and trusts. A London daily of the 1880s employed a dozen parlia-

16 The press developed slower in France than in England and slower in England than in the United States. Although France had popular newspapers in the early nineteenth century, a popular press could not obtain a firm foothold until after the 1881 press law swept away decades of legal regulations.

mentary reporters, six or seven court reporters, correspondents in European capitals, and a fleet of editorial and freelance writers. The cost of starting a London paper rose from £4,000 in 1818 to £100,000 in 1870. Nevertheless, the *Daily Telegraph* in London made a tidy profit of £120,000 in 1882.[17] In the United States, James Gordon Bennett began the *New York Herald* with $500 in 1835. The cost of starting an American daily in the 1880s was $1 million. By the 1890s, the largest U.S. papers produced weekend editions of over 100 pages, almost half advertising. In New York, Joseph Pulitzer employed over 1,300 people at his *World*, which made profits of $500,000 per annum in the late 1890s, on expenses of $2 million.[18]

Staggering hikes in circulation and advertising covered rising costs. From 1870 to 1900, the number of American daily newspapers jumped from 400 to 2,326. Total daily circulation leaped from 3.5 million to 15 million.[19] Annual advertising revenue increased from $16 million to $95 million. In England and Wales, the number of daily and weekly newspapers rose from 267 in the 1830s to 1,102 in 1861. London had 18 dailies in 1880; the provinces had 96, and Scotland 24. In Canada, there were only about 20 weekly journals in the early nineteenth century, with total circulation of not more than 2,000. But in 1900 121 dailies sold thousands of copies.

The American popular press developed in three phases. The original, penny papers gave way to larger newspapers after the Civil War and culminated in the huge, mass-circulation newspapers of the 1890s. American publishers, free from English-style taxes, were the first to reach out to a news-hungry populace, especially the tradesmen, working class, and immigrants who filled the cities.[20] In the 1830s they launched penny papers in Baltimore, Boston, New York, and Philadelphia. The egalitarian, liberal-democratic paper was born. The pennies poured scorn on the elite and its papers, such as Arthur Tappan's *New York Journal of Commerce.* They caught the spirit of a nation entering a period of urban growth, immigration, industrialization, westward expansion, and democratic reform.[21]

17 In the 1870s, London dailies made an annual profit of about £60,000, on spending of £260,000.

18 Mott, *American Journalism*, 546.

19 Baldasty, *The Commercialization of the News in the Nineteenth Century.*

20 See Leonard, *News for All.*

21 By 1850, three million American children were attending primary school – a huge potential audience for newspapers. From 1870 to 1900, an influx of immigrants, mainly from southern Europe, doubled the U.S. population to 75 million. Cities such as New York doubled or tripled in size.

The first successful penny paper was Benjamin Day's *New York Sun,* launched on 3 September 1833. It promised to "lay before the public, at a price within the means of every one, all the news of the day, and at the same time afford an advantageous medium for advertising." New York's shopkeepers, barbers, and craftsmen read the *Sun's* dramatic reports on crime, suicides, and disastrous fires. The paper's motto was "It Shines for All."[22] James Gordon Bennett's *New York Herald* appeared first on 6 May 1835.[23] The self-promoting Bennett offered everything from domestic news and political essays to commercial data and satire. Horace Greeley started his *New York Tribune* in 1841. His editorial restraint, compared with Bennett's lack thereof, earned him the reputation of a penny editor "with class." He brought the penny into the parlour. Greeley became one of the most famous Americans. People either ridiculed him as an eccentric or praised him as a principled reformer. He preached against slavery, alcohol, and war, while promoting women's rights, scientific agriculture, and trade unions. The two-cent *New York Times,* founded by Henry Raymond, joined the field just as the Civil War turned newspapers into large and efficient news organizations.

After the war, newspapers entered a "gilded age" of unparalleled growth. First came a new generation of publishers such as Charles S. Dana of the *New York Sun.* Then, in the 1890s, another generation, led by Joseph Pulitzer and William Randolph Hearst, took the press to greater profits and notoriety by employing the yellow journalism techniques of "scare" headline, jingoism, stunt journalism, and stories about pseudo-science, crime, and sports. Readers had a choice between the dramatic stories in Hearst's papers or the restrained reports of the *New York Times* under Adolf Ochs.

A popular press advanced quickly in Britain, especially in England, after removal of the newspaper taxes.[24] The stamp act and other newspaper

22 Not exactly for all. When Willis Hodges, a black American, protested the *Sun*'s opposition to voting rights for blacks, the editor replied: "The Sun shines for all white men, and not for coloured men." Quoted in Stephens, *A History of News,* 194.

23 In 1837, when Day sold the *Sun,* the paper had a daily circulation of 30,000. After one year of publishing, the *Herald* was selling 20,000 copies daily, despite a price increase to two cents.

24 Dominant dailies, such *The Times,* supported the stamp act because it limited competition. By 1815, the stamp tax was four pence on every copy sold. *The Times* in the 1820s had an unimpressive daily circulation of 10,000 copies in a city of two million people.

taxes had placed restrictions on the size of newspapers and the space available for the display of news. The newspaper of the first half of the nineteenth century was dense with copy and dull in appearance. The editor had to squeeze news into a limited space, below small headlines. The popular press in the second half of the century was, in comparison, visually exciting.[25] The first popular sheets were the Sunday papers of the middle decades, full of sports and other material for the working class. Then came the penny morning dailies and the half-penny evening dailies in the 1870s and 1880s.

Popular English journalism had pioneering editors such as W.T. Stead, whose *Pall Mall Gazette* began in 1881. Borrowing from American papers, Stead introduced large headlines, human-interest stories, gossip columns, and interviews. Some observers portrayed Stead as a muck-raker. Others, such as Matthew Arnold, called him the "clever" man behind a "new journalism" for a growing democracy. But Arnold also had his reservations. In 1887, he said that "the new voters, the *democracy,*" are full of generous spirit. But democracy's one great fault is that it is "feather-brained," as is its spirited "new journalism."[26]

Arnold's faint praise of Stead missed the mark. Stead, like Pulitzer in New York, did more than produce a spirited, superficial journalism. Stead *combined* intellectually respectable opinion with engaging news stories. He rejected the ponderous political discussion that filled the "quality" press, yet he campaigned for social causes, such as the abolition of white slavery. In 1886, Stead had argued that the time was ripe for "government by journalism," since the press represented the people better than Parliament. Editors "live among the people," Stead wrote. The press is "at once the eye and the ear and the tongue of the people."[27]

25 An illegal (unstamped) working-class press that combined radical politics and dramatic stories preceded the popular press. This weekly "pauper" press included William Cobbett's *Political Register* and Henry Hetherington's *Twopenny Dispatch.* In 1834, the *Twopenny Dispatch* promised news abounding in "Murders, Rapes, Suicides, Burnings, Maimings ... stuffed with every sort of devilment that will make it sell." More than 560 unstamped newspapers appeared between 1830 and 1836, and another 50 unstamped Chartist papers, led by the *Northern Star,* in the late 1830s.

26 Arnold, "Up to Easter," 346–7. Arnold noted that the upper class was selfish in politics, and the middle class narrow in interests. The members of democracy, the lower classes, were feather-brained because they believed what they wished to be true.

27 Stead, "Government by Journalism," 654, 656.

For all his attention to popular formats, Stead still accepted the elite liberal view that the press exerted its real influence on society not through reporting but through strong political comment. He railed against the cautious "impersonal" journalism of his day: "An extraordinary idea seems to prevail with the eunuchs of the craft, that leadership, guidance, governance, are alien to the calling of a journalist ... Their ideal is to grind out a column of more or less well-balanced sentences ... conflicting with no social conventionality or party prejudice ... [which] then utterly, swiftly, and forever vanishes from mortal mind. How can they help to make up other people's minds when they have never made up their own? The cant ... is inconsistent with any theory of civic responsibility. Before I was an editor and a journalist I was a citizen and a man."[28]

However, as Stead was writing, opinion journalism was giving way before a more impartial journalism of news.[29] From the 1840s to the 1890s, the English popular newspaper learned the business of news. This cheap press soon outsold the serious, opinion press. The evening papers, such as Lord Northcliffe's *Evening News,* took advantage of reduced telegraph rates to provide the latest news. Edward Lloyd's *Weekly News,* a Sunday paper begun in 1842, had a circulation of 100,000 by mid-century and a million in 1896. The *Daily Telegraph,* a penny morning daily, had 300,000 readers in 1880, compared with the *Times's* 60,000. In 1896, Northcliffe brought out the *Daily Mail,* a half-penny morning daily.[30] Distributed by newspaper trains, it had a million readers by the start of the First World War. A similar expansion in the newspaper was occurring in American centres. In New York, the morning and evening editions of Pulitzer's *World* had a combined circulation of one million in 1897. The mass-circulation paper was established on both sides of the Atlantic.

Tools for News

Technology is rarely a neutral means to determined ends. It changes ends and how people seek them. It usually favours one end over another. This

28 Ibid., 667, 669.

29 In his 1911 series on the American newspaper, Will Irwin noted that many editors believed that the power of the modern newspaper lay no longer in its editorials but in its news columns. Irwin, "The Power of the Press."

30 The *Daily Mail* was typical reading matter for the lower middle class. It was liberal-imperialist in tone. It became more conservative after the Boer War. The elites had nothing but disdain for this form of journalism. Lord Salisbury sniffed: "By office boys for office boys."

general truth applies especially to nineteenth-century journalism. Technology altered the way that journalists thought about the newspaper and the aims of journalism. The newspaper changed from an expensive medium of opinion for the elite to a cheap medium that provided news for all. Technology also altered the way journalists wrote, what they considered news, and how they made a distinction between news and commentary, facts, and opinion. Moreover, in changing the process of journalism, it shifted the relationship of journalist and reader.

Technology is never sufficient to implement far-reaching social change. The appeal of certain forms of technology needs the support of the right social attitudes and conditions. After all, it is people who must accept, adapt, and apply any new technology. Technology and society interact in complex ways. That is true for journalism's embrace of new technology in the nineteenth century. This technology-aided change in journalism's "ends" coincided with new beliefs about what liberal society required. The belief that the legitimate end of newspapers was the provision of reliable news went hand in hand with the idea that what a mass society needed to govern itself was not so much the circulation of turgid opinion among elites, but the dissemination of factual, impartial, useful information among members of the general public. Journalism's orientation towards news fit nicely with a simultaneous movement towards what I call "objective" society – a more impersonal society, built on science, impartial professionals, objective facts, and fair procedures. Technological values prosper when they fit hand in glove with new social and political values.

At the start of the nineteenth century, the printing press underwent its first substantial changes since the fifteenth century. By 1850, steam-powered rotary presses that printed on long sheets of paper could produce 20,000 pages an hour, compared with the hand press's 300 impressions an hour. The development of wood pulp reduced the price of paper. In the last third of the century, printers replaced worn-out type on printing machines with the help of "stereotypes." The linotype machine replaced the laborious task of setting type by hand. Railways gave reporters access to remote locations, expanded the newspaper's area of circulation, and ensured regular news delivery.

One of the most important advances was the electric telegraph.[31] Newspapers in North America and Europe began sending reports by

31 Kiever, *The Electric Telegraph.*

telegraph in the mid-1840s.[32] A transatlantic cable was established in 1866. The telegraph allowed reporters to file stories on the spot, without returning to the newspaper. News "updates" by telegraph helped to create the evening edition of the newspaper and a new species of journalist – the a deadline-driven reporter with a "scoop" racing for a telegraph office.

The telegraph made the pursuit of news more important than the construction of opinion. In 1894, C.F. Bell, a manager at the *Times*, instructed a war correspondent that "telegrams are for facts; appreciation and political comment can come by post."[33] Telegraph-based news agencies, either private companies or newspaper co-operatives, were functioning across Europe and North America by 1850 or so. They included Reuters in Britain, Havas in France, Wolff in Germany, the Associated Press (AP) in the United States, and later the Canadian Press news agency (CP). In 1900, AP was sending 50,000 words a day to 2,300 papers. Reuters had 47 foreign bureaus in 1906.

The rush for news forced reporters to abandon old genres of writing, such as the slow-paced chronology of events and the long, stenographic report. The telegraph encouraged the "inverted pyramid" story structure and the "5W" lead paragraph, both of which became central to objective reporting. The "inverted pyramid" put the most important facts at the top of the story and then added facts of descending importance. The 5W lead summarized the news event by putting who, what, where, when, and why in the first paragraph. This dry, concise style suited the transmission of news by telegraph. The telegraph charged by the word, and the communication link could break down at any time. The inverted pyramid sent all the crucial news first. Reporters even invented their own telegraph language with abbreviations for often-used words.[34]

The inverted pyramid suited the busy editors who received the reports. Stories were easier to edit because they had a standard form, and it was easy to add them to previous stories as updates. Editors' direc-

32 The first American news report went in 1844 from Baltimore to Washington, DC. In England, London's *Morning Chronicle* received its first telegraph report in May 1845 from Portsmouth.

33 Cited in Palmer, "The British Press and International News," 208.

34 Abbreviations were obvious money-savers at a time when a telegram from Britain to India cost one pound per word. News agency "language" still exists. Messages between agency journalists today use abbreviated words such as "wld' for "would" and cryptic phrases such as "Outpointing mistake para 5" instead of the longer, "I am pointing out a mistake in paragraph 5."

tives to "stick to the facts" reflected as much technological and newsroom considerations as ethical concerns. Textbooks as early as 1872 referred to the inverted-pyramid style as a basic skill of journalism.[35] The 5W lead was the "first and greatest commandment" of reporting.[36] By late century, the inverted pyramid was widespread in the United States and Canada. One study found that, from 1905 to 1914, 81 per cent of news stories in American newspapers had that form.[37] Theodore Dreiser, author and realist, recalled learning the style at the *Chicago Globe* in 1892. "News is information," explained his copy editor. "People want it quick, sharp, clear – do you hear?"[38]

The tools of news created the modern newsroom. The stream of data arriving via the new technology required a division of labour. The tasks of gathering news and editing it fell to assignment editors, copy editors, city editors, wire editors, and so on. Copyreaders wrote the headlines. Sports news demanded illustrators and photographers. Typewriters, first installed in newsrooms in 1884, sped up production. The telephone in the 1890s added another division of labour – a "legman" (reporter) who called the story in to a "rewrite" editor. Towards 1900, photography was becoming a special division of journalism, because of technological advances such as half-tone printing. The first pictures moved over the news wires in 1924.

Advances in reporting were already evident during the American Civil War. The *New York Herald,* which had sent one reporter to the Mexican War, sent 63 reporters to cover the Civil War. The *New York Times* fielded at least 20 reporters and spent $500,000 covering the conflict. Editors turned telegraph updates into "specials" or new editions. Horses, wagons, steamboats, and special trains moved reporters around the country. Reporters became famous for their "on-the-scene" accounts, some of them sitting in trees overlooking the action. Some reporters dressed as confederate soldiers to travel in the south. Photographs conveyed the drama and the bloodshed. The conflict showed that reporters had special skills and the newspaper had special methods. By war's end, there was little doubt that a paper's main business was news.

Mitchell Stephens has shown how reporting changed during the nineteenth century by comparing the slow, limited reporting of the

35 One writing guide that referred to the features of the inverted-pyramid style was [Chatfield?], *Hints to the Young Editor,* written probably by the book publisher Charles Chatfield of New Haven, Connecticut.

36 Edwin Shuman, *Steps into Journalism,* 60.

37 Stensaas, "The Objective News Report."

38 Dreiser, *Newspaper Days,* 52.

1819 "Peterloo" massacre of protesters by Manchester soldiers with the speedy, voluminous coverage of the overthrow of Napoleon III in 1870. Reporters at "Peterloo" acted as spectators, describing what they saw but not interviewing the principal players. In their follow-up stories, they did not investigate, although they followed the subsequent court cases and reported official statements. In contrast, for the advance of the Prussian army on Paris in 1870, newspaper and news-agency reporters reported, interviewed, and investigated incessantly. The *New York Tribune* had correspondents with the Prussian and French armies and in "leading capitals." Their telegraph reports described the emperor's whereabouts and provided eyewitness accounts of battles. Many of the reports had an immediacy that sounds modern. "I was with the King throughout the day on the hill above the Meuse, commanding a splendid view of the valley, of the river and the field," said an on-the-spot journalist in 1870. Clearly, the basics of modern reporting were coming into existence.[39]

A REVOLUTION IN ETHICS: TOWARDS OBJECTIVITY

Questioning Partiality

The revolution in the nineteenth-century newspaper caused a radical shift in the ethics of journalism. We have noted the change in how journalists thought about the newspaper and its "ends." The emergence of objectivity as a dominant ideal was a product of what I call the ethics of popularity. A prior ethics of persuasion, which sought, in a grave tone, to tell people what they ought to believe, gave way before an ethics of popularity, which used a more accessible style to tell readers what they wanted to know.

The evolution of ethical norms related closely to the evolution of the mass newspaper. As journalism practice changed, it invented, reinterpreted, or gave greater stress to a number of journalistic norms. Among the most important concepts were independence, factuality and impartiality. As newspapers' dependence on political parties declined, editors asserted their independence in opinion. As the pursuit of news led to staggering increases in circulation and advertising, newspapers trumpeted the speed, inventiveness, and factual accuracy of their reporters. They sought rhetorically to reinforce readers' confidence in the same

39 Stephens, *A History of News*, 220, 233.

way as the newsbook editor had tried to reduce readers' scepticism. As publishers sold their papers to a wide readership of varying political views, their editors made a virtue of political neutrality and the impartiality of their reports. In this manner, the idea developed that journalists were independent professionals, who wrote impartially for the general public.

The ideal of objectivity began with, and was an extension of, this attempt to practice an independent, impartial journalism. The practice initially was an attempt to reduce partisan bias in political reporting. Then editors tried to reduce partisanship or bias in other types of reporting. By 1900, the practice had evolved into an attitude of editorial independence and a strong empiricism – a devotion to facts in reporting. In the early twentieth century, this set of norms – independence, factuality, and impartiality – came to be called objectivity. Objectivity was reporting "just the facts" and leaving opinions out of the story. By the 1930s, many journalism associations had created codes of ethics. Among their principles were impartiality, objectivity, and the distinction between news and commentary. A revolution in ethics had occurred. After 300 years, modern journalism had come to question the presumption of partiality, at least for reporting. But it had done more than that. It had made impartiality, or objectivity, its dominant ideal, and it had begun to construct a set of strict rules and newsroom methods to ensure impartial reports and to police the distinction between objective reports and subjective opinion.

Towards Objective Norms

For centuries, until the late nineteenth century, partiality and subjectivity had defined journalism. The publisher used the newspaper to propagate his own ideas and values. The newspaper reflected the editor's personality and force of will. Newspapers were vehicles of persuasion. Observers evaluated a journalist's writing in large part by the subjective values of wit, eloquence, ability to attract readers, and sometimes ability to stir popular agitation. The shift towards objectivity introduced a new catalogue of values: rhetorical restraint, fairness to other views, fidelity to facts, authoritative sources, and independence from factions.

Norms of objectivity began to obtain a serious foothold on journalism with the adoption of the news model – the most profound influence on journalism ethics since the arrival of periodic news publishing in the seventeenth century. The nature of news called for a different set of values. News was empirical, changing, novel, observational, factual, a description of events in the external world. Collecting news required enterprise, frantic activity, travel, investigation, and good sources. Reporters had to leave the newsroom and venture into the world to find fresh news every day. Reporting was, in this sense, objective.

In contrast, opinion in the newspaper was internal to the newsroom, written by someone at a desk turning over ideas in his or her head. Opinion was not descriptive. It was discursive, analytical, and argumentative. Opinion writers constructed arguments on a pre-existing layer of news. Opinion making in newspapers was more rationalistic and subjective than empirical news reporting. It was a reflection more of someone's values and judgments than of events in the world. It was natural therefore for journalists to use the subjective–objective distinction to explain the central journalistic divide between news and opinion.

The newspaper as an organ of opinion lacked incentive to make objectivity its primary ethical norm. But once news became the main editorial purpose, the norms of factuality and independence moved to the heart of journalism ethics, in theory and in practice. The public came to expect news as a separate newspaper product. News was information stripped of partisan comment and overt bias. In response, editors emphasized the factuality of their news with a rhetorical strength rarely seen before and required an objective reporting style.

The new forms of journalism redefined the relationship of the newspaper to the public. The English liberal paper saw itself as a public educator on behalf of the liberal intelligentsia. A journalist was a teacher who tutored public opinion from "above," according to the norms of the middle and upper classes. "Serving the public" meant giving it what its members ought to know to become good, liberal citizens. The purpose of the press (and an open public sphere) was *not* to give equal weight to all opinion or to accept the opinion of the masses. The liberal newspaper should not simply voice the current "prejudices" of the masses. The editor aspired to be a *creator* and shaper of enlightened public opinion through persuasive editorials, political news, and "elevating" information. Liberal papers were not neutral communication channels between denizens of the public sphere or just a "forum" for exchanging views.[40]

40 The attitude of elite liberal papers to the business of news is clear in a comment by an employee of *The Times* who told a government committee on the Post Office in 1876 that the spread of telegraph reporting had made news a "slop article." Cited in Alan J. Lee, *The Origins of the Popular Press in England*, 62.

The popular paper was not so much a creator of public opinion "from above," according to a political ideology, but a voice of the masses "from below," an amplifier of existing popular opinion. In news, the reporter was supposed to be a neutral channel of communication. In opinion, the popular press launched campaigns on behalf of the "people," but usually not on behalf of a political ideology or party. It was independent, a potential critic of all governments and factions.

The popular press defined the journalist as a supplier of news "product" to a consumer, the reader. The public sphere was a competitive consumer market for information. It watered down the normative concept of the journalist as tutor. Telling people what they ought to know became only one part of the press's information package. The market, not elites, defined what was news and information. What was news or information expanded to include just about any aspect of life that might grab the imagination of the reader. The marketplace of ideas was no longer just a sphere for deliberation on ideas by "the best informed." More and more, satisfying the consumer took precedence over educating the citizen. Or, as some people argued, education was something that happened as a result of informing and entertaining. The popular press adopted the rhetoric of egalitarian democracy, claiming to be both educator and informer and to be empowering all classes through news and information.

The ethical revolution in journalism did not just identify news as a valuable commodity. Editors went further – to news as *objective information*, crucial to society and democracy. On this view, papers should restrain their age-old reforming zeal and political partisanship so as to provide the straight facts. Objective information was valuable not just to scientists. Democracy needed objective information through unbiased news reports. The public, to form rational opinions, required more than intellectual analysis. It needed facts obtained from non-partisan, independent reporters. The marketplace of ideas needed not only the free combat of ideas but also objective information. Reporters should put the facts in front of people and let them make their own judgments.

This theory of the objective reporter implied that the journalist should be a different type of voice in the public sphere. Instead of joining the chorus of partisan voices, the journalist should be a more detached, independent voice, mediating between perspectives through the provision of facts and the balancing of views. The journalist should be a special, impartial public communicator who informed the public from the point of view of the public. This was the political justification for the business of news, for a journalism of objective information. At bottom, the justification assumed an egalitarian, optimistic belief in the rationality and public-mindedness of ordinary people. It was a departure from the classic liberal newspaper, with its wariness about the judgment of the masses.

Ultimately, the journalism ideals of both elite liberals and popular liberals were vulnerable in theory and practice. Elite liberalism assumed that a free press would be a serious educator and not move to sensationalism and profits; the popular press assumed sufficient public interest in serious journalism rather than in softer news or in scandal. Both ideals presupposed that a rational and democratic public sphere was possible in a mass society through the press. The idea of informing citizens by publishing "raw data" or untainted facts was objectivity's ethical rationale. The press had come to embrace this ethical concept only after the economic and technological factors described above had dramatically changed it.

However, once in place, objectivity took on a life of its own, influencing the way of doing journalism. Here we have an example of how an ethical norm arises from underlying economic and social factors but is not simply a product of these factors, or "reducible" to them. Once the idea of objectivity took root in the culture of journalism, it influenced the attitude of journalists towards correct writing styles and the proper content of newspapers. The public came to see the journalist's function in terms of independently determined facts and independently formulated opinion. Objectivity also shaped attitudes towards further developments in journalism such as yellow journalism and radio broadcasting. In this ethical revolution of journalism, cultural norms interacted with economic and technological forces. To see how this interaction played out, we need to consider the norms of factuality, independence, and professionalism.

THREE SIGNPOSTS TO OBJECTIVITY

Factuality

Newspapers discovered the importance of espousing factuality, impartiality, and professionalism when they discovered the masses. Printing partisan propaganda for a select group was no longer a viable approach. The popular newspaper had to assert that it provided non-partisan news and opinion from a public perspective.

There was no shortage of editors in the nineteenth century who claimed that their purpose was "to record facts on every public and proper subject, stripped of verbiage and colouring."[41] But the public only gradually came to expect news columns to offer a factual chronicle of events. Readers also enjoyed the newspaper for its scandal coverage, which they took with a grain of salt. The press was an "aesthetic medium" that employed, to use a phrase from Ludwig Wittgenstein, "language games" that readers intuitively understood.[42] In 1835, Benjamin Day's *New York Sun* ran the famous "Moon Hoax," which announced on its front page the discovery of life on the moon, accompanied by a picture taken by a telescope of green men. The story sold amazingly well. But it stirred up no revolt among angry readers once the hoax was revealed. In 1836, James Gordon Bennett's *Herald* fabricated part of the lurid coverage of the murder of a prostitute, Helen Jewett. Despite his protestations to the contrary, Bennett was not committed to "just the facts." The sensational reports of a fire that destroyed P.T. Barnum's Museum in New York in 1865 went beyond delivering the facts to emotional descriptions and even satire. Reports of the fire poked fun at editors of rival newspapers by depicting them as various types of animals.

Nevertheless, there were powerful forces pushing journalism towards accurate reporting and working against the idea of a journalist as storyteller and partisan. Foremost among these forces were the news agencies, those sober leaders of factual journalism. Their neutral reports, acceptable to clients of varying ideologies, were a model for impartial reporting. The "origins of objectivity," said James Carey, "lie in the necessity of stretching language in space over the long lines of Western Union."[43] In 1866, Lawrence Gobright of the Associated Press in Washington, DC, explained his journalism: "My business is merely to communicate facts. My instructions do not allow me to make any comments upon the facts which I communicate. My dispatches are sent to papers of all manner of politics, and the editors say they are able to make their own comments upon the facts ... My dispatches are merely dry matters of fact and detail."[44]

This was a modern expression of journalism as a discourse of fact. It is an early statement of traditional objectivity. For the agencies, news was a neutral unit of information, transmitted down a telegraph wire for profit. News agencies look at information in the detached way that a modern computer scientist looks at information as so many "bytes."

41 James Gordon Bennett, quoted in Stephens, *A History of News,* 218.

42 Tucher, "The Sensational Nineteenth Century," 7. See Tucher's *Froth and Scum.*

43 Carey, "The Dark Continent of American Journalism," 164–5.

44 Quoted in Mindich, *Just the Facts,* 109.

Reuters instructed its senior people not to be in politics and told staff members to "leave their patriotism" at home. News was "independent, unbiased and impartial" and suitable for any paper "irrespective of the political view of the paper."[45]

The news agencies showed journalists how to provide "raw data" for citizens. The objective reporter was a new breed of independent "professional communicator," whose reports, unlike the writings of the partisan journalist, did not bear any "necessary relationship to his own thoughts and perceptions."[46] The reporter was factual, acting like a recording machine. "A reporter should be a mere machine to repeat in spite of editorial suggestion or dictation," wrote Bennett.

Meanwhile, the emphasis on news decreased the amount of space given to politics. Slavish, almost verbatim, coverage of political speeches gave way to summaries, often supplied by a news agency. Editors, from Pulitzer in New York to Hugh Graham at the *Montreal Star,* toyed with the idea of killing the editorial. Canadian newspapers began dropping their verbatim accounts of parliamentary debates by 1898. In the 1890s, F.A. Acland, business manager of the Toronto *Globe,* figured that the paper could double its profits if it dropped editorials.

If the telegraph promised objectivity in reports about the world, photography presented objective images of the world. Newspapers said that their photographs of fires, shipwrecks, and war showed the world as it is. Charles Dana claimed that the *New York Sun* would offer a "daily photograph of the whole world's doings." Photographs "proved" the factuality of the newspaper report because the camera copied the event without the intervention of human bias. Photographs were objective in the same way that the new X-rays were "mechanically objective" pictures for science.

Not all journalists thought mechanical, factual journalism a good thing. Julius Chambers, managing editor of the *New York World,* complained how he had to struggle to overcome the factual style, which he had learned in the 1870s at the *New York Tribune.* This style was: "Facts; facts; nothing but facts. So many peas at so much a peck; so much molasses at so much a quart. The index of forbidden words was very lengthy, and misuses of them ... was punishable by suspension ... or immediate discharge. It was a rigid system, rigidly enforced."[47] Muckraker

45 Read, *The Power of News,* 1, 197.

46 Carey, "The Communications Revolution and the Professional Communicator," 23–38.

47 Quoted in Schudson, *Discovering News,* 77.

Lincoln Steffens complained about the objective reporting style of Godkin's *New York Evening Post*: "Reporters were to report the news as it happened, like machines, without prejudice, color, and without style; all alike." But in England, C.P. Scott asserted, "comment is free but facts are sacred." Scott wrote: "Its [newspaper's] purest office is the gathering of the News. At the peril of its soul it must see that the supply is not tainted."[48]

A photographic realism and a telegraphic empiricism came together in the journalism of the late nineteenth century. Journalistic realism was consistent with the new culture of pure objectivity in science, utilitarianism in social policy, and realism in art and literature.[49] Newspapers reported on the latest wonders of science and portrayed themselves as part of the march towards scientific truth. Many writers had a science background. Clarence Darrow summed up the mood: "The world has grown tired of preachers and sermons. Today it asks for facts."[50]

Journalism, with its "veneration of the fact," was a rough-and-ready empiricism. But its expositions fail to stress the fact that there were two notions: a *passive* and an *active* empiricism. Reporters are passively empirical if they simply record comments and events and write in a stenographic manner. They are actively empirical if they seek out stories, investigate events, select news angles and sources, and eliminate material not germane to the news "hook." In practice, journalists of the nineteenth century were increasingly active, eschewing stenographic reports and searching for the best stories.

But when they explained their empiricism, they used the language of passive empiricism. Bennett's description of the reporter as a recording machine is a metaphor of passive empiricism. But it was a passivity that he did not practise. Bennett pioneered the use of the interview and the investigation of crime. The new objective forms of reporting, from the

48 Anthony Smith, *The Newspaper*, 130.

49 Richard Hofstadter has noted how American realists, such as Mark Twain, Stephen Crane, and Theodore Dreiser, were trained in journalistic writing and observation. Many journalists from the 1890s on had studied a scientific discipline or shared the popular admiration of science. Steffens did graduate work at Wilhelm Wundt's psychology laboratory in Leipzig. The penny papers carried science on their front pages, such as "The Minuteness of Atoms" in the *New York Sun* on 29 April 1834. See Daniels, *American Science in the Age of Jackson*; Shi, *Facing Facts;* and Hofstadter, *The Age of Reform*, 245.

50 Darrow, "Realism in Literature and Art," 109.

inverted pyramid to telegraphic news reports, appeared to provide a passive reflection of events as they occurred.

In reality, the objective techniques required the reporter to be active in constructing news stories. An inverted-pyramid story was not a "mirror" of an event. It was the event described concisely, according to a story angle, with many details omitted. The reporter had to choose the most important facts, the most reliable sources, and the pithiest quotations. Few editors stopped to explain how a reporter could be both an active selector of materials and a recording machine.

The reason for the gap between the theory and the practice of reporting was the prevailing, passive notion of objectivity. Popular culture interpreted scientific objectivity as the model of objectivity, and scientific objectivity apparently entailed passive, careful observation of facts. Editors drew, consciously or unconsciously, on this view when constructing their own version of "pure objectivity" in reporting. They too sought a metaphor in the apparent passivity and perfect impartiality of machines. The objective reporter should not taint data with subjective interpretation. Editors followed this conception of objectivity when defending their empiricism, despite the obviously active nature of reporting.

We reach a crossroads in the history of objectivity. Journalism could have based its theory of objective reporting on passive or on active empiricism. It chose the former. Editors defended reports as objective – allegedly the factual statements of a passive observer. They ignored the obvious activity of reporting and news editing and talked with amazing confidence about reports as similar to "photographs" that copied events "just as they were." In the long run, this was a fatal conceptual error for traditional objectivity. The theory of journalistic objectivity took on an epistemologically indefensible position and an inaccurate representation of the reporting process.

Independence

The dominance of the news model virtually guaranteed that the norm of independence would become a new and pervasive norm. Papers devoted to "news for all" shed their hidebound partisanship and began calling themselves independent. Initially, independence had a strictly political meaning. An independent paper, in theory, did not allow political parties to control its opinion or distort its news. Readers, it said, no longer required their papers to agree with them.

The idea of independence took on many meanings. In the early nineteenth century, the independence of an American penny paper might mean no more than a reduction in the paper's political vitriol, less bitter denunciations of rival editors, or a willingness to include comments from political opponents. By mid-century, some papers in England and North America called themselves "Liberal independent," "Republican independent," or "Democratic independent." This meant that they sympathized with a party but retained the right to criticize it or its leaders, as the occasion demanded. The attitude of independence expanded eventually beyond politics to include news and opinion on any topic. The news agencies defined independence as strict neutrality on all issues.

The evolution of independence reflected more than an economic imperative to serve a diverse readership. The norm had political and moral overtones. Independence meant different things for different social classes. For some early American pennies, such as Day's *Sun* and Bennett's *Herald*, it was a defiant non-partisanship that expressed the aspirations of the working class and the rising middle class. Independence was a critical detachment "from the old (political) order."[51] Greeley sought not full independence but rather a middle course between "servile partisanship" to a party and "mincing neutrality." Editors could "heartily advocate" a party's principles yet "frankly dissent from its course."[52] Penny editors criticized the elite journals for being smug mouthpieces of upper-class interests, with their expensive subscriptions creating a "monopoly" on knowledge.

The pennies' independence went beyond politics, however. It was an expression of the era's general desire for change. The flamboyant penny style was partly a matter of aesthetics and format. But it was also a visible sign that the editors rejected the "restraint" and respect demanded by the status quo. To many upper-class readers, penny independence seemed an impertinent, demoralizing influence and an ideological inconsistency. Bennett's paper, for example, lashed out at different times against Catholics, Protestants, and Jews, drunkards and temperance advocates. For the penny editor, independence was freedom from restrictive alliances.

In mid-century, the norm of independence came to respectable, middle-class papers, such as the *Times* of London, the *Manchester Guardian*, and the *New York Times*. Liberalism combined with independence. The *Times*, under Thomas Barnes, was from the 1840s on a "thunderer" for liberal reform. Barnes knew the British establishment as well as anyone, yet he battled for the paper's independence from government influence.

51 Mindich, *Just the Facts*, 24.

52 Dicken-Garcia, *Journalistic Standards in Nineteenth-Century America*, 114.

"There is nothing which they [government] so much dread as a free journal; unattached to any other cause than that of truth, and given to speak boldly of all parties," he declared.

Independence also evolved in another direction – scepticism towards all governments. Sceptical independence was apparent in the U.S. newspaper campaigns of the 1860s and 1870s, where editors ignored party lines to expose corruption on behalf of the public. After the Civil War, Charles Dana declared that his *New York Sun* would wear "the livery of no party, and [discuss] public questions and acts of public men on their merits alone."

The claim of independence became a badge of honour for the U.S yellow (and non-yellow) press of the late century. Since the main revenues came from readers and advertisers, it was sound editorial policy to boast loudly that one's newspaper was a champion of ordinary people. Pulitzer said that his *St. Louis Post and Dispatch* would "serve no party but the people ... no organ Republicanism but the organ of truth." In 1883, he took over the *New York World*, with the aim of making it a bright, cheap, and democratic paper dedicated to the people, not to the "purse potentates." The *World* was so independent that it had "no friends."

After 1896, Adolph S. Ochs combined factual news and independence to revive the *New York Times*. On 19 August 1896, he issued his first, and most famous, editorial, under the boring title "Business Announcement." Ochs said that the *Times* would "give the news impartially, without fear or favor, regardless of party, sect or interests involved."[53] The paper would be a "forum" for "all shades of opinion." Newspapers across the country printed the entire article. Ever since, journalists and news organizations have cited the creed of "without fear or favor." It would be cast in bronze under the bust of Adolph Ochs in the *Times's* executive offices. It amounted to a contract with readers, which the Ochs–Sulzberger family would nurture.

Ochs thought that his editorial had an impact because he "actually believed what he wrote." However, the explanation is more complex. Ochs issued the creed at a time when observers considered the paper an organ of the Democratic Party. Ochs wanted to reassure Republicans of the paper's "political objectivity." In addition, his editorial came at a time when many editors were worrying about the drift of popular journalism. It touched a nerve. Ochs wanted to distinguish his paper from the competition in New York – the yellow papers. In 1896, the huge circulations of the *World* and *Journal* forced the so-called quality press –

53 Quoted in Tifft and Jones, *The Trust*, xix.

James Dana's *Sun* and the Herald, now managed by James Gordon Bennett Jr – to lower their standards. On 18 August 1896, the day before Och's announcement, the *Sun* had published a story, "Body Sent to Morgue," about a man who supposedly narrowly escaped embalming alive, along with a "news report" called "A Fish That Plays the Piano."

In October 1896, Ochs asked readers to enter a contest for a new motto for the paper, to replace his own creation, "All the News That's Fit to Print." Entries showed concern about yellow journalism and a desire for respectability. Readers offered such mottos as "News for the Millions, Scandal for None," and "Free from Filth, Full of News." Newspapers all over the United States praised the *Times* for its denunciation of the "sewer and morgue fields" that provided the stories for the *World* and the *Journal*. The contest winner was "All the World's News, But Not a School for Scandal." Ochs, in the end, kept his original motto. In February 1897, "All the News That's Fit to Print" appeared in the upper-left-hand corner of the front page for the first time.[54]

Despite its economic appeal, independence faced formidable opposition. The lure of government printing contracts, party subsidies, and appointments for editors kept many papers attached to parties well into the late 1880s.[55] Centuries of practice had entrenched the notion that partisanship was necessary. Some editors attacked independence as a sign that the press was losing its vigour. Greeley had warned against "mincing neutrality." This worry continued into the twentieth century. In England in 1925, editor J.A. Spender complained, like Stead had in 1886, that the independent or neutral journalist had became "so other-minded ... [he] ceased to have a mind of his own."[56] Throughout the nineteenth-century, news organizations and editors committed to independence struggled to fend off political pressure. Politicians hounded editor J.S. Willison of the Toronto *Globe*, a supporter of the Liberal

54 Ibid., xix, 43, 42, 46.

55 President Andrew Jackson had 57 journalists on his payroll. Abraham Lincoln declined offers of help from editors because he did not want to anger other editors. Historians' attitudes to partisan journalism vary. Frank Mott called the early nineteenth century "the Dark Age of Partisan Journalism." Canadian media historian Paul Rutherford termed the first century of the Canadian press, from 1750 to 1850, a "glorious era of personal journalism." He describes how Canadians read eagerly the editorial battles between reform and conservative papers before Confederation. There was, he said, a "joyous disregard for objectivity." Rutherford, *The Making of the Canadian Media*, 13.

56 Quoted in Alan J. Lee, *The Origins of the Popular Press in England*, 195.

Party, for having the audacity to criticize Sir Wilfrid Laurier's Liberal Dominion government.

Nevertheless, despite the obstacles, the independence movement carried on. By the 1890s, one-third of American newspapers listed in newspaper directories identified themselves as independent. That figure rose to 50 per cent by 1940. In England, independents outnumbered partisan papers by the 1890s. In Canada, independence was a common editorial stance in the early twentieth century. It was popular, no doubt, because advertising made up 65 per cent of Canadian newspaper revenue in the late nineteenth century and was increasing. Trade journals in the United States and Canada praised independence almost as regularly as accuracy and factuality.

As codes of ethics made independence a requirement of objective journalism, the battle for independence in newsrooms carried on into the twentieth century, and it continues today. Even the major news agencies, paragons of neutral journalism, were dependent on government contracts or subsidies. Havas had close financial and editorial ties to the French government, receiving secret government subsidies. In times of war, governments pressed news agencies – and the entire press system – to support their foreign policies.

Buried in Canada's National Archives in Ottawa is a circular to the "press of Canada" dated 16 July 1915 from E.F. Slack of the *Montreal Gazette.* The memorandum states that editors of the major dailies had met with the Dominion secretary of state to implement the censorship law on the press. The resolution read: "The publishers of Canada have no desire to publish any news or comment that may embarrass or hinder the successful prosecution of the war. ... The daily newspapers in Canada have shown unanimous loyalty since the war began."

In London, the executives of Reuters struggled throughout the two world wars to be British and patriotic, yet objective and independent. Reuters needed government money to help compete against the Nazis' news agency, since only 10 per cent of its revenue came from British papers. Roderick Jones, its chair and managing director, wanted his organization to work *with* the government without becoming servile. Jones's attempt at this delicate balance caused tensions inside the news agency. He tried hard to reconcile patriotism and objectivity. In an interview on 24 October 1915, for London's *Observer,* he said that Reuters "should preserve a cold and judicial impartiality." However, he added that Reuters saw international affairs "through British eyes." Objectivity, it appeared, did not exclude writing from a British perspective. Was objectivity simply a matter of not taking sides *within* Britain?

In 1939, as Europe drifted towards war again, Jones and the British government reached an agreement that Reuters would "bear in mind any suggestions made to them on behalf of His Majesty's Government" on the orientation of the news service or on topics that required special attention. Jones assured his board that although the agency would take the official view into account, it would not give up final judgment.[57]

Looking back over the nineteenth century, one realizes that the movement towards independent opinion did not occur in isolation from the shift to factual news. The practices of factual news and independent opinion not only influenced each other; the ideas behind each were mutually dependent. In describing their newspapers, editors regularly put factuality and independence together in double-barrel ethical assertions. Good reporting, they said, was factual *and* impartial (or non-partisan). Editorial opinion was *both* independent and based on facts. Moreover, factuality and independence were part of a larger movement towards the autonomous newspaper, as an impartial, public voice. Support for these norms derived from a public that wanted independent reporting and independent opinion. It was not only communities of scientists that needed objective methods to facilitate communication across cultures and perspectives. Many journalists and citizens in a complex, modern world needed as much objective information and independent analysis as possible from the newspaper.

The claim to provide factual news and the claim to offer independent opinion were conceptually dependent. Independent opinion does not make sense without a commitment to objective facts, and factual reporting means nothing without journalistic independence. Logically, a reporter could not claim to be factual and impartial unless he or she also was independent from undue editorial or commercial influence. Independence was a necessary condition for objective reporting. Conversely, an editorial writer could not write plausible, independent opinion unless he or she based arguments on facts, logical reasoning, and a "public good" perspective that transcended partial viewpoints.

Taken together, willingness to be guided by facts, objective reasoning, and a broad public perspective amounted to a measure of objectivity in making opinion. Common to the ideals of factual reporting and independent commentary was the idea of autonomy. Journalists were to be rationally autonomous communicators, whether commenting or reporting. They should be employees of an independent newspaper. Behind the justification of independence lay a Kantian ideal of autonomy.

57 Read, *The Power of News*, 126–7, 187.

The popular paper brought fresh ideas to the liberal theory of the press and to journalism ethics. It offered a rich set of related norms – factuality, independence, autonomy, and a public perspective. Its duty was to be free, frank, factual, and autonomous. It contributed the idea of the press as an egalitarian informer that respected the masses and believed that all classes should help form public opinion.

The popular paper contributed the idea of the journalist as an independent voice in the public sphere, not beholden to political parties or to any faction and guided by facts and autonomous reasoning. Even the journalist who continued to act as a rhetor or promoter of causes was to provide reasons that appealed to the public good. Journalists were to put a critical distance between themselves and their beliefs (and personal allegiances). In their willingness to test facts and construct opinion from a public perspective, both the reporter and the opinion-maker adopted a broad, objective attitude. As scientists laid claim to reason and objectivity in the explanation of nature, the objective, independent newspaper staked "a preemptive claim to the exercise of reason in the public sphere."[58]

Professionalism

A nascent professionalism joined journalism's winding journey towards objectivity in the late nineteenth century, buttressing the movement towards independence. It is not surprising that an aspiration to professionalism emerged at the same time as journalists were adopting a more objective attitude and reminding themselves of their social obligations. A profession is a group of individuals who carry out an important social function, based on special skills, knowledge, and commitment to ethical standards.[59] For some professionals, such as doctors and lawyers, a licensing body, established under law, protects the relationship of trust between professional and client. The body regulates entrance to the profession and disciplines unethical behaviour by a code of ethics. Most professions promote two fundamental attitudes among their members: dedication to the public good over personal gain and an objective attitude in making judgments and in dealing with problems.

True professionals do not let personal interests, emotions, or conflicts of interest cloud judgment. They judge matters on the basis of objective

58 Schiller, *Objectivity and the News*, 15.

59 See Allison, "A Literature Review of the Approaches to the Professionalization of Journalists."

evidence and fair methods. Professional ethics raises ethical discourse from the level of the individual to that of the group. A professional ethic is not just a personal statement of values by one or more individuals, but a set of standards of behaviour that represent obligations that all members owe to society. By adopting a code, a profession becomes accountable. The code tells the public what it can expect from members of the profession.

The promotion of professionalism especially in U.S. and Canadian journalism about the turn of the century was therefore an ethical milestone. For the first time, journalists as a group were ready to commit themselves to a set of public duties, in addition to their long-standing claim to the right of free expression. Editors in the nineteenth century used the term "professional" in two senses – a set of technical skills in newspaper writing and editing and/or dedication to serving the public rather than a faction. In this latter sense, professionalism implied independence.

The motivations for professionalization in journalism were plentiful. Many journalists in Canada and the United States, and also in Britain, began to consider themselves a profession in the 1860s, as newsrooms expanded and attracted educated practitioners. Newspapers ceased to be the enterprise of one editor from the printing trade. Journalists desired professionalism to raise their social status and to express their pride in the expanding skills of reporters and editors. Professionalism was an obvious model. Journalists looked around and saw many other fields, from lawyers to historians, seeking professional status. Journalists believed that a professional attitude would raise standards and reduce the embarrassing partisan behaviour of editors. As college-trained journalists developed "beats," they too saw themselves as professionals with their own expertise.

This self-conscious professional attitude grew among journalists as they formed press clubs and associations, published trade journals, wrote training manuals, promulgated ethical codes, and established the first schools of journalism.[60] But professionalism was a hard sell in journalism. Some people thought it obvious that journalism had become a profession; others thought it a ridiculous idea. In 1879, the *Nation* magazine said that American journalism was not a profession because it required no special education. An ability to observe and write was a "gift."

60 The Canadian Press Association began publishing the *Canadian Printer and Publisher* journal in the 1860s. In 1884, two major journals with the same name appeared in America and in Britain: the New York *Journalist*, which was consolidated with *Editor and Publisher* in 1907, and the British *Journalist*.

In addition, journalism was too "commercial" to qualify as a profession. But reporter Junius Henri Browne noted in 1886 that journalists in large eastern U.S. cities were "regularly educated men." He concluded confidently: "Journalism has grown to be a profession."[61]

The popularity of professionalism had much to do with prevailing social attitudes. The Victorian value of social "respectability" shaped initial conceptions of the journalist as a professional. In Britain, upper-class attitudes defined a professional as a respectable gentleman. "Respectability" implied a set of moral and social attitudes – "decency," restraint, and "fair play." A newspaper was professional if it also acted like a restrained gentleman. Respectable journalists did not hold radical political views. They tended to share the upper-class biases of the time, such as the superiority of British law. Decent journalists did not reveal the personal problems of leading families, and they practised "fair play" – or balance – by printing the comments of people damaged by stories. Many of the early codes of ethics stressed fair play and decency.[62]

Leaders of the British liberal press, who considered themselves gentlemen, used concerns about respectability to oppose the spread of the popular press. They complained that journalism was surrending to a "host of nobodies" who worked for wages. Charles Mitchell, owner of the *Newspaper Press Directory*, argued in 1854 against the removal of the Stamp Act, because it would create papers whose editors were not gentlemen and would "completely reduce the respectability of the newspaper press, and reduce it from its present position, that of the highest in the world – to that of the American press." Champions of a free press, such as Henry Brougham, worried that the new journalism meant that "the Newspaper Press is thus degraded from the rank of a liberal profession." The press, he feared, was falling into the hands of men of "obscure birth, imperfect education, blunt feelings and coarse manners."[63] In Anthony Trollope's novel *He Knew He Was Right,* Sir Marmaduke Rowley reacts to the statement that journalism is a profession by saying: "But a barrister's profession is recognized as a profession among gentlemen."

For much of the nineteenth century, many members of the upper and middle classes saw journalists as bohemians in low-paying, unreliable

61 Mott, *American Journalism,* 489.

62 The code of ethics of the American Society of News Editors still insists on "fair play" – respecting the rights of people in the news, observing the "common standards of decency," the right of reply to accusations, and so on.

63 Alan J. Lee, *The Origins of the Popular Press in England,* 105, 53–4.

jobs; muckrakers who disclosed embarrassing facts; or radicals.[64] In the 1840s, only a few important English journalists with aristocratic connections had high social status. In 1860, a *Times* reporter was disqualified from becoming a judge because he was a reporter, an editor from joining a book club, and Barnes from joining the London gentlemen's club the Athenaeum. H.B. Thompson, who advised middle-class men on the professions, said that journalism was not a profession that "a man would willingly enter when a competence is open to him." Editor G.A. Sala complained in 1880 that the journalist had no "definitely ascertained social position."[65]

However, Victorian attitudes towards decency did provide support for the *Times* of London and the *New York Times.* Both papers did not focus on the "de-moralizing" details of scandal and crime. Ochs said that the *New York Times* "did not soil the breakfast cloth" and would be "clean, dignified and trustworthy." In Canada, many editors were good British subjects, with similar Victorian values. P.D. Ross wanted his *Ottawa Journal* to be a "gentleman" that was "anxiously honest in its presentation of news," giving it fairly, impartially, and "mercifully."[66]

The signs of professionalism – associations, codes, manuals, and courses – gradually emerged in the United States, Canada, and Britain. In the United States, there were no textbooks, training programs, or professional societies before the Civil War. Things changed quickly after the war.[67] By the 1890s, major cities had press clubs, almost every state had a press association, and national and international associations were forming.[68] In

64 In Britain, only the top journalists made salaries that approached those of the other professions. A top London editor in the 1830s earned between £600 and £1,000. By the 1870s, £1,000 was an average salary, with *The Times's* editor earning £5,000. In the United States, by the early 1890s, managing editors in New York made over $6,000 a year, and city editors between $3,000 and $5,000. But the police and court reporter wrote for $15 a week, and it was common for general reporters to make $25 a week.

65 Thompson, *The Choice of a Profession*, 339; Sala, *America Revisited*, 77. See also Aspinall, "The Social Status of Journalists at the Beginning of the Nineteenth Century," 219–20.

66 I. Norman Smith, *The Journal Men*, 58–9.

67 Banning, "Discovering a Mid-Nineteenth Century Drive for Journalistic Professionalization," 2–18.

68 Among the earliest American calls for professionalism and a code of conduct were two books of mid-century: Lunt, *Three Eras of New England*, and Pray, *Memoirs of James Gordon Bennett.*

England, there were press clubs in London and the provinces in the 1860s, preceding the National Association of Journalists (NAJ), formed in Birmingham in 1886.

Professionalism in Britain, however, was less supportive of higher education for journalists, because of the apprentice-training model.[69] In the United Province of Canada (now Quebec and Ontario), journalists formed the Canadian Press Association (CPA) in 1859 and a press gallery in the province's Parliament before Confederation in 1867. Other press associations spread across eastern Canada in the 1870s. Speeches at CPA meetings emphasized the newspaper's high purpose and the need for professionalism. In 1876, editor Goldwin Smith said that a professional "tone" would reduce misbehaviour by journalists, bring together a press "divided by party," and provide an "additional title of social respect." A "professional feeling" would make journalists conscious that they have a "corporate interest in the position, rights and privileges of their order."[70] The time for professionalism was ripe, Smith said, because the legal, medical, and military professions had organized themselves. Talk of professional duty was so prevalent that Mark Twain satirized such assertions: "Our duty is to keep the universe thoroughly posted concerning murders and street fights, and balls, and theatres ... to magnify their undue importance for the instruction of the readers of the great daily newspaper."[71]

Meanwhile, the rules of a professional press were being written down on paper. The 1869 annual meeting of the Missouri Press Association (MPA) suggested a principled journalism dedicated to the public good through factual, non-sensational reporting. At its 1876 convention, the MPA approved four rules: press independence, articles that omit useless details, stories based on "brain work," and the avoidance of partisan articles. The MPA's documents do not use the term "objectivity." However, press historian Stephen Banning has stated, "the concern of objectivity is addressed in the coverage of the issues of truth and accuracy."[72] In addition, leading editors, from Greeley to Dana, is-

69 English journalists started at small papers, and the best of them moved on to the larger Fleet Street dailies in London. By the 1860s, there were calls for the proper training of journalists. The first school of journalism, established in 1879 at Crewe, lasted only briefly. There was more pressure for training in the 1880s, but owners feared that more qualifications would raise wages. Alan J. Lee, *The Origins of the Popular Press in England,* 115.

70 Craik, *A History of Canadian Journalism in the Several Portions of the Dominion,* 3–4, 78–9.

71 Mott, *American Journalism,* 289.

72 Banning, "Truth Is Our Ultimate Goal," 22, 28.

sued lists of rules.[73] In 1864, William McKean of the *Philadelphia Public Ledger* wrote a guide for staff, which stipulated that reporters "deal fairly and frankly with the public," give "trustworthy information," and "have a safe voucher for every statement." In 1888, Charles Dana offered a set of principles that included "get nothing but the news," never attack the weak unless necessary, and never think that you have the whole truth.

Over the years, these lists changed from an eclectic set of narrow rules to codes of comprehensive principles. The rules of the 1860s and 1870s were an editor's personal directives, mixing ethical norms with technical tips on writing and how to be a loyal employee. The codes of the press associations from the late 1870s onward, however, linked the norms to journalism's democratic functions.[74]

Advocates of a profession of journalism insisted on higher education for practitioners. Despite ridicule from journalists and conservative-minded university officials, U.S. campuses were the first to establish journalism courses.[75] Journalism education developed from isolated courses to stand-alone programs to the first school of journalism in 1908 at the University of Missouri.[76] In 1912, a survey found that over 30 American colleges were offering courses in the field. An association

73 Bovee, "Horace Greeley and Social Responsibility," 251–9. Greeley had rules on presentation of readers' contributions, requiring printing of "all sides" to a dispute. His rules also forbade "immoral" material and personal attacks against individuals.

74 This shift in American codes is the subject of McConnell, "Journalism's Role in Society."

75 On the reception of journalism educators, see Hyde, "Taking Stock after 24 Years." Frederic Hudson noted how journalism courses at Washington College and Yale had ignited debate "all over the country." A Yale campus newspaper said that the real "professors" of journalism, working editors such as Bennett and Greeley, could "turn out more real genuine journalists in one year than the Harvards, the Yales, and the Dartmouths could produce in one generation." Quoted in Hudson, *Journalism in the United States,* 713.

76 The University of Missouri offered the first journalism courses, from 1878 to 1884. It called them "History of Journalism" and "Materials of Journalism." The first curriculum in journalism was in the Wharton School of Business at the University of Pennsylvania, between 1893 and 1901. The first four-year curriculum began at the University of Illinois in 1904. Meanwhile, there were journalism courses in schools of commerce and English departments across the country.

of journalism teachers formed the same year. Canada would not have schools of journalism until after the Second World War.

Such courses created a demand for manuals and textbooks with discussions on ethical behaviour. Joseph Milando, after analysing 12 journalism textbooks and manuals from 1867 to 1899, concluded that education in the field had already "embraced" objectivity as a central tenet, although it did not use the term.[77] In 1867, New York publisher Jesse Haney published a *Guide to Authorship,* which said that the editor should "chronicle the facts," giving his personal views in another portion of the paper.[78] *Hints to Young Editors* justified objectivity: "There is no reason why the news of a Republican paper should not be read by a Democrat with as much confidence as that of a paper of his own party, and vice versa. It is only by presenting clear, unbiased records of fact that any benefit can be derived from the accompanying comments."[79] In 1884, George Gaskell's *How to Write for the Press* stressed that reporters must cultivate "impersonality" and avoid words that "arouse the passions." *The Blue Pencil and How to Avoid It* by Alexander Nevins supported the division of news and opinion. "The facts, when concisely written, speak for themselves," argued Nevins.[80]

In 1894, Edwin Shuman, the *Chicago Tribune*'s literary editor, published the first comprehensive journalism textbook, *Steps into Journalism.* It was reprinted several times and was still in use when journalism schools started after 1900. *Steps* stressed authoritative sources and news-agency standards. The book contained the basics of traditional, objective journalism: the inverted pyramid, non-partisanship, detachment, reliance on observable facts, and balance. "It is the mission of the reporter to reproduce facts and the opinions of others, not to express his own." Schuman quoted approvingly an AP directive to employees:

> All expressions of opinion on any matter, all comment, all political, religious or social bias, and especially all personal feeling on any subject, must be avoided. This editorializing is the besetting sin of the country correspondent and a weariness of the flesh to the copy-reader who has to expunge the copy's colourings and invidious remarks about individuals. Opinions are the peculiar province of the editorial writer. The spirit of modern journalism demands that the news and

77 Milando, "Embracing Objectivity Early On," 23–32.

78 Haney, *Haney's Guide to Authorship,* 92.

79 [Chatfield?], *Hints to Young Editors,* 17.

80 Gaskell, *How to Write for the Press,* 12, 28; Nevins, *The Blue Pencil and How to Avoid It,* 11, 17.

editorials be kept distinctly separate. The one deals with facts, the other with theoretical interpretations, and it is as harmful to mix the two in journalism as it is to combine church and state in government.[81]

Calls for professionalism were also a reply to press criticism, which became popular in the nineteenth century. A trickle of articles on journalism early in the century swelled into a stream of books, magazine articles, and speeches by the late 1880s. Early American commentators, like their British counterparts, talked idealistically about the press. Whereas British critics tended to accept partisanship, U.S. critics argued that it tainted journalism. Edwin Godkin, founder of the *Nation,* noted in 1865 that the reporter should give to civilization "a plain, unvarnished, and veracious account of itself."[82]

The first full book of criticism appeared in 1859. It was *Our Press Gang or A Complete Exposition of the Corruptions and Crimes of the American Newspapers,* by veteran journalist Lambert Wilmer. Wilmer accused the press of provoking violence among the "rabble," and he decried press subservience to corrupt, monied interests. The first article of American press criticism to use the word "ethics" in its title appeared in 1889 – "The Ethics of Journalism."[83]

In Britain, conservative periodicals worried about the press's abuses, its effect on morals and on women, and the influence of its "unrestrained discussion of public affairs" on the masses. These concerns were part of a long tradition of elite criticism. From the 1850s on, many intellectuals, politicians, and editors of an elite press poured scorn on a cheaper labour press. Then they turned on the popular papers, which addressed readers who were neither fully respectable nor radical. Elite editors such as J.F. Stephen rejected the "new journalism" for pandering to a busy public with intellectual mincemeat: "Their food must be chopped up small before they eat it; and it must be so prepared as at once to tempt the appetite, and assist the digestion."[84] Matthew Arnold, as we saw above, called the popular press "feather-brained." John Ruskin rejected the "dirty printed falsehood every morning at breakfast." When Charles Dickens visited the United States in 1842, he objected to popular journalism as an

81 Shuman, *Steps into Journalism,* 65–6.

82 Quoted in Dicken-Garcia, *Journalistic Standards in Nineteenth-Century America,* 163.

83 Lilly, "The Ethics of Journalism," 503–12.

84 J.F. Stephen, "Journalism," 53–4.

"evil" power spreading "odium."[85] Anthony Trollope satirized the "fourth estate" as a Mount Olympus that issued "the only known infallible bulls for the guidance of British souls and bodies."[86] The same criticism surfaced against other forms of mass media as they appeared – the music hall, cinema, phonograph, and radio.

Media commentary turned bitter as the century ended. Over 100 magazine articles on the press appeared in the United States during the 1890s. Shuman's *Steps* condemned "independent journalism" for selling out standards for profits. Had the free press exchanged one master, the political party, for another, the corporate interest? Had the sensational press abandoned its liberal heritage of acting as a serious educator?

Major assumptions of the liberal theory of the press were in question. One could no longer assume a free press would propagate elevating opinion. Also, it was no longer evident that the formulation of public opinion through the press would lead to the triumph of the most rational, progressive ideas. The liberal paper was no longer omnipotent or extravagantly praised. A magazine article said in 1902: "No other profession is so wept over."[87] Professionalism and objectivity, it seemed, were the only bulwarks against the invading evil forces of sensationalism and commercial degradation of the once widely admired liberal press.

CONCLUSION: WAITING FOR OBJECTIVITY

By the end of the nineteenth century, the commercial popular press had transformed journalism into a business of news for the masses. A business model imposed on a craft had changed its practices and ethics. In ethics, the developments of a liberal paper and a liberal-democratic paper had resulted in a new theory of the press as autonomous, guided by factuality and a "professional attitude." These norms were both a response to the growth of journalism and a critical backlash against a lowering of standards by late century. Both egalitarians dismayed at the

85 In *Martin Chuzzlewit* (1843), Dickens provided two caricatures of American journalists: Colonel Diver, publisher of the *Rowdy Journal* in New York, and his chief writer, Jefferson Brick. In the dark *Hard Times* (1845), Dickens attacked his era's veneration of facts and utility. The novel opens with schoolteacher Thomas Gradgrind's oration on facts: "Now, what I want is facts. Teach these boys and girls nothing but facts."

86 Trollope, *The Warden*, 118.

87 Colby, "Attacking the Newspapers," 534.

yellow press and elite liberals who interpreted "responsibility" as a matter of upper-class respectability wanted a responsible press.

Journalism ethics became an explicit concern because journalism was undergoing dramatic change. Journalists practised a craft that was developing almost faster than they could comprehend. Former assumptions were becoming problematic, stimulating ethical debate. Journalists, for centuries the watchdog on other groups, began declaring standards by which they themselves were to be held to account. The convergence of independence, factuality, and professionalism marked the development of journalism ethics beyond the eighteenth century's focus on one issue – the liberty of the press. Journalists had responsibilities as well as freedoms. All future ethical debate would take place within this framework of rights and responsibilities.

In the United States and Canada, many of the practices of objective reporting were in place by 1900, along with the associated norms of factuality, independence, and impartiality.[88] This proto-objectivity had become a defining feature of the professional reporter. The 1890s was one of the last decades for the swaggering attitude of journalistic empiricism, before the self-doubts of modernity emerged after the First World War. By 1900, Western journalism was ready for the arrival of objectivity as one response to those doubts.

88 Stensaas, "Development of the Objectivity Ethic in U.S. Daily Newspapers," 50–60. Stensaas found that a decade after the Civil War, only 40 per cent of surveyed news stories were objective in style, but by 1900, two-thirds of news stories.

6

Objectivity and After: The Twentieth Century

Make your stuff hard.

J.F.B. Livesay

The effort to state an absolute fact is simply an attempt to give you my interpretation of the facts.

Ivy Lee

THE BRIEF REIGN OF OBJECTIVITY

The doctrine of journalism objectivity was invented in the 1920s – a North American invention of newspapers and journalism associations – after almost a century of anticipation in the popular press. Objectivity was never as popular in European journalism, where opinion continued to play a substantial role, even in news reporting. After the First World War, "objectivity" arrived as an explicit, common term in journalism. It occurred in numerous press codes, articles, and textbooks. One of its earliest known uses appears in Charles G. Ross's *The Writing of News,* published in 1911: "News writing is objective to the last degree in the sense that the writer is not allowed to 'editorialize.'"[1] Ross's comments reflected the reporting rules of his day when he told journalists to "keep yourself out of the story."

The formal recognition of objectivity as a fundamental principle goes back to the formulation of two major statements about ethics – the 1923 code of the American Society of News Editors (ASNE) and the 1926 code of Sigma Delta Chi, forerunner of the Society of Professional Journalists. Both documents enshrined objectivity as a canon of journalism and drew the distinctions that define traditional objectivity. The ASNE's code – the first national code – stressed responsibility, freedom of the press, indepen-

1 Ross, *The Writing of News,* 20.

dence, truthfulness, impartiality, and decency. Anything less than an objective report was "subversive of a fundamental principle of the profession." Impartiality meant a "clear distinction between news reports and expressions of opinion."[2] Objectivity was second only to truthfulness in the code of Sigma Delta Chi (1926). Its first two principles were: "Truth is our ultimate goal," and "Objectivity in reporting the news is another goal, which serves as a mark of an experienced professional. It is a standard of performance toward which we strive. We honour those who achieve it."[3]

The principle of objectivity was so widespread in journalism by the 1930s that it played a role in labour disputes. Editors contended that journalists could not be objective if they belonged to trade unions.[4] Philosophically, influential journalists such as Walter Lippmann argued that democracy needed professional journalists who provided objective information. Objectivity reached its zenith in the 1940s and 1950s. Brucker saluted objective reporting as one of the "outstanding achievements" of the American newspaper.[5]

Yet objectivity's career was stormy. Objectivity was dominant for only a few decades in the twentieth century, and journalists challenged the ideal almost as soon as it was espoused. Its proponents had to defend their views against the practitioners of other forms of journalism, such as investigative and interpretive reporting. Critics complained that newspapers slavishly followed a superficial objectivity that repeated official statements. Press theorist Theodore Peterson, in the 1950s, wrote that objectivity was "a fetish."[6]

2 Pratte, *Gods within the Machine*, 205–7.

3 Sigma Delta Chi, a professional journalistic fraternity, was founded in 1909 at DePauw University in Greencastle, Indiana, by a group of students to benefit the "noblest profession of all." Its 1926 code, modeled on the ASNE's code, would become one of the best known. Bostrom, *Talent, Truth and Energy*, 177.

4 Objectivity was part of a case that went before the U.S. Supreme Court in 1937 involving the Associated Press News Agency and the National Labor Relations Board. The court supported a board ruling that the AP had fired a reporter for his loyalty to the Newspaper Guild. The AP claimed that it dismissed him for biased, pro-labour news. Morris Ernst of the Newspaper Guild told the court: "the Constitution does not guarantee objectivity of the press, nor is objectivity obtainable in a subjective world." Also in 1937, the American Newspaper Publishers Association, the American Society of Newspaper Editors, and nine other publishers' groups opposed unionized "closed shops" because the "uncolored presentation of the news" required that employers be free to hire reporters from any walk of life. See Schudson, *Discovering the* News, 15–7.

5 Brucker, *Freedom of Information.*

6 Peterson, "The Social Responsibility Theory of the Press, 88.

The ideal of objectivity was hardly new. As we saw above, the concept in general went back to ancient philosophy and to early modern discourses of fact. Objectivity had been in common use outside journalism for about a century before journalists adopted the term. Modern science was the paradigm of objective knowledge, and much of Western culture in the nineteenth century paid homage to the objective fact. The prestige of objectivity in journalism grew with the development of egalitarian, democratic theory. Countless public figures repeated the claim that the press's most important social role was to provide citizens with enough objective information to govern themselves. Nor was the idea of objective reporting radically new in journalism. The "matter of fact" report went back to the seventeenth century. Nineteenth-century journalists claimed to provide impartial news.

So what was *new* about journalism objectivity? Its formulation in the early twentieth century differed in three ways from its predecessor – the nineteenth-century idea of factual reporting. The three differences were matters of degree – objectivity was stricter, more methodical, and more professional.

First, the norms of objectivity were stricter, with a clearer distinction between news and opinion. Thus the ideal of objectivity in the early twentieth century required a more demanding form of empirical reporting. The proponents of objectivity fashioned a stricter ideal of reporting by providing a more demanding interpretation of such existing norms as impartiality, independence, and factuality. In this sense, they exaggerated the meaning of existing norms, calling for greater journalistic restraint. Exaggeration and greater restraint – this was the way in which the advocates of objectivity invented a new ethical ideal. These tougher norms and sharper distinctions formed the conceptual core of the ideal of traditional objectivity in journalism.

Journalism's movement towards traditional objectivity matched a similar shift by science towards a stricter, "pure" objectivity. At the same time as journalism was moving from an informal empiricism to a strict positivism in reporting, empirical science was embracing a scientific positivism that sought the elimination of perspective and "metaphysical" opinion.

The reporting style of the nineteenth century, for all its talk of facts, still contained healthy doses of "colour" and interpretation. Editors did talk about the need for reporters to restrain their partisanship. But for most of the century, impartiality meant reducing – not eliminating – bias in political coverage. The same held for talk of independent journalism. In many newsrooms, independence did not imply complete journalistic neutrality on all matters. Impartial factual journalism was a loose, evolving set of general attitudes. The dual impulse to seek facts for the business of news and to reduce journalistic dependence on political parties did not amount to the objectivity of the early twentieth century. Empirical reporting did not involve a code of objectivity – strictly enforced principles and newsroom rules.

The editors who enforced objectivity after 1900 banned *all* comment or interpretation, raising questions about almost any adjective or verb in a report. To "editorialize" was the reporter's mortal sin. Editors detected a lapse in objectivity when they read interpretive paragraphs in news stories. They were suspicious of colourful language because it hinted at the reporter's attitude towards an event. In addition, objectivity expanded the nineteenth-century ideal of political non-partisanship to strict neutrality on all topics. Objectivity strengthened the demands on the reporter's attitude. The ideal was *complete* detachment from events, like Pythagoras's philosophical spectator at the Olympic games.

Proponents of objectivity drew a hard, clear line between news and opinion in the newspaper. This boundary replaced the more relaxed, sometimes fuzzy line that one finds in the nineteenth-century press. For objectivists, news did not differ from opinion by having *less* interpretation or comment – it had *no* interpretation or opinion. Advocates of objectivity argued that news was objective because it contained only statements of facts. They saw reporting and interpreting (or the expression of opinion) as completely different. Interpretations contained value judgments – one person's subjective "opinion."

The doctrine of objectivity implied that everything in the newspaper that was not a news report lacked objectivity because it went beyond facts into the arena of opinion, values, and interests. Non-objective journalism included analysis, interpretation, investigative reporting, dramatic description, theoretical speculation, strong comment, and campaigning. The doctrine of objectivity supported its news–opinion distinction, implicitly or explicitly, by appeal to a clear fact–value distinction.

Second, objectivity required a firm method for the policing of reports for subjective elements. It favoured a detailed method for gathering news, constructing facts into stories, and editing reports. This objective method supported, and had support from, the economic and technological pursuit of news. The objective method and style fit perfectly the stress on short, quick stories and the inverted pyramid. In time, it became hard to distinguish whether a newsroom rule was based on ethical concern for objectivity, on more pragmatic concern for brevity and ease of editing, or on both.

The objective approach developed into a more rigid and more detailed method than anything envisaged by newsroom editors in the previous century. Reporting came to follow an elaborate set of objective procedures. There was a list of rules for checking claims, testing facts, quoting sources, attributing comments, and balancing sources. Objectivity preached carefulness, restraint, and scepticism towards unverified claims. In busy newsrooms, the rules became easy-to-remember clichés, some serious, some funny. The clichés became part of newsroom folklore. If a reporter thought facts questionable, he should "when in doubt leave it out" of the story. As for the spirit of scepticism, "If your mother tells you she loves you, check it out."

These rules, both general and specific, operationalized the principle of objectivity. Newsroom manuals, such as the stylebook of the Canadian Press news agency, had so many rules that reporters and editors kept these "bibles" of the craft within reach for constant reference. The rules were evidence that a rough-and-ready empiricism was no longer enough. Reporters had to follow the correct method and the correct attitude.

Third, objectivity provided new and substantial support for professionalism. In the nineteenth century, journalists claimed to be professionals on other bases. For example, in England, journalists could be "professionals" if they were respectable gentlemen or acted like gentlemen, if they were not featherbrained and provided intellectual analysis of issues, or if they did not pander to the public's demand for salacious news. Even when the business of news created a rapidly growing class of reporters, the idea that they were professionals grew slowly, often meeting scepticism from within the craft.

The justification for the claim of professionalism shifted gradually from social status and intellectual writing to provision of objective public information. Even in 1904, Joseph Pulitzer would argue that journalists were part of the professions not because they provided objective news, but because they dealt with ideas and issues. They "are in touch with the public taste and mind, whose thoughts reach beyond their own livelihood to some common interest."[7]

A serious movement towards professionalization would wait until the early twentieth century, when the ideas of objectivity and professionalism would come together. Objectivity provided crucial support for journalists and their associations who saw professionalism as an ethical response to concerns about the press. Soon after 1900, when journalists sought evidence of their professionalism, they did not turn to the norms

7 Pulitzer, "The College of Journalism," 658.

of subjectivity that governed opinion making – wit, satire, and persuasive rhetoric. They pointed to forms of journalism that embodied the objective norms of fairness, balance, impartiality, and verified facts. Objectivity came to define what it meant to be an autonomous, impartial, public communicator – that is, a professional.

An explanation of the rise of the doctrine of journalism objectivity therefore involves these three features: the exaggeration of existing norms, the emphasis on correct method and attitude, and the idea of objectivity as a prime characteristic of a professional journalist. Only by examining the journalistic and social factors that encouraged these three features will we understand the many factors that turned journalism's robust empiricism of the nineteenth century into the more careful, rule-bound method of objectivity in the twentieth.

The emergence of objectivity provides further evidence for a rhetorical theory of journalism ethics. The evolution of stricter norms reflected yet another evolution in the relationship between journalist and reader. This shift reflected other changes in the practice of journalism and in the society that it served. This chapter examines each of the main changes: yellow journalism and press barons; the bifurcation of objective and subjective social realms; and new forms of reporting – muckraking, interpretive, and explanatory. A case study follows of Canadian journalism and its transition from breathtakingly partisan journalism to professional and objective reporting. The conclusion summarizes the emergence of traditional objectivity, and the epilogue looks at objectivity and ethical invention.

YELLOW JOURNALISM AND PRESS BARONS

The embrace of objectivity derived from worrisome trends within journalism. The virtues of objectivity loomed large from 1895 on because of the notoriety of the U.S. yellow journalism of Hearst and Pulitzer. "Yellow" became a term of abuse that ignored the strengths of yellow journalism. It covered indiscriminately just about any aggressive form of journalism or dramatic story telling.[8] Even magazine muckraking in the early twentieth

8 Campbell, *Yellow Journalism.* The term "yellow journalism" went into circulation in 1897 from an editorial written by Ervin Wardman, editor of the *New York Press.* Wardman used it as a dismissive epithet for the sensational journalism of Hearst's *Journal* and Pulitzer's *World.* Hearst and Pulitzer were in competition for the services of R.F. Outcault, who drew the popular yellow-coloured cartoon "The Yellow Kid," which depicted the antics of an irreverent, jug-eared child from the tenements of New York.

century, despite its admirable investigations, seemed irresponsible to many journalists. Unfortunately, yellow journalism's jingoism, scandal mongering, and lack of "respectability" overshadowed its strengths. Also, several unforgettable excesses, such as Hearst's apparent encouragement of an assassination attempt on President McKinley, tainted it. Conservative editors joined church and other groups in calls for a boycott of the yellow press. Mary Baker Eddy started the *Christian Science Monitor* in 1908 to counter these trends in journalism.

Then, in the "roaring twenties," as yellow journalism appeared to be dead and newspapers enjoyed prosperity, an unrestrained "jazz" journalism arrived.[9] Tabloids appeared with blaring headlines, large illustrations, and lively, brief stories that departed from the inverted pyramid.[10] In the late 1920s, a tabloid war broke out in New York. The "gutter journalism" of the *Daily News*, the *Daily Mirror*, and the *Daily Graphic* included photographs of executions, "confessional" stories attributed to participants in events (but written by reporters), and faked photographs. Sensational trials created media frenzies, drawing over 200 reporters. Once again, there were calls for a boycott of the tabloid press, which some critics referred to sarcastically as the "Daily Pornographic." Editors therefore were not naïve in calling for objectivity. They did not think that it would be easy to instil objectivity in newsrooms. They hoped, however, that objectivity would help to restrain the bias, subjectivity, and yellow journalism that they perceived in the press.

Concerns about content joined worries about new ownership patterns in the American, British, and Canadian press. Newspaper chains took commercialization to a new level. The mergers and closures of papers during and after the First World War concentrated ownership even further. By 1919, Hearst owned 31 papers (including Sunday papers), six magazines, two wire services, and several film

9 In 1926, *Editor and Publisher* congratulated the industry on "the greatest era in its history," with larger papers "lavish in service." Aggregate daily circulation in the United States reached 40 million in 1930, and the value of advertising that year exceeded $860 million.

10 The pharmaceutical industry coined the term "tabloid" in the 1880s for compressed, easy-to-digest medicine. English publisher Alfred Harmsworth introduced the tabloid newspaper in 1901 with his *Daily Mirror*. A tabloid was not just small – lots of early papers were small. A tabloid featured large and numerous illustrations, multi-column headlines, and short, dramatic stories. The first successful American tabloid was the New York *Illustrated Daily News*, founded in 1919.

companies. Edward Scripps by 1914 had a "league" of twenty-three papers, with its own news service, later known as the United Press. Chains ran newspapers according to business principles. They cut costs by centralizing editorial and administrative functions, by using news-agency reports, by sharing syndicated columnists, and by running boilerplate features. Scripps's legacy was the low-cost, centrally managed chain, run on the principles of market segmentation and vertical integration.[11]

A new generation of publishers in the 1940s and 1950s, such as John S. Knight, rejected what they saw as the crude journalism of men such as Hearst. A newspaper was a business whose proper management should not be sacrificed to the owner's inflated ego or political ambitions. These patterns helped to create a newspaper that valued the neutrality of objective reporting. In many papers, objective reporting deteriorated into a dry formula for writing all news stories. Each story used the "5W" lead, the inverted-pyramid structure, and careful attribution of comments to officials. This style, dull though it was, suited many of the new business-like owners and seemed to suit the readers of a more conservative time. The news stories were less libellous and tended to contain little partisan comment that would offend a diverse readership.

Journalism as big business worried some of the leading publishers. As he grew old, Pulitzer realized the danger of advertisers and business interests. In 1903, he endowed Columbia University with funding to start a school of journalism to train professionals with an "anti-commercial" attitude. Journalists must see themselves as workers for "the community, not commerce, not for one's self, but primarily for the public." He issued a warning that once the public came to regard the press as exclusively a commercial business, the press would lose its moral power. "Influence cannot exist without public confidence." Pulitzer added: "Nothing less than the highest ideals, the most scrupulous anxiety to do right, the most accurate knowledge of the problems it has to meet, and a sincere sense of moral responsibility will save journalism from a subservience to business interests, seeking selfish

11 Nine chains existed in the United States before 1900. E.W. Scripps bought or established more than forty papers between 1873 and 1908. Also, he created a telegraph news service (United Press Associations) and an illustrated news feature syndicate (Newspaper Enterprise Association). Baldasty, *E. W. Scripps and the Business of Newspapers,* 4, 2.

ends, antagonistic to public welfare."[12] Schools should promote a class feeling among journalists based on "morals, education and character." Journalists should emulate doctors and lawyers and find in the solidarity of their profession an independence of monied interests.

In writing his will in 1904, he made provision for Pulitzer Prizes in journalism, letters, and drama, first awarded in 1917. Pulitzer's will required descendants to operate the *World* as a public institution, from motives higher than mere gain. In Canada, Joseph Atkinson's will in 1948 left the *Toronto Star* to a charitable foundation so that it "shall not fall into private hands."[13]

Journalism as big business incited strong criticism.[14] Edward Ross said in 1910: "When the shares of a newspaper lie in the safe-deposit box cheek by jowl with gas, telephone and pipe-line stock a tenderness for those collateral interests is likely to affect the news columns." In 1911, muckraker Will Irwin criticized the influence of business and advertising on journalism in a series of articles for *Collier's* magazine. The eighth article included a code of ethics of four principles, summarized with the phrase: "The newspaper should be a gentleman." Irwin hoped that newspapers would incline more to following the code "with the passing of yellow journalism."[15]

The socialist press attacked and lampooned the corporate press. In December 1912, a cartoon by Art Young in the Marxist paper *The Masses* depicted the newsroom as full of whores (editors and business managers) and whoremasters (big advertisers). In response to such criticism, editors and publishers began to talk about the need for a "wall" between the newsroom and the business operations of the paper, described as a separation of "church and state." Robert McCormick, owner of the *Chicago Tribune*, and Henry Luce, founder of *Time* magazine, usually receive credit for promoting the "wall." The *Chicago*

12 Pulitzer, "The College of Journalism," 655, 659, 658.

13 "Portions from a Story Explaining Atkinson's Will," from a series celebrating the *Toronto Star's* 110th anniversary, www.thestar.com (6 Nov. 2002).

14 Marzolf, *Civilizing Voices.*

15 Irwin, "The Power of the Press," 47-8. First, a journalist should separate personal from professional life and not use information heard at a dinner party or similar social event. Second, a journalist, except when dealing with criminals, should publish nothing without the consent of the informant. Third, a journalist should not misrepresent himself or herself. Fourth, a journalist should respect people's privacy in their homes, especially in a tragedy.

Tribune tower reportedly had separate elevators – one for editorial staff and one for business personnel.[16]

The mounting criticism prompted a series of high-profile press inquiries that pointed ominously towards government regulation of the press.[17] For centuries, the press had challenged the "monopolies of knowledge" – the church, the state, the elites. Now, the public wondered whether the popular press was an information monopoly, owned by barons whom it could not trust with the public good. Between 1947 and 1981, there were three royal commissions on the press in England, the Hutchins Commission in the United States, and two major studies in Canada, including a royal commission on the concentration of newspaper ownership. American newspapers came under government pressure during the Depression, when the government called on all industries to adopt codes of practice or face licensing, by presidential edict. Pressure on newspapers to accept regulation came from new forms of media, such as radio and the cinema, which accepted the idea of the airwaves as a regulated "public domain."

To forestall government intervention, the broadcasting and movie industries developed codes based on the idea that government had a right to control content.[18] Codes of ethics, professionalism, and objective reporting were responses designed in part to persuade governments and the public that journalism could regulate itself. In Canada, formal inquiries recommended such initiatives as a press law that restricted mergers and limited newspaper ownership. Although government did not act on the recommendations, newspapers responded by creating press councils and ombudsmen in the 1970s and 1980s.

16 Historians have had trouble finding statements where the two publishers explicitly discuss an editorial "wall." See Leonard, "Lessons from L.A."

17 For ethical codes and press freedom, see Powe, Jr, *The Fourth Estate and the Constitution,* and Clayton, *Fifty Years of Freedom.*

18 The idea that radio operated on "public airwaves" justified government intervention and encouraged codes of ethics. In 1934, the Communications Act created the Federal Communications Commission to license the airwaves. The U.S. movie industry produced a code in 1930, the radio industry in 1937, and television in 1952. The codes were drawn up amid public concern about the influence of the media. In Canada, the government established a broadcasting commission in the 1930s to protect Canadian culture from powerful American radio stations whose signals crossed the border. See Nash, *The Microphone Wars.*

Objective and Subjective Society

The embrace of objectivity early in the twentieth century followed on fundamental changes in society. Two trends were of primary importance. One was confidence in public institutions run by impartial professionals who subscribed to the ideal of procedural objectivity. The other was loss of confidence in the public as capable of forming rational opinion in a democratic fashion. Such scepticism resulted from two factors. New public-relations techniques cast doubt on human rationality, and leading intellectuals worried that democracy was succumbing to the subjective, emotional opinion of the masses. Both trends – confidence in objective procedure and scepticism about public opinion – drove journalism into the arms of objectivity. Journalists sought to be part of objective society by acting like impartial professionals. They sought to avoid manipulation by public-relations agents by adopting the methods of objectivity.

In the early twentieth century, Canada and the United States were changing from partisan societies to objective societies. Large, urban, industrialized societies were replacing low-population, rural societies. Partisan society considered it legitimate to operate government, run institutions, and hand out public jobs on the basis of subjective criteria – the applicant's religion, ethnicity, social status, or political beliefs. Partisanship and patronage greased the wheels of society. Political parties assumed that they had the right to fill the civil service with white males who had supported them in the last election. People often romanticize the old partisan societies of North America as idyllic, small-town democracies. In fact, they were restrictive societies that favoured hierarchical structures, family connections, discriminatory traditions, and "old-boy" networks.

In the new objective society of the early twentieth century, traditions began to count for less. What the market economy valued was money, success, expertise, technology, and useful knowledge. The personal relationships and promises of partisan society gave way to impersonal (often legal) contracts between strangers based on purportedly fair procedures. A more educated populace demanded social mobility and equal opportunities. The diverse citizens of mass society did not share neighbourhoods. They shared abstract civil and democratic rights "guaranteed by administrative fairness and the courts."[19]

19 Schudson, *The Good Citizen*, 8.

In the objective society, procedural objectivity joined epistemological objectivity as central cultural norms. Over time, institutions and bureaucracies came under pressure to operate according to both objective procedures and objective knowledge, overseen by professional managers and experts. Even politics began to lose some of its passion. The press mediated between the people and distant leaders. Good citizens were no longer the fierce partisans of local politics. They were the more rational, non-partisan citizens who received information from the press and voted by secret ballot. Groups such as the (U.S.) League of Women Voters, established in 1920, encouraged reasoned debate. Partisanship and patronage came under attack. A long battle took place in Canada and the United States to eliminate patronage in the awarding of government contracts and civil-service jobs.

Objective society valued professionals.[20] It needed professionals to direct industries, manage the civil service, and conduct scientific studies of social issues. Booming cities needed expertise to manage their transportation systems and electric power. Professionals applied "scientific management" techniques to increase the efficiency of factories, government, and newspapers. In 1916, Frederick Taylor, founder of "scientific management," argued for an efficiency expert in the U.S. cabinet.

The natural scientist, with an objective attitude and knowledge, became the model professional, followed soon by the social scientists, with expertise in polling, statistics, and economics. By the 1920s, North American universities were busy training social scientists, armed with empirical data and objective attitudes. Private foundations and government bureaus gathered facts on economic and social issues. Pollsters surveyed the populace.[21]

Objective society needed objective knowledge in the form of scientific discoveries, inventions, and technology. A nation's prowess in areas such as medicine, industrial production, and international trade depended on information and technology. The key to progress in all areas of society, it seemed, was objective information, untainted by bias or subjective

20 On professionalism and objectivity, see Haskell, *The Emergence of Professional Social Science*; Banister, *Sociology and Scientism*; Purcell, Jr, *The Crises of Democratic Theory*; Furner, *Advocacy and Objectivity*; and Peter Novak, *That Noble Dream.*

21 On the rise of the expert, see Hofstadter, *Anti-Intellectualism in American Life,* 197–229. In the United States, 132 universities offered sociology courses by 1901. Sociologists were becoming professionals paid by universities, government, and foundations.

interpretations. The journalist too was to inform the public with value-free, objective information about current events – what editors called "hard news." Ideally, the reporter adopted an attitude toward events that was similar to that of Weber's objective sociologist.

The norms of objective society supported journalism's transition from partisan craft to objective profession. The public needed objective news and independent opinion that went beyond fawning coverage of political speeches or partisan diatribes. If journalists wanted to be part of objective society, they had to adopt the same objective approach as other professionals. The code of Sigma Delta Chi said that it would act as "a professional society" similar to "organizations serving the professions of medicine and law." Press historian James Melvin Lee wrote in the 1920s how the strong interest among American journalists in becoming a code-directed profession reflected a "trend of the times." President Woodrow Wilson encouraged journalists to adopt ethical codes. He noted that, before 1900, every newspaper was a "law unto itself, without standards of either work or duty: its code of ethics, not yet codified like those of medicine or of law, had been, like its stylebook, individualistic in character."[22] The tone of the "Journalist's Creed" of 1905 made the aims of professional journalism sound like a religious calling: "I believe in the profession of journalism. I believe that the public journal is a public trust; that all connected with it are, to the full measure of their responsibility, trustees for the public."[23]

An ethical professionalism was the claim of the new schools of journalism and journalism associations. Casper Yost, editorial-page editor of the *St. Louis Globe-Democrat,* discussed his "dream" of an ethical organization of journalists at a gathering of editors in 1912. Yost would go on to help found the American Society of Newspaper Editors and develop a code that stressed impartiality and independence. "There is a real and remarkable power of the press, and it is a power that inspires me always with a very solemn sense of responsibility," Yost wrote in 1924.[24] Gone were the days, he hoped, of "yellow journalism" and embarrassment at admitting that one was a journalist.

By the early 1940s, the idea that a free press had social obligations was common in journalism textbooks. The basic ideas of a responsible press circulated years in advance of the Hutchins Commission on the Ameri-

22 James Melim Lee, *History of American Journalism,* 388.

23 Walter Williams, the first dean of the University of Missouri School of Journalism, composed the creed.

24 Yost, *The Principles of Journalism.*

can press and its stress on "social responsibility."[25] The commission's chair, Robert Hutchins, acknowledged that its recommendation for a socially accountable press was not startling.[26]

Yet neither objective society nor journalism objectivity broke free from the shadow of their old nemesis, subjectivity. In fact, much of the impetus towards objective norms came from a new awareness of the extent to which subjectivity influenced human knowledge and social activity. In the early twentieth century, subjectivity became a burning question not just for psychological theories about humans but also for prevailing political theories of democracy. The age-old debate over subjectivity and objectivity was no longer a matter for philosophy or a discussion about the limits of accurate reporting. The issue was whether it made sense anymore to talk about rational public opinion and whether the press in general provided objective information for citizens.

The process of formulating public opinion in a mass society began to appear subjective, uninformed, and potentially irrational. Despite the rise of experts and objective procedures, it was difficult to believe that public opinion was the result of rational deliberation. The professional's calm advice was only one of the voices in a competitive public sphere. The other voices, often much louder and more biased, belonged to press agents, political apologists, interest groups, and sensation-seeking journalists. Would truth always win out in *this* marketplace of ideas? The popular press had disappointed elite liberals at the end of the nineteenth century. But now the disappointment went deeper. Some observers claimed that public opinion was a manufactured consensus or a matter of polling – of adding up individual opinions.

Two beliefs underlay this crisis of confidence – that the press and other agents tainted public information, and that individuals did not have the time, the interest, or even the capability of judging the issues of modern society. Both sides of the public-opinion process – the communicators and the people – were either corrupt or unable to carry out their democratic roles. The limitations of a mass society and a mass press ate away at the old liberal confidence in public-opinion as a means of self-governance.

The belief that public information was (or could be) systematically tainted gained credence during the First World War. The success of war

25 Cronin and McPherson, "Reaching for Professionalism and Respectability."

26 In *Four Theories of the Press*, an influential text that helped to circulate the theory of social responsibility, the authors note that "all the essentials of this theory were expressed by responsible editors and publishers long before the [Hutchins] Commission." Siebert, Peterson, and Schramm, *Four Theories of the Press*, 5.

propaganda in maintaining support for the slaughter showed how government and the press could manipulate public opinion. Historian Jack Roth called the war the "first modern effort at systematic, nation-wide manipulation of collective passions."[27] The new field of communications studies after the war used a propaganda model for explaining how the press affected public opinion. The messages of the press acted like "magic bullets" that directly entered the minds of citizens and altered their opinion. In the 1920s and 1930s, a cadre of American press agents, led by Ivy Lee and Edward Bernays, put the propaganda techniques to work for government departments, political leaders, and corporations. Lee and Bernays defended their activity by adopting a philosophical subjectivism, which held that everything was a matter of interpretation and presentation. They questioned even the idea of absolute facts. "We are prone to look at everything through glasses coloured by our own interests and prejudices," wrote Lee. In 1916, he told a group of railway executives: "It is not the facts alone that strike the popular mind, but the way in which they are published that kindle the imagination ... Besides, what is a fact? The effort to state an absolute fact is simply an attempt to ... give you my interpretation of the facts."[28]

Bernays, a nephew of Freud's, said that the public-relations counsel was "the creator of news." Political and moral judgments were "more often expressions of crowd psychology and herd reaction than the result of the calm exercise of judgment." The only test of ideas is "the power of thought to get itself accepted in the open competition of the market."[29] This was Milton adapted to the purposes of public relations. But war propaganda suggested the possibility of "regimenting the public mind." By the end of the 1920s, thousands of press agents stood between reporters and leaders. John Dewey tried to answer Lippmann's scepticism about mass democracy and a mass press. But he was not without his own

27 Schudson, *Discovering the News*, 142. Journalists in Canada and the United States did more than "accept" wartime censorship. Leading journalists helped to establish and operate the censorship process, serving on Allied boards of propaganda. Walter Lippmann directed American propaganda in Paris. In 1917, President Wilson appointed a muckraking editor, George Creel, to run the Committee on Public Information. It churned out 6,000 press releases and enlisted 75,000 "Four Minute Men" to deliver short speeches in movie theatres and other public places. For war propaganda in Canada, see Keshen, *Propaganda and Censorship during Canada's Great War.*

28 Ewen, *PR!*, 81.

29 Bernays, *Crystallizing Public Opinion*, 214.

doubts about the public sphere. He lamented that the press was an "organ of amusement that is part of a trend toward a collective mentality in society." He wrote: "We live exposed to the greatest flood of mass suggestion that any people has ever experienced." The publicity agent "is perhaps the most significant symbol of our present social life ... sentiment can be manufactured for almost any person or any cause." As a result, independent personal judgment was becoming impossible.[30]

Doubts about the rationality of public opinion found support in the writings of philosophers, scientists, and social psychologists. Intellectuals wrote about the subjective nature of the mind and knowledge, the power of non-rational forces over actions, and the irrationality of mass behaviour. Darwin had revealed the biological mechanism behind the evolution of all species, including human beings. Marx had shown the impact of economic structures on social conflict and class consciousness. Nietzsche had unmasked claims to truth as the expressions of a will to power. Freud revealed an unconscious mind underlying reason. Theories of knowledge investigated psychological and sociological influences on inquiry. As William James said in describing knowledge, "the trail of the human serpent" is everywhere. In art, rationality and representation were fading before impressionism and abstractionism. Stravinsky's *The Rite of Spring*, a shocking work of modernism when it opened in Paris in 1913, expressed a primitivism in life. The work had "no plot" but was a "musical choreographic work" that "represents pagan Russia" and "the mystery and great surge of the creative power of Spring."[31]

Conservative intellectuals whipped up fear of the masses. Many authorities associated popular movements, from trade unions to suffragettes, with a threatening socialism that justified a crackdown on strikes and socialist papers. French intellectual Gustave Le Bon wrote that the modern public, unlike the middle class in the eighteenth century, was "little adapted to reasoning."[32] Everett Dean Martin's popular *The Behavior of Crowds* of 1921 shared Le Bon's antiegalitarian social psychology. It portrayed the public as a dangerous eighteenth-century mob, except that the masses now had political power and their opinions mattered. The masses were intellectually lazy, or difficult issues cognitively overwhelmed them. They acted like an emotional "crowd," and demagogues could manipulate them. The *Revolt of the Masses* by philosopher Jose Ortega y Gasset and *End of Economic*

30 Dewey, *Individualism Old and New*, 42–3.

31 This is how Stravinsky described the work. Cited in Eksteins, *Rites of Spring*, 9.

32 Ewen, *PR!*, 66.

Man by Peter Drucker worried that the masses would follow fascist leaders and abandon democracy.

The First World War shattered Western Europe and its liberal belief in the assured progress of society. The war was a bloodbath over parched scraps of land between rat-infested trenches. In 1919, the prospect of an agreement to end all wars raised hopes. Woodrow Wilson's Fourteen Points, including his notion of "self-determination" and a league of nations, enjoyed great public support. But when Europe once again headed towards war in the late 1930s, disillusionment set in.[33] The mood among intellectuals was sombre, cynical, or nihilistic. Lippmann decried the superficiality and political apathy of the 1920s. H.L. Mencken lampooned democracy and "homo boobus" – the average person. T.S. Eliot's "Waste Land" (1922) expressed a world-weariness that became fashionable for characters in the novels of Hemingway and Fitzgerald. By the early 1930s, fascist and communist leaders were using emotional symbols, rituals, and media to bend the minds of millions to subjection before father figures who unleashed unimaginable brutality. In North America during the Depression, many people admired the way that Hitler and Mussolini reorganized their countries. They were men who created the public will, instead of following it. *Times* creator Henry Luce in 1937 called Mussolini "the ablest manager a poor nation ever had."[34]

The problem of public opinion was so widely recognized by the late 1930s that Louis Gallup offered his "scientific" method of polling to governments, political parties, and newspapers as a way to determine public opinion accurately. Polling was the "pulse of democracy," undistorted by powerful interests. Gallup presented himself as a democrat who trusted the citizen. Polling was a means by which ordinary people could regain control over government. Polling went further than the fourth estate in allowing the will of people to be known at all times. For Gallup, democracy required not that each citizen have information on every issue but only that "the sum total of individual views add up to something that makes sense."[35] A mathematical sum of opinions had replaced the more demanding ideal of deliberative democracy. But polling did not guarantee rational public opinion. On the contrary, it encouraged a politics that sought even harder to manipulate opinion through techniques of persuasion.

33 See MacMillan, *Paris 1919*, 3–35.

34 Baughman, *Henry R. Luce and the Rise of the American News Media*, 109.

35 See Gallup and Rae, *The Pulse of Democracy*, and Robinson, *The Measure of Democracy*.

These two conflicting features of modern society – an objective society and a subjective public sphere – provide the context for the writings of Lippmann, journalist and philosopher of the public sphere. Lippmann embodies nineteenth-century liberal disillusionment with the popular press. We also see twentieth-century scepticism about the public sphere. Before the First World War, he was a liberal rationalist of the Progressive Era, believing in reform, science, and the press. After the war, he became more conservative. He raised searching questions about the press, public opinion, and democracy. In a famous study, he and Charles Merz showed how the *New York Times*'s coverage of the Bolshevik Revolution was inaccurate and biased by wishful thinking.[36]

Lippmann's *Liberty and the News* (1920) argued that since government now acted on opinion, the crucial problem for democracy was whether the free press provided reliable news and opinion. The modern state has a crucial interest in keeping pure the "streams of fact which feed the rivers of opinion." Liberty depends on an independent press that disseminates "objective information." Unfortunately, Lippmann said, those streams are polluted. The news process is open to manipulation by powerful groups. Lippmann asked whether government by consent "can survive in a time when the manufacture of consent is an unregulated private enterprise." Part of the problem was the unprofessional state of modern journalism. The process of gathering news relied on unverified fact or rumour. "News comes from a distance, it comes helter-skelter, in inconceivable confusion; it deals with matters not easily understood; it arrives and is assimilated by busy and tired people who must take what is given to them." Journalists need a better education, and journalism must be more professional. Journalism should use objective methods and adopt a scientific attitude of impartiality. We cannot fight untruth by "parading our opinions," Lippmann wrote. "We can do it only by reporting the facts."[37]

In his *Public Opinion* (1922), Lippmann went further. Using social science, he raised the philosophical worry that the mind may be unable to discern objective truth, no matter what the press writes. He opened the book with a passage from Plato's analogy of the cave, where people see only the shadows of objects. He argued that people understand

36 Lippmann and Merz, "A Test of the News." The study examined the coverage over three years, beginning with the overthrow of the tsar in 1917. The paper reported events that did not happen and atrocities that never took place, and it reported 91 times that the Bolshevik regime was on the verge of collapse.

37 Lippmann, *Liberty and the News*, 5, 38–41, 103.

events through the prism of general ideas, or "stereotypes." They struggle to see the world from behind a veil of ideas, emotions, and interests. To make matters worse, democracy by public opinion is unrealistic because it asks citizens to be "omnipotent." It expects citizens to arrive at objective, informed opinions on matters far beyond their personal experience – military operations, international affairs, and economic policy. To formulate such opinions, citizens depend on the press. But the news is not a stable, whole picture of reality. The press shines "a searchlight that moves restlessly about, bring[ing] one episode and then another out of darkness into vision." To rectify this situation, Lippmann argued, society should assign the analysis of important issues to objective experts employed by "intelligence bureaus."[38] The press would relay their knowledge to the masses.[39]

Lippmann derived his notion of objectivity from science and the Socratic method of questioning beliefs. For him, objectivity in science and journalism was an answer to the menace of subjectivity. "The greater indictment against the reliability of human witnesses, the more urgent is a constant testing, as objectively as possible, of these results. When you consider how profoundly dependent the modern world is upon its news, the fragility of human nature becomes an argument not for complacency and apology, but for eternal vigilance."[40]

RESPONSES TO OBJECTIVITY: MUCKRAKE, INTERPRET, EXPLAIN

Other forms of journalism – other responses to the changing conditions of the press – shaped the progress of objectivity in the United States. These alternative forms forced objectivists to clarify or reaffirm their practices. These responses included muckraking, interpretive reporting, explanatory journalism (as exemplified by *Time* magazine), and radio and later television journalism.

The muckrakers wrote over 2,000 magazine articles between 1900 and 1915. Ida Tarbell prepared a long, critical, series on John D. Rockefeller's Standard Oil Company, and Lincoln Steffens's *The Jungle* exposed problems in the meat-packing industry. The muckrakers felt

38 Lippmann, *Public Opinion*, 182, 399.

39 Within a few years, Lippmann expressed even deeper doubts. "I hold that this public is a mere phantom. It is an abstraction," he wrote in *The Phantom Public*, 77.

40 Lippmann and Merz, "A Test of the News," 32–3.

objectivity's pull towards facts and personal journalism's pull towards a gripping story. Yellow journalism embarrassed them as much as objective reporting dissatisfied them.[41] Muckraking combined the clear, bold writing of story journalism with the factual methods of objective journalism. It was a reform journalism that was sensational and profitable, yet based on research and evidence, not on partisan diatribe.[42] Muckrakers turned the old campaign journalism into a "literature of exposure" that was a moral indictment of institutions.

Leading muckrakers criticized the objective reporting of their day. Irwin, in his series on the American newspaper, had said: "Every news report has some point of view, expresses some mission of God or of the devil."[43] However, the muckrakers showed how facts could add up to powerful opinion. Muckrakers shared with objective journalists a veneration of facts but pursued them with more vigour and method. These early investigative journalists established the journalistic tradition of systematic investigation of fact. They developed journalism as a discourse of fact to its fullest extent. Tarbell was "objectivity itself." In her history of Standard Oil, she built her case through detail, patience, and balance. "She wanted her story to be impartial, complete, definitive."[44] What the muckrakers disliked about the creed of objectivity was not its factuality but its neutrality. Facts needed interpretation and conclusions.

Another response to the limits of objectivity – interpretive reporting – came from the very news agencies and mainstream newspapers that had done so much to establish objectivity as a principle. Their editors could not deny that the complexity of the modern world called out for more interpretation. Their answer was to allow "interpretive reporting." Editors, from the 1920s on, published interpretive articles cheek-by-jowl with straight news reports. Interpretive journalists included the popular and powerful syndicated columnists, such as Lippmann and Walter Winchell.

41 Miraldi, *Muckraking and Objectivity*, 28.

42 See Filler, *The Muckrakers*. Muckraking articles sold millions of copies for magazines such as *Collier's*, *Cosmopolitan*, *Everybody's*, *McClure's*, and *Scribner's*. With a selling price of 10 to 15 cents, these magazines saw their circulations explode from 50,000 prior to 1890 to over one million for some of them between 1900 and 1912.

43 Irwin, "The Power of the Press," 8.

44 Filler, *The Muckrakers*, 103–4. Tarbell's series appeared in 1904 in two volumes. It had 550 pages of text, with several hundred more pages of appendix.

In addition, newspapers introduced more interpretation through the "beat" reporter. Beginning in the 1920s, newspapers extended their reporting beats beyond crime and into medicine, labour, science, and agriculture. By-lines of beat "experts," common by the 1930s, told the reader that the article contained a modicum of interpretation by someone in the know.

In the 1930s, AP and newspapers started providing interpretive news summaries for weekend editions. In 1932, Curtis MacDougall published a textbook entitled *Reporting for Beginners.* A reprint in 1938 had a new title, *Interpretive Reporting,* because of a new trend "in combining the function of interpreter with that of reporter."[45] In 1933, the American Society of News Editors (ASNE) passed a resolution which stated that editors should devote more space to "explanatory and interpretive news" to allow the reader to understand the "significance of events." Two years later, Gram Swing, who had spent 20 years as a foreign reporter with the *Chicago Daily News,* told the ASNE: "If European news is to be comprehensible at all it has to be explained. If it is explained it has to be explained subjectively ... That goes against the ethics of the profession, but it is absolutely essential to understand that."[46]

Liberalizing the rules of objectivity posed a problem. Asking reporters to provide the "truth" about facts, as the Hutchins Commission did, made the job more difficult. Journalist Elmer Davis said that interpretation in the news was often no more than the "prejudices of the reporter." The journalist "must walk a tightrope between two great gulfs – on one side the false objectivity that takes everything at face value and lets the public be imposed upon by the charlatan ... on the other, the 'interpretive' reporting which fails to draw the line between objective and subjective."[47]

45 MacDougall, *Interpretive Reporting,* 22, 5. MacDougall said that interpretive reporting was necessary because the factual reports of the wire services did not allow the public to understand the First World War and the Depression. MacDougall believed that interpretive journalism was consistent with objectivity. Its practitioners combined facts with the ability to "comprehend the meaning of immediate news events in relation to broader, social, economic, and political trends."

46 Schudson, *Discovering the News,* 147-8.

47 Elmer Davis, *But We Were Born Free,* 175.

Henry Luce had no qualms about interpretation. He saw a mix of fact and interpretation – explanatory journalism – as the future of journalism. In 1923, he and fellow Yale alumnus Briton Hadden started *Time* magazine as an interpretive summary of news.[48] They believed that busy people did not want to wade through the dull and detailed reports found in many newspapers. How dry were many of the objective reports? H.L. Mencken said that reporters at the *Baltimore Sun* wrote like "bookkeepers." The *New York Times* was "dry and detailed, and a burden to read." The *New Yorker* started in 1925 with the same intention as *Time* – to be "interpretive rather than stenographic." Luce had no love for neutral journalism. "Show me a man who thinks he's objective and I'll show you a man who's deceiving himself," quipped Luce. The son of a missionary, Luce thought journalism a "calling"; newspapers should put "intelligent criticism ... and evaluation" of public officials on the front page. Interpretive journalism freed editors from both partisan politics and neutrality.[49]

Time's non-objective style, which borrowed literary techniques from Homer and other august sources, was condensed but not dry. A *Time* narrative might begin with a quote, a metaphor, or a personal trait of a public figure. It might explain the meaning of a political summit by focusing on a private incident between leaders. Such techniques allowed writers to simplify events while creating the illusion of "being there." The secret lay in the editing. In the early days, *Time* had editors and writers, but not reporters. Facts came from news clippings. The *Time* "writer" was anonymous, and any piece was the work of several staff members. It was a group journalism of gifted rewrite men. Ironically, *Time's* style of interpretation often sounded objective and authoritative, not subjective. Good editing gave *Time* an all-knowing, detached tone. It seemed that *Time* looked down on humans each week, like an Olympian god. It

48 Luce and Hadden began the newsmagazine in 1923 for $86,000. By 1941, the annual revenues of Luce's *Time* and other ventures, such as the "March of Time" news reels and *Fortune* and *Life* magazines, reached $45 million, eclipsing the Hearst empire, which was in decline.

49 The objective style had become dull. The summary lead had to convey the "5Ws" even if it ran to over 25 words. For example, the *Chicago Tribune* of 24 September 1921 had a front-page story on the German–American peace treaty that began: "There will be no official participation by the United States except by the express authorization of Congress in the administration of German reparations, if the senate ratifies the German, Austrian, and Hungarian treaties with the reservations recommended by the foreign relations committee today." Baughman, *Henry R. Luce and the Rise of the American News Media*, 25–6, 29, 6.

praised the intelligent and ridiculed the idiots. One *Time* editor said that the magazine must have the "lunar detachment" of "the man in the moon at the end of the current century."[50]

Time anticipated a shift in mainstream reporting away from doctrinaire objectivity and the more personal journalism of broadcast media. In the 1950s, with objectivity at its height, mainstream editors pointed out the limitations of the dogma of objectivity. "The day is past when the superficial facts alone can tell the news," wrote Alan Gould, AP executive editor in 1954. Other observers lashed out at objectivity for being sterile or merely the quoting of half-truths of pretentious leaders. "I have no objection to the ideal itself but only to our rigid and almost doctrinaire interpretation of objectivity," remarked Wallace Carroll, executive editor of the Winston-Salem *Journal*.[51]

When radio and television began presenting news, they copied the objective style, reading wire reports over the air. But it soon became apparent that broadcast news was a more intimate and conversational medium that needed its own forms of narrative. The sounds and images of broadcast news had sensational or emotional impact. Reporters were audibly and visibly at the centre of the news story. They appeared on camera answering questions, offering predictions, and making mistakes. Sometimes events visibly shocked them – perhaps most memorably, the otherwise-imperturbable Walter Cronkite on announcing John F. Kennedy's death. Meanwhile, they might complete their reports with an interpretive "stand up." Meanwhile, the adversarial culture of the 1960s created a readership for an unrestrained personal journalism and a return of investigative reporting that refused to be neutral.

The effect of this competition from other forms of journalism was a decline in traditional objectivity. It seemed that no sooner had traditional objectivity arrived, then it went into decline. From the 1960s on, most of the reporting in the mainstream media did not reject objectivity outright. Instead, they watered down traditional objectivity. Pure objec-

50 *Time* writers, like many other journalists of this era, shared an enthusiasm for facts. Luce and Hadden had thought about calling their newsmagazine *Facts*. There was also the photographic realism of Luce's *Life*. For Luce, facts were the building materials for a well-crafted interpretation. Baughman, *Henry R. Luce and the Rise of the American News Media*, 42, 46.

51 Carroll made the comments in the *Nieman Reports* of July 1955, where he listed objectivity as one of the seven "deadly virtues." Gould and Carroll are cited in MacDougall, *Interpretive Reporting*, 13, 20.

tivity in journalism became an impure objectivity, allowing more interpretation and judgment. Journalism diluted "news objectivity" at about the same time as science abandoned its pure positivism of facts. Just as journalists recognized that values and interpretation were not separable from reporting, so scientists grasped that interpretation, theory, and values play an ineliminable role in the evaluation of hypotheses.

From the 1960s on, reporters sought alternatives to the inverted pyramid. They mixed facts with daubs of interpretation, colour, humour, and metaphor to create more appealing reports. During the 1970s and 1980s, even such bastions of objectivity as the Canadian Press (CP) news agency moved away from the dry reports of its early days toward better storytelling. CP editors urged reporters to experiment with inventive "leads" and to write gripping narratives that "took" readers to the scene. Journalists with storytelling skills did as well in the agency as the more traditional hard-news reporters.

A CASE STUDY: OBJECTIVITY IN CANADA: FROM PARTISANS TO PROFESSIONALS

Escaping the Political "Pap Bottle"

Canadian papers in the late nineteenth century were undergoing the same evolution from partisan organs to commercial newspapers as their American counterparts. The Canadian newspaper boom of the late nineteenth and early twentieth centuries built on the economic boom of the Laurier era (1896–1911). From 1901 to 1911, Canada was economically the fastest-growing country in the world, connected internally by a national railway and enlarged by new western provinces. Canada had an expanding population, immigrant settlement on the prairies, increased literacy, and a national market for consumer goods.

The newspaper boom of the late nineteenth century was a long time coming. Colonial authority, a small population, and low literacy rates had retarded development of Canadian newspapers. After the War of 1812, however, the press became more vigorous, shaking off its subservience to British governors. Up to the 1830s, nearly all papers were weeklies, run by an owner-printer and a couple of assistants. Penny tri-weeklies such as the Montreal *Transcript* (1836) and the Saint John *News* (1839) imitated the American pennies. For the first time, a substantial number of Canadian editors tried to attract lower-class readers. The first successful dailies appeared in the 1850s, and most promoted a political or religious cause. Many were "sectarian warriors" supporting religious groups. Toronto's *British Colonist*, for example, had the backing of conservative Scots and the Church of Scotland. Papers lined up on either side of the political divide. Conservative sheets supported the established colonial order, while reform papers campaigned for "responsible" (cabinet) government.

Partisan journalism was a natural ethic for editors, given limited news-gathering capabilities and the small circle of readers. The most popular newspapers in the 1840s struggled to reach more than 1,000 readers. The four-page papers were a "strange melange of politics, religion, abuse and general information." Short stories and poetry provided a smattering of entertainment, squeezed between advertising for businesses, professionals, retail products, and patent medicines. News and opinion mixed liberally. The editorials on page 2 were the heart of the paper. They abused politicians so as to appeal to readers. The rhetoric was part of the newspaper's purpose – "the advocacy of a dogma that thrilled ... the publisher's little public." The newspaper therefore "was a weapon of debate, not just a digest of facts."[52]

The first "popular" paper was George Brown's successful and influential *Globe*, begun in 1844 by political reformers and Free Kirk Presbyterians. It moved to daily publishing by 1853. Its ferocious editorials earned it the name of Canada's "thunderer" and made Brown an important player in negotiations leading to the formation of Canada.[53] Brown took advantage of the technologies of news, from the new printing presses and the development of wood pulp to the telegraphic wiring of British North America in the 1840s and 1850s. He harnessed the telegraph to scoop the rest of the press by publishing a draft version of the British North America Act (establishing Confederation) in February 1867. His circulation increased from 18,000 in 1856 to 45,000 in 1872.

Despite the telegraph, objectivity in news was a distant ideal, as shown by the biased coverage of Louis Riel's rebellion in Manitoba by anti-Riel papers in English Canada and pro-Riel papers in French Canada. Moreover, the appeal of facts was stronger for English papers, which provided a more complete array of information than the French press, which continued to stress philosophical argument and opinion.

By 1873, there were 47 dailies in Canada, including eight in Montreal and four apiece in Halifax, Saint John, Quebec and Toronto. The "new journalism" arrived in Canada in the 1870s with Hugh Graham's *Montreal Star* and its "people's journalism," followed by the penny evening

52 Rutherford, *A Victorian Authority*, 38.

53 See Careless, *Brown of the Globe*, 2 vols.

Telegram (1876) in Toronto, under John Ross Robertson. The *Star* deliberately targeted the "masses" with sensational stories, crusades, and short news items. Graham told reporters that he wanted stories that "you would be tempted to read aloud to the next person to you."[54] His paper campaigned for workers' rights, smallpox vaccination, tariff protection, and the end of political corruption. The formula worked. The *Star's* circulation was 100,000 in 1891, the largest in Canada.

As in the United States, the early popular papers in Canada were light on serious news, by modern standards. Their importance stemmed from their rejection of newspaper conventions and their tapping into lower-class resentment against economic privilege and social snobbery. By the 1880s and 1890s, the Canadian newspaper had become a "Victorian Authority." In 1892, there were 94 dailies, including seven in Toronto, a city of 182,000 residents.

The movement towards objectivity in Canadian journalism began in earnest in late century with claims by leading editors that a press run on business principles was more responsible. "Responsibility" became a mantra, playing a role similar to that of "respectability" in British journalism. Canadian editors asserted repeatedly that a commercial paper was more sober in its "tone" and more of a "gentleman." Many looked to the British press, not to the American, as a model of quality journalism. Of special influence was the *Times* of London. N.F. Davin praised the English press for its "impartial" editorials, "political intelligence," and support for a "cause," not a political party.[55] P.D. Ross, editor of the *Ottawa Journal*, echoed the elite liberal editors of England: "The outstanding glory of any journal is to create, to correct, to guide and mould public opinion."

Admiration of the British press tradition reflected conservative Protestantism in English Canada and colonial deference to hierarchy.[56] Most anglophone editors saw Canada as a dominion of the empire, distinguished from the American republic by its restraint and respect for authority. The editors were businessmen, a generation removed from the reform editors, such as William Lyon Mackenzie, the "firebrand" in Toronto, or the crusading Joseph Howe in Halifax.

"Responsibility" was more than a business strategy, more than a search for social status. It was also a rhetorical response to public criticism of the yellow popular press. Graham's *Star* looked south to popular

54 P.D. Ross, *Retrospects of a Newspaper Person*, 2.

55 Davin, "The London and Canadian Press," 118–28.

56 Newman, *The Canadian Revolution*, 7–10.

American newspapers, and the *Toronto Star* came to practise a "razzle-dazzle" journalism that historians have compared to that of Pulitzer's *World.* Some American influence was inevitable. Canadian and American editors belonged to the same associations and read the same trade journals. They crossed a common border to attend journalism conferences in both countries.

Popular papers in Canada adopted the techniques of their American counterparts, but in varying degrees. Canadian newspapers were never as yellow as Hearst's in their prime, because of a more conservative society and a less-heated newspaper market. Nevertheless, clergymen, politicians, and other critics blasted the Canadian popular press as a propagator of licentiousness. Even the introduction of comics set off protests. "This passion [for popularity]," remarked Thomas White of the *Montreal Gazette* in a public speech in 1883, "is so intense that in the effort to minister to it nothing is sacred." Editor Joe T. Clark, who had worked at *Saturday Night* magazine, described the popular newspaper as an ugly hag with insane eyes flinging slime at people in the public square. "The news of this paper is unclean and its views purchable."[57]

The *Canadian Printer and Publisher* admonished papers to be "dignified" in all their news and to omit items that made enemies. It also supported a version of objectivity: "Nor should they [news reports] contain opinions. The public should be left to draw its own conclusions from the facts stated." To counter criticism, defenders of the press exaggerated its virtues. The mayor of Truro, Nova Scotia, called journalists "gladiatorial educators" responsible for "good or bad government." Editors pointed to "an awakened sense of responsibility" among non-partisan newspapers, which had "buried their personalities in the anonymity of their columns."[58]

It was a commonplace by the early twentieth century that only a commercial press run on "impartial" editorial lines was economically viable. The failure of partisan papers such as the Toronto *Empire* and Montreal's *La Minerve* seemed proof that strident partisanship did not pay. So editors made a virtue out of a necessity. They argued that a press based on "solid business principles" delivered the untainted news that readers wanted and better represented the public interest. Atkinson agreed in 1899 to take over the struggling *Toronto Star,* recently purchased by a group of Liberals, only if he could run it as a business enterprise and

57 Clark, "The Daily Newspaper," 101–4.

58 Editorial, *Canadian Printer and Publisher,* Aug. 1895, 5; Editorial, *ibid.,* Sept. 1910; 27; *Ottawa Journal,* 1 May 1929, 6.

not face interference by owners. He told Prime Minister Wilfrid Laurier, "A newspaper is a good ally but soon becomes useless (among the public) as the subsequent organ of a party."[59] Walter Nichol, publisher of the Vancouver *Province*, noted in 1901 how, for publishers, "business and not (political) sentiment, was the watchword of the hour, and to this cry everything is made to conform." Enterprise, accuracy, and reliability would become the standards. "Only the best and most intelligent would survive, and those which hang on to existence through drafts on the party pap bottle would have to succumb."[60]

Others thought that profits were more important to newspapers than ethics. Robertson of the *Toronto Telegram* said, "a newspaper is published to make money, and its educational influence is merely an incident in the business of making money." J.S. Brierley, publisher of the *Montreal Herald*, wondered why the paper owner should be "a moral policeman, governed by the Sermon on the Mount." He asked: "What right has the public to demand that their business shall be conducted with a view to the interests of the state?"[61]

With the business paper came the idea of political independence. Robertson was perhaps the earliest independent editor when in 1862 he said that the *Telegram* would support whomever would "serve the interests of the city, irrespective of party." In 1878, the president of the Canadian Press Association declared that a "healthy business tone" among newspaper men meant that they were no longer "slaves of the party." "All of this infuses a spirit of independence among our newspaper men that is fraught with the best results. Editors are for the most part not afraid now-a-days to talk straight out even at the risk of offending some interested politician."[62]

In Halifax, conservative publisher William Dennis decided to run the *Herald* and the *Mail* as "pure business" in the late 1890s. Government funding had dried up after Laurier's Liberals took power. Dennis's papers offered ideas that went against the Tory party line. "As a consequence his publications are read by Grit and Tory alike," explained one commentator. "He gets the circulation, and circulation commands the advertising and the advertising commands the cash."[63] Independence

59 J. Atkinson to Wilfred Laurier, 1 Dec. 1899, personal correspondence, Wilfred Laurier Papers, MG 26, G, Vol. 132, National Archives, Ottawa.

60 Nichol, "Newspapers from a Business Point of View," 10–11.

61 Quoted in Sotiron, *From Politics to Profit*, 12; *Printer and Publisher*, July 1896, 2.

62 Craick, *A History of Canadian Journalism in the Several Portions of the Dominion*, 90.

63 Taunton, "The Man behind the Halifax Herald," 38.

also applied to reporting. The Toronto *Evening Telegram* in 1899 described the reporter's aim: "His primary object, and, indeed, his only one, is to get the news he was sent for, and this he does irrespective of his own likes and dislikes, whether they be of a personal, social or political character."

Achieving true independence was a struggle, even though there were 37 independent dailies in Canada by 1900. The greatest editors of the era – Atkinson, Dafoe, and Williston, – walked a difficult line between political commitment and editorial freedom, between grovelling service to party and personal integrity. John Dafoe, the great liberal editor of the *Winnipeg Free Press* in the first quarter of the twentieth century, had to battle for his own ideas against the paper's owner, the powerful Liberal cabinet minister Clifford Sifton. Dafoe defined an independent paper as "any journal whose opinions are made on the premises by its owners and officers, and the making of which is affected only by considerations of public interest so far as they make an appeal and by the interests of the property itself."[64]

The career of John S. Willison is a case study in the difficulties of independence. His struggle for independent journalism at the Toronto *Globe* earned him only personal attacks from Liberals and misunderstanding from other journalists. Willison grew up in the party press system. He supported the Laurier Liberals when he reported from the Press Gallery in Ottawa. But his penchant for departing from the party line brought him into heated personal correspondence with politicians, caught between his Liberal sympathies and his desire to speak up for what was right.

In 1901, Willison wrote a bitter letter to Clifford Sifton rejecting Liberal complaints that the *Globe* was not "savage" enough in its criticisms of the Conservatives and that the paper gave too much space to Tory speeches. Sifton complained about the *Globe's* Ottawa correspondents. "You never had a man in whom our strong party would confide ... who would score for the government," wrote Sifton, adding that the current *Globe* correspondent hung around the Conservatives too much. Willison replied that the *Globe* gave five columns to Liberal speeches for every column to a Tory politician. Canada was the only "civilized country" left where papers "venture to discriminate in their news columns" in favour of one party or another.[65]

64 Ferguson, *John Wesley Dafoe*, 3; Dafoe, "Review," 14–24.

65 Willison to Sifton, 29 Jan. 1901, personal correspondence, Willison Papers, MG 27 II D15, Vol. 91, Reel C-530, National Library, Ottawa.

Willison pointed out that they lived in an age of professionals and public men. Even politicians used arguments, not abuse. "Is it fair that I should be asked to do what the self-respecting public man will not do? Have I not as much right to respect myself and my profession as have my critics?" To "pursue" opponents, Willison writes, was "disgraceful and contemptible ... and simply insulting." He added that he would appreciate more thanks from a Liberal Party that had invested $400,000 in papers over the previous five years, but nothing in the *Globe.* "Personally, I resent the assumption of every Liberal politician that I am his hired gun, that he has the right to criticize and condemn me and that he has the right to dictate or shape my course as a journalist. I claim as much freedom as any other liberal."

Willison caused a sensation in Canadian journalism in 1902 when he resigned from the *Globe* "to enter independent journalism" and edit the Toronto *News.* He admitted that it was hard to criticize former Liberal friends, "But is it not possible that there may be such a thing as public duty?" In a note to a reporter, he defined his independence:

> The paper to be acquired or established shall not be the organ of any political party or of any organized interest; and shall be absolutely independent of all business and corporate enterprise. The only objects in view are free and frank discussion of public questions, in no spirit of hostility to any party; to debate public questions only on public grounds; to further in a sane, rational and practical way all movements which seem to make for the public betterment; and, above all, not to employ the paper for the promotion of the private interests of any individual or groups of individuals.[66]

Canadian newspaper independence in the early twentieth century was therefore a precarious doctrine that tried to hang on to partisanship while meeting readers' demands for independent news and opinion. The chief editors of the era declared their independence yet were frequent guests at the homes of party leaders. Such behaviour appears to us inconsistent, but it did not bother most of them. We operate with a much stronger notion of journalism independence, and we do not live in the partisan society of that era. These editors made no claim to be perfectly neutral. They did not dispute the idea that a newspaper had party connections. They saw that as natural. What they did dispute, as the nineteenth century ended, was how strong those connections should be.

66 Colquhoun, *Press, Politics and People,* 93.

Editors began to revolt against tight party control of opinion and news. John Copper, secretary of the Canadian Publishers Association, tried to explain the idea of editorial independence in 1899. Copper was impressed, not disturbed, by the fact that many editors were politicians or the companions of politicians. He explained the independent paper as "never subservient, but always sympathetic."[67] *Printer and Publisher* in August 1895 said that newspapers, if fair, could support a party yet earn opponents' respect "sufficiently to secure their subscriptions and a share of their advertising."

The non-partisan (or independent) popular press was not without its critics. Like editors in England, Canadians such as Willison and Dafoe feared that, as news became more important than editorials, the press would steer clear of strong opinions and abandon its political role. Dafoe complained that publishers were keen to replace the "useless luxury" of an editorial with the comics or other "real circulation builders."[68] On 26 August 1905, the *Toronto Star* raised the issue of "Does Capital Threaten Liberty of the Press?" only to dismiss it.

The virtues of non-partisan journalism were still provoking debate early in the new century. The difference in perspectives is visible in the editorial philosophies of two legendary editors of the Ottawa *Journal*, – P.D. Ross and M. Grattan O'Leary. For Ross, partisan journalism was the worst fault of newspapers, causing a paper to be unfair and untruthful. Ross, an independent Conservative, thought that a paper could support the policies of a party but would lose influence as a party "mouthpiece." In contrast, O'Leary was an ardent Tory who thought neutrality one of the "deadly sins" in politics and newspapers. Democracy was better off if the press promoted strong views. People who avoided partisan political activities were "freedom's hypocrites." In his maiden speech to the Senate in 1962, the aging O'Leary declared proudly: "I am a party man. I am a partisan."[69]

The drift of history, however, was against the old partisan editors. The commercial press, with its preference for impartial news, just kept growing. Canadian daily newspaper circulation increased from 650,000 in 1900 to more than 1.3 million in 1911. The Southam newspapers, Canada's first chain, played a role in spreading the doctrines of independence and impartiality. Between 1877 and 1923, the Southam family

67 Copper, "The Editors of the Leading Canadian Dailies," 336–52.

68 Dafoe, "The Press Blamed for National Paralysis," 39.

69 I. Norman Smith, *The Journal Men*, 167.

established six dailies from Ottawa to Vancouver. When William Southam bought the *Hamilton Spectator* in 1877, he told the Conservative Party. "I will buy this thing and support you people, but I am running the paper and I am not your servant."

In 1919, when the conservative *Calgary Herald*, owned by Southam, took an increasingly independent editorial stance, the "machine" Tories threatened to set up a party organ. Publisher J.H. Woods told William Southam that he would like to turn the Herald into an "independent paper" without party affiliation. The paper would fight for western Canada and criticize both parties with equal enthusiasm. "That is the kind of paper I would like best to run and I believe it is the kind that will pay best in this country," he wrote.[70]

In 1897, sons Wilson and Harry Southam took over the *Ottawa Citizen*. Their first issue said: "The change in management will have no effect upon the Citizen's policy. Conservative it was born and Conservative it would die."[71] Yet, over several decades, the brothers moved the paper towards independence. In 1907 they issued to staff a list of rules for non-partisan reporting. Keep reports free from the bias of the reporter or the newspaper. Verify the correctness of every term, when possible. Give the other side of the story. Do not sacrifice accuracy for sensational effect, and avoid "unsavoury" news unfit for home reading. In a memo to out-of-town correspondents, they wrote: "Although politically the *Citizen* supports the policy of the Conservative party, correspondents should not allow this to interfere with their giving the Citizen impartial copy ... The *Citizen* is not the organ of any political party."[72]

The Southam chain issued a statement on independence in 1945. "The practice of the company is to leave the direction of editorial policy of each paper to the discretion of its local publisher who is an executive officer of the company. The company's objective in all of its newspapers is to preserve complete political independence and to present the news fairly and accurately."[73]

As more and more papers reduced their partisanship, traditional objectivity became the newsroom standard. The Southam memo was traditional objectivity in all but name. Four additional factors helped to clear a path for traditional objectivity: a non-partisan Dominion government

70 Bruce, *News and the Southams*, 116–17.

71 Ibid., 72.

72 Ibid., 84.

73 By 1919, Southam Inc. was worth over $4 million, it made a profit of $186,000 in 1921.

during the First World War, the merger of newspapers from the war onward, the establishment of the Canadian Press (CP) news agency, and the arrival of an objective society in industrializing Canada.

The election of a Union (non-partisan) federal government during the First World War muted party squabbles and press partisanship. Dafoe's *Free Press* announced that it was "out of party politics" for the rest of the war and that its duty was "serving the country."[74] The war also introduced difficult economic times for newspapers. Between 1914 and 1922, 40 dailies closed. In many towns, rival papers merged into one newspaper. The Halifax *Chronicle* and the Halifax *Herald* became the Halifax *Chronicle-Herald.* The number of dailies dropped from 143 in 1911 to 113 in 1921.[75]

The tough times continued into the 1930s. The result was a demand for neutral reporting that did not offend Liberal or Conservative readers. In 1936, John Bassett, vice-president of the *Montreal Gazette,* said that the "number of purely party organs can be counted on the fingers of one hand," mainly for economic reasons. Newspaper costs were so high that papers had to amalgamate, and news columns became unbiased as partisan papers ceased to play.

The ethic of independence would never have lifted off the ground if readers had not wanted objective reporting and independent opinion. Like the United States, a modernizing Canada was an increasingly objective society that valued objective information and professionalism. Other Canadians shared Willison's weariness with partisanship. Critics who see the rise of objectivity as the sad tale of a safe, homogeneous reporting style replacing a "glorious" personal journalism fail to appreciate how inglorious partisan reporting really was.

Willison's struggles provide insight into the unsavoury aspects of party journalism and show why many editors saw objective journalism as a positive development. Objectivity was replacing a corrupt, vindictive opinion press where politicians had journalists under their thumb. The plain

74 Editorial, "Winnipeg Free Press Out of Politics," *Canadian Printer and Publisher,* Oct. 1917, 29.

75 The war economy meant less advertising as costs soared. Wages for editorial staff represented 57.3 per cent of total costs of the *Ottawa Citizen* in 1900. In 1899, the *Toronto Star* had a staff of 52; by 1905, it had over 100. The Toronto *Telegram's* staff increased from 79 in 1891 to 156 in 1908. It cost Hugh Graham $1,000 to start the *Montreal Star* in 1869. Robertson spent $10,000 to begin the *Telegram* in 1876. Nichol sold the Vancouver *Province* to the Southam family in 1923 for $2.5 million.

fact is that the objective newspaper, in the main, was a better newspaper. It was more informative, more balanced, and more responsive to the public. It was the sort of paper that Canadians wanted to read. Slowly, partisanship and patronage, the political "glue" of Canada since before Confederation, were breaking down.

The rise of objective journalism occured against a social background of patronage and partisanship. The overwhelming strength of patronage in the nineteenth century made Canadian politics almost unique and shocked both American and British visitors. John A. Macdonald used patronage to create a disciplined Conservative party after Confederation.[76] Partisanship seeped into every crevice of public life and caused deep divisions. Once in place, patronage was difficult to uproot because so many people either had an interest in the status quo or wanted to become part of the status quo. Much was at stake. A change in government meant a loss of jobs for thousands of workers hired by the previous government.

No wonder then that journalism and politics intertwined closely. Until the First World War, the press benefited from party sponsorship of papers, government printing contracts and ads, purchase of additional subscriptions for propaganda purposes, and government appointments for loyal journalists. Journalism catapulted some editors into political careers, while some politicians felt it necessary to start papers. Laurier spent hundreds of thousands of dollars to create a Liberal newspaper network across Canada.

By the early twentieth century, however, Canadian society was growing wary of partisanship. E.F. Slack of the *Montreal Gazette* put it succinctly: "Newspapers to-day are business propositions. The public expects them to give the news of the day as it happens, without color or bias." Soon papers would have a model of objectivity to imitate – the Canadian Press (CP) news agency, established as a newspaper co-operative in 1917. It was an opportune time to spread the gospel of objectivity. Canada society was more objective, the business model of newspapers was solidly in place, and newspapers were merging, disposing them more to impartial news. CP's ability to provide timely news guaranteed that it would be influential.

CP made traditional objectivity its defining principle. It showed how to do objective reporting, and it disseminated the rules of objectivity in its well-

76 Stewart, *The Origins of Canadian Politics*, 71. Also, Moore has shown how, from 1878 to 1891, Prime Minister John A. Macdonald worked to reduce his vulnerability to parliamentary opposition by building a disciplined and obedient party, mostly by patronage. Moore, *1867*, 219

used stylebook.[77] Robert Fulford said that the CP's approach "helped make the distinction between unopinionated news columns and opinionated editorials ... both evident and real."[78] CP was impartial for the same reason that AP was. Reports had to be above suspicion of political bias if the agency was to satisfy over 100 newspapers. Meanwhile, CP helped to kill off struggling partisan papers by requiring entrance and annual fees for its service and by favouring the commercial papers. Brian Beaven has noted that in the 1920s "a new ideal of objectivity or balanced coverage defined the professional ethos of career journalists."[79] Fulford has stated that Canadian journalists by the 1930s were beginning to hear from their editors that their reports should be objective.[80] CP was largely responsible for this ethos.

The establishment of a CP bureau in Ottawa was probably the most important event in the history of objective reporting in Canada. The old partisan reporting and the new objective style clashed in Ottawa, the nation's capital. From the beginning of CP, some journalists had hoped that the agency would rid Canada of partisan reports. But this was not the view of most politicians in Ottawa. Used to preferential treatment by sympathetic newspapers, they did not welcome CP's "sternly impartial reports of political proceedings."

Nor did CP reporters fit in easily with the partisan Ottawa press gallery. Until at least 1911, reporters had sat on opposite sides of the gallery, depending on what party they supported.[81] Papers sent reporters to Ottawa to assist parties. Politicians talked only to sympathetic reporters, and governments gave "exclusives" to party papers. But as the CP model spread, after the First World War, politicians had to tolerate a more objective approach by reporters. CP stories on Parliament filled the front pages of newspapers across Canada. CP's success put pressure on newspaper editors to adopt the objective approach. When observers compared a newspaper's partisan report with an objective CP report, the latter usually was more balanced and informative.

Moreover, newspapers that were members of the CP co-operative had to send their main stories to CP for distribution across Canada. Hence their reports were supposed to be as objective as possible. Finally, newspaper editors could hardly demand objective copy from CP without asking the same

77 The *Report of the Special Senate Committee on Mass Media* (Davie Committee) stated that CP was so reliable and objective that "even politicians trust it" (1:229).

78 Fulford, "A Sort of Reckless Courage," 1:13.

79 Beaven, "Journalism," 1221–2.

80 Fulford, "A Sort of Reckless Courage," 1:13.

81 Cumming, "Parliamentary Press Gallery," 1763.

from their own reporters. The practice of objectivity grew from these initial steps. CP had inaugurated nationally an objective form of reporting that could trace its roots back to the independence movement and the struggles of Willison late in the previous century.

We get an insider's glimpse at the development of the ideal of objectivity in the terse minutes of the CP's annual meetings. The minutes show constant concern for objectivity in the formative period of the 1920s. In 1921, E. Norman Smith, the CP president, told the annual meeting "that the reputation of CP for accuracy, thoroughness and absolute non-partisanship has steadily grown among the parliamentary representatives of the people in Ottawa." At the 1922 meeting, Smith said that CP's coverage of a recent federal election meant that "no general election campaign in Canada was ever covered so thoroughly and so fairly." Smith told CP editors: "Your staff was drilled in nonpartisanship – neither by omission nor commission must they falter."[82]

The personalities of the early CP senior editors embodied this adherence to careful, factual reporting. Livesay, who retired in 1939 after 20 years as general manager, was austere in appearance and spoke with a stammer. His aesthetics of writing news valued economy and clarity of expression. Every redundant word was to be hunted down like a criminal and eliminated. "Make your stuff hard," Livesay would tell his staff. Great writing was achievable only by "assiduous practice, repression and selection."[83] M.E. Nichols of the *Winnipeg Tribune*, a former CP president (1931–33), said that his history of CP tried to "strictly follow the historical facts without offending anyone unnecessarily with bluntness or harshness of expression."[84]

National elections put CP's objectivity to the test. Politicians would use any CP inaccuracy to accuse the agency of bias. Rules for election coverage were needed. In this way, CP in the interwar years gradually added to the rules of traditional objectivity. In 1935, Livesay issued an election circular to CP staff, saying that the CP had "no object to serve but the impartial presentation of fact." Reporters were to use quotations only for important statements, scrutinize sources for partisan motivations, and avoid colourful descriptions of political rallies. "Leads must be brief and factual ... The interpretive lead is a trap to be avoided." There would be

82 CP annual meeting, Toronto, 5 May 1921, 7; CP annual meeting, Toronto, 2 May 1922, 5. From the official minutes of the CP's annual meetings, provided by CP headquarters in Toronto.

83 Quoted in I. Norman Smith, *J.F.B. Livesay*, 11.

84 E. Norman Smith papers, Nichols to E. Norman Smith, personal correspondence, 30 Nov. 1948, National Archives, Ottawa. Nichols was commenting on his book about CP being well received in the newspaper industry.

no by-lines for campaign reporting because a by-line "adds nothing to the authority of the report."[85]

Objectivity was a widespread ideal by the 1930s. J.R. MacMillan of the Canadian Newspaper Association said in 1937 that national unity required "newspapermen to maintain an objective attitude towards life because ... honest information had become essential to the public as food and shelter."[86] As in the United States, in Canada editors repeated the clichés about how reporters should report the facts and let the chips fall where they may. Looking back on Canadian newspaper history, journalist George Bain complained that the colourful newspaper was on its way out in the late 1930s and had nearly disappeared by the end of the Second World War. It gave way to a paper "in which the key word was Objectivity, with a capital O."[87]

However, these so-called objective papers were not without bias or subjective forms of reporting. Objective reporting coexisted with campaigns for social reform in the pages of the *Toronto Star.* Atkinson in 1933 wrote that the *Toronto Star* would be a "tireless, unremitting, propagandist" for the slow advance of human justice, through social programs such as unemployment insurance and old-age pensions. In the 1930s, the Toronto *Globe* and *Telegram* reflected anti-Jewish sentiment in the city. They supported an anti-communist frenzy and used it to oppose the rights of workers to unionize or strike. The right-leaning *Telegram* dismissed the *Star's* reports of Nazi atrocities in Germany as "sensational" and inaccurate.

Too many papers failed to oppose draconian federal legislation making "unlawful assembly" a criminal offence with a maximum jail term of 20 years. The law defined "unlawful assembly" so loosely that it extended to just about anyone who was against the government. Police could arrest and send to jail, without a trial, people whom they suspected of being a communist.

In the 1950s, an all-out newspaper war in Toronto between the *Star* and the *Telegram* caused reporters to invent facts and even stories.[88] By

85 Livesay, "General Election Circular," 9 Feb. 1935.

86 *Montreal Gazette,* 11 March 1937, 13.

87 Bain, *Gotcha!,* vii.

88 Val Sears, who reported for the Toronto *Telegram,* has recounted the sensational scoops of the period. One story was about a young girl, Marion McDowell, who was kidnapped from a "lover's lane" in Scarborough, Ontario. The *Telegram* brought in a legendary Scotland Yard inspector to investigate, Robert Fabian. Sears wrote up his material. According to Sears, Fabian "hoked up a series of investigations," including a false report that they had found the woman's "knickers." The *Star's* reporters could not verify some of the Fabian–Sears alleged "facts" because, as Sears stated, these facts had come "from a Scotch bottle." Sears, "Star and Tely Duke It Out," part of a series on the *Toronto Star's* 110th anniversary, www.thestar.com (1 Nov. 2002).

the late 1950s, some publishers sought to wean their reporters off sensational reporting. Michael Pieri, a former *Toronto Star* reporter, recalled how publisher Beland Honderich spent many of his early years at the paper attempting to pound "his own code of ethics into the heads of *Star* editors more used to the razzle-dazzle, high octane brand of journalism." The stress on "truth" was so strong that it gave the impression that it was a novel concept in journalism. "Many journalists who couldn't – or wouldn't – change their ways from 1955 onwards simply lost their jobs if they did not see things Publisher Beland Honderich's way." Cub reporters and a "few old timers" attended evening lectures on style and logical thinking. The sessions included "heavy and frequent references to Greek and Latin scholars, and the British press."[89]

Making a Modern Code

To see how objectivity has fared since its heyday, we need only examine what role it played recently in the making of a code of ethics. In April 2002, the Canadian Association of Journalists (CAJ), with over 1,500 members, approved its first statement of principles at an annual meeting in Ottawa.

I chaired the committee that drafted the statement and an accompanying set of ethical guidelines. From the beginning, the committee wanted the statement to be succinct and positive in tone, expressing the best qualities of Canadian journalism. The committee believed that CAJ members would reject any mechanism to enforce the code as a threat to a free press. Its deliberations divided the committee between "empty" generalizations and a code that was too detailed. The answer was to add specific guidelines to the statement. Throughout the committee's work, no one advanced objectivity as a possible principle or guideline. Instead, members cited related concepts: accuracy, credibility, fairness, independence, and so on.

The committee, in not including the ideal of objectivity, indicated the ambiguous status of objectivity in journalism today. Criticisms of objectivity, combined with changing journalism attitudes, have taken a heavy toll on the concept's popularity. As we have seen above, even bastions of traditional objectivity, such as CP, enriched their objective style from the 1970s onward. Most journalists today do not reject the idea that a news reporter should *try* to be objective, in a loose sense; but they do not want objectivity as a formal principle. They no longer need the cry of objectivity to beat back the spectre of blatant political partisanship, as their predecessors did in the early twentieth century.

89 Michael Pieri, e-mail correspondence with author, 13 Nov. 2002.

In addition, many journalists believe that objectivity can restrict good storytelling and good journalism. They feel that journalism should no longer restrain itself with commitments to strict neutrality or stern, Livesay-like restrictions on interpretation. Other journalists think that "objectivity" is too ambitious a term. They believe that it entails absolute detachment, an impossible purity of motivation, or lack of passion. In short, they reject traditional objectivity and its exaggerated norms. Tom Kent, who led a royal commission on newspapers over 20 years ago, argued recently that truth in journalism must go beyond a recital of facts to include honest and fair investigation, as deadlines permit. In the end, "what is reached is truth as the writer sees it that day. There can be no claim to detached objectivity."[90]

This change in attitudes towards objectivity has affected other codes of ethics. Most major codes no longer use the word "objectivity."[91] In the mid-1990s, the Society of Professional Journalists removed the term from its code and added "accountability." In other cases, "impartiality" has replaced "objectivity." Code builders know that advocacy journalists, investigative reporters, and news reporters are more likely to agree with the norms of accuracy, fairness, and independence than with objectivity. What remains of objectivity in the codes is the older, less rigorous idea, as found in the code of the American Society of News Editors, of a "clear distinction for the reader between news reports and opinion." Or objectivity gives way to talk of a diversity of views in stories or a "respect for facts." The code of ethics of Quebec journalists refers to a "critical viewpoint" so that journalists "methodically doubt everything; impartially so they research and expose the diverse aspects of a given situation." A few codes in other countries use the word "objective." The Danish national code of ethics insists that court reporting "be objective." This is typical of what remains of the once proud language of objectivity.

What were the factors that prompted the CAJ code? Criticism within and outside journalism about a decline in standards was one. But it expressed itself as concern not for lack of objectivity but rather for accu-

90 Tom Kent, "A Public Trust," series on *Toronto Star*'s 110th anniversary, www.thestar.com (6 Nov. 2002).

91 The Canadian Daily Newspaper Association (now the Canadian Newspaper Association) wrote its first statement of principles in 1977, crafted mainly by former *Toronto Star* journalist Borden Spears. It updated the document in 1995. The code has sections on freedom of the press, independence, accuracy and fairness, community responsibility, and respect. Objectivity does not appear.

racy, fairness, and independence. Criticism created the need for a code as a rhetorical instrument to advance standards and defend journalism. In particular, CAJ executives wanted a set of approved principles that explained to the public what the association stood for and disarmed the charge that CAJ officials were only stating personal beliefs in their public statements.

Association members were also acutely aware that Canadian journalism was undergoing fundamental change. The future of independent, quality journalism was uncertain. On-line journalism, the 24-hour news clock, the proliferation of media, new technology, intense competition in a multi-media market, and a concentration of ownership were raising new issues or reviving old ones with new urgency.

Journalists worried especially about the editorial policies of the Winnipeg-based CanWest Global news corporation, which had purchased daily newspapers across Canada. Global already owned a national TV network. In Ottawa, numerous reporters told me confidentially about their fears of improper editorial interference in their work. What was crucial was the *perception* of potential interference. Even journalists who were sceptics about codes felt that it "wouldn't hurt" to have one.

Members' feedback to a draft of the CAJ's statement of principles revealed that professionalism and editorial independence were key concerns.[92] "The code will generate a lot of discussion and move our profession forward," said one journalist. "I think it is appropriate, especially in these troubled [journalistic] times, for the CAJ to articulate professional behaviour." One journalist said the code would help students know "what the professional ideal is. However, a document like this also shows how far some organizations have strayed from the ideal." Restraint on misbehaviour was another reason: "If every journalist followed these precepts, distortion in reporting would not be as prevalent as it is these days."

One journalist expressed the anxiety of today's practitioners: "I agree wholeheartedly with these statements ... But are they meaningful in the current concentrated ownership climate? It's all well and good for journalists to say this, but it's an entirely different thing ... when decisions on content come from much higher up the ladder – from people who probably aren't aware these guidelines are in the works and probably don't care either."

The reasons for constructing the CAJ's code differed little in principle from the ethical and professional concerns of the journalists of the late nineteenth and early twentieth centuries. Studies on the history of

92 These comments by CAJ members reached the author by e-mail between December 2001 and March 2002.

codes show that these documents are responses to cynical publics, the threat of government intervention, and calls for professional standards.[93] The CAJ code was no different. Professionalism, misbehaviour, criticism, commercial pressures, and the integrity of journalists continue to haunt journalists in the early twenty-first century. These concerns now rise amid global journalism, which is vying for a slice of a media-saturated market.

CONCLUSION: THE EMERGENCE OF TRADITIONAL OBJECTIVITY

We are now in a position to summarize the factors that explain the arrival of objectivity. The invention of traditional objectivity required two large steps. The first was establishment of a liberal press in the nineteenth century. The primary materials for the construction of objectivity came from two forms of this liberal press – the elite liberal press, idealistically defined as a serious-minded educator and elevator of public opinion, and a popular press devoted to the technology and business of news, not to the manufacture of partisan opinion. Papers claimed to be independent and to speak for the public at large. Their news articles combined "active empiricism" in factual reporting and love of a good story. Despite the sensationalism, a proto-objective journalism that believed in factuality, independence, and impartiality existed by the late nineteenth century, its philosophy forming the content of the first journalism codes.

The second step in objectivity occurred in the first half of the twentieth century. Journalists went beyond empiricism. They developed their reporting methods and formed professional associations. They strengthened their interpretation of the norms of factuality and independence until they arrived at the ideal of traditional objectivity.

Why did journalists accept the restraints of objectivity, after centuries of freewheeling journalism? Objectivity arose at the intersection of confidence and concern in the commercial newspaper. The success of the popular press led to confidence that reporters could (and should) devote themselves to the impartial gathering of news – the core business of the popular paper. Concerns about the popular press led to a stress on objectivity to counter-balance sensationalism and partisanship.

Cracks in confidence in the "new journalism" grew into a crisis of confidence in the early twentieth century. Could the press find a middle way between a debased commercial newspaper and a fading, elite upper-

93 Limor and Gabel, "Five Versions of One Code of Ethics," 136–54.

class press? Objectivity became dominant quickly because both journalists and publishers supported it, albeit for different reasons.

For publishers, objective news made business sense. The idea of impartial news was appealing to the business model of newspapers in the early twentieth century. Objective news suited the purpose of the commercial paper. It met reader's demand for reliable news and less partisan comment. It built up circulation and advertising revenue. It was less offensive and less libellous. The objective style suited the new technologies for gathering news and for manufacturing news in large newsrooms. A public commitment to objectivity promoted the view that journalism could be respectable and responsible and could regulate itself.

Journalists supported traditional objectivity for positive and negative reasons. Positively, objectivity became a defining feature of their progressive profession. Journalists exaggerated their norms and insisted on method so as to enhance their claim to be a profession. Objectivity would help them join the magic circle of professions. The popularity of journalism objectivity reflected the growth of an objective society that valued impartial experts and facts and devalued partisan attitudes towards public life.

Negatively, objectivity gathered support because it was a response to a range of worrisome developments. A strong dose of objectivity seemed an antidote to excessive yellow journalism. Objective, professional journalism appeared the only viable option to a corrupt, partisan press or to a sensational popular press. Only a stern objective press could cure the disease of irresponsible journalism apparently taking over the popular press.

Finally, objectivity provided an ideal and a method to protect journalists from manipulative agents in the public sphere and from manipulative press barons. It also protected them somewhat from public criticism. It looked as if only a stern, objective press could ensure that as much objective information as possible reached the public sphere.

Journalists did not react to subjectivity in journalism and in the public sphere by giving up on objectivity. Instead, they stressed the standards of objectivity all the more and added rules and methods. Instead of admitting that all news had a subjective element, they drew a hard line between objective news and subjective opinion. They claimed that reporters could clearly separate fact and value, fact and interpretation. They insisted that reporters could be independent only if they were perfectly detached. For objectivists, the "only thing safe in a newspaper ... was a fact," and to move beyond that was to trespass into "dangerous ground." Reporters who offered their opinion and interpretation interfered with the public's right to judge the facts for themselves. They forgot their "humble duties as reporters of the news ... [setting] themselves up as gods" who created news. In addition, the subjectivity of the public sphere required a stress on neutrality and balance. If all opinions were subjective, and if all parties claimed to have the facts, then the reporter could only balance the contending views.[94]

These many factors and social trends combined to turn empiricism into traditional objectivity – a doctrine constructed for a world grown complex and uncertain. If the image of the nineteenth-century journalist is that of an eager reporter in a fedora hunting down sensational stories, that of the twentieth-century objective reporter is one of a cautious professional with a positivist's suspicion of value judgments and bias. The objective journalist is a rule-bound Cartesian, searching for certainty and absolute facts in a confusing, deceitful world.

EPILOGUE: OBJECTIVITY AND ETHICAL INVENTION

Having followed the path of 400 years of journalism, we can better appreciate the idea that journalism ethics was, and continues to be, a sphere of invention. The ethical invention of objectivity may appear more obvious to us than the ethical inventions of the newsbook editor or the eighteenth-century public journalist. This is because the events that shaped objectivity are closer to us in time. Also, the invention of objectivity is more evident because journalism ethics in general became more explicit and self-conscious in the early twentieth century. With the rising power of the press, journalism ethics, including objectivity, became a subject of debate across society. Journalism ethics acquired a higher public profile with the creation of codes of ethics, professional associations, journalism schools, and public inquiries into the press.

The invention of objectivity followed the general pattern of earlier inventions, as I described above in my rhetorical theory of value change. Once again, the impulse for invention came from a change in the journalist–audience relationship. In the second half of the nineteenth century, the business of news altered that relationship radically. The primary role of the journalist changed from that of a liberal educator of the public, mainly through opinion, to that of a mass informer – a news "hound" who delivered the latest news. Early in the twentieth century,

94 Newbold Noyes, Jr, *Editor and Publisher,* 9 May 1953, and R.L. Spangler, *Publisher's Auxiliary,* 3 March 1955. Cited in MacDougall, *Interpretive Reporting,* 17. Noyes was national news editor of the *Evening Star* in Washington, D.C. His remarks were a recollection of the AP's founders and their belief in objectivity.

reporters had to become more than reckless news hounds – namely, responsible, objective reporters. Readers of a mass society increasingly dependent on accurate press information came to expect reporters to act more professionally. They expected objective information. More and more, readers grew impatient with the excesses of yellow journalism. They worried about the manipulation of journalists by their press owners, by "business interests," and by press agents.

To meet these changing expectations, and growing scepticism, journalists invented a tougher approach to factual reporting – objectivity. The rhetoric of the objective editor was, like that of the newsbook editor, aimed at reassuring the public and developing higher standards for journalism. Journalism ethics in the early twentieth century was awash in rhetoric about the neutrality of reports and the hard line between news and opinion. Editors never tired of "just the facts." This rhetoric may strike us today as incredibly naïve or exaggerated or cynical. But we are looking back after decades of scepticism about pure facts.

To appreciate the attraction of a stern objectivity in journalism, we need to remember that it was a reasonable rhetorical response to deep concerns about the press, within and outside journalism. Objectivity was not just a convenient ideology of press owners. It was an ideal sincerely advocated by a large number of journalists. It was a reaction to a chorus of criticism and threats of government intervention. Journalists could no longer claim, without serious challenge, that the press was omnipotent and a disinterested tribune of the people. The ideal of objectivity also responded to an acute awareness among journalists that they needed a firm set of standards to help them counter-balance the forces of subjectivity in the manipulative public sphere. At the same time, the espousal of objectivity was a rhetorical reply to objectivity's "other" – muckrakers, interpretive journalists, and sensational tabloid reporters. Objectivity was a rhetorical weapon by which journalists could articulate and defend their belief in impartial, factual journalism. It was a way to articulate their idea of the journalist as an impartial public communicator.

Although the doctrine of traditional objectivity was an over-reaction and conceptually implausible, we should not be uncharitable to its originators. For all its faults, it was a positive step in the development of a responsible, independent, modern journalism. Before we curtly dismiss traditional objectivity as a sham, we should place ourselves in the position of concerned journalists of the 1920s, 1930s, and 1940s. Buffeted by controversy and powerful crosscurrents in society, these journalists looked for a way forward for their profession. They invented objectivity as an ethical signpost in troubled times.

PART THREE

Pragmatic Objectivity

7

Pragmatic Objectivity

Within our own total evolving doctrine, we can judge truth as earnestly and absolutely as can be; subject to correction, but that goes without saying.

W.V. Quine[1]

BEYOND TRADITIONAL OBJECTIVITY

Having followed the thread of objectivity through the labyrinth of cultural and journalism history, we arrive at what appears to be a dead end. Traditional news objectivity is, by all accounts, a spent ethical force, doubted by journalist and academic. Two options loom for journalism ethics. One is the invention of a different norm that can take over objectivity's role of restraining and evaluating reports. Another is a redefinition of objectivity so that it is more appropriate for the journalism of today and the foreseeable future.

This chapter takes the second option. It provides a theory of journalism objectivity by analyzing how we evaluate inquiry in both theoretical and practical domains. Traditional objectivity is rejected as an incorrect theory of journalistic inquiry, built upon an indefensible epistemology and a false characterization of reporting as passively empirical. The epistemology of traditional objectivity presupposes epistemic dualisms of fact/value and fact/interpretation that distort our understanding of how we know, interpret and value. Traditional objectivity is flawed by the mistaken belief that objectivity requires claims to be based on absolute standards or facts, as ascertained by neutral, perspective-less agents. In practice, traditional objectivity lacks the ethical force to guide journalists because criticisms of objectivity have cast a pall of doubt over the ideal. Moreover, the relevancy of an old-fashioned objectivity of "just the

1 Quine, *Word and Object*, 25.

facts" to contemporary journalism is questionable. Journalists in both mainstream newsrooms and on the Internet experiment with more interpretive, interactive, story telling.

This charge against traditional objectivity puts the onus on pragmatic objectivity to offer an alternative epistemology and ethic of journalism. We have to march fearlessly into the contested area of normative analysis, armed with proposals on how we *should* conceive of objectivity and what journalism *should* be. We have to engage imaginatively in ethical invention. Most of this book describes how journalists came to espouse ethical norms. This chapter presents my own values. I begin by explaining the criteria that any new ideal of objectivity must satisfy and present the basic concepts of pragmatic objectivity. Then I explain why pragmatic objectivity is valuable.

Our historical survey indicates how to move beyond traditional objectivity by noting where it went astray. Chapter 5 stated that the fatal error came in the nineteenth century, when journalists started to explain their objectivity in terms of a recording of events, as they are, allegedly devoid of the reporter's interpretation, values, or perspective. Journalists were objective insofar as they were passively empirical. Only reporters who "merely" recorded the facts could claim to be objective. The epistemology of traditional objectivity grounds itself in the persistent metaphor of the journalist as a passive recorder who aspires to be a perfect recording instrument. As long as recording was the central notion, objectivity could be understood as the passive intake and transmission of information. Objectivity was about recording with "high fidelity," as phonographs promised. Ironically, reporters in the nineteenth century were never more active in selecting story angles, facts, and sources. As the new century got under way, the doctrine of traditional objectivity attempted to discipline this activity by exaggerating the norms of detachment and impartiality far beyond reasonable expectations. Traditional objectivity was sure to meet with scepticism once the cultural climate changed. And change it did.

By mid-century, defenders of objectivity faced scepticism about universal methods, pure facts, and a rational public sphere. Other forms of journalism, from muckraking to a more intimate broadcast journalism, challenged the dominance of objectivity. Journalism's new technology, its desire to tell good stories, and its romantic, self-expressive impulses could not fit within strict, traditional objectivity. Yet these changing attitudes did not lead to a serious reformulation of traditional objectivity. Since the profession had invested so much ethical capital in traditional objectivity as a defining principle, the natural reaction was to defend objectivity against all comers. The clash of objectivists and their critics produced heated rhetoric, not thoughtful reform. Long after the epistemology of positivism had died in academia, journalists continued to espouse a traditional objectivity.

From this historical vantage point, what are the criteria that any thoughtful reform of objectivity must satisfy? First, as I indicated in chapter 2, journalism objectivity needs to be fallible and practical. Objectivity must provide normative guidance for journalism conceived of as a way of practice. Objectivity in journalism should take its inspiration from attempts to be objective in other practical domains – professions such as law and public administration. It should seek models in modern ways of practice, where a fallible, imperfect sense of objectivity is dominant and the goal is reasonable judgment in a context.

Second, a reformed objectivity must be an inventive and relevant response to the changing rhetorical relationship between journalists and their audiences. This means that the history of journalism should inform any new theory of objectivity. Such a theory should retain what is of value in previous conceptions of objectivity, while keeping an eye to the new forms of journalism. Third, it must do more than criticize other conceptions. It must be a positive doctrine, putting forward its own distinctive standards and concepts.

The reinvention of journalistic objectivity begins with new epistemological foundations. Traditional objectivity built on discredited epistemic assumptions. A theory of news objectivity must be a more sophisticated empiricism that does not insist on drawing a hard line between facts and values and does not seek to eliminate all judgment and evaluation in reports. A new theory should incorporate recent insights from philosophy, history, and the social sciences into knowledge as an interpretive, social enterprise.

The epistemic challenge is to develop a coherent idea of how journalists can objectively evaluate interpretations that arise from inquiry, whether the interpretations involve news reports, analysis, or argumentation. Nothing short of a philosophical re-evaluation of journalism objectivity will produce a theory that is intellectually and practically defensible.

The aim of a theory of pragmatic objectivity is to find a place for objectivity in a world where fact, value, theory, and practical interests intertwine inextricably. Pragmatic objectivity does not require detachment from all values and perspectives – an impossible demand. Instead, it tests the essential activities of interpreting, evaluating, and adopting a perspective. Objectivity operates as an instrument of rational restraint within the pragmatic, purposive activity of journalism. Pragmatic objectivity is acutely aware of, and therefore allows for, human failings; it wears a human face.[2]

In what follows, I construct my theory of pragmatic objectivity by defining the notions of pragmatic inquiry, holistic interpretation, and objectivity in general. Then I explore the possible relevance of these concepts for journalism. Finally I explore their implications for the future of journalistic practice.

PRAGMATIC OBJECTIVITY

Pragmatic Inquiry

Pragmatic objectivity is the evaluation of the means and results of inquiry. Current beliefs, theories, and methodological norms are the tentative results of past inquiry, providing a platform for further inquiries. The emphasis on process – on tentative results and the seeking of truth – follows from the fact that, even though firm, objective truth is a worthy goal, there are many occasions when we are not sure of having reached it. In practical activities, rigorous proof is a rare achievement. In journalism, the practitioner occupies a precarious epistemological situation. He or she bases reports on limited data, imperfect methods, conflicting values, and changing conditions. Self-interested rhetoric assails him or her from all sides. Therefore a theory of journalism objectivity should talk about imperfect procedures and about standards that *point* in the direction of truth.

To summarize, my idea of objective evaluation of inquiry is as follows. Inquiry interprets events with the assistance of conceptual schemes. The inquirer can reform and improve his or her schemes of understanding but can never completely transcend them.[3] The inquirer understands phenomena holistically, against a background of preexisting ideas that

2 My theory of pragmatic objectivity owes much to the work of the Harvard philosophers W.V. Quine and Hilary Putnam and to their pragmatist predecessors, William James and John Dewey. My phrase "objectivity with a human face" echoes the title of Putnam, *Realism with a Human Face.*

3 The idea that our situation influences our understanding has been a major philosophical theme since Descartes's attempt to transcend the prejudices of his culture. More recently, the overcoming of one's situation has been a theme in the work of Hans-Georg Gadamer. See Gadamer's, *Truth and Method,* and Ipperciel, "Descartes and Gadamer on Prejudice," 635–52.

form the content of his or her conceptual schemes. The objective evaluation of ideas is holistic, also. Beliefs are objective insofar as they satisfy, to some degree, the best available epistemic standards. Objectivity comprises general standards for all modes of inquiry and specific standards that vary according to the domain in question. The objective standards can serve as criteria of justification because they have contributed to successful inquiry in the past.

My notion of objectivity as an imperfect test of belief presupposes a pragmatic view of inquiry. Inquiry is the natural activity of a highly evolved organism motivated to explore, understand, and control phenomena as it navigates a perilous natural and social environment. Both theoretical knowledge and practical wisdom are outcomes of that exploration. Careful observation is part of knowing, but the inquirer is not a passive spectator but an active, purpose-driven agent in a social setting. Similarly, the inquirer's mind is not a private theatre where the "mind's eye" passively views ideas. "Mind" is an umbrella term for a complex of skills, functions, and abilities that aid active inquiry of the world.[4] This cognizing, inquiring organism is pragmatic. He or she goes out into the world to test hypotheses, to solve problems, to find the best means to ends. Ideas are mental tools that organize and predict experience. He or she evaluates methods according to whether they help achieve goals.

Pragmatic inquiry is neither an intellectual elitism that privileges abstract thought over practical thinking (and action) nor a crude pragmatism that privileges action and "results" over thought. The mind's ability to construct cognitive representations of the world and its ability to reason practically about action are equally valuable features of human beings. Aristotle, who reached the height of abstraction in his *Metaphysics,* could recognize also the value of practical reason – the habit of forethought – as fundamental to life. Pragmatists should not devalue the ways of theoretical truth in favour of the ways of practice. Our ability to theorize about phenomena, for no practical purpose, is part of human flourishing. It is part of a continuum of stances that we can take towards the world. The continuum ranges from the instrumental use of physical materials to an intellectual engagement with abstract ideas. Valid inquiry can take place anywhere along the continuum.

4 Some psychologists and philosophers of mind have argued that the brain, or intelligence, is not just "one" thing or one faculty but a grab bag of many specific functions that have evolved over time. Some writers even question the idea of a unity of consciousness. See Dennett, *Consciousness Explained,* and Gardner, *Frames of Mind.*

Pragmatic objectivity sees contingency, vulnerability, and fallibility at the heart of all things human.[5] We, as a species, are a contingent product of a contingent evolutionary process. Biological evolution has been supplemented by a contingent cultural evolution that has resulted in modern society, language, art, science, and organized inquiry. Non-genetic learning defines much of what it means to be human.[6] Rational inquiry is the activity of one fragile species in a tiny part of an expanding universe. Inquiry is the activity of an organism that happened to develop a relatively large brain with remarkable cognitive abilities and self-consciousness. The contingency and imperfection of knowledge or society neither surprise nor dishearten the pragmatist. He or she believes that mature acceptance of contingency prevents us from fleeing into the arms of absolutism in knowledge and authoritarianism in politics. Pragmatism is the hard-won but modest wisdom that celebrates constructive activity in a contingent world. Humans give meaning to their lives through purposeful activity. No grand metaphysical plan bestows meaning on our earthly labours. The pragmatist is an imperfectionist, poised between naïve idealism and cynical despair.

Pragmatic inquiry is also situated inquiry. There is no hope of philosophically transcending all places and times to reach some universal, transcendent truth that exists apart from all human perspective and interest. Pragmatic inquiry does not require that we wipe our minds clean of all presuppositions and start fresh from absolute propositions. What is possible is a partial transcendence of our current situation through well-designed inquiry, questioning, imagination, and interaction with other ways of thinking.

The pragmatic inquirer, despite his or her awareness of contingency, should not be a denier or demoter of truth.[7] Truth is an indispensable ideal for genuine inquiry. But what conception of truth will suffice? Philosophers have offered definitions in terms of correspondence with fact,

5 Nussbaum, in *The Fragility of Goodness,* shows how notions of luck and vulnerability influenced ancient Greek ethics and drama.

6 On the importance of non-genetic learning and culture to an inquiry into truth, see Williams, *Truth and Truthfulness,* 22–30.

7 Williams argues against two approaches to truth – the "deniers" and the "common sense party." The common-sense party believes it an adequate response to the deniers to point out that it is only common sense to believe in many ordinary truths, from the fact that Moscow is the capital of Russia to snow is white. *Truth and Truthfulness,* 5–7.

coherence of ideas, well-justified belief, or successful prediction.[8] My view of pragmatic inquiry requires only a modest conception of truth that is close to common sense. The ordinary concept of truth that we use every day is straightforward: a statement (proposition, belief) is true if and only if what the statement says is actually the case.[9] What makes the statement that grass is green true is the case that grass is green. Aristotle said as much when he explained truth as a matter of saying of what is that it is.

This view of truth is realist because it expresses the intuition that the truth "maker" is external to the truth bearer – the belief or statement.[10] Truth is about something independent of our wishes and imaginings, about which we can be mistaken. As Dummett wrote: "The roots of truth and falsity lie in the distinction between a speaker being, objectively, *right* or *wrong* in what he says when he makes an assertion."[11]

My view of truth is minimalist because it contains a minimum of philosophical assumptions. It does not assume a metaphysical or scientific view about what actually is the case. It does not depend on a philosophical theory of truth or epistemology. It does not pretend to be a substantial definition of truth in more basic or clearer terms. Davidson has warned us about the "folly" of trying to find such a definition. We can elucidate truth only by other terms, such as belief, desire, and reference.[12] The idea of truth is as basic as we can go.

The fact that truth is basic does not mean that we cannot say interesting things about it. Once the minimalist conception of truth is in place, we can philosophize about truth to our heart's content. We can trace its web of connections to concepts such as justified belief, knowledge, facts, and "what is the case." We can investigate the kinds of truth and the kinds of justification. But these elaborations should not obscure our clear-eyed commitment to the simple idea of truth as what is the case.

8 Theories of truth are so numerous and technical that it is impossible to do justice to their variety in this short section. My aim is not a philosophical exegesis and critique of theories of truth but to identify a basic conception of truth that is useful and adequate for a pragmatic theory of inquiry and objectivity.

9 Alston, *A Realist Conception of Truth*, 5. Alston's book defends the idea of a minimalist and realist theory of truth.

10 Ibid., 7.

11 Dummett, *Truth and Other Enigmas*, xvii.

12 See Davidson, "The Folly of Trying to Define Truth," 264–5.

We do not pursue just any sort of truth. Inquiry seeks important and secure (or well-evidenced) truths.[13] The pursuit of significant truth is difficult. The world resists our attempts to discover or change it. We seek methods of discovery and standards of evaluation because truth is not directly accessible.[14] Truth does not reduce to justification. You may, by luck or hunch, have a true belief without justification; a justified belief can be false. Nor does truth reduce to the standards of objectivity. It is possible for a false belief to satisfy objective standards and objective evidence. The standards of objectivity are means to truth, not truth itself.

My pragmatic view of inquiry does not entail that investigators will converge on one, unique Truth through one, unique, Scientific Method. Truth and its methods are plural. There are many ways to investigate the world. Science deserves recognition as a distinct and impressive approach to truth. The unity of science is not the unity of one, rigorous method, but an informal association of evolving sciences with overlapping but not identical approaches. Often in science, there is only general agreement on what is rational and plausible or on what constitutes evidence.

Science provides many types of description of one and the same phenomenon. There are, for example, many levels of description of the brain – the levels of physics and chemistry, of biological functioning, and of explicit mental operations, such as the formation of belief and reasoning. Scientists seek lawful, causal theories of the world. Artists, in contrast, engage the world in a different manner, producing new insights. Rembrandt articulated his deep knowledge of the self, with all its fears and vanities, not in psychological theory but in self-portraits.

Pragmatic objectivity ascribes to a fallibilistic theory of truth. Our truths are not only plural; they are fallible. There is no guarantee that our most fundamental and seemingly secure beliefs will not need revision. Fallibilism walks between absolutism and extreme scepticism. Both absolutism and extreme scepticism agree that, if there are no absolute

13 There are goals for inquiry other than truth, from biological survival to intellectual pleasure. See Alston, *A Realist Conception of Truth*, 231-64, and Goldman, *Epistemology and Cognition.*

14 Bonjour, *The Structure of Empirical Knowledge*, 7–8. Rules for conducting inquiry are related to, but not identical with, objective criteria of justification. The standards of justification differ from rules of inquiry in the same way as criteria for judging a meal as nutritious differ from directions for cooking. Haack, *Evidence and Inquiry*, 204.

truths, than there is no knowledge – only relative opinion. If there are no guarantees of certainty, then it appears that no claim is more objective than any other. Fallibilism, in contrast, employs only a limited scepticism. It holds that we can question any belief if good reason arises. The fact that we are sometimes mistaken about particular beliefs does not entail that we should doubt every belief. Inquiry should not end in radical doubt. Fallibilism believes that inquiry should avoid a Platonic "craving" for absolute, objective knowledge. A perfectionist approach to inquiry often results in a philosophical theory that contradicts or demotes the value of ordinary experience. The aim of inquiry should be the illumination of experience, not its demotion. Pragmatic inquiry is a truth-oriented process that is fallible, situated, and pluralistic, yet non-arbitrary.[15]

There are many rival views about the nature of inquiry and the value of truth. The neo-pragmatist Richard Rorty, for example, has been a major influence on current scepticism about truth and objectivity. He has gone so far as to deny that truth is an important concept. Not surprisingly, his views have sparked controversy.[16] Rorty rightly inveighs against absolute notions of truth and objectivity, the sort of concepts that define the Platonic "way of truth."[17] He rejects the idea of truth as firm knowledge of "intrinsic reality" behind appearances. Similarly, he rejects objectivity as a correspondence with the "way things are in themselves."[18] He says that there is "nothing more" to truth and objectivity than justification and intersubjective agreement. "There is nothing to the notion of objectivity save that of intersubjective agreement – agreement reached by free and open discussion of all available hypotheses

15 For a pragmatic conception of fallibilism, see Putnam's *Pragmatism,* 21, and in *Words and Life,* 152. See also Putnam, "The Craving for Objectivity," in *Words and Life,* 120–31.

16 Opposition to Rorty's pragmatism varies from claims that he collapses the distinction between truth and socially approved belief and that he is guilty of "tribalism" – the belief that what one's group believes is the criterion of truth. For a fierce critique of Rorty, see chapter 9 of Haack's *Evidence and Inquiry*: "Vulgar Pragmatism: An Unedifying Prospect," 182–202.

17 Rorty inveighs against traditional understandings of truth and objectivity in many of his books, including *Contingency, Irony and Solidarity; Objectivity, Relativism and Truth; Philosophy and Social Hope;* and *Truth and Progress.*

18 Rorty, *Truth and Progress,* 1–2. Rorty states that we have "no criterion of truth other than justification."

and policies."[19] Truth as justification is relative to our purposes and conceptual schemes. This is relativism, but relativism for Rorty is not a "menace."[20]

Rorty contends that truth is not a goal of inquiry.[21] Truth can appear to be a goal only if we interpret it wrongly as the metaphysical quest of moving closer to reality.[22] So what *is* the goal? Rorty states that inquiry has many non-metaphysical goals: obtaining what we want, improving humankind's situation, convincing as many audiences as possible, and solving problems.

Rorty's readiness to reformulate basic concepts derives from his view of philosophy as a conceptually inventive enterprise. Philosophy jettisons or redefines ways of speaking that have become obstacles to progress in inquiry. Rorty regards the traditional conceptions of truth and objectivity as obstacles. They mischaracterize inquiry. They assume dubious metaphysical dualisms such as appearance and reality, certain knowledge and mere opinion. Historically, the demand for absolute truth and objectivity has stimulated a futile search for absolute truth and produced an oscillation between dogmatism and scepticism.

Most important, absolute notions of truth and objectivity misconstrue the aim of philosophy as an intellectual grasp of timeless truths. Rorty adopts Dewey's perspective that philosophy is cultural problem-solving. Philosophy, where vibrant and relevant, grows out of contemporary issues within a culture. Its purpose is to shed light on these fundamental issues. Rorty believes that philosophy progresses to the extent that it integrates "the worldviews and the moral intuitions we inherited from our ancestors with new scientific theories or new socio-political institutions and theories and other novelties." He cites Dewey's belief that philosophy offers "hypotheses" that hope to "render men's minds more sensitive to the life about them."[23]

Given Rorty's influence, I want to note where he and I agree and disagree. We agree on the pragmatic view of inquiry as purpose-driven and

19 Ibid., 6–7.

20 Rorty, "Hilary Putnam and the Relativist Menace," 43–4. One reason why relativism is not a menace is that we are not locked inside our conceptual schemes. We can transcend them by encountering other schemes and other cultures.

21 Rorty, *Truth and Progress*, 3–11.

22 Rorty, "Is Truth a Goal of Inquiry?" 39.

23 Cited by Rorty in *Truth and Progress*, 5.

philosophy as problem-solving. We agree that judgments of truth and objectivity are possible only from within conceptual schemes. We both reject traditional notions of truth and objectivity, and we concur that justification and intersubjectivity are essential features of truth and objectivity. In fact, this book attempts to follow Dewey by applying the conceptual inventiveness of philosophy to redefine epistemic notions surrounding the problem of journalism objectivity.

Where I disagree with Rorty is over the idea that truth cannot be a goal of inquiry because we must interpret truth in an abstract, metaphysical manner. Contra Rorty, I keep truth as a goal of inquiry and redefine truth in a modest, realist manner. The search for truth does not require the presumption of an absolute truth or reality. We can understand truth as the slow process of coming to know more and more things about our empirical world and to grasp them in a more accurate and comprehensive manner. At any time, our set of beliefs determines our overall view of the way that the world is – a worldview that we win by non-mysterious empirical means. It is not a special insight of Reason into a fixed reality, behind the appearances.

Truth is important to inquiry because it acts as a presupposition and an ideal of serious inquiry.[24] Truth is a presupposition for embarking on study. One inquires about phenomenon *x* to find out some truths about *x*. "Every man is fully satisfied that there is such a thing as truth, or he would not ask any question," wrote C.S. Peirce.[25] If one really believed that all standards and methods were only arbitrary conventions, then why inquire? As Haack says, to believe p is to accept that p is true.[26]

We require the idea of truth to make sense of inquiry's adherence to difficult methods and careful evaluation. One presumption is that the higher the degree of justification, the greater the likelihood of truth. It is hard to understand why we would struggle to follow objective methods and standards unless we believed that they were "truth-directed" or "truth-conducive."[27] If justificatory procedures are not "truth-acquiring,"

24 Here I consider only the importance of truth to theoretical inquiry. Below in this chapter I argue that truth and rational evaluation are important elements in practical deliberation.

25 Quoted in Haack, *Manifesto of a Passionate Moderate*, 22. In the same way, the assumption of an external world is not an inductive inference from experience. It is a precondition for any inquiry.

26 Haack, *Evidence and Inquiry*, 192.

27 Alston, *A Realist Conception of Truth*, 242. See Moser, *Knowledge and Evidence*, 42-3.

why prefer rigorous scientific methods to other, dubious methods of acquiring beliefs, such as brainwashing or consulting oracles?[28] Part of the concept of justification is that it "counts toward truth."[29] The same considerations apply to other epistemic distinctions. The distinction between accuracy and inaccuracy (or distortion) must, at some point, rely on a distinction between truth and falsity. The distinction between rational belief and ideology, or between rational persuasion and manipulation, must appeal in some manner to truth or truth-conducive methods.

Finally, truth is an important concept because it acts as a regulatory ideal. It gives us something to point at or strive for. The ideal regulates how we inquire – it demands that we inquire honestly and diligently. The ideal motivates disinterested inquiry by requiring us to devote our energies to discovering the truth, to "getting it right." Truth is not a comforting ideal. It is a hard taskmaster. We cannot acquiesce in wishful thinking or platitudes. As Nietzsche said: "Truth has had to be fought for every step of the way, almost everything else dear to our hearts ... has had to be sacrificed to it."[30]

Moreover, truth serves as a real-world restraint on our other goals. The quest for solidarity, inclusiveness, and solutions to problems is important. However, we should base our pursuit of solidarity and problem-solving on rigorous, well-evidenced truths.[31] The idea of truth *is* abstract. But it is an important abstraction that does not have to carry the baggage of absolutism.

Holistic Interpretation

Truth is plural and fallible because incomplete modes of thinking inhibit our attempts to know. We base our beliefs and actions on our representations of what the world is like. The medium of representation is not the isolated concept but the conceptual scheme. A conceptual scheme is a mental grid of intelligibility – a set of ideas that helps us to interpret experience. Causal, logical, and hierarchical relationships link concepts to each other.[32] Different conceptual systems can cover the

28 Williams, *Truth and Truthfulness*, 127–9.

29 Audi, *The Structure of Justification*, 300-1.

30 Nietzsche, *The AntiChrist*, 50.

31 For a rethinking of the goal of solidarity in a global era, see Gunn, *Beyond Solidarity*.

32 On conceptual schemes in science, see Thagard, *Conceptual Revolutions*, 30.

same phenomena – there are several systems for categorizing library books. Conceptual schemes never capture all that there is to know. External objects out-distance what we can know of them at any given time. They admit of many perspectives and reveal unexpected depths. The world exhibits a "cognitive opacity" that inquiry cannot eliminate.[33]

A conceptual scheme can fit within other schemes, like figures inside a Russian doll. The conceptual scheme for dogs fits into the conceptual scheme for mammals, which is part of the scheme for animals. Conceptual systems can be normative, descriptive, or explanatory. Utilitarianism is a normative scheme, while classical (Newtonian) physics is explanatory. A conceptual system may be loosely organized or precise. Euclidean geometry is a tidy conceptual system. Our understanding of how ordinary objects behave – "folk physics" – is imprecise. A shift in a conceptual scheme can spark a conceptual revolution. In the sixteenth century, Galileo's new way of thinking about the motion of bodies challenged the centuries-old Aristotelian model. Galileo's revolution contained a seemingly simple conceptual change – think of motion, not rest, as natural.

My claim that interpretation depends on conceptual schemes is not equivalent to the truism that we think by using concepts. My claim contains three non-trivial theses: ubiquitous interpretation, holistic understanding, and holistic verification. The first thesis asserts that all statements about the world are interpretations. All statements, even factual ones, contain some element of conceptualization, theorizing, and evaluation. Statements of fact differ from other statements by being more responsive to empirical stimuli and by containing a minimum of theory and speculation. We tend to label a statement an "interpretation" (as opposed to a fact) when we are sceptical about its evidence. We tend to call a statement an interpretation if it is highly theoretical or when we are cognizant of rival interpretations. But, strictly speaking, all statements are interpretations.

Interpretation is ubiquitous because we have no direct, cognitive contact with reality. Even our seemingly direct perceptions of objects are the result of much processing of stimuli by our perceptual system. The mind must interpret the stimuli according to our categories, beliefs, and expectations. We interpret stimuli effortlessly and almost without notice. A few black streaks on the sea's horizon become smoke from a ship. Simple statements such as "this is a sparrow" and "this is copper" depend on relatively sophisticated conceptual schemes for

33 Rescher, *Objectivity*, 97.

birds and natural elements. In inquiry, how we categorize is not just a matter of observation but a pragmatic decision on which category scheme is the most useful, given our purposes.[34] Elements of the world and of the mind intertwine in interpretation.

What is this mental act that we call interpretation? To interpret is to perceive, understand, or explain something in a specific manner. In its simplest form, an interpretation places an object (event, phenomenon) under a descriptive or explanatory category. Interpretation is a judgment that, for example, x is F or is understood *as* F. We perceive x *as* a lion in the dark, we interpret x *as* a mocking gesture, we conceive of light *as* quanta of energy. Psychologically, the interpretation, as an explicit judgment, is only the tip of the iceberg. Why we adopt *this* interpretation, and how we understand it, usually depend on a good deal of existing theory and fact.

We do not construct an interpretation by first experiencing uninterpreted data and then applying a set of concepts to it – the way we apply a cookie cutter to dough. We do not first experience an unmediated "given" or "raw data" and then apply our concepts. Instead, we experience a fusion of perceptual stimuli and concepts.[35]

There are always plenty of interpretations for any event, given our conceptual creativity. We can see drawings that are no more than a series of dots as a duck or as a rabbit.[36] We can interpret mental problems

34 A biologist prefers a category scheme that makes dachshunds and Dobermans similar but horses and zebras dissimilar because the latter pair cannot breed with each other. The ability to breed is an important category because it correlates with the biologist's interest in fundamental genetic similarities and differences. Scientific research leads to new categorization schemes that conflict initially with common sense but suit the purposes of biology, physics, and so on. Scientists look for categorizations that enable them to express general causal laws. For example, Jerry Fodor argues that economists categorize monetary transactions abstractly in terms of people's intentions because that allows the formulation of economic laws. Fodor, *Representations*, 143.

35 The empiricist C.I. Lewis gave a classic formulation of knowledge as a combination of stimuli "given" to the senses and the active interpretation of the given by the mind, through concepts. What we experience is the "thick experience of the world of things, not the thin given of the immediacy ... We do not see patches of colour, but trees and houses; we hear, not indescribable sound but voices and violins." The given is "in, not before, experience." Lewis, "The Given in Experience," 36–66.

36 One of the most famous examples of how the mind can interpret perceptual data in different ways is Wittgenstein's duck-rabbit drawing in *Philosophical Investigations*, 194.

as a sign of personal weakness, *as* God's punishment on us, or *as* a chemical imbalance in the brain. A firm statement by a political leader on the dangers of global warming we can interpret *as* empty words to deflect criticism or *as* preparing the public for a tough new environmental law. My backyard digging can be interpreted *as* the burying of a body, *as* preparing the ground for flowers, or *as* the search for a leaking pipe.

Interpretation is ubiquitous because the brain is an organ of representation and information processing. It mediates between a potentially overwhelming cascade of stimuli and bodily responses. Some of this mediation is hard-wired. We must quickly understand stimuli as threatening or pleasurable. For example, I duck bricks without logic. Other forms of mediation occur through abstract mental representations or formulas that Bruner has called "coding systems." These codes allow humans to represent economically the many details of experience and to anticipate similar experiences in the future. Through codes, cognition goes "beyond the information given."[37]

Codes can take the form of grammatical rules, memory schemata, cognitive maps, theories, mathematical formulas, modes of inference, or hierarchically arranged categories. Codes compress data into meaningful patterns.[38] Anyone confused by the renovation of a grocery store realizes the importance of knowing the pattern of product display. We are a pattern-recognition species. We are all aware of the predictable narrative pattern of romance novels. In music, we grasp quickly the pattern of chords called the "blues." Other codes are highly abstract. Logical laws and scientific laws compress patterns of phenomena into general principles.

Ubiquitous interpretation is holistic. Any interpretation gains its sense by being part of a larger, mainly implicit, conceptual scheme. The concept of a sparrow is part of a web of mental representations about sparrows' behaviour, their environmental niche, their biological relatives and enemies, and so on. The place of a concept (or belief) in a conceptual scheme depends on at least four properties: its distance from stimuli, its degree of generality, its relative immunity from revision, and its "interanimation" with other concepts.[39]

37 Bruner, *Beyond the Information Given*, 218–37. The idea of an organizing mind is old. Eighteenth-century British empiricists attempted to chart the organizing powers of the mind, through the association of ideas.

38 Dennett, "Real Patterns," 32. For Dennett, random data are data that defy an economical, summarizing description.

39 Quine, *Word and Object*, 1–25.

Various concepts and beliefs differ in their relative distance from external stimuli (or observation). The concept of a quark is further from observation than that of a rabbit. "It is raining" is closer to observation than "Human aggressiveness is due to inherited genetic factors that are a product of centuries of evolution." Similarly, "The moon is large and yellow tonight" is closer to observation than "The red shift by the galaxies in our expanding universe shows that the galaxies are moving towards a great attractor." Yet even the last statement, despite its theoretical nature, is closer to observation than "God is everywhere."

The notion of being "closer to observation" means that the attribution of a concept or the acceptance of a statement is more likely to be prompted by a specific range of stimuli than some other concept or statement. Also, the generality of a concept or belief helps to determine its place in a conceptual scheme. Our beliefs extend from specific sentences – for example: "There was a green tint in this tube at 7:05 p.m on 3 December 2002" – to the sweeping generalities of physics typified by $E = mc^2$. Logical laws are so general that they apply to all sentences of a certain form, regardless of subject matter.

The place of a concept or belief in our conceptual scheme depends on its epistemic importance. It depends on whether we treat the concept or belief as basic or non-basic. Strawson defined basic concepts as a set of general, irreducible notions that form a "structure which constitutes the framework of our ordinary thought and talk."[40] Basic concepts come in at least three types: concepts used to understand sensory experience, such as space, time, causality, and external body; concepts to understand the social realm, such as personhood, morality, and responsibility; and methodological and normative concepts about how we should think, such as truth, evidence, fact, logical inference, and objectivity.

I argued above that truth was a basic concept for inquiry. Basic beliefs are our fundamental assumptions. Basic beliefs logically support other, less basic beliefs. Darwinian natural selection, for example, is a fundamental principle for the entire science of biology. Wittgenstein compared the basic beliefs of a person's worldview to a riverbed where "hardened propositions" (or basic beliefs) function like the bed of a river, shaping the rest of our ever-changing belief system. Yet the river-

40 Strawson, *Analysis and Metaphysics*, 24.

bed can change too, through a gradual evolution in ideas or a conceptual revolution.[41]

The test of the centrality of a belief to our scheme comes when we are under pressure to change it, because of negative evidence or a rival theory. Faced with negative results, we normally have a number of choices as to which part of our theory to change. We incline to revising some beliefs more quickly than others. Some beliefs of logic, mathematics, or experience are so basic that we can barely imagine what it would be like to alter them. Some beliefs become so important to our view of the world that they become an inflexible ideology. In the grip of a political ideology, such as Marxism, we may ignore or explain away counter-evidence to the theory. In the grip of fundamentalist faith, we can resist changing our belief that God created the world 6,000 years ago by denying empirical evidence and scientific theory.

Finally, there is an important, dynamic relationship or "interanimation" between the parts of a conceptual scheme. A scientist mixes the contents of two tubes, observes a green tint, and says, "There is copper in it." The scientist's assertion derives from something more than the perception of a green tint – knowledge of chemistry. The stimulus elicits the observation sentence only in conjunction with other, more theoretical beliefs. There is an interanimation between the observable and theoretical concepts of the scientist's conceptual scheme.

Similarly, my decision to drain an Equatorial swamp makes sense relative to my theory of malaria. There is a dynamic relationship among my theory of malaria, my observations of malaria locations, and my beliefs about what inhibits the spread of malaria. This dynamic relationship operates on the most prosaic level of experience. Each morning, I interpret a yellow ball in the sky *as* a rising sun, given my background beliefs about gravitation and a heliocentric universe.

The fact that we interpret events through a multi-levelled, dynamic conceptual scheme means that observation is not passive watching. It is an active, skilled performance guided by background knowledge. An experienced astronomer easily identifies comets in the sky; a veteran bird-

41 Wittgenstein, *On Certainty*, 15. The modern idea of conceptual schemes derives from Kant and his claim that people could not understand their experience unless their minds came equipped with basic general concepts such as space, time, and causality. See chapter 2, above. My view of conceptual schemes is closer to Quine's than to Kant's. I see the mind as having a plurality of conceptual systems that change, even at the most basic level. Like Wittgenstein, I see these conceptual schemes as reflecting "forms of life." See Lynch, *Truth in Context*, 31–54.

watcher "sees more" than the novice; a physician quickly recognizes a mole on the skin as potentially cancerous.[42]

Holism of conceptual schemes means that isolated facts do not play a significant role in our cognitive life unless my conceptual scheme links them to other facts and beliefs. There is perhaps no more succinct debunking of the idea that isolated facts have a special power by themselves than John Dewey's introduction to *The Public and Its Problems*.[43] In a few pages, Dewey throws cold water on the idea that facts "carry their meaning along on themselves on their face."

There may be disagreement on the facts or on what they mean. There may be insufficient facts to establish a claim. The same facts may support rival interpretations. Purported facts may be false or manipulated. We need to select facts for relevance and importance, organize them into coherent statistical patterns, and place them in their proper context. In science reporting, for example, journalists need to compare the cancer rate of a group in a clinical trial with background levels of cancer in the general population. In political reporting, the "facts" of opinion polls are worthless unless correctly interpreted.[44]

Dewey points out that a few recalcitrant facts need never force a person to accept or abandon a particular theory about what the facts mean. Quine argued that facts never "prove" an empirical theory. There is always the possibility of an equally good, rival theory. Yet-to-be-discovered facts may undermine a theory. Just as facts "under-determine" scientific theory, so they under-determine our news reports.[45]

Holistic interpretation leads to holistic evaluation. The evaluation of the truth or evidential strength of our beliefs is holistic in two senses. First, in most cases the evaluation concerns not one sentence but a group of beliefs that cohere together. The evaluation of a scientific hypothesis, for example, will depend on the plausibility of the theory

42 For the idea of scientific observation as active intervention in nature, see Hacking, *Representing and Intervening*, 180.

43 Dewey, *The Public and Its Problems*, 3–8.

44 Scepticism towards a realm of value-free facts (or interpretation-free description) has become so prevalent that in 1997 the Annenberg Public Policy Center of the University of Pennsylvania held a conference on "The Future of Fact." Leading scholars claimed that there are no "facts out there" independent of some conception of how the world really is. Another theme was that "facts follow interpretation." See Strange, ed. *The Future of Fact*.

45 The notion of under-determination of theory by fact comes from Quine. See Quine, "On the Reasons for the Indeterminacy of Translation."

that contains it. Hypotheses have empirical implications that we can test scientifically only in conjunction with other beliefs and assumptions. Quine expressed this sense of holistic evaluation by his dictum that theories approach experience for verification as a "corporate body."[46] Second, the standards of evaluation are themselves plural. We must consider various types of standards together. Sometimes the standards conflict and need weighing against each other.

One aim of holistic evaluation is what John Rawls called a "reflective equilibrium" within one's conceptual scheme. Rawls used the idea of reflective equilibrium to describe the construction of ethical theory and the evaluation of ethical rules. If we are constructing a theory of justice, we seek a theory that accords with "our considered convictions, at all levels of generality." If we are evaluating an ethical rule, we examine how well it applies to a range of cases. Does it fit with our intuitions about these cases? In addition, we examine whether the rule fits with basic ethical principles. Where there is a lack of fit, we alter our intuitions or principles until we achieve a new intellectual equilibrium in our ethical conceptual scheme.

For Rawls, ethical construction and evaluation proceed by this constant activity of mutual adjustment of principles, rules, facts, and judgments. Any concept or rule is interpreted and evaluated holistically, in terms of its overall fit within a conceptual scheme. When difficult cases arises, the goal is a considered judgment based on a reflective equilibrium between the elements of the conceptual scheme.[47]

The idea of reaching considered judgments by holistic evaluation and reflective equilibrium extends beyond ethics to wherever one seeks considered judgments. As Elgin states: "A system of considered judgments in reflective equilibrium is neither absolute nor arbitrary: not absolute, for it is fallible, revisable, revocable; not arbitrary, for it is tethered to antecedent commitments. Such a system neither is nor purports to be a distortion-free reflection of a mind-independent reality. Nor is it merely

46 Quine, "Two Dogmas of Empiricism," 41. Quine rejected the view of the logical positivists that verification was a matter of determining the observations implied by a single statement. Groups of sentences have empirical content. Quine attributed this view to the French philosopher of science Pierre Duhem.

47 Rawls, *Political Liberalism,* 8, 20, 89–90. He advocated "constructivism" in ethical theory. He believed that, since humans cannot agree on a metaphysical basis for ethics, they must construct the most plausible set of ethical principles through impartial and reasonable deliberation. Valid ethical principles are the "outcome of a certain procedure of construction."

an expression of our beliefs. It is rather a tool for the advancement of our understanding."[48]

Philosophers have provided metaphors that convey the idea of holistic evaluation within evolving conceptual schemes. Otto Neurath compared the inquirer to a sailor who repairs his boat while he sails along. Quine added that scientific inquirers are sailors whose boat they "must rebuild plank by plank while staying afloat in it."[49] Epistemically, this means that inquirers cannot start from scratch by rejecting all standards and beliefs. Rather they employ a limited scepticism that questions specific beliefs from within their evolving conceptual scheme. In effect, they stand on planks to repair other planks.

Holism and Objectivity

Given this view of our cognitive life, I arrive at my concept of pragmatic objectivity: objectivity is the epistemic evaluation of situated inquiry. More precisely, objectivity is a fallible, context-bound, holistic method of testing interpretations. We judge an interpretation to be objective if it has good support, according to the best available standards of a conceptual scheme. We determine "what is objective from the point of view of our best and most reflective practice."[50]

The evaluation of inquiry by objective standards is a form of standard-guided thought, of disciplined rationality. The mind turns back on itself; it monitors and corrects its activity. The standards of objectivity specify conditions for being rational. My notion of pragmatic objectivity is compatible with Popper's idea of critical rationality as a practical form of "reasonableness" analogous to scientific rationality.[51] Popper describes his rationalism as a "modest and self-critical rationalism," which recognizes the limitations of human nature. The attitude of critical rationality involves being ready to listen to critical arguments and to learn from experience. The rationalist attitude, Popper says, is characterized by a desire for objectivity and impartiality.[52]

48 Elgin, *Between the Absolute and the Arbitrary*, 198.

49 Neurath used this metaphor in "Foundations of the Social Sciences," 47. Quine's gloss on the metaphor is in *Word and Object*, 3.

50 Putnam, *Words and Life*, 177.

51 Popper, *The Open Society and Its Enemies*, 2:224–40. Popper also called his view "pragmatic rationalism." We recognize that the world is not rational but still try to subject it to reason as far as possible. Popper quotes Carnap *(The Logical Structure of the World)*: pragmatic rationalism is "the attitude which strives for clarity everywhere but recognizes the never fully understandable or never fully rational entanglement of the events of life" (2:237n).

52 Ibid., 2:225.

My theory of pragmatic objectivity goes beyond an attitude of reasonableness. It conceives of objectivity in more detail, as having a relatively complex structure that is both generic and domain-specific. Objectivity is generic because it has features that apply to all forms of rational inquiry. The generic features consist of an objective stance and an accompanying set of broad epistemic standards. Objectivity is specific in the sense that different domains of inquiry apply the generic standards of objectivity in different ways. Domains, such as law, journalism, and the sciences, interpret the general standards to suit their purposes. This adaptation of objectivity results in an additional set of distinct and detailed norms. Specific forms of objectivity are extensions of generic objectivity into areas of distinct subject matter, specific problems, and special practices. Therefore we can say that there are different forms of objectivity. As this book has argued, objectivity in theory is different from objectivity in practical enterprises. Within practical enterprises, there are differences in the application of objectivity among professions. For example, objectivity in journalism relates to but is not identical with objectivity in law.

The Objective Stance

Let's begin with the dispositions of the objective stance – what Aristotle called the intellectual virtues.[53] The objective stance consists of a set of mutually supportive dispositions. There are at least four: dispositions towards open rationality, towards partial transcendence, towards disinterested truth, and towards intellectual integrity. I call this web of dispositions a "stance" to indicate that it is a general attitude that one adopts for certain purposes.

An objective inquirer is willing to open rationality if he or she accepts the burdens of rationality. He or she is open to the demands of others to be logical, to face the facts squarely, and to give reasons for one's beliefs that others could accept.[54] Rescher puts the point this way: "To proceed objectively is, in sum, to render oneself perspicuous to others by doing what any reasonable and normally constituted person would do in one's place, thereby rendering one's proceedings intelligible to anyone."[55]

53 Aristotle, *Ethics*, 203–25.

54 Philosopher Joseph Raz has defined objectivity in a way that is compatible with my dispositional analysis: "People are objective about certain matters if they are, in forming or holding opinions, judgments, and the like, properly sensitive to factors epistemically relevant to the truth or correctness of their opinions or judgments, that is, if they respond to these factors as they should." Raz, "Notes on Value and Objectivity," 195.

55 Rescher, *Objectivity*, 8.

Open rationality is related to the disposition towards partial transcendence. Open rationality assists the objective inquirer in partially transcending his or her current epistemic situation. To transcend partially one's epistemic situation is to expand, enhance, and deepen one's current understanding of the issue in question. When our critical faculties encounter the experience of others, we enlarge our perspective.

To practice open rationality and achieve partial transcendence requires support from another disposition – the willingness to be disinterested in the pursuit of truth. Disinterestedness means not allowing one's interests to subvert one's truth-seeking. One way to explain disinterestedness is to use the metaphors of space and distance. We begin to be disinterested when we step back, metaphorically, and put a "critical distance" between our beliefs and us. We can adopt a critical distance in a number of ways. In philosophy, we can practise scepticism and self-doubt. In literature, we can exhibit this distance by the way we write and discuss issues. We have seen how the early modern scientists displayed their disinterestedness by using plain language, avoiding heated rhetoric, and making modest claims about the philosophical implications of their experiments.[56]

Unfortunately, disinterestedness is one of the most misunderstood and maligned of the intellectual virtues. Some people incorrectly think that disinterestedness entails complete emotional detachment. They confuse disinterest with lack of interest, or of caring. To the contrary, disinterestedness is not radical detachment, leading to a "view from nowhere."[57] Instead, it is an extension of our common and important ability to step back and reflect on the grounds of our beliefs, apart from our partialities and interests. Disinterestedness does not mean that the objective stance is without passion. Disinterestedness is the correct use of our passion for truth.

Pragmatic objectivity is a passionate commitment to dispassionate inquiry. Genuine inquiry derives from a disinterested search for the truth, "regardless of what the colour of that truth may be."[58] Disinterestedness

56 Mark Phillips has described the writing styles of historians by looking at how they place varying degrees of distance between themselves and their subject. He notes that David Hume, in *History of England*, attempted to maintain readers' interest in various passages by getting "closer" to the historical events through the use of emotional and detailed language. However, when Hume passed historical judgment on a monarch or era, he placed a distance between himself and the topic by using more abstract philosophical language. See Phillips, *Society and Sentiment*.

57 Nagel, *The View from Nowhere*.

58 Cited in Haack, *Manifesto of a Passionate Moderate*, 10.

is not neutrality. It is not uncaring. It means caring so much for the honest truth that one does not allow personal interests to subvert inquiry or to prejudge the issue. Disinterestedness implies an impersonal use of reason. One puts "aside one's idiosyncratic preferences and parochial preferences in forming one's beliefs, evaluations, and choices." To be disinterested is to prevent the passion for truth from succumbing to other interests. One nurtures a Platonic "eros" for truth.

The importance of disinterestedness is clear when we consider what happens when inquirers reject this disposition or lack it in sufficient degree. A good deal of pseudo-inquiry is the reasoning of an inquirer who has a "prior and unbudgeable commitment to the proposition for which he tries to make a case."[59] Another variant of the pseudo-inquirer is what Harry Frankfurt called frankly the "bullshitter." That person is indifferent to the truth of the proposition that he or she is advancing, so long as he or she can make an impression on others with verbal pyrotechniques.[60]

At the bottom of all these dispositions is the inquirer's intellectual integrity. This is a trait of character that disposes the inquirer to admit wishful thinking, to face up to the toughest questions, and, where necessary, to admit that one's ideas are flawed.

Objective Standards

One cannot be objective simply by having a set of dispositions. One has to put those dispositions to work in real inquiry and in concrete situations. One needs correct methods and standards.

The standards of objectivity are both generic and specific. There are three types of generic standards by which we judge the objectivity of any claim or judgment. There are *empirical standards,* which test a belief's agreement with the world; *standards of coherence,* which evaluate how consistent a belief is with the rest of what we believe; and *standards of rational debate,* which test how fair we have been in representing the claims of others and in opening up our claims to the scrutiny of others.

First, both common sense and the sciences use general epistemic standards. The empirical standards of common sense are implicit in our daily activities: the value that we place on direct observation, on observation under good conditions, and on repeated perceptions by unbiased observers. The empirical standards of science take these informal standards and

59 Ibid., 9.
60 Frankfurt, "On Bullshit," 11–33.

make them more formal, more precise. Experiments must satisfy standards and methods that are rigorous, controlled, quantifiable, replicable, and mathematically correct.

The generic standards of coherence include the rules of logic, such as the principles of logical consistency and non-contradiction, the support that a belief receives from other beliefs, and the way a hypothesis fits with established knowledge.[61] Coherence standards include aesthetic values such as the simplicity or mathematical elegance of a theory. We use coherence standards every day, such as when we try to make sense of a surprising perception. As I drive down my street at sunset, I am surprised to see that my house appears to be pink when I believe it to be beige. Do I accept this perception as correct or objective? No, because the perception does not cohere with previous perceptions of my beige house. Also, this perception of pink does not cohere with my firm belief that I painted the house beige last summer. Furthermore, it is improbable that someone painted my house pink while I was at the office. A more likely explanation is that the pinkish colour is the result of the sunset, and I set about verifying that hypothesis by making further observations.

Second, standards of coherence are at work in assessments of theory. For instance, I am sceptical about a new book that claims that science can show that nature exhibits a mysterious sort of "intelligent design," perhaps by a deity. I am suspicious not only because of the logical implausibility of the theory and its evidence but also because it does not cohere with my basic belief in design by natural selection. Take another example, from law. A jury refuses to believe that Jim murdered Mary because evidence shows that he was not at the murder scene at the time of the killing. The proposition that Jim is guilty does not cohere with a basic belief of logic – no one can have the property A and the property not-A at the same time. That is, Jim cannot be in two places at the same time. The case against Jim is logically incoherent. The same preference for coherence applies in theology. Coherence considerations are essential to constructing reasonable interpretations of conflicting passages in the Bible.

One might assume that only empirical standards are relevant to evaluations of objectivity, since we presume objectivity to be ontological – what exists in the world. However, our beliefs about what exists objectively must also pass the standards of coherence. In physics, we believe in the existence of unobserved (theoretical) sub-atomic entities mainly

61 Many of these standards appear in the writings of William James, such as *The Meaning of Truth* and *Pragmatism.*

because these postulates cohere with the experimental evidence and prevailing theory.

Third, standards of rational debate consist of the norms of rational deliberation and criticism among groups, disciplines, and societies. They include diversity, equality, and inclusiveness. For the attainment of objective beliefs, it is important that all rational voices in the debate receive fair and respectful treatment, that the process of debate be inclusive, and that hierarchies of power do not distort deliberation. The process of deliberation should not "block the paths of inquiry" by preventing the formulation of hypotheses or criticisms.[62] As with standards of coherence, one may wonder why "satisfying standards of rational debate" is a criterion of objectivity. Why not consider the standards of rational debate as norms of communication, rather than norms of objectivity? The reason is that our empirical and coherence standards must be applied in a context of inquiry that is as open and democratic as possible. Democratic values for rational debate are crucial because of the essentially social nature of inquiry. We support standards of rational debate not only because we want to be fair to participants but because we want to ensure presentation of a full range of facts, theories, perspectives, and possible objections during the objective evaluation of any claim.

A century and a half ago, John Stuart Mill, in *On Liberty,* recognized the importance of living in a society that encouraged open criticism of beliefs. More recently, leading liberal philosophers have made standards of rational deliberation an essential part of the construction of acceptable ethical rules, fair principles of justice, and objective scientific theory. Hilary Putnam, following Dewey, has stressed that science "requires the democratization of inquiry."[63] Open and fair rational debate is just as vital for rational inquiry in science as it is for rational deliberation on public policy in democracies. Norms for rational deliberation are central to Rorty's theory of objectivity. The norms are central to Habermas's theory of communicative action and his "discourse ethics." We saw above that Rorty defined objectivity as "agreement reached by free and open discussion of all available hypotheses." For Habermas, communicative action is communication governed by the ideals of rational discourse – ideals that define discourse ethics. In communicative action, participants perform speech acts that presuppose such norms as sincerity, telling the truth, and asserting what

62 Putnam, *The Collapse of the Fact/Value Dichotomy and Other Essays,* 105.

63 Putnam, "Pragmatism and Moral Objectivity," 173. Dewey believed the democratization of inquiry crucial for the application of "social intelligence."

reason warrants.[64] In discourse ethics, problems in moral argumentation cannot be "handled monologically but require a cooperative effort." Habermas states that people attempt, by entering into norm-governed moral discourse, to restore "a consensus that has been disrupted."[65]

The ideal of rational standards of debate supports Rawls's appeal to "public reason." Public reason is the means by which a society fairly and openly discusses fundamental political issues. Rawls argues that citizens in a pluralistic democracy must agree on the sort of reasons that they will give each other when basic principles are at stake. If each group insists on the unique truths of its worldview, the issues are unsolvable. Rawls recommends that the groups debate according to public reason – put forward reasons that are politically acceptable to all citizens as citizens. What reasons might those be? For Rawls, they must be consistent with their country's fundamental principles of justice. Through the exercise of public reason, the principles of justice attain some degree of objectivity.[66]

The three types of generic standards correspond with the three senses of objectivity. Empirical standards express the ontological sense of objective facts; they anchor an interpretation in experience and worldly facts. Coherence standards express the epistemic sense of careful, systematic method and make sure that the interpretation is part of a meaningful and consistent conceptual system. Standards of rational debate express the procedural sense of objectivity – the idea of fair process – and ensure impartiality and openness to criticism.

All three types of norms may come into play in the objective evaluation of a belief or theory. Paul Thagard's concept of "explanatory coherence" provides a model of how these norms interact. Thagard uses the notion of explanatory coherence to explain conceptual revolutions in science. According to Thagard, scientists throughout history have adopted a new theory, such as Darwin's natural selection or Lavoisier's oxygen, because it satisfies empirical and rational (coherence) standards better than rival theories. Thagard recognizes that there is a "data priority" in theory evaluation. Yet there is more to evaluation than collecting data. "Theories are enmeshed in conceptual systems, just as rationalists have argued, and such systems are not open to simple empirical challenges." To "data priority" we must add such norms as the explanatory breadth of a theory, the coherence of its propositions, and

64 Habermas, *The Theory of Communicative Action*, 1:ix, 1:86, 1:94.

65 Habermas, "Discourse Ethics," 67.

66 Rawls, *The Law of Peoples*, 132–3. Rawls limited public reason to the "public political forum," which included the discourse of senior judges and elected officials and the public oratory of candidates for political office.

the simplicity of its assumptions. Acceptance of a theory is an inference to the best explanation – the one that satisfies multiple constraints.[67]

Objective evaluation therefore employs not only a diversity of types of standards but a range of standards, from the general to the specific. For example, a study of the objective efficacy of a new drug requires health researchers to subject the drug to a multi-phased clinical trial. Researchers must of course act rationally. They must adhere to the generic standards of objectivity. In addition, they follow specific standards and methods developed for (or applied to) their domain of inquiry. For example, they must disprove the null hypothesis, test the drug against a control group, apply triple-blind procedures, and evaluate results according to standards of statistical significance.

The ideal of pragmatic objectivity, as a combination of objective stance and disposition, has three far-reaching implications. First, a holism of interpretation and evaluation undermines the fact–value dichotomy. Epistemically, it does not make sense to insist on a strict distinction between fact and value, fact and theory, or fact and interpretation. Psychologically, it does not make sense to try to draw a hard line between what we know by observation, what we know by theorizing, and what we know through valuing and interpreting. Even objective science evaluates claims, by using a rich mixture of facts, theories, aims, and epistemic values.

My entire discussion of holism has presupposed the collapse of the fact–value dichotomy,[68] which flows from the view that pragmatic inquirers gather facts in the service of various purposes. The collapse of

67 Thagard, *Conceptual Revolutions*, 251, 97.

68 As Putnam emphasizes, it is important not to confuse a distinction and a philosophical dichotomy (or dualism). It is important not to confuse a difference between two phenomena and a dichotomy that draws a "hard line" between two phenomena. A distinction notes that two things are different in some regard and to some degree. A dichotomy (or dualism) attempts to make the difference between two phenomena so extreme or complete that there is no significant or interesting relationship between them. The problem with a dichotomy is that it exaggerates the differences, distorting our understanding of the phenomena. In this sense, we can speak of the positivists as promoting a dichotomy between observation and theory and a dichotomy between the analytic truths of language and the synthetic truths of science and observation. The whole idea of pure facts is another attempt to create a dichotomy between our ways of knowing facts and non-facts. Pragmatic holists do not deny that there is a difference between perception and imagination, between observing and theorizing. But they do deny that observation, theorizing, and valuing can be radically separated in epistemology and psychology. See Putnam, *The Collapse of the Fact/Value Dichotomy and Other Essays*, 9–13.

the dichotomy followed too from the idea of holistic cognition – judgments as the result of the interanimation of elements of conceptual schemes. It is a consequence of the idea that epistemic evaluation involves the convergence of many types of standards. If this view is correct, it appears that objectivity is in effect a species of holistic evaluation.

Second, objective standards are as fallible as the beliefs that they govern. Pragmatic objectivity does not assume the existence of absolute standards or pure facts. True, the standards of objectivity are basic. They belong to the third class of basic concepts – epistemic norms. But they are not universal and unchanging, known a priori by reason. At the same time, we do not invent the standards of objectivity *ex nihilo*, nor do they simply pass on uncritically from one generation of inquirers to another. The standards refer to epistemic features of previously successful inquiry. They represent our best judgment on how to conduct and evaluate inquiry, given our experience. We learn how to learn, and objective standards are one of the results of this learning. Future experience may warrant their redefinition.

Third, objectivity is a complex property, ascertained by a second-order, comparative judgment. The result of objective evaluation is a judgment that "x is objective" where "x" can be a belief, theory, journalism report, or bureaucrat's decision. It is a judgment about a judgment. It is a second-order epistemic judgment about a first-order belief or decision. Given the complexity of this judgment, appeals to brute fact rarely settle the objectivity of a claim. "Objectivity" does not refer to a simple, easily recognized property. We cannot 'perceive' directly that a claim is objective the way we perceive an object to be red. Instead, we judge indirectly a claim to be "objective" after we have applied generic and specific standards. On most occasions, the judgment of objectivity is a matter of degree and comparative. The judgment says that interpretation *X* satisfies standards 'x', 'y,' and 'z' to degree 'd.' It says that interpretation *X* is more objective than interpretation *Y*, given certain standards.

PRAGMATIC OBJECTIVITY AND JOURNALISM

This section applies the notion of pragmatic objectivity to reform the idea of objectivity in journalism. We can profitably reconceive journalism objectivity as a species of pragmatic objectivity for three reasons. First, the core features of pragmatic inquiry appear in objective journalism. Second, we can reinterpret current procedures for testing the objectivity of reports as procedures of pragmatic objectivity without doing too much violence to existing concepts. Third, pragmatic objectivity is an attractive conceptual option for journalism, because it avoids the problems of traditional objectivity while continuing to express the best practices of responsible journalism.

I begin by discussing the social context within which journalism occurs before examining truth-seeking in journalism. I then look at the elements of journalism inquiry in turn: pragmatic inquiry, holistic interpretation, and objective evaluation.

Rhetoric and Social Truth

To understand truth-seeking in journalism we have to comprehend the society in which truth-seeking occurs. In particular, we need to consider how that society gathers information and deliberates collectively on issues. We must keep two facts in mind. First, journalism is both the product and one of the creators of an "infosphere" – the worldwide media system of information exchange, which exists in addition to the biosphere and the social sphere. Second, groups in a public sphere use and contest whatever news journalists dig up and exchange.

The first fact is easy to grasp. Journalism is an organized cultural expression of a biological fact – that all creatures have informational needs. Biologically, humans have an epistemic hunger for new and accurate information about their environment. The development of information-dependent societies has strengthened that biological need. Humans, through their information-processing brain, language, and culture, have become "informavores."[69] Each day they ingest large quantities of data and opinion. We might consider journalists to be professional informavores – with by-lines.

The second fact – that journalism provides material for public discussion – is also evident. But *how* this process occurs is difficult to analyse. Journalism does not produce just a stream of data on the stock markets, tomorrow's weather, or the price of gas in Vancouver. It generates information and opinion that become part of a system of social discussion that determines public policy. News is not just facts for individuals – it is material for the politics of citizens.

The social structure by which a society discusses these facts and opinion is what I call its "public rhetorical system"[70] – a process by which elements of the system, using the media, attempt to determine which beliefs are most credible, or true. This process determines what a society (or its

69 Dennett, *Consciousness Explained,* 181.

70 The structure of the system includes the way the news media circulate the material and the openness, accuracy, and diversity of that circulation. It includes the most influential groups, the norms and values that restrain or support the various players, the way that political institutions respond to public pressure, and structural imbalances between powerful and less-powerful commentators.

dominant parts) counts as rational policy and fair behaviour by institutions. I refer to its results as "social truth" – a temporary resting place in an endless debate under changing circumstances.

The process by which elements of the system engage in discussion is primarily rhetorical. The aim is to persuade the public of one's position through appeal to plausible beliefs, accepted values, and what is useful and realistic. Persuasion also appeals to a range of facts and, on the whole, to what appears to be a reasonable argument. The rhetorical process combines both collaborative and competitive reasoning. Much of the rhetoric of individuals and groups is strategic. Groups position themselves advantageously with respect to rival groups. They construct their public reasoning with a view to the strengths and weaknesses of other views and with regard to their opponents' counter-moves.

I call my approach to understanding this system a "rhetorical theory of social truth." I conceive of the reasoning, the strategies, and the interaction of the system's elements as rhetorical exercises. I see the process of truth-seeking in society as the coming together of different voices with different interests to engage in persuasive speech – to propose, to rebut, to posture, to accommodate, to reconsider, and to try to reach a compromise. A rhetorical theory of social truth does not hold that truth is whatever the loudest or most manipulative voice says that it is. It holds instead that truth in society is what emerges from an informal, interest-laden public discourse on topics that elude certainty.

Models of rational discourse governed by strict logic, rigorous standards, and well-controlled methods provide limited help in explaining the process of social truth. While absolute truth would be preferable to plausibility, the model of a rigorous mode of truth is not appropriate (or realistic) for many areas of human activity. Aristotle recognized as much in his *Rhetoric* when he noted that there were parts of human experience where philosophical truth does not play a part. Humans base actions on probability rather than on truth.[71] Politics, for example, requires collaborative inquiry into the relative just or unjust nature of actions, given socially constructed laws and their accompanying punishments. Societies base politics and law on "communal truths-as-probabilities rather than universal truth."[72] The exercise of "public reason" in the public sphere is not the constrained, rational discourse

71 Aristotle, *On Rhetoric*, 34–45.

72 McComiskey, *Gorgias and the New Sophistic Rhetoric*, 32–52.

of supreme courts. It is the messy, everyday discourse of people in the streets, of people engaging in the ways of practice.

What is the situation of journalists in this rhetorical process? It is a multi-faceted role, with internal tensions. Journalists generate factual information and opinion every day. This material provides fodder for social discussion. Journalists circulate this material across society and allow groups to talk to each other. In addition, journalists, especially reporters, mediate between conflicting claims. They try to ascertain objectively the most plausible truth from participants in the rhetorical system. Journalists are both communicators attempting to determine the truth about events and one of the voices in the debate. Journalists report on the rhetorical system and are part of it. They shape the system, and it shapes them.

Ideally, what should journalism's role be in the rhetorical process? Journalism, I contend, should help to make rhetorical debate on public issues as rational, inclusive, and objective as possible. As democrats, we should want public discussion to adhere to standards of rational debate. But we should not expect the process to satisfy the ideal norms of rational discourse noted above. At best, we can hope for a journalism that gradually clarifies issues, airs important views, and exposes dubious claims. We can hope for a journalism that focuses on public discussion of serious issues, objective facts, credible sources, and consequences for society. Journalism should expose and fight the forces that manipulate public debate. It should assist a society's inquiry into its ailments and its future promise by allowing a robust give-and-take among a diversity of citizens at many locations across the public sphere. Journalism should assist the slow emergence of a more complete truth.

A rhetorical theory of social truth is optimistic but not naïve. It does not assume that if we have a free press, truth in the marketplace will always win out over falsity. A rhetorical theory of journalism truth is optimistic in that it continues to believe (and hope) that journalism can help public argumentation be rational and objective. To abandon that hope would only make matters worse for journalism and for society. Yet the theory is acutely aware that the arts of rhetoric offer no royal road to truth. One cannot eliminate bias or limited knowledge or the advantages of money and power. The arts of rhetoric can serve either democracy or self-interested factions. Journalism is one of those arts.

The quality of journalism and the public sphere tend to rise and fall together. The limitations on collective truth-seeking in society affect the quality of journalism, and the limitations on journalism truth-seeking affect the quality of public discourse.

Pragmatic Inquiry in Journalism

Inquiry and evaluation in journalism occur in the context of the public sphere and the media-saturated infosphere, where self-interest, ideology, and the pressure to promote one's interests can diminish social truth. The forces of subjectivity and self-interest only make it more difficult for truth-seeking in journalism.

Journalists have to deal with the same obstacles facing all inquirers in their search for truth: the cognitive opacity of the world, the plurality of limited perspectives, the threat of bias, and the limitations on inquiry in practical fields. In addition, they face hindrances inherent in the nature of their craft. Often, they lack the specialized knowledge needed to inquire critically. They labour under deadlines, powerful publishers, and finite newsroom resources. Journalists attempt to ferret out the most plausible accounts from a gradual accumulation of facts that begins as a jumble of unconfirmed reports or strong assertions by manipulative sources. Even where facts are available, as in official reports, the journalist faces an abundance of interpretations of the facts. Most of the day's news is about issues that are not remote and academic but directly affect people's lives. Many stories deal with matters where no consensus exists and where controversy, bias, and conflict surround the issues.

The precarious epistemic position of journalism in the public sphere makes it imperative that we conceive of truth-seeking in journalism as the diligent application of fallible methods over time. That is why many journalists and journalism codes stress the telling of truth or the attempt to approach the truth. The principles of the *Washington Post,* drafted by Eugene Meyer in 1933, advocated "telling the truth as nearly as the truth may be ascertained."[73] The *Post*'s Carl Bernstein described the reporting process as striving to provide "the best obtainable version of the truth."[74]

Given this informational environment, one of the best ways for journalism to contribute to a healthy public sphere is to adhere to the standards of pragmatic objectivity. Such adherence begins with a reconception of journalists as pragmatic inquirers and holistic interpreters. We should think of them not as passive recorders of events but as truth-oriented inquirers. All good journalism, including reporting, is active inquiry. It consists of searching and interpreting, of verifying and testing, of balancing and judging, of describing and observing. Good journalists possess re-

73 Meyer, "The Post's Principles," 7.

74 Quoted in Kovach and Rosenstiel, *The Elements of Journalism*, 44.

search skills that reveal reclusive facts. They have interpretive skills that explain complex events. Journalism inquiry, like all inquiry, is not just the search for any and all facts. Like the scientist, the journalist looks for important truths, secured by evidence.

Journalists are beginning to use the computer to analyze large amounts of data. But journalism does not have a rigorous method of verification. Its method is a non-systematic hodgepodge of common sense, scepticism, and informal rules that newsrooms follow with varying consistency. The best journalism is a judicious blend of two fundamental impulses – the romantic and the objective. The romantic impulse consists of the passion for interesting stories and substantial revelations. It is the impulse to seek out stories that give the journalist an opportunity for creative writing, interpretation, and self-expression. The objective impulse is the concern to verify what the romantic impulse finds and make sure that it is fair.

The fact that truth in journalism is a work in progress is evident to foreign reporters. In war zones, the fog of war severely hampers journalists' search for truth. Obstacles include lack of access to conflict areas, a plethora of dubious atrocity stories, a dearth of hard evidence, and many well-orchestrated efforts to mislead the media. In January 2002, journalist Claude Adams flew to Kathmandu to do a story on Nepal's Maoist insurgency for the CBC-TV news program *Foreign Assignment*. Adams's description of his efforts to produce an accurate story speaks volumes for the fragility of truth and the limitations of method in journalism:

> Working with a local reporter, Guna Raj Luitel, we quickly determined that doing a comprehensive story on the war itself would be impossible – climate, lack of access, lack of co-operation by the Army, the rebels in hiding: All were reasons that prevailed against us. But the government's Human Rights Commission had a great stack of alleged human rights violations (mostly by the security forces) that they were unable to verify, so the commission co-chairman gave me the list and I went through it. I decided to focus on the killing of Khet Lamichhane, described as a peasant farmer in the mountain village of Bageswari, about four hours drive west of Kathmandu. When we arrived there, townspeople gave us their version of the story: Soldiers and police had arrived early in a December morning, looking for a rebel unit that had spent the night in the village. There was some kind of altercation and they opened fire. Khet Lamichhane was shot in the mid-section and another man, a peddler, was chased into the woods and killed. Lamichhane, bleeding profusely, begged for help and water. The soldiers prevented anyone from helping him, and then told the townspeople to go inside and close their windows and doors. One witness said she heard a soldier asking an officer: "Should we give this man medical treatment?" The officer reportedly answered: "Give him another bullet." Then

there was a shot. When the people came out of their homes, Lamichhane's body was gone. A day or two later, his family arrived at the nearby headquarters town of Trisuli and asked for his body so they could bury it. They were told Lamichhane, father of a baby girl, had been cremated. A half-dozen townspeople told me the story.

A local politician insisted that Lamichhane was not a Marxist supporter, as did his family. A police official in Trisuli, however, said the soldiers fired because they were ambushed, and that Lamichhane was taken back to hospital where he died. Could I see the weapon he was carrying? No. Could I meet the doctor who declared him dead? Could I talk to an army officer who had been on the scene? No. Could I see any evidence that Lamichhane was a terrorist? No. I would have to go to the Interior Ministry. I repeatedly, phoned, faxed AND emailed both the interior ministry and the army headquarters in Kathmandu for more information on the killing, and got no response. Guna Raj Luitel, who was the head of reporters for a major Kathmandu newspaper, called it a clear case of "murder" based on what we had learned, but said he could not publish the story because it would violate the terms of Nepal's state of emergency. I went back to the Human Rights Commission, but they could give me nothing more, other than to say that there were many similar cases of civilian deaths and disappearances. Weeks later, I contacted Amnesty International in London, but their inquiries on my behalf also could not raise any more information on the case.[75]

Adams eventually included the story of Khet Lamichhane in a report on civilian killings in Nepal for both the CBC and Star TV Asia. He also wrote freelance pieces for the *Globe and Mail* and *National Post* newspapers in Toronto. In all stories, he gave the police official's version of events, as unlikely as it sounded. Adams was trying to put a "human face" on terrible allegations. But the selecting and sifting process, frustrated by uncertainty and obstacles at every turn, never reached anything approaching certainty. Adams accumulated facts, testimony, and perspectives until the balance of probabilities tipped in favour of reporting the story.[76]

75 Claude Adams, e-mail correspondence to author, Feb. 2003.

76 The balance of probabilities sometimes leads to a false story, as Nancy Durham, a CBC TV reporter in London, England, found out to her chagrin. In 1999, CBC aired her retraction of a story about a young Albanian girl whom she had featured in one of her reports from the Balkans called "The Truth about Rajmonda: A KLA Soldier Lies for the Cause." The girl, Rajmonda, had told Durham that she had joined the Kosovo Liberation Army in part to avenge the death of a sister at the hands of the Serb military. Durham discovered later that Rajmonda's sister was very much alive. Durham had been the victim of Rajmonda's propaganada and of the restrictions on travel and verification during war.

The process of truth-seeking in journalism gradually strips away error, inaccuracy, or exaggeration from the initial descriptions of events. The process of truth involves a sifting out of fact from innuendo, the identification of spin, and refocusing on what is true and significant for the public. Journalists follow leads, add up probabilities, compare what they think they know with what others say, and receive feedback from the community. Journalism truth is a "protean thing which, like learning, grows as a stalagmite in a cave, drop by drop over time."[77]

Interpretation in Journalism

Truth-seeking in journalism proceeds via the interpretation of events. All forms of journalism, including objective news reports, are implicit or explicit interpretations. A report saying that the police chief was "stung" by accusations of wrongdoing and "struggled" to reply is an interpretation. Rival descriptions of an armed standoff between Natives and police as an "illegal Native act" or a "legitimate affirmation of Native rights" are rival interpretations. If I report that "The defence minister is a zealous, misguided opponent of any budget cuts that might hurt retired soldiers," I mix facts and evaluation. Journalists interpret both the language and the behaviour of leaders. What is the meaning of an awkward handshake between the prime minister of Israel and the leader of the Palestine Liberation Organization? Headlines also summarize and interpret. On 24 January 2003, Canadian newspapers reported the comments of Prime Minister Jean Chrétien on whether he supported an American plan to attack Iraq. The *Globe and Mail* headline read: "PM to Bush: Hold Off On War." The *Toronto Star* blared: "Chretien Supports U.S. Push For War."

Deciding on the news of the day is an interpretive editorial exercise influenced by newsroom culture, news judgment, and the form of media. News is information deemed to be novel or significant, according to the interests of the journalist, the news organization, its readers, and society at large. Journalists do not traffic in information per se. Lots of information is not news. The idea of information in journalism is not the idea of information in biology, computer science, communication theory, or psychology. Journalists traffic in a type of information called

77 Kovach and Rosenstiel, *The Elements of Journalism*, 44.

news.[78] News is not a natural kind. News is a social category that journalists have constructed over several centuries. Nature does not carve the world into things that are news and things that are not. Journalists divide the world into news and non-news.

Like all interpretation, journalism interpretation uses Bruner-like codes to organize information into meaningful stories. The inverted-pyramid structure and the human-interest feature are examples of journalistic codes for story composition. These forms of narrative belong to what psychologists call "interpretive cognition."

Journalists use codes to compress data into relatively short stories. When reporters cover a complex event, such as a federal budget, they organize a blizzard of information by selecting the most important facts, picking the relevant issues, and choosing story angles. Editors construct an elaborate editorial plan that reduces the glut of material to a manageable package of stories. This selecting, categorizing, and organizing of material are essential components of a coherent interpretation that readers can understand.

Codes also come into play when journalists supply context. "Context" refers to the history, causes, and impact of an event. Context for a federal budget includes information on previous budgets, the economy, an upcoming election, and so on. A foreign reporter realizes that meaningful reports depend on readers and reporters sharing background knowledge and a social context. For example, I was never completely successful in my attempts to explain Canada's constitutional complexities to Europeans.

Another form of interpretation is the frame of a story – its general, organizing perspective. Journalists can frame a report on heroin addicts as a story about criminals or a story about people with a health problem. Stories may "frame" Latin American revolutionaries as dangerous rebels or as freedom fighters.

The ubiquity of interpretation prevents clear division of journalism into reports of fact and reports that interpret the facts. We can, however,

78 Information in computer technology is a sequence of binary code in digital language. Information in biology refers to DNA gene sequences. Communication theory measures information as an objective quantity between signal and receiver, based on the surprise value of a piece of information. See MacKay, "Information Theory," and Dretske, *Knowledge and the Flow of Information*, 45. The locus classicus of mathematical communication theory is Shannon's "The Mathematical Theory of Communication." For the cognitive sense of information, see Young, *Philosophy and the Brain*, 26–50. For information and mass communication, see DeFleur and Ball-Rokeach, *Theories of Mass Communication*, 8.

say that some journalism reports are more interpretive than others. In some contexts, journalists intentionally strip away most of the interpretation. For example, Canadian reporters tend to write careful descriptions of court trials. Judges tell witnesses at trials to "stick to the facts" in their testimony. Yet some vestiges of interpretation always remain. Stories that stick to the facts are not pure, factual (non-interpretive) reports but stories that restrain extrapolation, speculation, and unwarranted inferences. They hover close to the level of observation.

Journalistic interpretation therefore is ubiquitous and holistic. The journalist constructs reports by bringing together facts, concepts, values, probabilities, presumptions, and background knowledge. Holistic interpretation is a complex encounter between the world and a journalist's cognitive, emotive, and perceptual abilities. Journalists neither manufacture news nor simply record stimuli. They interpret their experiences against the background of their conceptual schemes. Observations and theories interanimate and influence each other. The reporter's concepts affect how he or she interprets what he or she sees, which in turn alters how he or she conceives the event. To use jargon from cognitive psychology, the process of interpretation is both "bottom–up" and "top–down."

A simple question brings out the importance of interpretation to journalism. What is the difference between the journalist as a reporter and the tape machine as a recorder? Imagine that I go into a news conference and turn on a tape recorder while taking notes. What is the difference between the recorder and me? If reporting is the passive recording of information, then the answer is: not much. But if reporting is active, holistic interpretation, there is a large difference. I differ from the tape recorder in the way in which I handle the input conceptually. I select it and edit it. I place it in context, seek evidence, and consider implications. I compare isolated facts with the rest of what is known. In sum, I interpret. Journalism interpretation is this rich mix of percept and stimuli, code and experience, mind and world.

Objective Evaluation in Journalism

Pragmatic objectivity is the epistemic evaluation of truth-seeking inquiry in journalism. It guides the difficult search for verified truths, and it restrains partiality. Journalists and their reports are objective to the degree that they satisfy two levels of objectivity. On the first level, reports must satisfy, to some tolerable degree, the requirements of objectivity in general. That is, reports must be constructed by an objective stance in accordance with three types of generic standards – empirical standards, coherence standards, and standards of rational debate. On the second level, reports must satisfy, to some tolerable degree, the standards and rules specific to journalism. The same applies when we consider the objectivity of journalists and news organizations. Journalists are objective to the degree that they adopt the objective stance and adhere to the two levels of objective standards in composing their stories.

Let us examine each level separately. On the first level, objective journalists have adopted the objective stance if they display the general dispositions of open rationality, partial transcendence, disinterested truth, and integrity. Objective journalists practise open rationality in their domain of inquiry by accepting the burdens of rationality – to listen to all sides, to learn from criticism, and to be accountable to the public for the content of their reports. Objective journalists seek partial transcendence by attempting to improve their current understanding of issues by engaging other viewpoints. They exhibit partial transcendence by putting aside their biases and parochial preferences. They practice partial transcendence by putting a critical distance between themselves and their beliefs and by approaching stories with a healthy scepticism. As we saw with writers of science and history, journalists display their objectivity by their professional attitude, the carefulness of their reporting, and the restrained tone of their reports.

The objective journalist is disposed towards disinterested truth if he or she refuses to prejudge a story and follows the facts to the truth, wherever the facts lead. The disinterested journalist does not allow personal interests to overwhelm passion for truth. He or she is willing to correct errors and to admit that a story idea is wrong-headed and should not be published. Objective journalists let integrity guide their work.

The journalist is not objective simply because he or she has a set of dispositions. Objective journalists put these general dispositions to work by adhering to three types of generic standards. They evaluate their reports for their overall fit with the generic objective standards for all inquiry, mentioned above. They should base any report on sufficient evidence derived from reliable observations and, where possible, from solid empirical studies. A report should not contain logical inconsistencies, manipulative rhetoric, or fallacies. If claims violate well-known facts and established knowledge, the objective journalist investigates this incoherence.

The three generic standards correspond with three traditions in the history of journalism: empirical standards of inquiry, with the emphasis on factuality in reporting; standards of coherence, with the long tradition of comparing claims with existing knowledge and experts; and standards of rational debate, with the idea of fairness, openness, and impartiality.

Pragmatic objectivity also requires reports to satisfy, to a tolerable degree, second-level requirements – rules and standards specific to journalism – in the same way that health researchers apply specific standards to drug trials. These rules and standards interpret the meaning of objectivity for the domain of journalism. Many of them exist already as informal rules of practice in newsrooms or occur in journalism codes of ethics. In newsrooms, specific empirical standards take form in editors' directives to reporters to gather accounts from eyewitnesses or to go and observe events themselves. The journalist should check findings against available facts and sources.

Accuracy, verification, and completeness are prime empirical standards in journalism. Accuracy calls for accurate quotations and paraphrases of statements and correct numbers. It forbids manipulation of news images and use of misleading dramatizations and "reconstructions" of events. Verification calls on reporters to cross-check claims of potential whistleblowers against original documents. Its standards include rules on the number (and quality) of anonymous sources. The standard of completeness means that stories should be substantially complete by including the essential facts, main consequences, and major viewpoints. Good newsrooms have empirical standards for types of recurring stories, such as the reporting of opinion polls. The standards demand that reporters check the poll sponsors, the polling agency, the sample size, the margin of error, the wording of questions, the dates when the poll was taken, and other information. Good newsrooms support these reporting standards with a layer of tough editing standards that take nothing for granted and challenge assertions.

Codes of ethics for journalism do not spell out standards of coherence. They do not contain directives to "be logical" or "test your claim against other beliefs." But quality journalism tests for coherence at every turn. Any journalist who has tried to construct a complex story, such as Claude Adams in Kathmandu, knows that the coherence of evidence from many sources is a prime consideration. Any journalist who has tried to report on an alleged scientific breakthrough knows how important it is to evaluate the claim by appeal to other experts and existing scientific knowledge.

Coherence considerations take centre stage when journalists attempt to weigh diverse perspectives on a controversial issue.

Journalists cannot avoid selecting and evaluating viewpoints. They must ask questions. How does this viewpoint fit prevailing knowledge in the field in question? Is it credible? Does it fit with previous, similar studies? This is Thagard's "explanatory coherence" at work in journalism. Some degree of subjectivity and uncertainty will surround such selections. What is the "appropriate" number of diverse views? Who is a bone fide expert? Is there an authoritative consensus on this issue? May today's "fringe" viewpoint be tomorrow's majority opinion? Despite these difficulties, the responsible, objective journalist makes every effort to reach a fair judgment on the credibility of viewpoints.

Objective journalists adhere to the standards of rational debate in their work. Newsroom practice follows the ideal of rational debate when reporters include a diversity of views in their reports and are careful to represent fairly the views of all groups. Some newsrooms have rules that reduce or eliminate stereotyping by race, gender, age, and religion. The code of ethics for the Society of Professional Journalists, under its principle to seek the truth, urges journalists to "tell the story of the diversity and magnitude of the human experience." In recent years, journalists have interpreted the standard of rational debate to mean that reporters should make a special effort to represent the voices of the less powerful and the marginalized.

In summary, pragmatic objectivity in journalism is a holistic, fallible, rational evaluation of reports. A report is objective to the degree that it derives from an objective stance and satisfies the two levels of standards – those generic to inquiry and those specific to journalism practice. In some cases, the standards will collide, making objective judgment difficult. For example, a journalist may find that, by some empirical standards, a new scientific study appears valid and important. Yet the study goes against existing knowledge and the opinion of most experts. Empirical and coherence standards appear to clash. The best that the objective journalist can do in such a circumstance is to weigh the standards and evidence against each other and include any uncertainty in his or her report. Similarly, tension may arise between the journalist's desire to report with diversity and fairness and his or her commitment to reporting the truth. For example, a journalist may be tempted to ignore or play down some damaging facts about a struggling minority. Once again, the objective journalist can only do his or her best to weigh the conflicting standards while maintaining the primary obligation to tell the truth, independently, to the public.

IMPLICATIONS OF PRAGMATIC OBJECTIVITY FOR JOURNALISM

At least three major questions, addressed in this section, arise about pragmatic objectivity in application to journalism. First, does it, by stressing holistic evaluation, undermine the role of facts in journalism? Second, is it inconsistent in combining objective standards and subjective values? Third, does it apply to many forms of journalism, some of which reject objectivity? This section looks as well at the role of journalists's attachments.

Facts and Values

Pragmatic objectivity does not diminish the role of gathering and verifying facts. It recognizes, for instance, the importance of facts to investigative journalists in their efforts to expose corruption. Facts provide a vital test of interpretations, from the simplest of news reports to the most complex stories about foreign affairs. But pragmatic objectivity regards the appeal to facts as only one test of objectivity. Facts are a small part of our corpus of knowledge. Nevertheless they anchor our conceptual systems in experience. They force interpretations to face the test of an external world.

A more difficult issue arises in the second question. Is the theory of pragmatic objectivity inconsistent by speaking of both facts and values? Is "objective evaluation" or "objective interpretation" a contradiction in terms? The feeling that there exists some inconsistency springs from deep-seated intuitions about the intrinsic subjectivity of valuing and interpreting. We are dealing here with fundamental philosophical assumptions. These mistaken intuitions give rise to confusions on two levels. On the first, there is a common presumption that particular statements cannot be objective if they contain valuings and interpretations. On the second, there is a common presumption that the objective stance in general must be "value-free."

Consider the first level of confusion – that reports cannot be objective if a reporter inserts his or her evaluations or interpretations into the story. One source of this view is belief in the discredited fact–value dichotomy – only pure statements of facts are objective. This view leads to traditional objectivity. I do not repeat my arguments against the dichotomy or against traditional objectivity. I note simply that my discussion so far has argued that interpretation can be objective to the degree that it satisfies the two levels of standards of objectivity.

It is fortunate that we can conceive of ways to assess objectively statements that contain more than fact, because journalism is replete with value judgments. The daily news is full of implicit or explicit value judgments – tales of winners and losers, good guys and bad guys. Reporters cannot avoid evaluative language in reporting on unfair bosses, brutal massacres, vicious murders, notorious pedophiles, and dangerous terrorists. Journalists employ evaluations in selecting credible sources or displaying scepticism towards a new scientific theory. To enter journalism is to enter a value-laden craft. New journalists learn more than the skills of writing news and gathering information. They acculturate into a realm of reporting routines, news values, and peer attitudes. Thus a theory of objectivity must provide standards by which to assess these value-laden activities.

To remove lingering doubts about the compatibility of objectivity and valuation we need a sea change in our views about the nature of values and valuation. The assumption at the root of most of the trouble is this: the act of valuing is not a rational act that one can assess by objective standards. The act results in a judgment determined by subjective factors, such as our interests, emotions, and biases. Psychologically, what I value is the result of emotion or a self-interested attitude that is not based on reason or objective thinking. Valuing is the product of an encapsulated faculty of emotion or desire.[79] To value anything is a brute psychological fact that has causes, but eludes objective evaluation.[80]

Historically, this subjectivism has drawn support from a dualistic psychology that divides humans into two parts – cool, factual reason and a hot, irrational (or arational) set of emotions and impulses. Traces of this psychology go back as far as Plato's depiction of the rational soul as a dominating chariot driver in the *Phaedrus*.[81] For subjectivism, value judgments are subjective because they are "merely" expressions of an irrational or a-rational part of the psyche. They express only a positive or negative attitude (or emotion) towards actions or objects. The assumption is that one cannot evaluate these attitudes in an objective manner – they are idiosyncratic and personal.

Subjectivism does not have to hold that reason plays no role at all. Although emotions and desires set our "ends" and what we value, reason

79 By "encapsulated" I mean a psychological operation not influenced in its processing of information by other psychological operations. For an explanation of encapsulation in psychology, see Fodor's *The Modularity of Mind.*

80 I do not claim that all people who are suspicious about the objectivity of valuation embrace this psychology. However, I believe that some form of this psychology, or some of its assumptions, is part of this attitude towards valuation.

81 Plato, *The Collected Dialogues of Plato,* 499-500 (253d–254e).

can tell us how to achieve these values or how to try to control the emotions and desires, where they conflict. But an instrumental notion of reason does not eliminate the inherently subjective nature of our valuing. If we share values, it is possible for us to reason together and co-operate. But if we disagree on basic values, there is no way for us to determine objectively that my values are better or "more true" than yours. At best, I can try to persuade you to see the superior nature of my values through exhortation, emotion, and rhetoric.

There is no rational, objective method of evaluating the ends and values that we happen to prefer. In contrast, judgments of fact are objective descriptions of the world, arrived at by observation of external objects. They are the products of the rational psyche. Where we disagree, we can appeal to external, objective facts. We can see how deeply such assumptions have entered our culture by the popularity of the rebuttal, "But that's *just* your own value judgment." The word "just" gets its force from the presumed subjective nature of value judgments.[82]

The theory of pragmatic objectivity rests on three contrary assumptions. First, our evaluations have a subjective component, but they are not intrinsically or inescapably subjective or "personal." In many cases, our valuations are not just the expression of subjective biases or emotions. Second, our valuations are susceptible to rational influence and to rational, objective assessment. Third, our valuing is not the product of encapsulated psychological faculties. In coming to judgments of any kind, individuals combine valuing, observation, interpreting, and theorizing. Value judgments can be as rational and as holistic as other types of judgments.

The first step in supporting these three assumptions is to question directly the presumption that value judgments are merely subjective. When we look carefully at our acts of valuing, we realize that this view is an exaggeration of the subjectivity inherent in valuing. It is a platitude that does not agree with much of our moral experience. To be sure, part

82 When dressed up in philosophical language, this ethical subjectivism has taken on several forms. One of them is emotivism, which was popular among logical positivists such as A.J. Ayer and other philosophers in the mid-twentieth century. In 1923, Ogden and Richards, in *The Meaning of Meaning*, made an influential distinction between emotive and descriptive language. Charles L. Stevenson developed the distinction in 1944 in his *Ethics and Language*. Ogden and Richards said that the ethical sense of "good" was a "purely emotive sense" that expressed an attitude and might be used to persuade other people to adopt a similar attitude.

of valuing *is* to adopt a favourable or unfavourable attitude towards something. Values are subjective and personal in the obvious sense that they are *my* values or *our* values. Also, some value judgments and some actions based on value judgments can be irrational because intense impulses prompt them.

There is, all told, an undeniable affective component in valuing. Yet a good deal of our valuing displays a rational and social component. Unless we are totally in the grip of passion or egoistic impulses, or we are sociopaths, our valuing displays an openness to influence from reflection on our values and the views of others. It is not true that values are inert, subjective facts immune to the influence of external facts or objective forms of thought. Changing external circumstances cause us to reconsider our value judgments. New circumstances may challenge my values. For example, my idea that life is an absolute value may be questioned by the development of medical technology that prolongs the lives of severely deformed newborns. The consequences of acting on certain values may cause us to reflect on our values and the values of society. Initially, I may be indifferent to the plight of a group of people. But I may begin to care about them from an examination of their plight and by rational arguments that call for assistance. Initially, I may be a strong supporter of the values of social stability and obedience. But I may reconsider the primacy of such values by reflecting on societies where stability entrenches unjust hierarchies and where unquestioned obedience may lead to war or genocide.

Subjectivism fails to appreciate the influence of these rational considerations in the evolution of a person's values. As an agent in a changing world, I have values that reflect an evolving set of preferences. I use these values to guide my actions, and I observe the results. I test my values and adjust them in light of new experiences and new goals. Ultimately, our ability to act ethically is due in large part to our ability to view our subjective preferences and partial perspectives from more rational, objective perspectives.[83] Much of what we value is not personal but lies outside ourselves. Rational arguments encourage us to embrace transpersonal values – the values of human rights, democracy, and social justice.

A subjective theory of values oversimplifies the role that valuation plays in the lives of individuals and in social deliberation about issues. A common view is the "standard desire model" of practical deliberation,

83 For the role of the objective perspective in ethics and political theory, see Nagel, *Equality and Partiality*.

which sees desires not as the conclusions of practical reasoning but as its starting points. They are subjective states that simply occur or not, and when they do they provide an independent and sufficient impetus (and reason) to promote their fulfilment.[84]

The model lacks the idea of evaluation. Rarely do desires occur without a judgment that there is something good, rational, or advantageous about acting on the desire. As Dewey said, deliberation is the active evaluation of what we experience as good – to *know* that it is good. Valuation means to prize and appraise, to have a pro–attitude, and to give reasons for the attitude.[85]

Scanlon has argued that many so-called subjective attitudes are really "judgment-sensitive attitudes" – things of which we can ask reasons.[86] There are some feelings and states that are not judgment-sensitive, such as being thirsty, hungry, or tired. We do not ask for reasons for having them. But beliefs, intentions, hopes, fears, respect, and contempt are attitudes of rational agents that are judgment-sensitive. As evaluative attitudes, they are attitudes for which we can be responsible.[87] In the realm of value and action, we should do more than express our feelings. We should seek rational desires. We should seek truth-informed attitudes and values as determinants of choice.[88]

Subjectivism is also an inadequate explanation of the role of valuation in the professions and in social deliberation on public issues. In the professions, the existence of some measure of subjectivity in a domain of inquiry or practice does not mean that this is an area where objectivity cannot apply or where all judgments are arbitrary. In important areas of public life, such as law and professional ethics, glib talk of one interpretation being as good as any other does not rate serious attention. Instead, professionals work hard to develop reasonable, objective restraints on interpretations and value-laden decisions. There is no room for the intellectual luxury of extreme scepticism about interpretations or a thorough-going subjectivism about value judgments.

84 Scanlon, *What We Owe to Each Other*, 43.

85 Cited in Weissman, *Truth's Debt to Value*, 323.

86 Scanlon, *What We Owe to Each Other*, 20. "Reasons" here is used in the normative sense – what good reasons a rational agent may have for believing x or doing y.

87 Ibid., 21.

88 For the role of truth and reasons in valuing, see Weissman, *Truth's Debt to Value*, 297–330.

On complex social issues, especially where many people may be affected, we must engage in public reasoning. It is not enough simply to express a preference for *X* over *Y*. Other people will not allow us to rest content with an appeal to a subjective emotion. We must formulate a rational, considered judgment about the issue and about the values involved. Weighing the conflicting values in any reasonably complex situation is *not* analogous to preferring chocolate ice cream to strawberry. My preference, as an employer, to hire only white, male employees is not just a personal preference or judgment. It is a preference that is challenged by both ethics and the law. Thoughtful positions on issues, such as global warming or the treatment of heroin addicts, are rational evaluations open to public scrutiny. The positions link facts and theories with goals and values. They are not arbitrary expressions of feeling. In all these situations, I need to argue that value *X* is worthy of rational support by showing that my value judgment satisfies the best available evidence and rational standards. I need to provide reasons that others could accept. In other words, we adopt the objective stance towards our valuations.

Reasoning *about* values and reasoning *with* values are therefore part of good inquiry, a coherent life, and a democratic society. By questioning the objective basis of my values, I transform my values from unconscious prejudices to explicit values consistent with my beliefs and goals. Rational inquiry and rational living by individuals, and by society as a whole, require the habit of objective appraisal. This is why the idea that values are merely subjective is pernicious. It undermines the crucial project of value evaluation in all spheres of life.

Given this view of valuing, I draw two conclusions. First, pragmatic objectivity can play an important role in assessing value judgments and evaluative language, within and outside of journalism. Pragmatic objectivity asks: do the facts of the case support the value judgment? Does the value judgment cohere with my other values and goals? Have I come to my judgment with a sufficient degree of critical distance and impartiality? Do I provide reasons acceptable to other rational agents? Second, valuations and interpretations can be objective to varying degrees, depending on how well they satisfy objective standards. Some evaluations are more objective than others. Therefore a report is not completely subjective just because it contains evaluative language. What matters is whether such elements have an objective basis.

Yet, even if we accept these conclusions, we do not entirely remove the intuition of an inconsistency. There exists a second level of confusion. It has to do with the attitude of objectivity in general, rather than with the objectivity of particular statements. It stems from the view that objectivity must be "value-free." The vagueness of "value-free" encourages many misunderstandings about what objectivity requires. One interpretation is that the objective stance must be completely neutral not only towards all sides in a dispute but towards all values or preferences. To be non-neutral introduces, almost automatically, an unacceptable subjectivity into objective judgment.

But the demand that the objective stance be a value-free zone is an impossible, mistaken demand. Objectivity is itself a major value of journalism, embraced as a means to other values such as truthful reporting. Objectivity is a set of standards and dispositions that expresses values. The issue of a value-free objectivity, or a remote, detached journalism, is a pseudo-issue. It is not necessary theoretically, or a major problem practically. The idea of journalists being *too* objective today is hardly a pressing issue. The real issue theoretically is the relative value of objectivity in inquiry and journalism. The real issue practically is whether the personal interests or narrow partialities of journalists undermine their commitment to objective standards in their daily practice. The main concern is whether various real-world influences, such as pressure from sources and unconscious biases, are distorting the accuracy, balance, and fairness of reports.

Talk of value-free or "neutral" objectivity is misleading for another reason. It confuses objective methods and partial goals. All practical activities have goals, and to have a goal is, by definition, to have a value. To have a goal is to be partial towards one objective over another. But it is still possible to adhere to objective standards and methods in the pursuit of goals. Objective journalism has goals and values. One of journalism's main values is truthful, independent reporting for the public. That does not make the ideal of objectivity inconsistent or subjective. What is objective about journalism is not its goals but its methods. What is objective about journalism is its methodological commitment to following the facts where they lead, to not prejudging a story, to representing viewpoints fairly, and so on. Practitioners can apply these impartial standards even though broad goals, such as the well-being of the public, motivate them. In the same way, judges and scientists serve the larger goals of justice and truth by following impartial methods.

The importance of not confusing goals and objective methods is evident in times of uncertainty and war. Under such conditions, journalists come under pressure to report in a patriotic manner – to compromise their standards of truth-seeking and independence. Patriotism encourages journalists to use partial methods. Rationalizations of patriotic journalism note that a goal of journalism is to support one's country. Don't codes of ethics state that journalism serves the public? This type of rationalization gets wrong both the goal and the methods of journalism. The goal of journalism is to a democratic public, not to the "country," often defined as the current policies of the government. In addition, journalists serve the public best, especially in times of conflict, by adhering to objective methods. Just because journalists are partial to serving the public, they do not have to use partial methods.

Ecumenical Ethics

The third question about pragmatic objectivity casts doubt on the scope of pragmatic objectivity as an ethical theory. How can any theory of objectivity pretend to provide guidance in an era of multiple forms of journalism?

Consider just a few varieties of journalism – activist or committed journalism; civic journalism, aimed at enhancing democratic community; and investigative journalism that takes sides. On the internet, many web sites feature "point-of-view" journalism. More and more, mainstream reporters use a lively, opinionated style or adopt an interpretive stance towards stories. They see themselves as providing meaning to a glut of news items.

These differences within journalism stem from the many possible functions of journalism and from the differing interests of journalists and news organizations. Many of these forms of journalism reject the ideal of objectivity, or they do not adhere rigidly to all of its standards. Investigative journalists, for example, reject the presumed neutrality of objective journalism. Other journalists stress the need for passion and attachment in journalism, which they oppose to passionless and unattached objective journalism. Civic journalism urges practitioners to be "fair participants" and "catalysts" of public discussion, not detached observers.[89]

My response to these attitudes towards objectivity is to take a step back and consider the enterprise of journalism ethics. Should journalism ethics have principles that apply to all forms of journalism? How universal can any principle be? The issue of different approaches to journalism is not specific to objectivity. It is an issue for journalism ethics as a whole.

89 Rosen, *Getting the Connections Right.*

In answering these questions, we should start by resisting any view of journalism that tends to divide it into competing camps. It is unproductive for investigative journalists to look down their noses at straight news reporters or for news reporters to pour scorn on activist journalists. It is equally unproductive to attempt to set up one value, such as objectivity, as a supreme and exclusive principle of journalism.

I believe that it is better to start from what I call an "ecumenical" view of journalism. Such a view recognizes that a healthy public sphere needs different forms of journalism and a plurality of journalism values. Different forms of journalism fulfil different public functions. An ecumenical approach believes that most forms of responsible journalism *should* share a moral framework that allows for commonalities and differences.[90] To a certain extent, those principles exist: principles such as truth-telling and independence occur in most codes of ethics.

One candidate for an ecumenical moral framework is contractualism. According to it, journalism as a profession has a social contract. Society provides journalism with guarantees of freedom. In return, society expects journalism to act responsibly and provide a range of public benefits. The responsibilities include informing the public fairly, fully, and accurately. I place the many responsibilities of journalism under three general principles – credibility, justifiable consequence, and humanity. Credibility requires the journalist to be a truthful and credible informer. It takes in the many ways of truth-seeking in journalism.[91] Justified consequence requires journalists to be able to justify any harm that they might do by their reporting and to avoid unjustified consequences. Humanity urges journalists never to treat others as only means to ends and to respect and recognize our common humanity.

The principles are general enough to accommodate most approaches to journalism. For example, credibility – the idea of doing one's best to provide reliable information and opinion – should obtain the agreement of both objective and committed journalists. No matter what approach one uses in journalism, from factual reporting to the "partici-

90 I say "most" because, given the worldwide differences in journalism, it is unlikely that all journalists will accept one set of principles.

91 As chapters above have shown, credibility has been a primary concern of journalists since the start of the periodic news press. It has an obvious economic and practical utility to journalists. In journalism ethics, it becomes part of the public's legitimate ethical expectations of the news media. The news media provide credible information as one of the conditions of the social contract. Credibility applies not only to reporting but also to analysis and commentary.

pant observations" of documentary journalism, the result should be credible communication for the public. I cannot provide a detailed elucidation of these principles here. My only purpose is to suggest what an overarching framework might look like.

My ecumenism holds that all journalists, despite their differing purposes and techniques, should fulfil their social contract with their publics by adhering to the principles of credibility, justifiable consequence, and humanity. The purposes of satirical journalism are not those of objective reporting; the approach of the investigative reporter is not that of the campaigning editorial writer. These differences are healthy as long as some general principles of responsible journalism apply and readers are aware of which forms of journalism are operating in different contexts.

Ecumenical ethics allows us to see more clearly the place of pragmatic objectivity in journalism. Pragmatic objectivity is a principle of responsible journalism and a requirement of the social contract. Pragmatic objectivity concerns itself mainly with credibility – journalists' efforts to provide accurate and balanced news and analysis to the public.

I would argue that pragmatic objectivity is a type of objectivity that most forms of journalism could accept. Traditional objectivity, with its rigid rules on all forms of editorializing, applies only to a narrow range of journalism – straight news reporting. Pragmatic objectivity can apply to more types of journalism because it provides standards by which people can judge reports that contain differing amounts of context, interpretation, and value.

Instead of dividing journalism into objective reports and subjective opinion, it is better to see it as a continuum. At one end of the continuum are accounts that stay close to the facts, such as reports about car accidents, fires, and petty crime. Those in the middle contain more context and assessment about the significance of events, such as protests, government decisions, and social issues. At the other end are stories about highly complex topics such as civil wars and foreign lands. Moving across the continuum, we encounter accounts with increasing distance from known facts, increasing amounts of interpretation, and decreasing degrees of objectivity.

How strictly to enforce the standards of objectivity in any case depends on the type of story, the intentions of the journalist, and the expectations of readers. The restraint of objectivity should affect most strongly news reports where careful, accurate informing is crucial, such as criminal trials, or where the truth is unknown and contested. In investigative reporting, objectivity will be present in the stress on verified facts, but there will be more allowance for judgment and evaluation. Even commentary in the news media can be evaluated for how well it satisfies objective standards. *New York Times* columnist Anthony Lewis has argued that good columnists have a point of view but "still prize facts above all."[92] Strictly speaking, pragmatic objectivity is not a specific style of writing or reporting. It is a method that forms of journalism can apply well or poorly and in varying degrees.

Pragmatic objectivity has the potential for acceptance by a wider range of journalists than traditional objectivity for one other reason. It does not oppose passion in journalism. It refuses to accept a stark opposition between a bloodless, detached objective journalism and a caring, attached journalism. It recognizes that journalists need to be passionate about what they do and why they do it. We need the eros for truth in journalism. But journalists also need the restraint of objectivity to test their claims. Passion and objectivity should work together to produce engaging *and* objectively tested journalism. Objectivity controls our penchant to speculate and promote our interests, while the passion for important truths lifts journalism above superficial coverage of events. It is natural that passionate reporters will chafe at their editors' demands for fact, documentation, and fair treatment. This chafing is the coming together of passion and objectivity. This tension is exactly how it should be.

Attachments

So far I have been stressing the commonalities among journalists and the wide applicability of pragmatic objectivity. But we should not gloss over the significant differences within the practice of journalism. One important source of difference, which requires separate treatment, is the belief that journalists cannot (and should not) avoid attachment to causes, groups, and ideologies. Most journalists, from the seventeenth to the nineteenth centuries, would have agreed with this modern doctrine of partiality. To a certain extent, contemporary journalism, disappointed with objectivity, has relegitimized partiality in journalism.

How does the theory of pragmatic objectivity perceive this call for attachments in journalism? If the claim is only that journalists have attachments, such as values and goals, then pragmatic objectivity agrees. As we have seen, all journalists have values and goals. Everything

92 Quoted in *Kovachi Rosentiel, The Elements of Journalism*, 97.

depends on *how* they define those goals and *how* they seek them. Attached journalists differ from journalists who adhere to pragmatic objectivity in two ways. They promote goals that are narrower than the goal of serving the public or democracy. They see their goal as promoting a specific group or social cause. In addition, they tend to prefer forms of journalism that are more interpretive, evaluative, and opinionated than objective reporting. Activist journalists attempting to protect the environment or to advance the rights of gay people may favour advocatory articles over mainstream objective reports. As a whole, the values of reforming, persuading, and critiquing take priority in attached journalism.

However, journalism from a point of view does not have to be cheap rhetoric, blatant bias, or propaganda. Quality attached journalism provides objective support for claims, sharp arguments, and a variety of perspectives. Responsible, attached journalists make it clear to their readers that they are writing from an attached perspective. They adhere to at least some of the standards of pragmatic objectivity.

In practice, however, attached journalism can violate the ideal of pragmatic objectivity. Pragmatic objectivity is not so flexible as to sanction all forms of journalism. It insists that all journalists make their primary attachment to the public at large. Where serving a particular group clashes with serving the public, the latter must prevail. If it is in the public interest to inform society about problems within a minority or marginalized group, pragmatic objectivity insists that it is the ethical duty of any journalist – even one "committed" to helping this group – to report these facts.

The same applies to method. Pragmatic objectivity expects attached journalists to adhere as closely as possible to the standards of objectivity. It considers use of partial methods to achieve one's goals a violation of a journalist's ethical duty. An attached journalist contradicts pragmatic objectivity if he or she avoids uncomfortable facts, distorts rival views, and so on. Pragmatic objectivity flatly opposes attachments if they leave journalists free to abandon their commitment to accurate and fair truth-telling.

Pragmatic objectivity's attitude towards attached journalism will always be one of caution. The ideal of pragmatic objectivity is a reminder to journalists to be wary of narrow attachments, because they can weaken the journalist's primary commitment to the public and to independent truth-telling. For example, a journalist with a strong attachment to environmental values may prejudge a story about a logging company accused of pollution. Positive talk about attachments, combined with emotional appeals to social justice, can rationalize an unbalanced journalism of ideology, of faction, and of prejudgment. At its worst, attached journalism is irresponsible, non-credible journalism.

A journalism of attachment that stresses feelings and opinion, without the restraint of objectivity, is reckless. A moralizing attached journalist may get the facts wrong or arrogantly presume to have the answers. For example, what is *the* truth about the conflicts in the Balkans or in Northern Ireland? Who are the "good guys" that an unflinching, attached journalism should support? Without the critical perspective of objectivity, journalists, as eager participants, may fall into the dogmatic belief that they have the one truth or the uniquely right moral standard. An unfettered journalism of attachment, in the hands of unethical reporters, would devolve into unsubstantiated journalism, where biases parade as moral principles.

It is crucial that journalists not confuse their attachments as citizens with their attachments as professionals. As citizens, it is natural for journalists to have a large number of attachments, ranging from ethnic group and religion to local school board. But to act as a professional is to assume other duties, other attachments, and other priorities. As a professional, the journalist is a special communicator to the public, for the public. *That* attachment trumps personal attachment to factions and special causes. Pragmatic objectivity does not deny that journalists have a stake in the fate of their society. As Robert MacNeil puts it: "We [journalists] are not social engineers but each one of us has a stake in the health of this democracy. Democracy and the social contract that makes it work are held together by a delicate web of trust, and all of us in journalism hold edges of the web. We are not just amused bystanders, watching the idiots screw up."[93]

True, but the engagement of journalists who adhere to pragmatic objectivity is different from the engagement of advocate or partisan journalists. Objective journalists are engaged in public life as agents who inform the public from an independent perspective. Pragmatic objectivity does have an "agenda" – that of an open public sphere. It is an engaged objectivity, in service to a democratic public.

93 MacNeil, "Regaining Dignity," 110–11.

SUMMARY: THE VIRTUES OF PRAGMATIC OBJECTIVITY

Has my exercise in ethical invention produced a stronger, more attractive framework for objectivity than traditional objectivity? Two questions are crucial. Does pragmatic objectivity advance a more defensible epistemology of journalism objectivity? Is this epistemology a more useful and appropriate theory for journalism today? I believe that the answer to both questions is yes. To support my contention, I review the strengths of pragmatic objectivity as a theory.

This chapter defines journalism as a practical, truth-directed form of inquiry. Objectivity is the evaluation of how well this inquiry, and the stories that it produces, satisfy epistemic standards that are truth-conducive. Pragmatic objectivity starts from the premise that journalism is an active empiricism, full of judgments, selections, values, and decisions under conditions of uncertainty. It does not begin with the inaccurate view of traditional objectivity that journalism is a passive recording of events and objectivity a matter of expressing the recorded fact. It avoids traditional objectivity's exaggerated norms of neutrality and detachment. It rejects the epistemic dualisms of traditional objectivity.

Instead, pragmatic objectivity makes "interpretation," "conceptual scheme," and "holistic evaluation" fundamental notions for a more plausible epistemology of journalism. Using this richer conceptual base, it can explain how to test acts of interpretation and valuing for objectivity. Some journalists criticize objectivity on the ground that they need to interpret the meanings of complex events. But one's "meaning" may be biased or ideological. Journalists need a theory of objective interpretation to guide their forays into interpretive journalism.

The conceptual orientation of pragmatic objectivity is ideal for journalism. An objectivity of fallible, holistic judgment is more appropriate for the hurly-burly of reporting than absolute, philosophical notions of objectivity. Pragmatic objectivity does not relinquish the ideal of truth-seeking, but it never loses sight of the precarious epistemic position of journalists.

Pragmatic objectivity also brings arid, acrimonious debates over objectivity down to earth. It shifts the debate away from irresolvable, abstract disputes about the theoretical possibility of a perfect objectivity to more concrete questions about the degree of objectivity of a specific report, relative to other reports on the same event. Pragmatic objectivity turns metaphysical questions about whether a report "mirrors" reality into more manageable epistemic questions about whether it meets certain basic tests in a specific context. Pragmatic objectivity clarifies what objectivity really requires, dispelling confusions that have been a persistent source of debate.

The theory of pragmatic objectivity, with its focus on concrete questions, is open to further psychological and epistemological inquiry. It encourages the study of bias and of how to avoid it in specific situations. We turn from metaphysical questions of objective reality to psychological questions about how certain forms of journalism communication can lead readers to a hasty conclusion or about the way in which language can stereotype social groups. Common sense tells us that everyone has a point of view. Pragmatic objectivity goes further to ask how, in concrete cases, our conceptual schemes lead us astray. Journalism objectivity would benefit from scientific study into the cognitive, social, linguistic, and emotive processes by which journalists interpret the world.

Pragmatic objectivity is not vulnerable to standard objections to traditional objectivity. For example, critics charge that objectivity is an ideal that requires an impossible detachment. Pragmatic objectivity replies that objectivity is a matter of good practice, available to ordinary humans. It presumes no superhuman attitudes other than the ability to adopt the objective stance. Every day, judges, labour-dispute arbitrators, administrators, and ethical journalists adopt the objective stance. An objective stance is not too onerous a demand of citizens with public duties, such as journalists. As for the impossibility of eliminating interpretation, pragmatic objectivity agrees, but insists on standards to test interpretations. The same applies to the truism that everyone is prone to biases. This fact is an argument *for* objective testing, as Lippmann understood.

One line of criticism mistakenly saddles objectivity with an unrealistic standard and then points out that journalism cannot live up to the standard. For example, Herbert J. Gans attacked objectivity as impossible because there is no "perfect and complete reproduction (or construction) of external reality."[94] But reproducing reality is too strong a requirement. Another objection is that objectivity is undesirable even if it is possible, because it encourages superficial, formulaic reporting that media owners or other powerful interests can manipulate. Theodore L. Glasser

94 Gans, "Multiperspectival News," 190.

ridiculed objectivity as a lazy citing of obvious facts and quoting of officials.[95] Formulaic, unreflective objectivity is a *faux* objectivity. Pragmatic objectivity is critical, self-conscious evaluation. Objectivity requires constant reflection on the practice of journalism and its assumptions. The fact that objectivity can serve as a rationalization for political or personal agendas, or for bad practice, is not unique to objectivity. The ideal of advocacy journalism is as vulnerable to misuse as the ideal of objectivity.

Another virtue of pragmatic objectivity is that it is a method of evaluation that is applicable to many forms of journalism, beyond straight reporting. It is compatible with an ecumenical ethics that allows many forms of journalism to recognize a core of common ethical values. As we see in the epilogue, this recognition of commonality is the first step towards the development of global journalism ethics.

95 Glasser, "Objectivity and News Bias," 181.

EPILOGUE

The Future of Objectivity

Principles are no less sacred because their duration cannot be guaranteed.

Isaiah Berlin[1]

Tho' the rules of justice be artificial, they are not arbitrary.

David Hume[2]

Our journey to pragmatic objectivity has travelled a long and winding road through 400 years of journalism history. In this epilogue, I first look at the timeliness of objectivity today and then consider the emerging world of interactive global media and the possibility of a global journalism ethics.

I believe that objectivity, in theory and in practice, will persist for the foreseeable future. It is possible that we will invent forms of practice unguided by objective standards, for better or for worse. The term "objectivity" may become unpopular in academia and other circles. Intellectual fashions come and go. But objectivity has deep roots in human nature. Humans have the ability to adopt a partial or an impartial perspective on events and issues. The tension between these two perspectives cuts across almost every aspect of our lives and is unlikely to disappear entirely. Standards of objectivity will persist so long as humans strive for rigorous, rational understanding and fair social arrangements. Some notion of objectivity will continue to underwrite epistemic and logical notions, whether it is "intersubjective validity" or "manifest rationality."[3] In journalism, objectivity may be maligned in theory, but in practice journalists will continue to use objective standards to evaluate stories.

1 Berlin, "Two Concepts of Liberty," 172.

2 Hume, *A Treatise of Human Nature,* 484.

3 Ralph H. Johnson, *Manifest Rationality,* 143–4.

PRAGMATIC OBJECTIVITY TODAY

Objectivity as Ethical Choice[4]

Throughout this book, I have presented objectivity as a stance that is useful for specific purposes. I do not demean the value of objectivity by making the stance voluntary. On the contrary, I believe that the decision to adopt the objective stance is one of the most important choices that we can make, as individuals and as a society. The decision is not restricted to a group of scientists or professionals. The decision has far-reaching ethical consequences because it is linked to thinking, acting, and valuing in a rational and coherent manner.

To be objective is to favour a rational perspective that follows experience, facts, logic, and public standards. Objectivity is part of our culture's attempt to say what knowledge is and how to pursue truth in the many domains of inquiry. Objectivity, properly understood, is a bulwark against authoritarianism in belief and practice. It is a defence against an obscurantism that allows the clever to manipulate the naïve or vulnerable. The attitude of objectivity stands squarely against the many forms of obscurantism in our culture, propagating themselves through the media. It opposes irrationalism, emotionalism, extreme religious fundamentalism, occultism, and fraudulent mysticism. For all the faults attributed to a detached, "cool" objectivity, I fear more a mindless emotionalism and an inability to assess critically beliefs inculcated by a media-saturated world.

The objective stance is part of that noble phenomenon called the liberal mind – a mind that is autonomous and critical and respects the autonomy of other minds. An objective disposition is a manifestation of rational, liberal agency at work. Citizens with objective dispositions, with their sense of fairness, insistence on evidence, and intellectual honesty, help public deliberation. The disposition to give reasons supports a peaceful resolution of disputes.

Objectivity encourages respect for the views of others. To be objective is to give reasons for and against views, rather than attacking the person or his or her class. The equating of truth and objectivity with the agenda of a social group or with an intolerant rationality is not

4 Popper calls the choice between rationalism and irrationalism a "moral decision." The decision to make critical rationality one's intellectual attitude is part of the decision to adopt the objective stance. See Popper, *The Open Society and Its Enemies,* 2:232.

only false – it is an insidious claim. It uses logic and rationality to eat away at the basis of our commitment to rationality. It blurs the distinctions between reason and cause, rational persuasion and propaganda. To adopt the objective stance is to incur a responsibility to communicate freely, clearly, and rationally. To become suspicious of reason and argument is in effect to lose a measure of respect for humans and the process of sharing ideas.

Objectivity is an ethical choice because its dispositions are "virtues of truth."[5] The dispositions of accuracy and sincerity, for example, are not just dispositions to pick up reliable information and to express "inner information states" correctly. They are virtues, because they must overcome obstacles to their operation. The virtues of truth and objectivity operate "in a space that is structured by motivations to conceal or dissimulate."[6] Internal and external obstacles make necessary an objectivity of method and evaluation. Externally, the world resists our intellectual probing. Internally, we must overcome our weakness for wishful thinking, mental laziness, and self-deception. Epistemic standards are closely associated with ethical norms of honesty, integrity, and respect for others. To follow objective standards and to practise objectivity's virtues are to express one's rational autonomy.

Psychologically, pragmatic objectivity represents a mature attitude towards the fact that knowledge is an interpretive achievement. It is a maturity that is able to live between the certain and the arbitrary. Our struggles to reach this psychological attitude, individually and as a society, are evident in our cultural history. Psychological studies on the development of epistemic attitudes have indicated that adolescents, after much struggle, tend to adopt a "post-sceptical rationalism" that is, I believe, similar in spirit to pragmatic objectivity. Boyes and Chandler have found that epistemic attitudes develop in stages, from naïve realism in childhood to swings between dogmatism and scepticism in early adolescence. Finally, the adolescent realizes that rational belief does not require unmitigated truth. There are methods that determine which beliefs are better than others.[7]

5 Williams, *Truths and Truthfulness*, 124.

6 Ibid., 124.

7 Boyes and Chandler, "Cognitive Development," 277–304. Psychologist Michael Chandler of the University of British Columbia has written on how youths grapple with doubt, objectivity, and relativism. See his "Relativism and the Problem of Epistemological Loneliness," 171–80, and "The Othello Effect," 137–59.

Isaiah Berlin concluded his *Two Concepts of Liberty* by linking an acceptance of pluralism with moral maturity: "Principles are no less sacred because their duration cannot be guaranteed. Indeed, the very desire for guarantees that our values are eternal and secure in some objective heaven is perhaps only a craving for the certainties of childhood or the absolute values of our primitive past." This craving may be a deep metaphysical need. But to allow it to influence practice is, for Berlin, "a symptom of an equally deep, and more dangerous, moral and political immaturity."[8] This book has argued that our culture should move towards this wiser, more mature attitude by adopting the notion of pragmatic objectivity.

When to Be Objective

The objective stance is not necessary in every moment of our lives. When I chat amicably with friends at a social event, it is inappropriate and annoying to insist that we subject everything said to a rigorous test for objectivity. If I watch a hockey game with a friend and we cheer for opposite teams, we are happily partial in our banter. If two groups of people debate what type of pizza they should order, their debate is about a small matter of taste. In the creation of an intense musical work, such as Beethoven's *Diabelli Variations,* or in the scientist's creation of an elegant hypothesis, objectivity plays either little or no role. If the purpose is to create a radical breakthrough in art, objectivity is not relevant.

Objectivity, however, looms large where we are dealing with knowledge-seeking and fair decision-making. Where we want to verify a scientific theory, inform truthfully, or make defensible claims, the objective stance is crucial. In society, the public expects its legislatures, government agencies, universities, and other institutions to make decisions that can be defended from an objective point of view. If I, as a teacher, evaluate your term paper, or if I, as a government bureaucrat, consider your application for employment, you will insist that I act objectively. If I am appointed to chair an inquiry into an urgent social problem, society will expect me to adopt the objective stance. Judges, labour arbitrators, Red Cross workers, university administrators, teachers, referees, dispute-resolution experts, peacekeepers, responsible public communicators, and most professionals practise their skills with at least some degree of objectivity. Objectivity is important in these situations for two reasons. We are dealing with decisions that have important consequences for others; and we live in a pluralistic, democratic

8 Berlin, "Two Concepts of Liberty," 172.

society where public representatives must appeal to objective criteria to justify their exercise of power.

Objectivity is an essential norm for responsible journalistic communication in the public interest. However, unlike judges, journalists do not need always to adopt the objective stance or to do so in full measure. Objectivity is not the only valuable tradition in journalism, nor is it an ethic that one must follow rigidly in all contexts. Social context determines in part the decision to adopt objectivity. Under brutal regimes, journalists may feel that it is more important to crusade for social justice. Objectivity is most effective in relatively stable liberal democracies, where an informed electorate is an important part of the political process. In chapter 6, I noted the varieties of attached journalism, where the adherence to objective standards is not always robust. In addition, opinion columnists, campaigning journalists, and editorial writers have considerable freedom to write from their perspectives. I indicated that some types of stories, such as reports on criminal trials, require strenuous application of objective standards. Other types, such as analysis and explanatory features, allow more interpretation.

Few people would care to live in a society that had no respect for the concept of objectivity, that saw no virtue in adopting the objective stance, and that refused to guide inquiry by the best available objective standards. Few critics of objectivity would want journalism to abandon objectivity *tout court*. It is one thing to cavil in academia about the myth of objectivity; it is quite another to live in a society that lacks the ideal.

OBJECTIVITY AND GLOBAL JOURNALISM

Of late, a new form of scepticism towards journalism objectivity has arisen, grounded in advances in communications technology, especially the internet. One line of thought argues that old-fashioned objectivity is inappropriate for the more personal and interactive journalism found on the internet. Another maintains that objectivity is not relevant to global news media. What global journalism needs, the theory goes, is more perspective, analysis, and interactive discussion. There is less need for neutral or objective reporting. To some extent, these arguments commit the same mistakes about objectivity that I canvassed in chapter 7. However, they contain novel features worth examining.

In the rest of this epilogue, I indicate how and why the ideal of pragmatic objectivity should be a major ethical principle of "new media" journalism. I argue that objectivity's future lies as a principle of "global journalism ethics" – a work in progress.

New Media Journalism

Two trends will affect the evolution of journalism ethics: the development of new media journalism and the establishment of global news media in a radically plural world.[9] In this section, I deal with the former trend.

Driving the communications revolution is the advent of digital multimedia, by which I mean three things:

- a quantitative increase in the number and forms of media and information providers, created by the internet and other communications technology,
- the convergence of media through a common digital language. Computer web sites, for example, present information in multiple forms – text, audio, video, and images,
- the multi-skilled journalist. Journalists increasingly produce reports for newspapers, television, and web sites using "notepads," recorders, personal digital assistants, cell phones, and digital cameras.

The explosion of forms of media has altered journalism and the media marketplace. Mainstream news organizations are now part of a larger, more competitive infosphere of web sites, specialty TV channels, and so on. Journalism is a small component of that large, ill-defined sphere that we call "media." Professional journalists share the public sphere with a host of interloping "content providers." Many media providers divide up the audience. In response to a fragmented market, some media organizations seek to attract a small slice of the total audience. Mass media move towards niche media. Other organizations pursue a "convergence" strategy. They reassemble an audience by offering content across types of media – newspapers, magazines, TV and radio networks, and web sites.

Among the new forms of media, journalism on the internet, or "online journalism," is having the greatest impact on the relationship between journalists and their audiences. On-line journalism is popularizing an interactive model of communication that differs from the older transmission model that dominates traditional news media such as newspapers. On the transmission model, the journalist is active and the audience is relatively passive. The journalist, as reporter, gathers sources,

9 For a theory of how media evolve, see Fidler, *Mediamorphosis.*

does research, and verifies facts. Reporting is not a dialogue; it is the transmission of results. The journalist, as commentator or editorial writer, transmits a message. The editorialist communicates with presumed authority, offering what appears to be the "last word" on an issue. The commentator constructs a linear argument. Communication is one-to-many, linear, and non-interactive.

On the new interactive model, however, the on-line journalist is more the initiator of a conversation than a transmitter of pre-digested facts or settled opinion. The journalist is a sherpa, guiding the reader through a blizzard of information and directing the reader to other on-line resources. Feedback to articles, shared with other readers, encourages further discussion. Stories on the internet combine text, audio, and video, supplemented by hyperlinks and chat forums. A reader may go back and forth between the components of the presentation. Interactive communication is many-to-many, non-linear, and multi-media. Interactive communication develops new audience expectations of journalism. Audiences expect fresh news when they want it. They want to engage in debate, to pursue their own on-line research, and to respond immediately by e-mail to news items.

The impact of these changes on journalism and journalism ethics is already apparent. All forms of media today, from newspapers to web sites, attempt to attract audiences by offering interactive features, from web opinion polls to TV town-hall meetings, where the audience supplies questions by e-mail. With so much information available to newsrooms, observers apply new, quasi-ethical terms to journalism, such as "transparency." Transparency refers to a news organization's readiness to inform readers on how it put stories together. Transparency can also mean "let the audience decide" about the credibility of information. Some newsrooms provide the audience with available information before they verify it. They say how they obtained information – for example, a video clip – and warn that the information may not be entirely reliable. They expect audience members to make up their own minds about the credibility of information.[10] This new ethics of "transparency" and "access" is a response to changes within and outside of journalism.

10 The issues of access and transparency are urgent because people can use the internet to send newsrooms their video, pictures, and alleged eyewitness reports on military coups, disasters, and other events in remote areas of the world. Editors must decide quickly whether to use unsolicited material that they have not verified by traditional methods.

It assumes that news consumers are media-savvy, and it moves some of the burden of responsibility away from the journalist to the audience.

On-line journalism is starting to redefine traditional ideas of balance and the process of truth-seeking. Balance in on-line journalism is not the formulaic inclusion of a couple of major viewpoints in one story. It is the progressive inclusion of multiple perspectives over many articles over many days. Also, on-line journalism uses the powerful resources of the computer to provide mountains of context to a story, through hyperlinks and hypermedia. Here, balance is the availability of multiple perspectives and endless background.

John Pavlik thinks that the internet's ability to provide layers of information and interactive communication should result in a more "contextualized journalism."[11] Given the dialogic nature of on-line communication, some on-line columnists do not claim to write the last word on any subject. Instead, they acknowledge frankly that their articles are "spins" or interpretations of events. They encourage on-line readers to use the multiple online perspectives available on the internet to triangulate their way to a more enhanced understanding of an event.

This ethic of perspective, this incessant talk of spin and attitude, is not necessarily the expression of an extreme relativism (or scepticism) about truth or a denial of all standards of pragmatic objectivity. The situation is ambiguous. On-line journalists talk about how their writing evolves towards a more inclusive and nuanced perspective. Jon Katz, the American on-line columnist, has described how preparing commentary on-line contrasts with writing columns for a newspaper. Within minutes of posting his articles on the internet, a host of experts from around the world use e-mail to provide him with counter-evidence, counter-arguments, original documents, graphics, and the latest academic studies. He finds himself writing not one article on a topic, but a series of them, with updated facts and alternative perspectives. He says that interactivity can be humbling: "The only thing I can compare it to is being tied to the back of a car and dragged through the street."[12]

Whither pragmatic objectivity amid these changes? Is it flexible enough to act as an ideal for these new forms of journalism? I find it difficult to be precise about its future because media forms are in transition, and new standards are slowly developing. Nevertheless, we can make some tentative comments. To begin with, technological change in

11 Pavlik, *Journalism and the New Media*, 23.

12 Quoted in A.L. Shapiro, *The Control Revolution*, 39.

journalism does not suspend the ethical responsibilities of professional journalists. Journalists cannot abandon a social contract that expects them to continue to provide the public with credible news and informed commentary. The fact that news organizations face commercial pressures in no way changes the ethical imperative of journalism to maintain its standards. In fact, complaints about the 24-hour news clock and profit-driven media owners only increase the need for new editorial controls on gathering of news and new public measures to make owners accountable. These changes do not threaten the legitimacy of pragmatic objectivity.

Similar remarks apply to the blurring of journalism and non-journalism by the proliferation of media. The blurring supports an increased emphasis on standards. Awash in media, the public needs a core of objective news reporting. It needs quality news organizations that serve as islands of credible, verified reporting in a sea of bias and opinion. More than ever, news organizations must alert their audiences to the difference between news and commentary, between reporting and "attitude."

The fact that on-line journalism is expanding quickly does not undermine the ideal of objectivity. It may be that no one can control the thousands of on-line writers who call themselves journalists but in fact treat media technology as merely a means to self-expression, self-aggrandizement, and ideological rants. Perhaps no one can control the proliferation of alleged news sites on the internet that are in fact unreliable, one-person operations or the propaganda tool for political groups. Yet ethically there is something that responsible journalists can do. They can insist that the profession of journalism remain true to its public responsibilities and to the standards of pragmatic objectivity.

Pragmatic objectivity in new media journalism is not merely a negative, constraining force. Its openness to perspective and interpretation makes its standards applicable to appraisal of new forms of journalism. Moreover, there are analogies between some of the practices of new media journalism and those of objective traditional journalism. For example, consider the journalism of writers such as Katz, with their enthusiasm for evolving stories and perspectives.

One can regard this form of on-line journalism as resembling the attempt by mainstream journalists to move closer to the truth. On the one hand, the manner in which on-line writers seek a more complete truth is different. It involves a more interactive journalism and a more interactive technology. On the other hand, this is a difference of degree. Is the sharing of perspectives on-line only a new twist on the rhetorical process of truth-seeking, described in chapter 7? Since journalism is in transition, we cannot press these analogies too hard. We have to wait and see how on-line journalism develops. I see this ambiguity of similarities and differences as a sign that changes in journalism are putting pressure on existing ideas of good journalism. Under such conditions, we can anticipate ethical invention.

What we *can* say, without ambiguity, is that pragmatic objectivity is not compatible with any form of journalism that abandons the responsibility to verify and balance information. On-line journalism that is nothing but a witty expression of an attitude is no more compatible with pragmatic objectivity than is uninformed bias in traditional news media. Journalism ethics cannot sanction rumour and unsubstantiated reports, in traditional or on-line journalism. As for the ethics of transparency, it is true that there are circumstances, such as major breaking stories, where one may use carefully important information, not fully verified. But this is an exception, not the rule.

Journalism should not embrace uncritically a general philosophy of "let the audience decide." News organizations should not hide unethical or irresponsible reporting under the cover of trendy phrases. Talk of transparency and interactivity should not function as an ethical fig leaf to hide a naked bias or to rationalize a caving in to competitive pressures. Journalists should not worship at the feet of new media. On-line journalism can disseminate unreliable rumour, manipulated images, and racist ranting. The edgy writing style that is popular on the internet can devalue logic and reasonable deliberation. The challenge is to prevent this powerful new medium from degenerating into a fragmented, self-contained sphere where bias dominates.

Pragmatic objectivity can provide a much-needed ethical compass in the midst of this disorienting change. Enthusiasm for interactive, multimedia stories should not overwhelm the objective impulse. My rhetorical theory predicts that such fundamental change will result in the invention of new values. It does not follow that the need for objectivity will disappear.

Global Journalism Ethics

Some ethicists see the development of new forms of communication as the main challenge to responsible journalism and traditional standards. However, beyond technology, there is another social fact that challenges journalism – the tension between pluralism and globalization. The news media constitute a global phenomenon that operates in a world marked by political and cultural pluralism. Under these conditions, the question of the future of objectivity becomes: what should be the role of pragmatic objectivity in a global journalism?

To answer that question we begin by considering what globalization means for the ethics of journalism. I argue that the global nature of news media implies new global responsibilities to a global audience. Journalism ethics can incorporate these new responsibilities only by redefining its principles. This reinterpretation of principles has two implications for objectivity. First, it redefines journalism objectivity as an international impartiality that leaves behind the last vestiges of parochialism. Second, it makes pragmatic objectivity central to the ethics of global journalism.

The news media are global in structure, content, and impact. Journalists increasingly work for global news organizations that obtain news from around the world. Their reports, via satellite or the internet, reach people around the world and influence the actions of governments, armed forces, humanitarian agencies, and warring ethnic groups. Their reports help to shape the way that countries or regions see the world and their place in it. Journalists, through the internet, report for a largely unseen, virtual community that extends beyond their local audiences. The audience is no longer local or national. It is international. The impact of a story carries over borders.

With global impact comes global responsibilities. Given global media, irresponsible and parochial journalism can wreak havoc. Unless media report stories accurately and with diversity, North American readers may fail to understand the causes of violence in the Middle East or a drought in Africa. Jingoistic reports can portray other regions of the world as possible combatants or as representing an undefined threat; they may incite groups to violence against other groups. In times of insecurity, news media can amplify the views of fear-mongering leaders who may stampede populations into approval of war or the removal of civil rights for minorities.

The impact of news media grows at a time when the world is struggling with poverty, environmental degradation, technological inequalities, and political instability. Global journalism takes place in a context of tension between the forces of pluralism and those of globalization. Our world is not a cosy, McLuhan-style global village where the media bring us closer together in a benign manner.[13] Our world is connected electronically like never before, yet this grid of connections coexists with a collision of

13 McLuhan, *Understanding Media*, 3–6.

cultures, values, and philosophies of life. The assertion of universal human rights and the spread of a global commercial culture coexist with communal attitudes that value particular traditions and cultures. The world is more global and more divided, more cosmopolitan and more parochial.[14] Journalists appear to face new and onerous ethical demands. They need to explain and explore plurality on a global scale so that colliding traditions can live together. Journalists need to help the world understand its daunting problems.

How should journalism ethics respond to these new conditions and demands? It is not enough to say that a global journalism needs to take ethical standards seriously. We are dealing with new forms of journalism that challenge the adequacy of existing ideals. Standards developed for a regional and national journalism of the previous century do not suffice to guide journalists today.

The conclusion that I draw is that we have to reinterpret the principles of journalism ethics from a global perspective. But what is that perspective, and what changes does it require? One change is a reconception of journalism's social contract and its public. The social contract of global journalism is not a contract with a regional or national public. It is a "multi-society" contract with citizens in many countries. The journalist's role as special public communicator becomes transnational. This new social contract requires that we add what I call the "claim of humanity" to the principles of journalism. The claim states that journalists' primary journalistic allegiance is to truthful, independent informing of a global public – humanity. When considering one's journalistic duty, a reader's place of birth, residence, race, or cultural group is morally irrelevant.

The claim of humanity derives from the Western tradition of cosmopolitan ethics, which regards all people as "citizens of the world." Cosmopolitan ethics enjoins us to make our primary ethical allegiance to the moral community of humankind. Ethical principles apply to a borderless community of humanity that respects human beings' rational and moral capacities.[15] Kant is a philosophical inspiration for modern cosmopolitan

14 For a thoughtful discussion of the challenge of pluralism, see Geertz, *Available Light*, 68–88 and 218–63. See also Ignatieff, *The Warrior's Honour*.

15 We find this cosmopolitan attitude in the stoics of antiquity, in the civic law of the Roman Empire, and in the universal brotherhood of Christian humanism. Cosmopolitanism has influenced Adam Smith, the American founding fathers, the human rights movement, the Red Cross, the Geneva Conventions, and the development of international law and the United Nations.

ethics.[16] In recent years, Martha Nussbaum has put cosmopolitanism forward as an antidote to parochialism in ethics and education.[17]

To respond to the globalization of news media, I believe that we have to go beyond the claims of humanity. Journalists should work towards the articulation of a new set of principles for a *global journalism ethics* – the next step in the invention of journalism ethics. A global journalism ethics is the project of another book. I can only offer three imperatives that sum up the thrust of such a perspective.

Act as global agents: Journalists should see themselves as agents of a global public sphere. The goal of their collective actions is a well-informed, diverse, and tolerant global infosphere that challenges distortions by tyrants, abuse of human rights, and manipulation of information by special interests.

Serve the citizens of the world: The global journalist's primary loyalty is to the information needs of the world's people. Journalists should refuse to define themselves as attached primarily to factions, regions, even countries. Serving the public means serving more than one's local readership or audience or even the public of one's country.

Promote non-parochial understandings: The global journalist frames issues broadly and uses a diversity of sources and perspectives to promote a nuanced understanding of issues from an international perspective. Journalism should work against a narrow ethnocentrism or patriotism.

What do these three imperatives imply for the ideals and standards of journalism, such as objectivity? To borrow an idea from music theory, we can say that we need to transpose these ideals and standards into a new, international key. We need international interpretations of standards such as balance and objectivity. Under global journalism ethics, objectivity becomes the ideal of informing impartially from an international stance. Objectivity in journalism has usually involved the duty to avoid bias towards groups within one's own country. Global objectivity takes on the additional responsibility of avoiding bias towards one's country or culture as a whole, especially when dealing with international issues and events. Objective reports, to be accurate and balanced, must contain all relevant international sources and cross-cultural perspectives. Global objectivity will

16 Kant's cosmopolitanism is evident in his pursuit of universal moral imperatives, his notion of humanity as a "kingdom of ends," and his proposal for an international federation of states to establish a perpetual peace for humanity. See his *Groundwork of the Metaphysics of Morals* and *The Metaphysics of Morals.*

17 For a debate on cosmopolitanism between Nussbaum and her critics, see Cohen, ed., *For Love of Country.*

require journalists to be more conscious of how they frame the global public's perspective on major stories and of how they set the international news agenda. The aim of global journalism should be more than helping the public sphere "go well" at home, as civic journalists say. Its goal should be to facilitate rational, objective deliberation in a global public sphere.

Pragmatic objectivity should be at the centre of a global journalism ethics. The objective stance is a means to satisfy the imperative to seek non-parochial understandings of issues. The objective dispositions of open rationality, partial transcendence and disinterested pursuit of truth are the dispositions that we want in a global journalist. The objective stance asks journalists to rise above their parochialism and to question critically the beliefs of their society. It asks them to consider their society's actions, policies, and values from a more impartial, global perspective.

Global pragmatic objectivity insists that journalists reject the inward-looking attitudes of extreme patriotism. It was disturbing to see how some U.S. news organizations during the Iraq war of 2003 so quickly shucked off their peacetime commitments to independent, impartial reporting as soon as the drums of war started beating. This parochial journalism is dangerously out of step with the emerging global world. Global pragmatic objectivity asserts that the primary ethical duty of a journalist in times of uncertainty and conflict is not to a patriotism of blind allegiance or to muted criticism. It involves a commitment to credible, independent news on the conflict, viewed from many perspectives. The transition to a global journalism should not threaten the future of pragmatic objectivity. Rather, it should reaffirm its importance as an ethical anchor.

The construction of a global journalism ethics faces many theoretical and practical obstacles. Conceptually, global journalism ethics must show in detail how to define standards and what that means for newsrooms. Ethically, it must explain what journalists in one country "owe" citizens in a distant land. It needs to explain how journalists can promote positive global development while remaining impartial public communicators.

There are also practical obstacles. Building a conceptual framework is only the theoretical part of ethical reform. There is also the slow, complex, practical task of developing new media institutions and practices. Exhorting individual journalists to be global-minded and objective is futile unless there is an institutional climate that supports these values.

Some journalists may doubt whether most news organizations would devote the extra resources needed to achieve a high-quality, cosmopolitan, objective journalism. Nevertheless, it is the duty of ethicists to show leadership, reject cynicism, and articulate new principles. Much is at stake. Only if we embrace the values of pragmatic objectivity and global journalism ethics will globalization in journalism mean something more than the development of broadband connections and converging media. Only if journalists re-examine their ethical role will they survive as critical informers, a force for humanity.

Our world needs objective journalists who care about responsible communication. The urgent problem of journalism today is not sterile objectivity but economic and technological forces that encourage subjective and irresponsible journalism, which does nothing to address our global future as a species. To devalue objectivity accomplishes nothing. It only leaves the public vulnerable to more manipulation. If journalism dismisses objective standards and ignores global responsibilities, demagogues will prosper and the public sphere will suffer.

AND IN THE END

My achievement in this book is modest. I have not written a practical manual for implementing pragmatic objectivity. I have not analysed news articles or news organizations. Instead, I have constructed a philosophical framework for understanding the evolution of journalism ethics and the concept of objectivity. It is up to the journalists themselves whether they wish to adopt pragmatic objectivity as an ethical theory. As for the application of pragmatic objectivity to specific stories, that will depend on the practical wisdom and holistic judgment of journalists in the field. This practical wisdom is part of the art of life.

References

Adorno, Theodor, and Max Horkheimer. *Dialectic of Enlightenment.* London: Verso, 1992.

Allison, Marianne. "A Literature Review of the Approaches to the Professionalization of Journalists." *Journal of Mass Media Ethics* 1, no. 2 (spring/summer 1986).

Alston, William P. *A Realist Conception of Truth.* London: Cornell University Press, 1996.

Anderson, Benedict. *Imagined Communities.* 2nd ed. London: Verso, 1991.

Andrews, Alexander. *The History of British Journalism.* 2 vols. London: R. Bentley, 1859.

Andrews, Richard. *Teaching and Learning Argument.* London: Cassell, 1995.

Arendt, Hannah. *Between Past and Future.* New York: Penguin, 1993.

Aristotle. "De mirabilibus auscultationibus," In *Opuscula.* Vol 6, *The Works of Aristotle.* 12 vols. Ed. W.D. Ross. Oxford: Clarendon Press, 1913.

– *Ethics.* Trans. J.A.K. Thomson. London: Penguin, 1976.

– *On Rhetoric: A Theory of Civic Discourse.* Trans. George A. Kennedy. Oxford: Oxford University Press, 1991.

– *The Works of Aristotle.* Ed. W.D. Ross. 12 vols. Oxford: Clarendon Press, 1913.

Arnold, Matthew. "Up to Easter." In Fraser Neiman, ed., *Essays, Letters, and Reviews by Matthew Arnold,* 338–54. Cambridge, Mass.: Harvard University Press, 1960.

Aspinall, Arthur. *Politics and the Press, 1780–1850.* London: Home and Van Thal, 1949.

– "The Social Status of Journalists at the Beginning of the Nineteenth Century." *Review of English Studies* 21, no. 83 (July 1945): 216–32.

Audi, Robert. *The Structure of Justification.* Cambridge: Cambridge University Press, 1993.

Audi, Robert, ed. *The Cambridge Dictionary of Philosophy.* Cambridge: Cambridge University Press, 1995.

Ayto, John. ed. *Bloomsbury Dictionary of Word Origins.* London: Bloomsbury Publishing, 1990.

Bain, George. *Gotcha! How the Media Distort the News.* Toronto: Key Porter, 1994.

Bainton, Roland. *Here I Stand.* Oxford: Lion, 1990.

Baker, Keith. "Politics and Public Opinion under the Old Regime: Some Reflections." In Jack R. Censer and Jeremy D. Popkin, eds., *Press and Politics in Pre-Revolutionary France,* 204–46. Berkeley: University of California Press, 1987.

Baldasty, Gerald. *The Commercialization of the News in the Nineteenth Century.* Madison: University of Wisconsin, 1992.

– *E.W. Scripps and the Business of Newspapers.* Urbana: University of Illinois Press, 1999.

Banister, Robert C. *Sociology and Scientism: The American Quest for Objectivity.* Chapel Hill: University of North Carolina Press, 1987.

Banning, Stephen A. "Discovering a Mid–Nineteenth Century Drive for Journalistic Professionalization." Paper presented to the annual meeting of the Association for Education in Journalism and Mass Communication, Atlanta, 2 Aug. 1994.

– "Truth Is Our Ultimate Goal: A Mid–Nineteenth Century Concern for Journalism Ethics." *American Journalism* 16, no. 1 (winter 1999).

Barnes, Barry, and David Bloor. "Relativism, Rationalism and the Sociology of Knowledge." In Martin Hollis and Steven Luke, eds., *Rationality and Relativism,* 21–47. Oxford: Blackwell, 1982.

Baughman, James L. *Henry R. Luce and the Rise of the American News Media.* Boston: Twayne Publishers, 1987.

Beaven, Brian. "Journalism." *The Canadian Encyclopedia.* 2000 edition. Toronto: McClelland and Stewart, 1999.

Beiser, Frederick. *The Sovereignty of Reason: The Defence of Rationality in the Early English Enlightenment.* Princton, NJ: Princeton University Press, 1996.

Bell, Martin. "The Truth Is Our Currency." *Harvard International Journal of Press/Politics* 3, no. 1 (1998): 102–9.

Berkeley, George. *Siris.* 2nd ed. London: Innys, Hitch and Davis.

Berlin, Isaiah. "Two Concepts of Liberty." In *Four Essays on Liberty.* Oxford: Oxford University Press, 1969.

Bernays, Edward L. *Crystallizing Public Opinion.* New York: Horace Liveright, 1923.

Billington, James H. *Fire in the Minds of Men: The Origins of the Revolutionary Faith.* New York: Basic, 1980.

Black, Jeremy. *The English Press in the Eighteenth Century.* London: Croom Helm, 1987.

Bloor, David. "A Sociological Theory of Objectivity." In S.C. Brown, ed., *Objectivity and Cultural Divergence.* Cambridge: Cambridge University Press, 1984.

Boardman, John, Jasper Griffin, and Oswyn Murray, eds. *The Oxford History of Greece and the Hellenistic World.* Oxford: Oxford University Press, 1991.

Bonjour, Laurence. *The Structure of Empirical Knowledge.* Cambridge, Mass.: Harvard University Press, 1985.

Bostrom, Bert. *Talent, Truth and Energy: Society of Professional Journalists Sigma Delta Chi.* Chicago: Society of Professional Journalists, 1984.

Boswell, James. *Life of Johnson.* 2 vols. Ed. G.B. Hill. Oxford: Oxford University Press, 1934.

Bouwsma, William J. *John Calvin: A Sixteenth Century Portrait.* Oxford: Oxford University Press, 1989.

Bovee, Warren G. "Horace Greeley and Social Responsibility." *Journalism Quarterly* 63 (summer 1986): 251–9.

Boyce, George, James Curran, and Pauline Wingate, eds. *Newspaper History from the Seventeenth Century to the Present.* London: Constable, 1978.

Boyes, Michael C., and Michael Chandler. "Cognitive Development, Epistemic Doubt, and Identity Formation in Adolescence." *Journal of Youth and Adolescence* 21, no. 3 (1992): 277–304.

Brewer, John. *The Pleasures of the Imagination: English Culture in the Eighteenth Century.* London: HarperCollins, 1997.

Briggs, Asa, and Peter Burke. *A Social History of the Media: From Gutenberg to the Internet.* Cambridge: Polity, 2002.

Brown, James Robert. *Who Rules in Science? An Opinionated Guide to the Wars.* Cambridge, Mass.: Harvard University Press, 2002.

Brown, Leslie, ed. *The New Shorter Oxford English Dictionary.* 2 vols. Oxford: Clarendon Press, 1993.

Bruce, Charles. *News and the Southams.* Toronto: Macmillan, 1968.

Brucker, Herbert. *Freedom of Information.* New York: Macmillan Co., 1949.

Bruner, Jerome. *Beyond the Information Given.* Ed. Jeremy M. Anglin. New York: Norton, 1973.

Burke, Peter. *The Italian Renaissance: Culture and Society in Italy.* Cambridge: Polity Press, 1991.

– *A Social History of Knowledge.* Cambridge: Polity, 2000.

Burtt, E.A. *The Metaphysical Foundations of Modern Science.*

Garden City, NY: Doubleday, 1954.

Butterfield, Herbert. *The Origins of Modern Science, 1300–1800.* Rev. ed. Toronto: Clarke, Irwin and Co., 1968.

Buxton, R.G. *Persuasion in Greek Tragedy.* New York: Cambridge University Press, 1982.

Calhoun, Craig. ed. *Habermas and the Public Sphere.* Cambridge, Mass.: MIT Press, 1993.

Campbell, W. Joseph. *Yellow Journalism: Puncturing the Myths, Defining the Legacies.* Westport, Conn: Praeger, 2001.

Careless, J.M.S. *Brown of the Globe.* 2 vols. Toronto: Macmillan, 1959, 1963.
Carey, James. "The Communications Revolution and the Professional Communicator." *Sociological Review* 13 (1969).
– "The Dark Continent of American Journalism." In Robert Manoff and Michael Schudson, eds., *Reading the News,* 146–96. New York: Pantheon Books, 1986.
– "Some Personal Notes on US Journalism Education." *Journalism: Theory, Practice and Criticism* 1, no. 1 (2000): 12–23.
Carlyle, Thomas. *On Heroes, Hero-worship and the Heroic in History.* Notes and introduction by Michael Goldberg. Berkeley: University of California Press, 1993.
Carnap, Rudolph. *The Logical Structure of the World and Pseudoproblems in Philosophy.* Trans. Rolf A. George. Berkeley: University of California Press, 1967.
Censer, Jack R. *The French Press in the Age of Enlightenment.* London: Routledge, 1994.
Chandler, Michael. "The Othello Effect: An Essay on the Emergence and Eclipse of Skeptical Doubt." *Human Development* 30, no. 3 (1987): 137–59.
– "Relativism and the Problem of Epistemological Loneliness." In K.F. Riegel, ed., *The Development of Dialectical Operations.* Basel, Switzerland: Karger, 1975.
[Chatfield, Charles?]. *Hints to Young Editors.* New Haven, Conn.: Chatfield, 1872.
Christians, Clifford. "Ethical Theory in a Global Setting." In T.W. Cooper et al., eds., *Communication Ethics and Global Change.* White Plains, NY: Longman, 1989.
Clark, Joe T. "The Daily Newspaper." *Canadian Magazine of Politics, Science, Art and Literature* 7, no. 2 (June 1896): 101–4.
Clavelin, Maurice. *The Natural Philosophy of Galileo.* Trans. A.J. Pomerans. Cambridge, Mass.: MIT Press.
Clayton, Charles C. *Fifty Years of Freedom, 1909–1959.* Carbondale: Southern Illinois University Press, 1959.
Cohen, Joshua, ed. *For Love of Country: Debating the Limits of Patriotism, Martha C. Nussbaum with Respondents.* Boston: Beacon Press, 1996.
Colby, F.M. "Attacking the Newspapers." *Bookman* 15 (Aug. 1902): 534–6.
Colish, Marcia L. *The Stoic Tradition from Antiquity to the Early Middle Ages.* Leiden: E.J. Brill, 1985.
Colquhoun, A.H.U. *Press, Politics and People: The Life and Letters of Sir John Willison.* Toronto: Macmillan, 1935.
Connor, Steven. *Postmodernist Culture.* Oxford: Blackwell, 1989.
Cook, Timothy E. *Governing with the News: The News Media as a Political Institution.* Chicago: University of Chicago Press, 1998.
Copper, John A. "The Editors of the Leading Canadian Dailies." *Canadian Magazine of Politics, Science, Art and Literature,* no. 12 (Feb. 1899): 336–52.

Craick, William. *A History of Canadian Journalism in the Several Portions of the Dominion, with a Sketch of the Canadian Press Association, 1859–1908.* Toronto: Ontario Publishing, 1908.

Cranfield, G.A. *The Development of the Provincial Newspaper, 1700–1760.* Oxford: Clarendon Press, 1962.

Crombie, A.C. *Science in the Middle Ages.* Vol. 1, *Medieval and Early Modern Science.* Garden City, NY: Doubleday, 1959.

Cronin, Mary, and James McPherson. "Reaching for Professionalism and Respectability: The Development of Ethics Codes in the 1920s." Paper presented at the annual conference of the American Journalism Historian's Association, October, Lawrence, Kan., 1992.

Cumming, Carman. "Parliamentary Press Gallery." *The Canadian Encyclopedia.* 2000 edition. Toronto: McClelland and Stewart, 1999.

Dafoe, John. "The Press Blamed for National Paralysis." *Canadian Printer and Publisher* (July 1917): 39.

– "Review: Press, Politics and People." *Canadian Historical Review,* no. 17 (March 1936): 14–24.

Dahl, Folke. *A Bibliography of English Corantos and Periodical Newsbooks, 1620–1642.* Boston: Longwood Press, 1977.

Daniels, George. *American Science in the Age of Jackson.* New York: Columbia University Press, 1968.

Darnton, Robert. *The Literary Underground of the Old Regime.* Cambridge, Mass.: Harvard University Press, 1982.

Darrow, Clarence S. "Realism in Literature and Art." *Arena 9,* no. 49 (Dec. 1893): 98–113.

Darwall, Stephen. ed. *Contractarianism/Contractualism.* Oxford: Blackwell Publishing, 2003.

Daston, Lorraine. "Baconian Facts, Academic Civility and the Prehistory of Objectivity." In Allan Megill, ed., *Rethinking Objectivity,* 37–63. London: Duke University Press, 1994.

– "Fear and Loathing of the Imagination in Science." *Daedalus* 127, no. 1 (winter 1998): 73–95.

– "Objectivity and the Escape from Perspective." *Social Studies of Science* 22, no. 4 (Nov. 1992): 597–618.

Daston, Lorraine, and Peter Galison. "The Image of Objectivity." *Representations* 40 (fall 1992): 81–127.

Davidson, Donald. "The Folly of Trying to Define Truth." *Journal of Philosophy* 113, no. 6 (June 1996): 263–78.

Davin, N.F. "The London and Canadian Press." *Canadian Monthly and National Review,* 5 (Feb. 1874): 118–28.

Davis, Edward B., and Michael Hunter. *Robert Boyle: A Free Enquiry into the Vulgarly Received Notion of Nature.* New York: Cambridge University Press, 1996.

Davis, Elmer. *But We Were Born Free.* Indianapolis, Ind.: Bobbs-Merrill, 1954.

DeFleur, Melvin L., and Sandra Ball-Rokeach. *Theories of Mass Communication.* 5th ed. New York: Longman, 1989.

Dennett, Daniel C. *Consciousness Explained.* London: Penguin, 1992.

– *Freedom Evolves.* New York, Viking, 2002.

– "Real Patterns." *Journal of Philosophy* 88, no. 1 (Jan. 1991): 27–51.

De Quincey, Thomas. *Confessions of an Opium Eater.* Vol. 3. In David Masson, ed., *The Collected Writings of Thomas De Quincey.* Rev. ed. 14 vols. Edinburgh: Adam and Charles Black, 1890.

Descartes, René. *The Philosophical Works of Descartes.* 2 vols. Trans. Elizabeth S. Haldane and G.R.T. Ross. Cambridge: Cambridge University Press, 1986.

Dewey, John. *Individualism Old and New* (1929). 8th impression. New York: Capricorn Books, 1962.

– *The Public and Its Problems.* New York: Henry Holt, 1927.

– *Reconstruction in Philosophy.* Boston: Beacon Press, 1948.

Dicken-Garcia, Hazel. *Journalistic Standards in Nineteenth-Century America.* Madison: University of Wisconsin Press, 1989.

Dickinson, H.T. *British Radicalism and the French Revolution, 1789–1815.* Oxford: Basil Blackwell, 1985.

Doyle, William. *The Oxford History of the French Revolution.* Oxford: Oxford University Press, 1990.

Dreiser, Theodore. *Newspaper Days.* New York: Horace Liveright, 1922.

Dretske, Fred I. *Knowledge and the Flow of Information.* Cambridge, Mass.: MIT Press, Bradford, 1981.

Dryden, John. "Astrea Redux: A Poem on the Happy Restoration and Return of His Sacred Majesty Charles the Second (1660)." In David Marriott, ed., *The Works of John Dryden.* N.P., Hertfordshire: Wordsworth Poetry Library, 1995.

Dummett, Michael. *Truth and Other Enigmas.* London: Duckworth, 1978.

Eisenstein, Elizabeth L. *The Printing Press as an Agent of Change.* 2 vols. Cambridge: Cambridge University Press, 1979.

Eksteins, Modris. *Rites of Spring: The Great War and the Birth of the Modern Age.* 2nd ed. Toronto: Lester and Orpen Dennys Ltd., 1989.

Elgin, Catherine Z. *Between the Absolute and the Arbitrary.* Ithaca, NY: Cornell University Press, 1997.

Epictetus. *The Enchiridion.* Trans. Thomas W. Higginson. Indianapolis, Ind.: Boobs-Merrill, 1948.

Ewen, Stuart. *PR! A Social History of Spin.* New York: Basic Books, 1996.

Ferguson, G.V. *John Wesley Dafoe.* Toronto: Ryerson Press, 1948.

Fidler, Roger. *Mediamorphosis: Understanding New Media.* Thousand Oaks, Calif.: Pine Forge Press, 1997.

Filler, Louis. *The Muckrakers.* Stanford, Calif.: Stanford University Press, 1968.

Flew, Anthony. *An Introduction to Western Philosophy.* London: Thames and Hudson, 1971.

Fodor, Jerry A. *The Modularity of Mind: An Essay on Faculty Psychology.* Cambridge, Mass.: MIT Press, 1983.

– *Representations: Philosophical Essays on the Foundations of Cognitive Science.* Cambridge, Mass.: MIT Press, 1983.

Foot, Michael, and Isaac Kramnick, eds. *The Thomas Paine Reader.* London: Penguin, 1987.

Foss, Sonja K., and Cindy L. Griffin. "Beyond Persuasion: A Proposal for an Invitational Rhetoric." *Communication Monographs,* no. 62 (1995): 2–18.

Fox, Robin Lane. *Pagans and Christians.* London: Penguin, 1986.

Frank, Joseph. *The Beginnings of the English Newspaper, 1620–1660.* Cambridge, Mass.: Harvard University Press, 1961.

– *Cromwell's Press Agent: A Critical Biography of Marchamont Nedham, 1620–1678.* Boston: University Press of America, 1980.

Frankfort, Henry, et al. *Before Philosophy.* Baltimore, Md.: Penguin, 1971.

Frankfurt, Harry G. "On Bullshit." In *The Importance of What We Care About: Philosophical Essays.* Cambridge: Cambridge University Press, 1988.

Fulford, Robert. "A Sort of Reckless Courage." In *The Journalists: Research Publications on the Newspaper Industry,* Vol. 1, 3–17. *Royal Commission on Newspapers.* Ottawa: Minister of Supply and Services, 1981.

Furner, Mary. *Advocacy and Objectivity: A Crisis in the Professionalization of American Social Science, 1865–1905.* Lexington: University of Kentucky Press, 1975.

Gadamer, Hans-Georg. *Truth and Method.* London: Sheed and Ward, 1975.

Galileo. *Dialogues Concerning Two News Sciences.* Trans. H. Crew and A. de Salvio. London: Dover Books, 1954.

Galison, Peter. "Constructing Modernism." In Ronald Giere and Alan Richardson, eds., *Origins of Logical Positivism,* 17–44. Minnesota Studies in the Philosophy of Science. Vol. 16. Minneapolis: University of Minnesota Press, 1996.

Gallup, George, and Saul Forbes Rae. *The Pulse of Democracy.* New York: Simon and Schuster, 1940.

Gans, Herbert J. "Multiperspectival News." In Elliot D. Cohen, ed., *Philosophical Issues in Journalism.* New York: Oxford University Press, 1992.

Gardner, Howard. *Frames of Mind.* New York: Basic Books, 1983.

Garin, Eugenio. *Science and Civic Life in the Italian Renaissance.* Trans. Peter Munz. Garden City, NY: Anchor, 1969.

Gaskell, George A. *How to Write for the Press: A Compilation of the Best Authorities.* New York: Penman's Gazette, 1884.

Geertz, Clifford. *Available Light.* Princeton, NJ: Princeton University Press, 2000.

Giffard, C.A. "Ancient Rome's Daily Gazette." *Journalism History* 2, no. 4 (winter 1975–76): 106–9.

Gigerenzer, Gerd, et al. *The Empire of Chance: How Probability Changed Science and Everyday Life.* Cambridge: Cambridge University Press, 1989.

Gilbert, Neal. *Renaissance Concepts of Method.* New York: Columbia University Press, 1960.

Glasser, Theodore L. *The Idea of Public Journalism.* New York: Guilford, 1999.

– "Objectivity and News Bias." In Elliot D. Cohen, ed., *Philosophical Issues in Journalism,* 176–85. New York: Oxford University Press, 1992.

Goldman, Alvin I. *Epistemology and Cognition.* Cambridge, Mass.: Harvard University Press, 1986.

Gottlieb, Anthony. *The Dream of Reason.* New York: Norton, 2000.

Graves, Robert. *The Greek Myths.* London: Penguin, 1992.

Groarke, Leo. *Greek Skepticism: Anti-Realist Trends in Ancient Thought.* Montreal: McGill-Queen's University Press, 1990.

Gunn, Giles. *Beyond Solidarity: Pragmatism and Difference in a Globalized World.* Chicago: University of Chicago Press, 2001.

Guthrie, W.K.C. *The Fifth Century Enlightenment.* Vol. 3, *A History of Greek Philosophy.* Cambridge: Cambridge University Press, 1969.

Haack, Susan. *Evidence and Inquiry: Towards Reconstruction in Epistemology.* Oxford: Blackwell Publishers, 1997.

– *Manifesto of a Passionate Moderate: Unfashionable Essays.* Chicago: University of Chicago Press, 1998.

Habermas, Jürgen. "Discourse Ethics: Notes on a Program of Philosophical Justification." In *Moral Consciousness and Communicative Action.* Trans. Christian Lenhardt and Shierry Weber Nicholsen, 43–115. Cambridge, Mass.: MIT Press, 1990.

– *The Structural Transformation of the Public Sphere: An Inquiry into a Category of Bourgeois Society.* Trans. Thomas Burger, with the assistance of Frederick Lawrence. Cambridge: Polity Press, 1989.

– *The Theory of Communicative Action: Reason and the Rationalization of Society.* Vol. 1. Trans. Thomas McCarthy. Cambridge: Blackwell, 1991.

Hackett, Robert A., and Yuechi Zhao. *Sustaining Democracy? Journalism and the Politics of Objectivity.* Toronto: Garamond Press, 1998.

Hacking, Ian. *The Emergence of Probability.* London: Cambridge University Press, 1975.

– *Representing and Intervening.* Cambridge: Cambridge University Press, 1995.

– *The Social Construction of What?* Cambridge, Mass.: Harvard University Press, 1999.

– *The Taming of Chance.* Cambridge: Cambridge University Press, 1990.

Hampden, John. ed. *The Beggar's Opera and Other Eighteenth-Century Plays.* London: Dent, 1984.

Hampson, Norman. *The Enlightenment.* Harmondsworth, England: Penguin, 1968.

Haney, Jesse. *Haney's Guide to Authorship.* N.P.: Jesse Haney and Co., 1867.

Harris, Michael. "The Structure, Ownership and Control of the Press." In George Boyce, James Curran, and Pauline Wingate, eds., *Newspaper History from the Seventeenth Century to the Present,* 182–97. London: Constable, 1978.

Haskell, Thomas. *The Emergence of Professional Social Science.* Urbana: University of Illinois Press, 1977.

Hawkesworth, Mary E. "From Objectivity to Objectification." In Allan Megill, ed., *Rethinking Objectivity,* 151–77. London: Duke University Press, 1994.

Herd, Harold. *The March of Journalism: The Story of the British Press from 1622 to the Present Day.* London: Allen and Unwin, 1952.

Herodotus. *The Histories.* Trans. Robin Waterfield. Oxford: Oxford University Press, 1998.

Hill, Christopher. *The World Turned Upside Down: Radical Ideas in the English Revolution.* London: Temple Smith, 1972.

A History of Canadian Journalism in the Several Portions of the Dominion, with a Sketch of the Canadian Press Association, 1859–1908. Toronto: n.p. 1908.

Hofstadter, Richard. *The Age of Reform: From Bryan to F.D.R.* New York: Knopf, 1955.

– *Anti-Intellectualism in American Life.* New York: Alfred A. Knopf, 1964.

Hohenberg, John. *Free Press, Free People: The Best Cause.* New York: Free Press, 1971.

Hookway, Christopher. *Scepticism.* London: Routledge, 1990.

Hudson, Frederic. *Journalism in the United States, from 1690 to 1872.* New York: Harper and Brothers, 1873.

Hume, David. "Of the Liberty of the Press." In *Essays: Moral, Political and Literary.* Oxford: Oxford University Press, 1963.

– *A Treatise of Human Nature.* 2d ed. Oxford: Clarendon Press, 1978.

Hyde, Grant M. "Taking Stock after 24 Years." *Journalism Quarterly,* 6 (1929).

Ignatieff, Michael. "Is Nothing Sacred? The Ethics of Television." In Ignatieff, *The Warrior's Honour,* 9–33.

– *The Warrior's Honour: Ethnic War and the Modern Conscience.* Toronto: Penguin, 1999.

Inwood, Brad. *Ethics and Human Action in Early Stoicism.* Oxford: Clarendon, 1985.

Inwood, Brad, and L.P. Gerson, eds. *The Epicurus Reader.* Indianapolis, Ind.: Hackett Publishing, 1994.

Ipperciel, Donald. "Descartes and Gadamer on Prejudice." *Dialogue: Canadian Philosophical Review* 41, no. 4 (fall 2002): 635–52.

Irwin, Will. "The Power of the Press." In Clifford F. Weigle and David G. Clark, eds., *The American Newspaper.* Ames: Iowa State University Press, 1969.

Israel, Jonathan I. *Radical Enlightenment: Philosophy and the Making of Modernity, 1650–1750.* Oxford: Oxford University Press, 2001.

Jackson, Mason. *The Pictorial Press: Its Origin and Progress.* London: Hurst and Blackett, 1885.

James, William. *The Meaning of Truth and Pragmatism.* Cambridge, Mass.: Harvard University Press, 1978.

Johnson, Paul. *A History of* Christianity. London: Penguin, 1976.

Johnson, Ralph H. *Manifest Rationality: A Pragmatic Theory of Argument.* Mahwah, NJ: Lawrence Erlbaum, 2000.

Johnson, Samuel. "The Rambler." In E.L. McAdam and George Milne, eds., *A Johnson Reader,* 159–98. New York: Random House, 1964.

Jolowicz, H.F. *Historical Introduction to the Study of Roman Law.* 2nd ed. Cambridge: Cambridge University Press, 1954.

Kant, Immanuel. *Critique of Practical Reason* (1788). Trans. L.W. Beck. New York: Bobbs-Merrill, 1956.

– *Critique of Pure Reason* (1781). Trans. Norman Kemp Smith. New York: St Martin's Press, 1965.

– *Groundwork of the Metaphysics of Morals* (1785). Trans. H.J. Paton. New York: Harper and Row, 1964.

– "Idea for a Universal History from a Cosmopolitan Point of View." In Lewis White Beck, ed., *On History: Immanuel Kant,* trans. Lewis White Beck, Robert E. Anchor, and Emile L. Fackenheim, 11–26. New York: Bobbs-Merrill Inc. for Library of Liberal Arts, 1963.

– *The Metaphysics of Morals* (1797). Trans. Mary Gregor. Cambridge: Cambridge University Press. 1991.

Katz, Jon. "No News Is Good News." *Hotwired.* www.hotwired.com (9 Oct. 1996).

Kent, Tom. "A Public Trust." In a series on *Toronto Star's* 110th anniversary. www.thestar.com (6 Nov. 2002).

Keshen, Jeffrey A. *Propaganda and Censorship during Canada's Great War.* Edmonton: University of Alberta Press, 1996.

Kidder, R.M. *Shared Values in a Trouble World.* San Francisco: Jossey-Bass, 1994.

Kiever, J.L. *The Electric Telegraph: A Social and Economic History.* Devon, England: David and Charles, 1973.

Kirk, G.S., J.E. Raven, and M. Schofield, eds. *The Presocratic Philosophers.* Cambridge: Cambridge University Press, 1966.

Kitto, H.D.F. *The Greeks.* Harmondsworth, England: Penguin, 1973.

Knight, Charles. *The Old Printer and the Modern Press.* London: Knight, 1854.

Korsgaard, Christine M. *Creating the Kingdom of Ends.* Cambridge: Cambridge University Press, 1996.

Kovach, Bill, and Tom Rosenstiel. *The Elements of Journalism.* New York: Crown Publishers, 2001.

Kristeller, Paul Oskar. *Renaissance Thought: The Classic, Scholastic and Humanistic Strains.* Rev. ed. New York, Harper, 1961.

Kuhn, Thomas S. *The Structure of Scientific Revolutions.* Chicago: University of Chicago Press, 1962.

Kung, Hans, and Helmut Schmidt. *A Global Ethic and Global Responsibilities.* London: SCM Press, 1998.

Kupperman, Joel J. *Value … and What Follows.* Oxford: Oxford University Press, 1999.

Lee, Alan J. *The Origins of the Popular Press in England, 1855–1914.* London: Croom Helm, 1976.

Lee, James Melvin. *History of American Journalism.* New York: Garden City, 1923.

Lenin, Vladimir Il'ich. *Where to Begin? Party Organization and Party Literature, the Working Class and Its Press.* Moscow: Foreign Languages Publishing House, n.d.

Leonard, Thomas C. "Lessons from L.A.: The Wall: A Long History." *Columbia Journalism Review* (Jan. 2000): 23–4.

– *News for All: America's Coming-of-Age with the Press.* London: Oxford University Press, 1995.

Lewis, C.I. "The Given Element in Empirical Knowledge." *Philosophical Review,* 61 (1952): 168–75.

– "The Given in Experience." In *Mind and the World Order,* 36–66. New York: Dover, 1929.

Lewis, Sian. *News and Society in the Greek Polis.* London: Duckworth, 1996.

Lilly, W.S. "The Ethics of Journalism." *Forum* 4 (July 1889): 503–12.

Limor, Yehiel, and Ines Gabel. "Five Versions of One Code of Ethics." *Journal of Mass Media Ethics* 17, no. 2 (2002): 136–54.

Lippmann, Walter. *Liberty and the News.* New York: Harcourt, Brace and Howe, 1920.

– *The Phantom Public.* New York: Harcourt, Brace, 1925.

– *Public Opinion.* New York: Macmillan, 1922.

Lippmann, Walter, and Charles Merz. "A Test of the News: Some Criticisms." *New Republic* (Aug. 1920): 1–42.

Lloyd, G.E.R. *Magic, Reason and Experience: Studies in the Origin and Development of Greek Science.* London: Cambridge University Press, 1979.

Locke, John. *An Essay Concerning Human Understanding.* 2 vols. New York: Dover, 1959.

Lunt, George. *Three Eras of New England.* Boston, n.p., 1857.

Lynch, Michael P. *Truth in Context: An Essay on Pluralism and Objectivity.* Cambridge, Mass.: MIT Press, 1998.

MacDougall, Curtis. *Interpretive Reporting.* 3rd ed. New York: MacMillan, 1957.

MacIntyre, Alasdair. "Epistemological Crises, Dramatic Narrative and the Philosophy of Science." *Monist* 60, no. 4 (Oct. 1977): 453–72.

MacKay, Donald. "Information Theory." In Richard L. Gregory, ed., *The Oxford Companion to the Mind,* 369–71. Oxford: Oxford University Press, 1987.

Mackinnon, William A. *On the Rise, Progress and Present State of Public Opinion in Great Britain and Other Parts of the World.* 2nd ed. London: Saunders and Otley, 1828.

MacMillan, Margaret. *Paris 1919: Six Months That Changed the World.* New York: Random House, 2003.

MacNeil, Robert. "Regaining Dignity." *Media Studies Journal* 9, no. 3 (summer 1995): 110–11.

Marzolf, Marion T. *Civilizing Voices: American Press Criticism, 1880–1950.* New York: Longman, 1991.

Matthew, H.C. "The Liberal Age (1851–1914)," In Kenneth O. Morgan, ed., *The Oxford Illustrated History of Britain,* 463–522. Oxford: Oxford University Press, 1989.

McAdam, E.L., Jr, and George Milne, eds. *A Johnson* Reader. New York: Random House, 1964.

McComiskey, Bruce. *Gorgias and the New Sophistic Rhetoric.* Carbondale: Southern Illinois University Press, 2002.

McConnell, Jane S. "Journalism's Role in Society: Ethics Codes' Framework of Responsibility." Paper presented to the History Division of the Association of Educators in Journalism and Mass Communication, Miami Beach, Aug. 2002.

McCracken, David. *Junius and Philip Francis.* Boston: Twayne Publishers, 1979.

McLuhan, Marshall. *Understanding Media: The Extensions of Man.* New York: McGraw-Hill, 1965.

McMullin, Ernan, ed. *The Concept of Matter in Greek and Medieval Philosophy.* Notre Dame, Ind.: University of Notre Dame Press, 1965.

Megill, Allan. *Rethinking Objectivity.* London: Duke University Press, 1994.

Meyer, Eugene. "The Post's Principles." In *The Washington Post Deskbook on Style,* 4–7. 2nd ed. New York: McGraw-Hill, 1989.

Milando, Joseph A. "Embracing Objectivity Early On: Journalism Textbooks in the 1880s." *Journal of Mass Media Ethics* 16, no. 1 (2001): 23–32.

Mill, James. "Liberty of the Press." In Ted Franklin, ed., *Essays on Government, Jurisprudence, Liberty of the Press and Law of Nations,* 21–8. New York: Kelly, 1967.

Mill, John Stuart. *Autobiography.* In Max Lerner, ed., *Essential Works of John Stuart Mill,* 11–182. New York: Bantam, 1965.

– "Civilization." In J. Schneewind, ed., *Essays on Literature and Society,* Notre Dame, Ind.: Notre Dame University Press, 1965.

– *Principles of Political Economy.* 2 vols. Ed. W.J. Ashley. New York: Longmans, Green and Co., 1929.

Mindich, David T.Z. *Just the Facts: How "Objectivity" Came to Define American Journalism.* New York: New York University Press, 1998.

Miraldi, Robert. *Muckraking and Objectivity.* New York: Greenwood Press, 1990.

Moore, Christopher. *1867: How the Fathers Made a Deal.* Toronto: McClelland and Stewart, 1997.

Morison, Stanley. *Ichabod Dawks and His Newsletter.* Cambridge: Cambridge University Press, 1931.

Moser, Paul K. *Knowledge and Evidence.* Cambridge: Cambridge University Press, 1989.

Mott, Frank Luther. *American Journalism: A History, 1690–1960.* 3rd ed. New York: Macmillan, 1962.

Muddiman, J.G. *The King's Journalist, 1659–1689.* London: John Lane, 1923.

Nagel, Thomas. *Equality and Partiality.* Oxford: Oxford University Press, 1991.

– *The View from Nowhere.* Oxford: Oxford University Press, 1986.

Nash, Knowlton. *The Microphone Wars: A History of Triumph and Betrayal at the CBC.* Toronto: McClelland and Stewart, 1994.

Neurath, Otto. "Foundations of the Social Sciences." In *International Encyclopedia of Unified Science* 2, no. 1. Chicago: University of Chicago Press, 1944.

Nevins, Alexander G. *The Blue Pencil and How to Avoid It.* New York: Forman, 1890.

Newell, R.W. *Objectivity, Empiricism and Truth.* London: Routledge and Kegan Paul, 1986.

Newman, Peter C. *The Canadian Revolution: From Deference to Defiance, 1985–1995.* Toronto, Viking, 1995.

The New Oxford Annotated Bible. 3rd ed. Ed. Michael D. Coogan et al. Oxford: Oxford University Press, 2001.

Nichol, Walter. "Newspapers from a Business Point of View." *Canadian Printer and Publisher* (Dec. 1901): 10–11.

Nietzsche, Friedrich. *Beyond Good and Evil.* Chicago: Henry Regnery, 1959.

– *The Twilight of the Idols* and *The AntiChrist.* Trans. R.J. Hollingdale. Harmondsworth, England: Penguin, 1968.

Novak, Maximillian. *Daniel Defoe: Master of Fictions.* Oxford: Oxford University Press, 2001.

Novak, Peter. *That Noble Dream: The "Objectivity" Question and the American Historical Profession.* Cambridge: Cambridge University Press, 1988.

Nussbaum, Martha C. *Cultivating Humanity: A Classical Defence of Reform in Liberal Education.* Cambridge, Mass.: Harvard University Press, 1997.

– *The Fragility of Goodness: Luck and Ethics in Greek Tragedy and Philosophy.* Rev. ed. Cambridge: Cambridge University Press, 2001.

– *Women and Human Development.* Cambridge: Cambridge University Press, 2000.

Ogden, Charles K., and Ivor A. Richards. *The Meaning of Meaning.* London: Paul, Trench, Trubner and Co., 1923.

Palmer, Michael. "The British Press and International News, 1851–99: Of Agencies and Newspapers." In George Boyce, James Curran, and Pauline Wingate, eds., *Newspaper History from the Seventeenth Century to the Present,* 205-19. London: Constable, 1978.

Passmore, John. *A Hundred Years of Philosophy*. Harmondsworth, England: Penguin, 1966.

Pavlik, John V. *Journalism and the New Media*. New York: Columbia University Press, 2001.

Peabody, Charles. *English Journalism and the Men Who Have Made It*. London: Cassell, 1882.

Peirce, Charles Sanders. "A Critical Review of Berkeley's Idealism." In Philip Wiener, ed., *Values in a Universe of Chance: Selected Writings of C.S. Peirce (1839–1914)*, 81–3. New York: Dover, 1958.

Penrose, Roger. *The Emperor's New Mind*. Oxford: Oxford University Press, 1989.

Perelman, Chaim. *The New Rhetoric: A Treatise on Argumentation*. Trans. John Wilkinson and Purcell Weaver. Notre Dame, Ind.: University of Notre Dame Press, 1969.

Perkins, Michael. "International Law and the Search for Universal Principles in Journalism Ethics." *Journal of Mass Media Ethics* 17, no. 3 (2002): 193–208.

Peterson, Theodore. "The Social Responsibility Theory of the Press." In Fred Siebert, Theodore Peterson, and Wilbur Schramm, eds., *Four Theories of the Press*, 73–103. Urbana: University of Illinois Press, 1956.

Phillips, Mark. *Society and Sentiment: Genres of Historical Writing in Britain, 1740–1820*. Princeton, NJ: Princeton University Press, 2000.

Plato. *The Collected Dialogues of Plato, including the Letters* (1961). Ed. Edith Hamilton and Huntington Cairns. 11th printing. Princeton, NJ: Princeton University Press, 1982.

– *The Republic*. Trans. Francis Cornford. London: Oxford University Press, 1968.

– "The Symposium." In *The Republic and Other Works*. Trans. B. Jowett. New York: Anchor, 1973.

Poovey, Mary. *A History of the Modern Fact*. Chicago: University of Chicago Press, 1998.

Popkin, Jeremy. *Revolutionary News: The Press in France, 1789–1799*. Durham, NC: Duke University Press, 1990.

Popkin, Richard. *The History of Scepticism from Erasmus to Spinoza*. Berkeley: University of California Press, 1979.

Popper, Karl R. *The Open Society and Its Enemies*. 5th ed. 2 vols. Princeton, NJ: Princeton University Press, 1966.

Porter, Roy. *Enlightenment: Britain and the Creation of the Modern World*. London: Penguin, 2001.

Porter, Theodore M. "Objectivity as Standardization: The Rhetoric of Impersonality in Measurement, Statistics and Cost–Benefit Analysis." In Allan Megill, ed., *Rethinking Objectivity*, 197–237. London: Duke University Press, 1994.

– *The Rise of Statistical Thinking*. Princeton, NJ: Princeton University Press, 1986.

– *Trust in Numbers: The Pursuit of Objectivity in Science and Public Life*. Princeton, NJ: Princeton University Press, 1995.

Powe, Lucas A., Jr. *The Fourth Estate and the Constitution: Freedom of the Press in America.* Berkeley: University of California Press, 1991.

Pratte, Paul Alfred. *Gods within the Machine: A History of the American Society of Newspaper Editors, 1923–1993.* Westport, Conn.: Praeger, 1995.

Pray, Isaac. *Memoirs of James Gordon Bennett.* New York: Stringer and Townsend, 1855.

Proctor, Robert. *Value-Free Science?* Cambridge, Mass.: Harvard University Press, 1991.

Pulitzer, Joseph. "The College of Journalism." *North American Review* 178, no. 570 (May 1904): 641–80.

Purcell, Edward A., Jr. *The Crises of Democratic Theory: Scientific Naturalism and the Problem of Value.* Lexington: University of Kentucky Press, 1973.

Putnam, Hilary. *The Collapse of the Fact/Value Dichotomy and Other Essays.* Cambridge, Mass.: Harvard University Press, 2002.

– *Pragmatism.* Oxford: Blackwell Publishers, 1996.

– "Pragmatism and Moral Objectivity," In *Words and Life,* 151–81. Cambridge, Mass.: Harvard University Press, 1994.

– *Realism with a Human Face.* Ed. James Conant. Cambridge, Mass.: Harvard University Press, 1990.

– *Words and Life.* Cambridge, Mass.: Harvard University Press, 1994.

Quine, W.V.O. "On the Reasons for the Indeterminacy of Translation." *Journal of Philosophy* 67 (March 1970).

– "Two Dogmas of Empiricism." In *From a Logical Point of View.* New York: Harper and Row, 1963.

– *Word and Object.* Cambridge, Mass.: MIT Press, 1960.

Rawls, John. "Kantian Constructivism in Moral Theory." In Steven Darwall, ed., *Contractarianism/Contractualism,* 190–218. Oxford: Blackwell Publishing. 2003. Reprinted from *Journal of Philosophy* 77 (1980).

– *The Law of Peoples.* 4th printing. Cambridge, Mass.: Harvard University Press, 2002.

– *Political Liberalism.* New York: Columbia University Press, 1993.

– *A Theory of Justice* (1972). Twelfth impression. Oxford: Oxford University Press, 1992.

Raymond, Joad, ed. *Making the News: An Anthology of the Newsbooks of Revolutionary England, 1641–1660.* New York: St Martin's Press, 1993.

– "The Newspaper, Public Opinion, and the Public Sphere." In Joad Raymond, ed., *News, Newspapers and Society in Early Modern Britain,* 107–40. London: Frank Cass, 1999.

Raz, Joseph. "Notes on Value and Objectivity." In Brian Leiter, ed., *Objectivity in Law and Morals,* 194–233. Cambridge: Cambridge University Press, 2001.

Rea, Robert R. *The English Press in Politics, 1760–1774.* Lincoln: University of Nebraska Press, 1963.

Read, Donald. *The Power of News: The History of Reuters, 1849–1989*. Oxford: Oxford University Press, 1992.

Reeve, Henry. "The Newspaper Press." *Edinburgh Review* (Oct. 1855): 470–98.

Report of the Special Senate Committee on Mass Media. Vol. 1. Ottawa: Queen's Printer, 1971.

Rescher, Nicholas. *Objectivity: The Obligations of Impersonal Reason*. Notre Dame, Ind.: University of Notre Dame Press, 1997.

Retat, Pierre. "The Revolutionary Word in the Newspaper in 1789." Trans. François Le Roy. In Jeremy D. Popkin, ed., *Media and Revolution*, 90–7. Lexington: University Press of Kentucky, 1995.

Richardson, Alan. *Carnap's Construction of the World: The Aufbau and the Emergence of Logical Empiricism*. Cambridge: Cambridge University Press, 1998.

Robinson, Daniel J. *The Measure of Democracy: Polling, Market Research, and Public Life, 1930–1945*. Toronto: University of Toronto, 1999.

Rogers, Nicholas. *Crowds, Culture and Politics in Georgian Britain*. Oxford: Clarendon Press, 1998.

Rorty, Richard. *Contingency, Irony and Solidarity*. Cambridge: Cambridge University Press, 1992.

– "Hilary Putnam and the Relativist Menace." In *Truth and Progress*, Vol. 3. In *Philosophical Papers*, 43–62. Cambridge: Cambridge University Press, 1998.

– "Is Truth a Goal of Inquiry?" *Truth and Progress*, Vol. 3. In *Philosophical Papers*, 19–42. Cambridge: Cambridge University Press, 1998.

– *Objectivity, Relativism and Truth*. Vol. 1. In *Philosophical Papers*. New York: Cambridge University Press, 1991.

– *Philosophy and Social Hope*. London: Penguin, 1999.

– *Philosophy and the Mirror of Nature*. Princeton, NJ: Princeton University Press, 1979.

– *Truth and Progress*, Vol. 3. In *Philosophical Papers*. Cambridge: Cambridge University Press, 1998.

Rosen, Jay. *Getting the Connections Right: Public Journalism and the Troubles in the* Press. New York: Twentieth Century Fund Press, 1996.

– *What Are Journalists For?* New Haven, Conn.: Yale University Press, 1999.

Ross, Charles G. *The Writing of News: A Handbook*. New York: Henry Holt, 1911.

Ross, P.D. *Retrospects of a Newspaper Person*. Toronto: Oxford University Press, 1931.

Rude, George. *Wilkes and Liberty*. Oxford: Clarendon, 1962.

Russell, Bertrand. *A History of Western Philosophy*. London: George Allen and Unwin, 1946.

Rutherford, Paul. *The Making of the Canadian Media*. Toronto: McGraw-Hill Ryerson, 1978.

– *A Victorian Authority: The Daily Press in Late Nineteenth-Century Canada*. Toronto: University of Toronto Press, 1982.

Sala, G.A. *America Revisited*. 5th ed. London: Vizetelly, 1885.

Scanlon, T.M. "Contractualism and Utilitarianism." In Amartya Sen and Bernard Williams, eds., *Utilitarianism and Beyond,* 103–28. Cambridge: Cambridge University Press, 1982.

– *What We Owe to Each Other.* Cambridge, Mass.: Harvard University Press, 1998.

Schiller, Daniel. *Objectivity and the News: The Public and the Rise of Commercial Journalism.* Philadelphia: University of Pennsylvania Press, 1981.

Schouls, Peter A. *The Imposition of Method: A Study of Descartes and Locke.* Oxford: Clarendon Press, 1980.

Schudson, Michael. *Discovering the News: A Social History of American Newspapers.* New York: Basic Books, 1978.

– *The Good Citizen: A History of American Civic Life.* Cambridge, Mass.: Harvard University Press, 1998.

Seigel, Jerrold E. *Rhetoric and Philosophy in Renaissance Humanism.* Princeton, NJ: Princeton University Press, 1968.

Sextus Empiricus. *Outlines of Pyrrhonism.* Trans. J. Annas and J. Barnes. Cambridge: Cambridge University Press, 1994.

Shaaber, M.A. *Some Forerunners of the Newspapers in England, 1476–1622.* London: Frank Cass, 1967.

Shannon, Claude. "The Mathematical Theory of Communication." *Bell System Technical Journal* 27, nos. 3 and 4 (July and Oct. 1948): 379–423 and 623–56.

Shapin, Steven, and Simon Schaffer. *Leviathan and the Air-Pump: Hobbes, Boyle and the Experimental Life.* Princeton, NJ: Princeton University Press, 1985.

Shapiro, A.L. *The Control Revolution.* New York: Century Foundation, 1999.

Shapiro, Barbara. *A Culture of Fact.* Ithaca, NY: Cornell University Press, 2000.

– *Probability and Certainty in Seventeenth-Century England.* Princeton, NJ: Princeton University Press, 1983.

Shi, David. *Facing Facts: Realism in American Thought and Culture, 1850–1920.* New York: Oxford University Press, 1995.

Shuman, Edwin. *Steps into Journalism: Helps and Hints for Young Writers.* Evanston, Ill.: Correspondence School of Journalism, 1894.

Siebert, Fredrick S. *Freedom of the Press in England 1476–1776.* Urbana: University of Illinois Press, 1965.

Siebert, Fredrick S., Theodore Peterson, and Wilbur Schramm. *Four Theories of the Press.* Urbana: University of Illinois Press, 1963.

Smiles, Samuel. "What Are the People Doing to Educate Themselves?" *People's Journal 1* (1846): 222–4, 229–30.

Smith, Adam. *The Theory of Moral Sentiments* (1759). Ed. D.D. Raphael and A.L. Macfie. Oxford: Oxford University Press, 1976.

– *The Wealth of Nations* (1776). Books I–III. New York: Penguin, 1981.

Smith, Anthony. *The Newspaper: An International History.* London: Thames and Hudson, 1979.

Smith, I. Norman. *J.F.B. Livesay: A Memory*. Ottawa: Mortimer, 1944.

– *The Journal Men: P.D. Ross, E. Norman Smith and Grattan O'Leary of the Ottawa Journal.* Toronto: Macmillan, 1974.

Smith, Nigel. *Literature and Revolution in England, 1640–1660.* New Haven, Conn.: Yale University Press, 1994.

Sotiron, Minko. *From Politics to Profit: The Commercialization of Canadian Daily Newspapers, 1890–1920.* Montreal: McGill-Queen's University Press, 1997.

Sprat, Thomas. *History of the Royal Society* (1667). Ed. Jackson Cope and Harold Jones. London: Routledge and Kegan Paul, 1959.

Stead, William Thomas. "Government by Journalism." *Contemporary Review* 49 (May 1886): 653–74.

Stensaas, Harlan S. "Development of the Objectivity Ethic in U.S. Daily Newspapers." *Journal of Mass Media Ethics* 2, no. 1 (fall–winter 1986–87): 50–60.

– "The Objective News Report: A Content Analysis of Selected U.S. Daily Newspapers for 1865 to 1954." Ph.D. dissertation, University of Southern Mississippi, 1987.

Stephen, J.F. "Journalism." *Cornhill Magazine* (July 1862): 52–63.

Stephen, Leslie, and Sidney Lee. *The Dictionary of National Biography.* Vol. 14. Oxford: Oxford University Press, 1917.

Stephens, Mitchell. *A History of News: From the Drum to the Satellite.* New York: Viking, 1988.

Stevenson, Charles L. *Ethics and Language.* New Haven, Conn.: Yale University Press, 1944.

Stewart, Gordon. *The Origins of Canadian Politics: A Comparative Approach.* Vancouver: University of British Columbia Press, 1986.

Stigler, Stephen M. *The History of Statistics: The Measurement of Uncertainty to 1900.* Cambridge, Mass.: Harvard University Press, 1986.

Strange, Jeffrey, ed. *The Future of Fact: An Annenberg Scholars Conference.* Philadelphia: Annenberg Public Policy Center, 1997.

Strawson, Peter. *Analysis and Metaphysics.* Oxford: Oxford University Press, 1992.

Striker, Gisela. "Following Nature." In Gisela Striker, ed., *Essays in Hellenistic Epistemology and Ethics*, 221–80. Cambridge: Cambridge University Press, 1996.

Sutherland, James. *The Restoration Newspaper and Its Development.* Cambridge: Cambridge University Press, 1986.

Taunton, W.D. "The Man behind the Halifax Herald." *Canadian Printer and Publisher* (Nov. 1911): 35–40.

Taylor, Charles. *Sources of the Self.* Cambridge: Cambridge University Press, 1992.

Thagard, Paul. *Conceptual Revolutions.* Princeton, NJ: Princeton University Press 1992.

Thomas, P.W. *Sir John Berkenhead, 1617–1679: A Royalist Career in Politics and Polemics.* Oxford: Clarendon Press, 1969.

Thompson, H.B. *The Choice of a Profession.* London, n.p., 1857.

Thucydides. *History of the Peloponnesian War.* Trans. C.F. Smith. Cambridge, Mass.: Harvard University Press, 1991.

Tifft, Susan E., and Alex S. Jones. *The Trust: The Private and Powerful Family behind the New York Times.* Boston: Little, Brown and Company, 1999.

Tindale, Christopher W. *Acts of Arguing: A Rhetorical Model of Argument.* Albany, NY: State University of New York: 1999.

Todd, S.C. "The Purpose of Evidence in Athenian Courts." In P.A. Cartledge et al., eds., *NOMOS: Essays in Athenian Law, Politics and Society,* 19–39. Cambridge: Cambridge University Press, 1990.

Toulmin, Stephen. *Return to Reason.* Cambridge, Mass.: Harvard University Press, 2001.

Trollope, Anthony. *The Warden.* London: Penguin, 1986.

Tucher, Andie. *Froth and Scum: Truth, Beauty, Goodness, and the Ax Murder in America's First Mass Medium.* Chapel Hill: University of North Carolina Press, 1994.

– "The Sensational Nineteenth Century." Paper presented to the Association for Education in Journalism and Mass Communication, New Orleans, Aug. 1999.

Tuchman, Gaye. *Making the News: A Study in the Construction of Reality.* New York: Free Press, 1978.

Ward, Stephen J.A. "Answer to Bell: Objectivity and Attachment in Journalism." *Harvard International Journal of Press/Politics* 3, no. 3 (1998): 121–5.

Ward, Stephen J.A., and Christopher Tindale. 2002. "Rhetorical Argumentation and the New Journalism." Paper presented at fifth conference of the International Society for the Study of Argumentation, Amsterdam, 26 June 2002. Forthcoming in conference proceedings.

Weinberg, Steven. *Facing Up: Science and Its Cultural Adversaries.* Cambridge, Mass.: Harvard University Press, 2002.

Weissman, David. *Truth's Debt to Value.* New Haven, Conn.: Yale University Press, 1993.

Westfall, Richard S. *The Construction of Modern Science: Mechanisms and Mechanics.* Cambridge: Cambridge University Press, 1977.

Williams, Bernard. *Descartes: The Project of Pure Enquiry.* Hassocks, Sussex: Harvester, 1978.

– *Truth and Truthfulness: An Essay in Genealogy.* Princeton, NJ: Princeton University Press, 2002.

Wittgenstein, Ludwig. *On Certainty.* Oxford: Blackwell, 1969.

– *Philosophical Investigations.* Oxford: Blackwell, 1953.

Woods, Oliver, and James Bishop. *The Story of the Times.* London: Michael Joseph, 1983.

Yost, Casper. *The Principles of Journalism.* New York: Appleton, 1924.

Young, J.Z. *Philosophy and the Brain.* Oxford: Oxford University Press, 1987.
Zaret, David. *Origins of Democratic Culture: Printing, Petitions, and the Public Sphere in Early-Modern England.* Princeton, NJ: Princeton University Press, 2000.
Zinman, John M. *Reliable Knowledge.* Cambridge: Cambridge University Press, 1978.

Index